SEXUAL ETHICS

Sexual Ethics

An Evangelical Perspective

Stanley J. Grenz

Westminster John Knox Press
Louisville, Kentucky

To Joel and Corina.
May they grow to find in their life choices
the same sexual fulfillment their mother and I enjoy.

Book design by Jennifer K. Cox
Cover design by Alec Bartsch

Published by Westminster John Knox Press
Louisville, Kentucky

This book is printed on acid-free paper that meets the
American National Standards Institute Z39.48 standard. ♾

PRINTED IN THE UNITED STATES OF AMERICA
99 00 01 02 03 04 05 06 — 10 9 8 7 6 5 4 3 2

Library of Congress Cataloging-in-Publication Data

Grenz, Stanley, date.
    Sexual ethics : an Evangelical perspective / Stanley Grenz.
        p.   cm.
    Originally published: Dallas : Word Pub., c1990, in series: Issues
of Christian conscience.
    Includes bibliographical references and indexes.
    ISBN 0–664–25750–X (alk. paper)
    1. Sex—Religious aspects—Christianity.   2. Marriage—Religious
aspects—Christianity.   3. Sexual ethics—Biblical teaching.
I. Title.
[BT708.G72 1997]
241'.66—dc21   97–1383

Contents

Preface to the Westminster John Knox Press Edition

"Dating just ain't what it used to be," screamed the opening line of an article written for this year's Valentine's Day edition of the daily newspaper *The Vancouver Sun*. The essay, bearing the title "Be still, my tacky heart," introduced what the writer claimed would be a series exploring "the changing landscape of love, sex and romance in the age of AIDS, political correctness and increasing isolation." As the article indicates, sex retains its perennial place at, or near, the top of today's "hot" topics.

In this context of keen interest in sex and sexuality but of a profound sense of "increasing isolation" as well, Christians have good news. We declare that human sexuality belongs to our essential nature as created by God. Consequently, the authors of "tacky heart" articles are not the only ones concerned about sex. In fact, no one is more interested in our "sex life" in all its dimensions than the Creator! But in contrast to the typical newspaper or magazine essay, which generally reveals a truncated understanding, our God-given sexuality involves more than genital sex. Nor is individual happiness or self-fulfillment its chief purpose.

Although she is somewhat misguided in the specific advice she offers, the "tacky heart" author is nevertheless on to something. Given the realities of our world, sex can never be the same. This is even more the case when it is viewed from a Christian perspective. Acknowledging a biblically informed understanding of ourselves as sexual beings can free us from the slavery to sex that so often seems to plague our society. Such an understanding can lead us to move beyond our isolation into truly meaningful relationships and thereby to live as persons of sexual integrity. And whether we are married or single, this awareness can release us to express ourselves as the sexual creatures we are, in a manner that accords with the intentions of our Creator and Savior.

My goal in this volume is to set forth a theological understanding of humans as sexual beings and of the sex act itself, and to explore the theological significance of marriage and singleness as contexts in which we express our sexuality. I then attempt to draw out some of the crucial ethical implications of this theological understanding. At the foundation of the discussion is the conviction that a biblical view of human sexuality carries ramifications for how we relate to one another as sexual beings, whether we are married or single. Hence, the following pages seek to address the ethics of fidelity vs. adultery, divorce, dating, and homosexual relationships. I explore other issues as well, however, including such practical questions as birth control and technological procreation. The recent creation of the cloned sheep "Dolly" suggests that these issues may take on even greater, and perhaps more ominous, importance in the near future.

The significance of the task of setting forth a theological understanding of sexuality and exploring its ethical ramifications has not diminished since this book first appeared in 1990. Therefore, I am grateful to Westminster John Knox Press for its interest in publishing a new edition of the volume and to Stephanie Egnotovich for her gracious support of the project. My thanks goes as well to Paul Chapman and Paul Martins for taking on the task of updating the indexes. And as always, I am indebted to Carey Theological College for its support of my writing endeavors, as well as to my colleagues at Regent College and more recently Northern Baptist Theological Seminary (Lombard, Illinois) for their interest in my work.

With the exception of slight editing of the text, the present book is identical to the original 1990 edition. The desire of Westminster John Knox Press to keep the work substantially in its original form is for me a gratifying indication of the continuing value of the positions I sought to articulate seven years ago.

Stanley J. Grenz
Vancouver, B.C.
Lent 1997

Preface to the First Edition

Humans are undeniably sexual beings. As Christians, we declare that this sexuality belongs to our existence as creatures of God. For this reason, it is crucial for us to articulate a specifically Christian understanding of this central dimension of our being. The need for a Christian delineation of human sexuality is augmented by the tumultuous nature of the times in which we live. Among the various ethical issues we face in the modern world none are more crucial or more demanding than those related to our sexuality. And the issues related to this human dimension are diverse, ranging from the possibilities created by modern scientific advances (such as abortion and technological procreation) to perennial questions related to lifestyle (e.g., adultery and homosexuality).

My interest in issues of human sexuality was heightened significantly when I joined the faculty of the North American Baptist Seminary in 1981 and found that courses in Christian ethics would become part of my teaching portfolio. Then in the spring of 1987 I was invited by Lyn Cryderman to participate in a Christianity Today Institute focusing on this topic. The discussions of those three days caused me to realize the importance of placing the difficult contemporary issues related to human sexuality in the context of a theological understanding of humans as sexual beings.

The opportunity for me to think through a theology of human sexuality and to set forth a restatement of the Christian sex ethic came in 1989. Vernon Grounds, editor of the Word series, Issues of Christian Conscience, and my ethics professor at Denver Conservative Baptist Seminary, invited me to write the volume on sexual ethics. The composing of this book gave me the occasion to explore the underlying thesis that human sexuality, as the basis for the human drive toward bonding, is related to the divine goal of establishing community among humans and between humans and God. This foundational thesis, in turn, forms the basis for viewing the great contemporary ethical questions concerning sexuality.

I acknowledge a debt of gratitude to many persons who have contributed to the publication of this volume. I thank Vernon Grounds for his expression of faith in entrusting to me the joyous privilege of writing this book. My thanks go to the editors of *Christianity Today* and to my coparticipants in the March 1987 Institute for the helpful dialogue that preceded my work on the project. At each stage the North American Baptist Seminary in Sioux Falls provided helpful personnel support. Faculty secretary Joy Huisman worked diligently on manuscript corrections. The students who participated in a course on issues in human sexuality during fall semester, 1989, became a valuable sounding board for my ideas. My capable research assistant, Marcia Moret Sietstra, provided an invaluable service by checking sources and offering suggestions at various stages of the project. I thank Carey Moore of Word, Inc., who undertook the task of manuscript editing.

Above all, I am grateful to my wife, Edna. As my life's partner she provides a daily object lesson concerning the joy that can be experienced through the community of male and female found in a Christian marriage.

Stanley J. Grenz
Sioux Falls, South Dakota
Summer 1990

Introduction:
The Church Amid Sexual Revolution

To an extent unparalleled since the early centuries of the Christian era, Christians at the close of the twentieth century find themselves living in a sex-oriented—or perhaps more accurately, a sexually *disoriented*—culture. Sex and sexual expression are among the dominant characteristics of contemporary Western society. We are continually bombarded with sexual messages. The advertisement industry and the media have often gone to great lengths to exploit the theme of sexuality[1] and have given the impression that to be sexually attractive and to express one's sexuality is the key to personal happiness and success. In the midst of this emphasis, people are increasingly confused both about their sexual identity and the proper context and the proper means for expressing their sexuality.

One of the most far-reaching results of the elevation of sexuality in contemporary society has been the questioning of what some would term the traditional sex ethic, a moral code which has dominated Western culture for over a millennium. This sex ethic focuses on marriage as the proper context for sexual expression. In recent years, however, this ethic has come under attack; many have rejected the older link between marriage and sexual expression. As a result, important questions have been raised, including the meaning of marriage itself, whether the sex act should be reserved for marriage, and whether marriage ought to form the boundary for personal sexual activity. At the same time, with the rise in the number of single persons, the single life has received increasing emphasis, yet without the development of guidelines for the role of sexual expression among single people.

Beyond the general questioning of the older sex ethic, modern technology has raised additional issues. In fact, many of the sticky moral dilemmas we face today are the result of the combination of technology and human sexuality. The explosive, emotional issue of abortion stands as a crucial example, especially as related to the use of abortion as a birth control measure or in cases of sexual abuse. Although capturing less public attention, issues surrounding artificial insemination have become increasingly important as well. As *Donum vitae,* the 1987 Vatican statement on human sexuality sought to indicate,[2] these issues are also closely bound to personal and public conceptions of the relationship between sexual expression and procreation.

Christians are called by their Lord to live as the people of God in the midst of the present situation. Jesus' statement to his first-century disciples, "You are the salt of the earth" (Matt. 5:13), applies to Christians in every age and in every culture. At this crucial point in history, therefore, the church must shoulder the responsibility to think through the sexual ethic it gleans from the Bible so as to determine its implications and application to the sex-intoxicated world of today.

Changing Views of Sexuality in Church History

Although contemporary society poses a situation that in many ways is unique, the task of determining a response to the question of human sexuality by looking to the pages of the Bible has been present with the church throughout its history. The church's viewpoint concerning this dimension of life, however, has not remained constant throughout its history, but has been the result of a lively dialectic between church and culture. So on the one hand, the understanding of human sexuality given by the church at various junctures has been determined in part by the situation posed by the mores of the surrounding culture. On the other hand, as the church came to be a dominant influence in society, its attitude toward sexuality was an important factor in the shaping of culture. Three basic viewpoints have characterized the church's understanding toward human sexuality.[3]

1. The Affirmation of Sexuality Within the Context of Morality

The church in the first Christian centuries characteristically placed sexuality within the context of concern for moral living. During the subapostolic era, theologians accepted sexuality and marriage as part of the good creation of God. This attitude was based on such biblical texts as the Genesis creation narratives, John's account of Jesus' presence at the wedding in Cana, and the several admonitions concerning marriage in the Epistles. But more important than the basis in creation was the context of morality for the early Christian understanding of marriage and sexual matters. The church fathers were concerned for moral living in all areas of life, a concern which formed an important theme in much of the literature of that era. This concern was applied to the sexual dimension and marriage (e.g., Heb. 13:4).

This emphasis on the basic goodness of sexuality and marriage, together with the call to moral living in the realm of sexual conduct, did not arise in a vacuum. As the New Testament era was drawing to a close and the subapostolic era dawned, the church found it necessary to do battle with a tenacious foe that invaded from the surrounding culture—Gnosticism. Inherent in the Gnostic outlook on human sexuality was the antimaterial bias that formed a central tenet of its philosophical foundation. Gnostic teachers disparaged the body as inherently evil. They offered to the "spiritual," to those initiated in Gnosticism, a special "knowledge." As a result of this rejection of the body (because it was material and not spiritual), these teachers would, according to the characterization of the Pastoral Epistles, "forbid people to marry and order them to abstain from certain foods, which God created to be received with thanksgiving by those who believe and know the truth" (1 Tim. 4:3).

In response to the Gnostic heretics, the early church theologians, following Paul, emphasized the created goodness of the body. This emphasis found a theological basis in the incarnation. In Christ, God had seen fit to assume human flesh, thereby affirming the material body as capable of housing the divine essence. In keeping with the heritage of the Old Testament and in contrast to certain aspects of the Greek philosophical tradition, the church's position affirmed likewise a basically holistic outlook toward the human person as spirit and body. This meant that the body and its functions, and not merely the soul, belong to the originally good creation of God. As a result, the church theologians viewed marriage, together with procreation, as divinely ordained, an outlook they believed Jesus himself had confirmed by his presence at the wedding at Cana.

The integral relationship between the physical and the spiritual dimensions of human existence also meant that what a person did "in the body" was important for his or her relationship to God. The body could not simply be indulged with no fear of affecting the soul, as certain Greek philosophers had taught. In this way the church continued the Pauline critique of the proto-Gnostic Corinthians, found in his admonition to "flee from sexual immorality." The Christian's body is "a temple of the Holy Spirit," Paul asserted. From this principle he drew the resultant command: "Honor God with your body" (1 Cor. 6:18–20). The sex-affirming, morality-demanding position of the church was capsulized by the simple injunction of the author of the Epistle to the Hebrews: "Marriage should be honored by all, and the marriage bed kept pure, for God will judge the adulterer and all the sexually immoral" (Heb. 13:4).

2. The Elevation of Celibacy

Already in the subapostolic era, however, the seeds of a changed viewpoint were being sown. This change would result in the elevation of virginity as an ideal and celibacy as the preferred lifestyle for the truly spiritual in the church.

One factor that contributed to the coming change was the growing emphasis on martyrdom that arose in the face of civil persecution. In this context, the church came to regard being put to death for one's testimony as the highest expression of devotion and faithfulness to Christ. By its very nature, martyrdom had a tendency to discourage entanglements with the world, including marriage. With the increased emphasis on the glories of martyrdom, the tone of Christian teaching became increasingly death-affirming and world-denying. This tendency gave birth to the fully developed asceticism which followed in later centuries.

A second seed of change came through the success of the Christian proclamation in the Roman world. As the church became increasingly more Gentile and less Jewish in membership, it became more Hellenistic and less Hebrew in outlook. This fostered a more Greek-oriented understanding of the New Testament Scriptures. As a result, when read apart from the context of the Old Testament affirmation of marriage, Paul's expressed preference for the celibate state—"because of the present crisis" (1 Cor. 7:26)—came to be viewed as a permanent injunction for all situations.

The growing influence of Greek thought is visible in the writings of the third-century Alexandrian father, Origen. Origen extolled the virtues of the celibate life. Choosing to follow literally Jesus' declaration that some had made themselves eunuchs for the kingdom (Matt. 19:12), he chose to be castrated prior to his ordination. Although he later regretted this radical action, Origen nevertheless continued to lead a life of strict austerity, emphasizing the pleasure of the rational soul's contemplation of God, as opposed to the pleasures of the body.

The seeds that sprouted in the subapostolic age produced a harvest in the post-Constantinian era. The focus of attention shifted away from an emphasis on marriage and personal sexual morality within marriage, to the single, celibate life. As this occurred, the theological understanding of human sexuality came to center almost exclusively on celibacy and virginity. In their writings, the church theologians generally continued to view sexuality as part of God's good creation, but they deemphasized sexual activity. This is visible already in Clement of Alexandria (early third century). Although affirming that marriage was instituted by God, he maintained that sexual intercourse ought to be practiced only with a view toward procreation.[4]

Although the biblical declaration of the goodness of human sexuality was not generally denied, the emphasis was now clearly placed on the other aspect of the biblical story of the genesis of humankind, the Fall. Through the Fall, human sexuality was marred. In this way the church fathers came to associate sexuality with the realm of sin. As a result the sex act, theologians declared, was always tainted by lust and thereby by sin, even when practiced within the marriage bond. Sexual activity carried a further negative aspect. Because it meant marital commitments and the raising of children, marriage by necessity brought involvement with the world. The mood of the times was captured in the writings of Jerome, whose teaching can be summarized by this quip:

Marriage populates the earth, virginity populates heaven.

The emphasis on the fallenness of human sexuality meant a growing emphasis on celibacy as the way to avoid the trap of sin bound up with the sex drive and even marriage itself.[5] This was paralleled by a developing Mariology. As Mary came to be the paradigm of obedient humanity, her obedience in the context of virginity gained significance as a model to be emulated, at least by the spiritual in the church. As a result, attempts were made in the West, climaxing with the First Lateran Council in A.D. 1123, to impose celibacy on the clergy.[6] The East was somewhat more lenient in this regard; yet, even the Eastern Church came to view celibacy as the preferred lifestyle.

The growing asceticism of the era found a more radical expression in the monastic movement, which often added hermitage to celibacy. Yet seclusion could not free the hermit from sexuality and sexual battle. The renowned hermit, Anthony of Egypt, for example, retired into the wilderness, where he discovered to his dismay that he could not escape his passions. While not following the life of a hermit, Jerome nevertheless did battle against lust even while in seclusion in the desert.

Although many theologians touched on the theme of human sexuality, Augustine of Hippo deserves a special place in the development of the theology of sexuality in this era. More than any other church father he became the leading theological authority for subsequent discussions. Augustine's theology was affected by his personal turbulent history as well as by the turbulence of his time. Prior to his conversion he followed a promiscuous lifestyle, and therefore he was well acquainted with "the temptations of the flesh." At one stage he embraced Manicheism, a dualistic philosophy that, similar to Gnosticism before it, held that the flesh was evil.

Although as a Christian he affirmed against the Manicheans the goodness of every aspect of God's creation including the body, Augustine also gave great emphasis to the dark side of human nature. He reformulated the Pauline concept of the universality of sin and, based on what is now often seen as a faculty exegesis of Romans 5:12, viewed this universality as the direct result of Adam's transgression. So pervasive were the effects of original sin, in Augustine's understanding, that every human act is tainted by it. Because of birth in Adam's lineage, each person quite naturally is captive to concupiscence, that is, the cravings of the will toward lower goods rather than for the highest good, God.

The emphasis on human fallenness spilled over into Augustine's understanding of human sexuality. The effects of the Fall are present in sexual activity in two ways, he maintained.

First, sexual intercourse is the transmitter not only of life from one generation to the next, but also of original sin. Second, because of its unavoidable link to passion and thus to compulsiveness, every act of coitus is tainted by evil, he asserted. Even limiting the practice of the sex act to the boundaries of marriage could not free it from this bondage to lust. In this way Augustine's view coincided with a quite literal interpretation of the cry of the Psalmist, "in sin did my mother conceive me" (Ps. 51:5 KJV). At best, marriage was useful as a way of channeling passion toward a useful end, procreation.

Despite this pessimistic attitude toward sexuality, Augustine did develop a positive understanding of marriage. The union of husband and wife could carry the blessing of God. The goodness of marriage came about in three ways: through the faithfulness of the spouses to each other (*fides*), through procreation and the education of children (*proles*), and through the sacramental importance of marriage as a sign of the grace of God (*sacramentum*).[7]

The Middle Ages mark the climax of the development of an emphasis on celibacy. The medieval church embraced fully the monastic ideal as the Christian's higher calling. Marriage may have been afforded sacramental status, but celibacy was clearly the preferred option, at least for the more spiritually attuned Christians. At the heart of the monastic life lay the vows—chastity, obedience, and sometimes poverty—that would bind the neophyte to the chosen pattern of existence. The vow of chastity not only meant renunciation of sexual activity, but also of marriage itself, in that love between spouses would only distract the believer from the higher calling of love for God. To sexual purity in act was added purity in mind, for only with the spirit clear of passion could the Christian gain a clear vision of God.

By the Middle Ages the community of the monastery had largely displaced the isolation of the desert. At this stage the monastic ideal emphasized friendship apart from sexual relations. Communities of the celibate, whether limited to a single gender or mixed, sprang up and became important agencies in the church. The mystics elevated the monastic outlook as the central model for the union with God that was to be desired by all Christians. As a result, sexual relations were deemphasized or even disparaged as being potentially sinful, addictive, and distortive. The common people, those who were not able to follow the more rigorous route to spirituality, could receive forgiveness of their sins of passion through the confessional, as they described to the celibate priest the details of their passionate exploits.[8]

3. Marriage as the Norm

The Reformation inaugurated a marked reversal of several trends in outlook toward human sexuality which had developed during the Middle Ages.[9] These changes focused on a rejection of the ideal of virginity and a reaffirmation of marriage as God's design for humanity, yet not as a sacrament of the church but as belonging to the order of creation.

The Reformers rejected the medieval ideal, which elevated virginity as superior to the married state. This move was precipitated in part by the Protestant rejection of justification by works, which the Reformers found in the sexual rigorism of the Middle Ages, in favor of justification as God's gracious gift received by faith alone. As a result, they attacked both the demand that clergy remain celibate, as well as the monastic vows of lifelong chastity.

The Reformation rejection of the elevation of celibacy was likewise the result of another theological understanding, namely, a return to a more holistic anthropology. Protestants came to regard the will of God as including that humankind be a sexual creation. This understanding of human sexuality as based in creation meant that to regard sexual expression in every form as at best unimportant and at worst fundamentally evil (which view Protestants found in medieval theology) was to contradict the divine will.

These two themes, anthropology and grace, worked together in Protestant ethics in an interesting fashion. Because the human person was created as a whole being and had fallen as an entire being, the person in every aspect of existence—body as well as soul—must be the object of the transforming grace of God. God's grace, therefore, could extend even to the sexual dimension of human existence. At the foundation of the medieval practices of monasticism and celibacy, the Reformers perceived a specific understanding of the Christian life, namely, that true Christian piety entailed the attempt to live up to the standards of the next life. In the place of this emphasis they taught the principle of obedience to one's true calling within the orders of creation. As a result, they viewed marriage as receiving value as one of several institutions belonging to the created universe.

This understanding, like the rejection of the ideal of celibacy, marked a radical move away from the Middle Ages; thereby the Reformers reasserted the positive contribution of marriage to the life of the Christian. Medieval ethics had afforded to marriage and sexual relations a place derived largely from their function as the remedy for sexual concupiscence and as the necessary context for procreation. In this way, marriage had gained a status within the structure of the sacramental system of the church. For the Reformers, in contrast, marriage was a means of being obedient to one's spiritual vocation to exemplify true charity and authentic chastity. It was a way of being a Christian in the created world.

As the Reformation unfolded, marriage became increasingly important, being elevated nearly to the point of developing into a positive duty. Yet, the concern that motivated the Protestant emphasis on the duty of marriage was quite different than what often motivates entrance into the marital state today. The Reformers viewed marriage as a vocation. Therefore, service, and not self-fulfillment and personal pleasure, formed the basis for enjoining marriage. In the Reformation era, marriage and raising a family were seen as one important way through which God wanted Christians to serve the present order.[10]

Despite the teaching and example of Reformers such as Luther and Calvin, some Protestants—including George Herbert and William Law—voiced a preference for a celibate clergy, a viewpoint that was defended even into the eighteenth century. Yet, their calls for a continuation of the older practice were overpowered by the newer mood. Protestant thinkers completed the Reformation challenge to the medieval system by arguing that the celibate life is not somehow purer than marriage. On the contrary, some even extolled the advantages of marriage for spirituality, in that those who share in the marital state are free from many carnal temptations.

The Puritans moved the Reformation understanding to a climax, exalting marriage, just as the Middle Ages had elevated celibacy.[11] They viewed sexual activity as more than a physical drive, for it was an expression of deep love, the love that is to exist between Christian spouses. As a result, the Puritans did not limit the function of the sex act to procreation. Instead they celebrated the relational aspect of the marital bond and the attentive care spouses were to give to one another. Sociologists Milton Diamond and Arno Karlen summarized the impact of Puritan attitudes in this manner:

> The real Puritan revolution was to move the passions of love and sex from adulterous romances into the marriage bed.[12]

The Puritan viewpoint concerning human sexuality was built on a central aspect of Puritan theology in general, namely, the concept of covenant. God had ordained a variety of covenants that are to form the context for human relationships, the Puritans taught. Among the most significant of these was the marriage covenant. By placing both marriage and general human social relationships under the rubric of the covenant, they catapulted marriage and the family to center stage for the rightly ordered society.

The Current Situation: An Era of Transition

The modern era, the epoch of Western history that began in the Enlightenment, has witnessed the demise of the Reformation understanding of society in general and marriage in particular. The breakdown of the older consensus, while a process that began with the intellectual shifts of the Enlightenment, came to enjoy wide influence within the broader society only in the twentieth century and with accelerated swiftness only since the Second World War. In some respects, recent developments have been positive. Contemporary attitudes have sought to redeem sex from the bondage to sin that characterized earlier stages in Western history.[13] But this liberation, with its attendant emphasis on the ecstatic and on "quality" sex, has not been without negative effects. It has brought heightened expectations to sexual relationships and a performance orientation to the practice of sex. And it has marked an additional example of the general undermining of the religious orientation of life, characteristic of the modern era.

1. Sex and Secularization

A central hallmark of the era that has resulted from the Enlightenment is a process generally termed "secularization." This process entails a movement away from religion as a basis for understanding life. People view increasingly fewer dimensions of personal and social existence by means of reference to, or in terms of, religious symbols and stories. As secularization advances, religion is relegated to the fringes of life. It becomes a private matter, seen as having little bearing on life beyond the realm of personal convictions.

The sexual revolution of the second half of the twentieth century is an important step in the larger process of the secularization of sexuality. In previous epochs, people interpreted sex acts and sexuality in general in theological categories and as having public implications. Recent decades, in contrast, have brought a decrease in the religious and public interpretation of sexuality. Underlying this phenomenon is the demise of the theological world view lying at the foundation of the older outlook toward sexuality. In earlier eras the sexual dimension was seen as an integral aspect of the human person, and people viewed themselves as standing in relationship to God. But when sexuality came to be divorced from its theological context, sexual acts, like religious belief in general, were severed from the public domain and made exclusively private.

The secularization of sexuality is closely related to the general secularization of human life, which process has included the loss of a theological perspective on existence as a whole. But as significant as this theological shift has been, it could not have become so pervasive in society without the aid of certain technological factors that have also contributed to the development of our secularized world.

One contributing technological factor is the advent of privacy itself. Persons raised in the twentieth century might not realize that separate rooms in houses (not to mention the anonymity offered by hotels and automobiles) is a recent phenomenon. This seemingly minor development—the advent of privacy as a presupposed context for human living—has had far-reaching impact on sexual mores and attitudes. Prior to the era of privacy, sexual activity could not be as completely hidden as is now possible. Sneaking off to have an illicit affair was not as readily accomplished. And even sexual relations between marriage partners could not always be shielded from the cognizance of children and others in the family. Modern living conditions, in contrast, allow sexual activity to transpire in private, thereby making sex, which was once a public concern, largely a private matter.

Technological advances produced by modern medicine have also contributed to the secularization of sexuality. Penicillin has reduced the chances of persons contracting sexually transmitted diseases. And recently developed artificial means of birth control, especially the pill, have reduced the risk that sexual activity will result in pregnancy. Such developments now give the impression that sex can occur without consequences. As a result, in the minds of many persons sexual activity has been effectively disengaged from the context of permanent relationships where it had been placed, at least ideally, in past eras. Disengaged from relationship and consequence, sex has become a free-standing activity engaged in solely for the purpose of pleasure.

2. The Sexual Revolution

The secularization of sex came to a climax in the 1960s in the so-called sexual revolution. That decade witnessed the sounding of the death toll of the older morality. The double standard was overturned, women were liberated to join men in practicing promiscuity, a call for the throwing off of all sexual restraints was issued, and a new era of enjoyment of sex was proclaimed.

Beginning in the 1980s, however, a new mood became evident. "Caution" and "commitment" replaced "freedom" and "experience" as the watchwords of the day. *Time* magazine even declared "The Revolution Is Over."[14] Statistics indicated that weddings and births were on the rise and divorce on the decrease. And even playboy guru Hugh Hefner joined the ranks of the married.

Several factors have been cited as contributing to the newer conservatism. "The sexual revolution was born in the mid-60s, the product of affluence, demographics and the Pill," postulated the *Time* report. But in the eighties and nineties attention turned in other directions. An uncertain economy is one factor. People today are concerned with job and career, and young people are concentrating on preparation for a profession. Second, the sputtering of the revolution was caused by concern over sexually transmitted diseases. Genital herpes and AIDS added a sobering dimension that demands a more cautious stance. A third factor is demographic: in the 1980s and 1990s the baby boomer generation passed into an age bracket in which stability and conservatism are more pronounced.

As important as these changes have been, many observers cite a different development as the most significant factor, the new search for commitment. The 1960s' quest for new sexual conquests came to be replaced by the search for what is termed "intimacy." Yet, the commitment that is touted today is not that of a lifelong, monogamous marriage relationship. Rather, it maintains certain features of the sexual revolution of the 1960s, including the primacy of the independent individual, the privacy of sex, and sex without any necessary consequences.[15]

3. Transition and the Church

The impact of secularization on sexuality has nearly run its course, many observers are declaring. But the new conservatism does not necessarily entail a return to the traditional morality or to a specifically Christian understanding of human sexuality.

As the authors of the *Time* report concluded, "No sexual counterrevolution is under way. The sexual revolution has not been rebuffed, merely absorbed into the culture." This reality means that Christians today are living in a transitional era, one in which they dare not grow complacent by assuming that they have won the sex ethics battle. The challenge for the church remains as acute today as in previous decades. We must rethink and reassert a biblically based sex ethic in this new era. We can no longer simply appeal to some ethical consensus which supposedly characterized earlier generations. Despite rumors of the end of the sexual revolution, people today are not simply affirming a consensus of a previous age. On the contrary, any past consensus has been discarded by a generation bombarded by the media's romanticizing of the necessity of sex for self-fulfillment and by the exploitation of sex by the gurus of advertising.

More than at any other time in Christian history, the present generation has been cast on its own resources. The freedom of private decision offered by secularized culture means that persons living in contemporary Western society find themselves entrusted with unparalleled responsibility for shaping and expressing their own sexuality. We may be discovering to our regret that the possibilities of the present have outpaced the moral capabilities of many persons, perhaps even of society as a whole.

All transitional eras are frightening. As the old norms are thrown aside—and not always in the name of higher norms, but in the overturning of the normative life as such—an ethical void develops. The presence of such a void is dangerous. It can readily lead to antinomianism and the casting off of all restraint. At the same time, transitional eras are challenging and exhilarating. Such times of change are characterized by iconoclastic tendencies. As old orthodoxies are questioned, all the old props of tradition are pulled out from under us. But when this happens, transitional eras offer us opportunity to read the classics anew, with opened eyes and a searching mind.

For the church, the present era of transition affords an opportunity to offer a fresh statement of God's design for human beings. The Scriptures assert that God created us as sexual beings. The current situation in Western culture challenges the people of God to think through the implications of our created maleness and femaleness and apply to the questions and issues of our day the biblical declaration that our sexuality is a divinely given aspect of our humanness which demands that we live together as the community of male and female.

Male and Female

The Nature of Human Sexuality

Generally the first statement made at the birth of a baby is an assertion of the sex of the newborn. Among the first characteristics we notice in encountering other humans, whether children or adults, is their sex. And we do not simply put aside our awareness of the sex of another after the first glance; rather, it continues to exercise a powerful, even pervasive influence in our ongoing social interactions.

But what exactly is this universal human dimension called *sexuality* which is evident in the distinctions, male and female? How pervasive of our being is our sexuality? And what does the Creator intend in constituting us as sexually determined beings? Questions such as these offer the beginning point for the attempt to provide a Christian perspective on the phenomenon of human existence as male and female. The task of developing a Christian response to the ethical issues surrounding human sexuality must begin with an understanding of our sexuality in the light of the Christian faith.

This chapter and the next develop the thesis that humans are a sexual creation, a thesis which carries both an individual and a social or corporate dimension. The task of this chapter is to explore the individual aspect of human sexuality—the human person as a sexual being. In the next, the corporate or social dimension will be considered, before turning to the implications for human sexuality of the dynamic of Creation and Fall which is so significant for Christian anthropology. In the entire discussion, our eyes must remain fixed on certain biblical texts that seek to shed light on the divine design in creating us as sexual beings.

What Is Sexuality?

The most readily perceived dimension of human sexuality is the individual dimension. We cannot help but see each other and ourselves as sexual entities. But the observation that humans are sexual beings only serves to raise questions, not provide answers, concerning our identity. Our cognizance of human sexual differentiations leads us to ask basic questions concerning this

PART 1 HUMAN SEXUALITY AND CHRISTIAN THEOLOGY

phenomenon: What do we mean by sexuality? And are the gender distinctions, male and female, an integral part of our essential being? These questions require further reflection and thereby form a basis for the development of a Christian theological understanding of human sexuality.

The question that arises first and becomes foundational is that of definition. What are we talking about when we use the term *sexuality?* What is this dimension of our existence that becomes visible in the distinctions "male" and "female"?

1. Sexuality, Biological Sex, and Reproduction

The initial response many people give to the question, what is sexuality? focuses on the physical characteristics associated with biological structures and on reproductive roles. Such a response is, of course, correct, at least in part. But we cannot simply look to biological sex, viewed solely in terms of certain distinctive features of the physical body that separate male and female, thinking thereby that we have come to grips with the essence of human sexuality.

Sexuality is closely related to physical sex, of course, and thus to our reproductive capacities. The thesis of this chapter, however, is that our sexuality, our fundamental maleness or femaleness, runs deeper than the physical features that separate male and female and allow the reproductive function.[1] Sexuality is an aspect of our being that lies behind, produces, and is given expression by physical sexual characteristics and reproductive capacity. To understand this fuller dimension of sexuality we must look both to the human sciences and the biblical narratives concerning human origins.

a. Sexuality in the human sciences. The assertion that sexuality is not merely our physical sex (male or female), but lies deeper in our being, is in keeping with the findings of the human sciences. Psychologists, for example, generally assert that children do not suddenly become sexual beings with the development of their reproductive capacities. On the contrary, sexuality is both present in the child and given expression prior to the onset of puberty. Roman Catholic theologian George Tavard succinctly summarized the conclusions of the analysis of human sexuality by modern depth psychology:

> Whether it remains latent or becomes active, sexuality pertains to the deepest levels of personality . . . from earliest infancy humans are sexually oriented . . . their sexual inclinations are predetermined by their earliest experiences.[2]

The priority of sexuality to reproductive capacity in developing humans is confirmed as well by biological findings. The development of the procreative capability in an adolescent is the product of biological sex, which is set already in the womb. In fact, even though the chromosome heritage of a fetus usually is not manifested until the sixth or seventh week so that in the first stage of development the fetus appears neuter or indifferent, the male or female potentiality is fixed at conception and is already present in the "neuter" stage.[3] Recent studies indicate that certain biologically based differences between males and females are evident in early infancy.[4]

Not only does sexual differentiation predate reproductive capacities in human beings, it is also present after the cessation of that capacity. Older adults, for example, remain sexual beings even after their reproductive capacities have ceased, as do persons who for physical reasons or because of mental malfunction will never be capable of reproduction. Recent research has documented the presence of interest in sexual expression in older persons.[5]

These factors all suggest that sexuality, while related to function in the process of reproduction, is actually a deeper dimension of our existence. For this reason, Milton Diamond and Arno Karlen define human sexual development as "everything in body, mind, and behavior that rises from being male or female."[6] In keeping with this understanding, many psychologists differentiate between "affective" and "genital" sexuality, a differentiation that dates to Freud.[7] "Genital sexuality," of course, refers to the physiological or biological dimension. The affective aspect, in contrast, goes deeper. It includes the emotional and psychological dimensions of our sexuality, lies behind the mystery of our need to reach out to others,[8] and is the basis for affection, compassion, tenderness, and warmth.[9]

b. Sexuality and Genesis. The opening chapters of Genesis indicate a similar orientation point and lead to a similar conclusion. The Creation and Fall sequence in Genesis 2—3 portrays sexual distinctions as being present already from the beginning with the creation of the woman from the man. The narrator indicates that upon creating the woman God brought her to the man. At this point, however, she is not viewed in terms of her function in reproduction. She is simply 'ishshāh, "female," just as he is 'îsh, "male,"[10] a point that is unfortunately lost by the English term *woman* with its explicit reproductive connotation (womb-man). In the narrative, actual mention of procreative capabilities comes only after the Fall. Only then does the man call his wife, Eve, a name that denotes her status as the mother of all the living. Adam then "knows" his wife, and she gives birth to a son.

This observation raises a crucial question. Does the Genesis narrative intend to indicate a relationship between sexuality and sinfulness? More specifically, is procreation itself to be viewed as a result of the Fall? The sequence of the narrative of Genesis 2—3, which only makes explicit reference to sexual activity after the Fall, has exerted a powerful influence in theological history. Although the motif of sexual consummation prior to the Fall was present in the rabbinic tradition and predates the Christian era, the church was more influenced by another Jewish tradition, the Levitical, which viewed Eden in terms of priestly purity within the temple.[11] This theme formed an important foundation for the Augustinian-medieval attitude toward human sexuality with its cautious stance toward sexual relations and its elevation of celibacy. Gregory of Nyssa, for example, held explicitly to this view, declaring that original creation was sexless and that sexuality resulted from the Fall. Augustine postulated that sexuality was present from the beginning of Creation. Nevertheless, he placed the exercise of sexuality under the sphere of sin. Even within the context of marriage, he maintained, the sex act was tainted with lust, because it participated in the Fall.

Two considerations, however, point us in a different direction.

First, the Creation account of Genesis 1 forms the context in which to understand that of Genesis 2. The shorter statement concerning the creation of humankind found in Genesis 1:27 includes the human procreative potential apart from any mention of the Fall. God creates humankind as male and female from the beginning. And he commands them to "be fruitful and multiply," implying the presence of reproductive capacities as a corollary of their existence as male and female.

Second, likewise in the second Creation narrative sexual distinctions, division into male and female, are evident already in the creation of the first human pair, being visible in the use of the similar sounding masculine and feminine terms, 'îsh and 'ishshāh. In the narrative, it is first after the Fall that Adam and Eve give expression to their sexuality through the birth of offspring. Nevertheless, the narrator does not mean to suggest that the procreative potential itself is a product of sin. On the contrary, it predates the Fall. Both accounts, then, follow a similar sequence. Sexual differences are presented as existing from Creation. This fundamental sexuality, in turn, forms the basis for the procreative function, which in Genesis is in view from the beginning, even though in Genesis 2—3 this function is not explicitly mentioned until the two humans are expelled from the garden.

While procreation (and thus genital sexuality) ought to be seen as implicit already from the beginning with the creation of humankind as male and female, it is not without significance that the text explicitly mentions the actual expression of the procreative function only after the Fall. Its importance may be seen when this observation is placed within the context of the main theme of the Bible as a whole—namely, God's salvific action. Already in the *proto-evangelium* of Genesis 3:15 a foregleam of the purpose of human procreation in the divine plan of salvation is evident. God promises that the seed of the woman will bruise the head of the serpent. The church has consistently interpreted this as a veiled reference to the Coming One who would be victorious over God's foe. The Victor would be the offspring of the woman.

Genital sexuality, then, is present from the beginning. But with the Fall it takes on a new, significant meaning which can move in either of two directions. On the one hand, human sexuality with its procreative potential, like all aspects of human existence, can now be used as an instrument of sin. History is filled with examples of this denegration of the potential found within human sexuality. On the other hand, after the Fall God employs the human procreative capacity as a vehicle of divine grace. This aspect of human existence comes to play a central role in God's purposes in bringing to humankind redemption from the effects of sin and the Fall, for through the procreative potential of humanity, God's Son enters the world.

c. Sexuality as the link to the order of life. Human sexuality both forms a link to the order of created life and sets humankind apart from that order. As a result, to employ the assertion of V. A. Demant, "sex in mankind has a dual aspect."[12] Demant divides the two levels of human sexuality into the drive to propagate the species through procreation, which humans share with many other life forms (*venus*), and the communion which the sex act nurtures between the sex partners, which sets humans above the world of nature (*eros*).[13]

The dual dimension of human sexuality is visible already in the procreative potential present in humans as a result of their existence as sexual beings.[14] Because procreation through the sex act links humankind with the animal world, sexuality mediates human participation in a reality in the created order that is not limited to humankind. Rather, propagation through sex acts is a feature of the divine plan shared by many species, being one specific expression of the survival instinct that pervades all life forms. This participation in the realm of nature provides a point of departure for an understanding of the nearly instinctual pervasiveness of sexual expression in humans.

At the same time, the procreative potential that arises from sexuality places humankind in a category apart from the rest of creation. God calls humans to participate in the divine work in salvation history. One dimension of this participation lies in the expression of human sexuality. After the Fall the begetting of children through the procreative function became the vehicle that linked the first human pair to the coming of the Messiah. And procreation continues to the end of the age, an understanding of which, within the context of the mandate to the church, we will develop subsequently.

The role of human procreation in God's salvific purpose in bringing the Son into the world and its importance as a part of the mandate of the church offer a clue as to why this capacity, which is present in humankind from the beginning, plays no apparent role in the eschatological kingdom, even though the broader aspect of human sexuality remains a part of human existence. As will be argued later, in the age to come we remain sexual creatures and give expression to our sexuality in various ways. But as Jesus' statement to those who attempted to test him with the dilemma of the woman who had been married to seven brothers quite clearly indicates, marriage and procreation will no longer be among these expressions (Matt. 22:30).[15]

The procreative potential that arises from sexuality both links and separates humankind from the rest of the order of life. But human sexuality encompasses more than procreation, more than the drive to perpetuate the species. As will be developed subsequently, sexuality also forms the dynamic which unites male and female together to form a unity of persons. This dynamic likewise both links and separates humankind and the rest of the life order. Sexually derived bonding is evident among some of the higher species in the animal world, indicating the participation of humankind in a wider reality. But human sexuality offers a potential for forming personal unity that goes beyond that found among animals. In humans sexually derived bonding is less strictly orientated to procreation and the rearing of offspring, for it can develop into the type of unity of persons which is spoken of as love.

This potential for the sharing of love, which has its basis in sexuality, gives to humankind a special status in creation. According to the Bible, only humans are designed to be the image of God. This theme will be developed in the next chapter.

d. The nature of human sexuality. Although sexuality is closely related to biological sex and procreation, they are not to be simply equated. Sexuality refers to our fundamental existence as male or female. The sexual distinctions we note in relating to one another, in contrast, focus most readily on the physical differences between the sexes. Differing functions in the human reproductive potential are one specific capacity that these physical differences make possible. Yet, the distinctions that give expression to our sexuality, our fundamental maleness or femaleness, run deeper than the procreative function.

Our sexuality is a basic datum of our existence as individuals. Simply stated, it refers to our way of being in the world and relating to the world as male or female. Studies within the social sciences indicate that males and females view the world differently; they "have different modes of orientation."[16] Our sexuality is related to this fundamental difference.

Further, sexuality is a dimension of our existence as embodied persons. As we will see later, at its core this embodied existence includes a fundamental incompleteness, one which is symbolized by biological sex and is based in our sexuality. Through sexuality we give expression both to our existence as embodied creatures and to our basic incompleteness as embodied persons in our relationships to each other and to the world. Our sexuality, then, calls us to move toward completeness. It forms the foundation for the drive which moves male and female to come together to form a unity of persons in marriage. But this yearning toward completeness also lies at the basis of the interpersonal and religious dimensions of human existence as a whole.

The concept of sexuality presented here suggests that a distinction exists between sexual desire and the desire for sex,[17] both of which arise out of our basic sexuality. "Sexual desire" refers to the need we all share to experience wholeness and intimacy through relationships with others. It relates to the dimension often called *eros,* the human longing to possess and be possessed by the object of one's desire. Understood in this way, *eros* ought not be limited to genital sexual acts, but encompasses a broad range of human actions and desires, and it participates even in the religious dimension of life in the form of the desire to know and be known by God. For many people, the desire for sex, the longing to express one's sexuality through genital acts (*venus*), is psychologically inseparable from sexual desire. Nevertheless, for the development of true sexual maturity, a person must come to terms with the difference between these two dimensions and learn to separate them both in one's own psychological state and in overt action.

This understanding of human sexuality is gaining broad support across the theological spectrum. A study commissioned by the Catholic Theological Society of America concluded from the Vatican *Declaration on Sexual Ethics:*

> The experience of people today supported by contemporary behavioral and theological sciences understands sexuality much more broadly. Sex is seen as a force that permeates, influences, and affects every act of a person's being at every moment of existence. It is not operative in one restricted area of life but is rather at the core and center of our total life-response.[18]

A similar statement was adopted by the Tenth General Convention of the American Lutheran Church:

> Human sexuality includes all that we are as human beings. Sexuality at the very least is biological, psychological, cultural, social, and spiritual. It is as much of the mind as of the body, of the community as of the person. To be a person is to be a sexual being.[19]

Sexuality, then, belongs to the mystery of personhood and the mystery of the image of God.

2. The Expression of Sexuality

While being related to both, human sexuality is not to be equated with either physical sexual characteristics or procreative capacity, for it is that dimension of human existence that lies behind physical features. Sexuality comprises all aspects of the human person that are related to existence as male and female. Our sexuality, therefore, is a powerful, deep, and mysterious aspect of our being. It constitutes a fundamental distinction between the two ways of being human (i.e., as male or female). This distinction plays a crucial role in our development toward becoming individuals and our existence as social beings.

We give expression to the fundamental sexual dimension of our being in many ways. The most obvious, of course, is through sexual attraction and sexually determined acts. Such acts include the way we speak and touch others, especially those to whom we are sexually attracted, and ultimately in genital sexual relations. But there are other ways of expressing our sexuality. These may range from the seemingly mundane—how we dress, comb our hair, etc.—to the more sublime—the appreciation of beauty, as well as cultural and artistic preferences and activities. The sexual aspect of our existence likewise forms the basis for our sensuousness. Letha Scanzoni aptly described this dimension as

> our capacity for enjoying and celebrating all kinds of bodily sensations, whether it be the fuzzy warmth of a new blanket, the bracing splash of a summer rainshower, the tender hug of a friend, or the playful nuzzling of a puppy.[20]

In a sense, our sexuality pervades all our relationships. We constantly relate to others as male or female. And our relationships to persons of the same sex differ from our relationships to the opposite sex.[21] This relation-pervading aspect of human sexuality forms the basis for the development of societal understandings of sex roles and of proper and improper sexual behavior. Such social mores, in turn, give rise to the task of expressing our sexuality in positive, beneficial ways.

Sexuality and Our Essential Being

Sexuality denotes more than the physical distinctions that allow for the differentiation in reproductive functions. Instead, the sexual dimension of the human reality encompasses all the various aspects of the human person that are related to existence as male or female. This understanding of human sexuality is relatively noncontroversial. It calls forth, however, a further question that in contrast to the first generates a variety of responses: Is sexuality an essential feature of our being?

In recent times much sympathy has been building for a positive response to this question. As noted above, many observers both in the human sciences and in the theological disciplines agree that sexuality is so all pervasive of the human person that it must be considered an essential dimension of what it means to be human. How we think, how we view the world, and how others view us are all affected by our sexuality. We can be human, therefore, only as male or female.

This viewpoint, however, has not generated a consensus. Throughout history there have been strong voices declaring in various ways that the true human essence lies beyond sexuality and gender distinctions.

1. Sexual Distinctions
as Peripheral to Essential Humanity

Christian thought has repeatedly denied the essential importance of human sexual distinctions. In the Middle Ages, for example, theologians generally described the essential nature of the human person in terms of the soul, seen as a nonmaterial substance constituting the core of each individual. In the same way, the image of God was viewed as a structure of the human person located in the human soul. This viewpoint tended to minimize bodily existence, and thus sexuality. Body (and sex) was separated from the soul and thereby was made ultimately superfluous to individual personhood, localized in the soul. The soul lay above sexuality. Both sexes, it was asserted, participate in the common essence of humankind apart from their existence as sexual creatures, although the scholastic theologians also differentiated between the sexes, asserting that women were in some sense inferior to men. Although the idea may seem humorous to us, medieval divines such as Thomas Aquinas accepted Aristotle's declaration that the rational soul is present in a female fetus eighty days after conception, in contrast to the forty-day interval in the case of a male fetus.

The medieval view is seldom articulated today in the categories of the scholastic theologians. Yet a somewhat similar understanding can be detected in the contemporary concept of androgyny. This view posits only one fundamental human essence lying beyond but also encompassing the sexual distinctions of male and female. The implication is, of course, that sexual differentiations are ultimately peripheral.

Although popularized recently by certain feminists, androgynous anthropology was present in the ancient world. Among the myths of the Greeks, for example, is a story that explains human origins in androgynous categories. According to Plato's retelling of this myth through the character Aristophenes in *The Symposium,* the original humans were unified wholes and globular in shape. As a punishment for their pride after their foiled attempt to conquer heaven by force, they were split into two halves. Now individuals are incomplete until they find union with their complements.

The Greek myth has exercised great influence in Western thought. It has at times colored the exegesis of the second creation account in Genesis 2, which is understandable in that God's creating the woman from a rib of Adam lends itself to the Greek myth. As a result, some exegetes view the original human as an androgynous being who becomes sexual only through the act of division into male and female.[22]

A contemporary variant on the theme of androgyny builds on Jungian depth psychology. Jung spoke of two dimensions of the soul related to gender (*animus* and *anima*) which all persons share, albeit to differing degrees depending on the sex of the individual.[23] Based on this theory, George Tavard argued that "men and women are complementary in sexual activity, yet identically human in everything else." Thus, he advocated a "harmonization of masculine and feminine," which he conceived "not as two modes of human nature or two ways of being human, but as two dimensions of every human person, the balance of each dimension varying from person to person."[24]

This viewpoint is helpful, especially as it seeks to avoid any identification of some virtues as essentially male and others as female. Nevertheless, it appears that the distinctions between the sexes run deeper into the individual psyche than is indicated by Tavard's suggestion that apart from sexual activity men and women are identically human.

2. The Basis for Affirming the Essential Nature of Sexuality

Despite their popularity, anthropologies that reject the essential nature of human sexuality are unable to account for the extent to which male and female differ. Sexuality, it seems, constitutes an essential dimension of the human person.

As noted earlier, the essential nature of our existence as sexual beings is becoming increasingly evident from the findings of the human sciences. Biology offers an example. John Money, a medical psychologist from Johns Hopkins University, to cite one example, concluded from his research that individuals go through four stages in the prenatal development of biological sexual identity. Most crucial to this process, however, is conception. At this point, one's biological sex is already determined, set by the coming together of chromosomes from sperm and egg, even though subsequent stages sometimes produce a situation in which the four bases for biological sex determination are at odds with each other.[25] In most cases, a person's genetically based sex forms the foundation out of which normal psychological sexual identity emerges.[26]

Our essential sexuality is supported likewise by theology.[27] Specifically, the assertion that sexuality belongs to the essential nature of the human person arises from two Christian doctrines, creation and resurrection. God created us as embodied beings, and in the resurrection recreates us in like fashion. Together the two doctrines confirm a basically holistic anthropology that includes our sexuality.

a. The doctrine of creation. The Old Testament fulfills a foundational role for the Christian doctrine of creation. The outlook concerning human origins that arose among the ancient Hebrew people formed the context for, and came to be reaffirmed in its basic form in, the New Testament. In contrast to that of the Greek philosophical tradition, the Hebrew understanding of creation resulted in a basically holistic or unitary anthropology. Greek anthropology was dualistic; it understood the human person in terms of two distinct substantial entities, generally termed "body" and "soul." The Hebrews viewed the human person as a unitary, embodied being. Although references to creation are scattered throughout the Old Testament, the most succinct statement of the forming of humankind is found in the opening chapters of Genesis.

In the first creation story, God is presented as simply making humankind, just as he had made the other aspects of the universe, including other living things. There is no indication that humans are anything but a part of the material world. They are created in the divine image, but their special creation entails no fundamental dualism in the human person that gives higher status to one part of the person, a nonmaterial soul, in contrast to the material body. The soul constitutes the "real" person. In fact, the only dualism in the text is the male/female distinction.

The second narrative offers more detail. God's creation of the man occurs in two steps. He forms him from the dust of the ground (material) and breathes life into him. But even this is not to be interpreted as meaning that God constituted the man as an ontological dualism. Rather, the emphasis falls on the fact that he is an animated being, a material creature animated by the life principle from God. The Pentateuch subsequently indicates that the animals are likewise animated, for they too are spoken of as "soul."[28] In this narrative, as in the first, the important distinction that arises from creation is the dual aspect of the first human pair as male and female.

From the perspective of the Genesis stories, then, humans are the creation of God in their entire being. God fashioned animate material creatures, each of whom comprises a unity of being. Genesis offers no indication that there are two substantial entities in the human person, as postulated by Greek anthropology, no indication of a soul/body dualism. In the narrative the human person is the whole person, the embodied person; the real human being is not localized in some spiritual principle standing within the material body. Rather, each human is an embodied creature.

b. The doctrine of resurrection. The basic holistic or unitary anthropology of the Old Testament forms the context for, and is reaffirmed in, the doctrine of resurrection. In fact, the resurrection offers the ultimate critique of all dualist anthropologies, for it declares that the body is essential to human personhood. Rather than the body being shed in order for the person to enter eternity, as in the Greek philosophical tradition, the human being comes into fullness of life as an animated body, as an embodied person transformed in one's entire being through the resurrection.

This doctrine indicates that God's creation of humankind as animated material beings is not a temporary act. Instead, the creation of the first human as a synthesis of the material from the earth and the animating principle, evidenced in Genesis, actually belongs to the human destiny as God's creation. God's intent is that humans exist as embodied persons.

The divine intent that our sexuality participate in the eschatological transformation of the person is confirmed by the resurrection of Jesus. The main purpose of the postresurrection stories of the Gospels as well as the Pauline appeal to the appearances of the Risen Christ is to indicate that the Risen Lord was recognized as none other than Jesus of Nazareth, the one who had been crucified. He had passed through the event of transformation into the new existence described metaphorically as eternal life, the apostolic tradition declared. Yet, according to the Gospel narratives Jesus remained an embodied reality. His disciples touched him, ate with him, and conversed with him. And they knew who he was. The Risen Lord had remained the recognizable Jesus.

The appearance traditions give no indication that Jesus had shed his maleness in the hours between Good Friday and Easter Sunday. He is presented as recognizable by sight to those who had known him. This would seem to suggest that the basic male physical features of Jesus of Nazareth were preserved through the transformation experience of the resurrection.

If in the paradigm of the eschatological resurrection the external maleness of the Risen Jesus is preserved (albeit only as it is transformed) so that he remains physically recognizable, then how much more are the deeper characteristics of maleness/femaleness preserved (yet again only as transformed) in the glorified state entered through the general resurrection at the consummation of history.

Some theologians assert the nonsexual nature of the resurrection state by means of an appeal to Jesus' statement, "At the resurrection people will neither marry nor be given in marriage: they will be like the angels in heaven" (Matt. 22:30).[29] However, two considerations indicate that Jesus' intent is not to deny the presence of sexuality in the eschatological community. First, Jesus does not explicitly declare that sexuality will be absent, only that marriage will no longer be practiced. Human sexuality will no longer be expressed in genital sexual acts, and the sexually based drive toward bonding will no longer be expressed through male-female coupling. This is not to suggest, however, that the deeper dimensions of sexuality will be eradicated. Second, Jesus declared that humans will be like the angels. Although some theologians see in this statement an assertion of a nonsexual existence, to do so is to go beyond Jesus' point, which is to assert only the nonmarital nature of the kingdom society. Even though they do not marry, the angels might in fact be sexual beings. This understanding can claim a long exegetical tradition of certain biblical texts (e.g., Gen. 6:4; 1 Cor. 11:10; Jude 6).

c. Implications for human sexuality.

The unitary anthropology inherent in the Hebrew-Christian doctrines of creation and resurrection indicates that sexuality is a constitutive part of the human reality as an embodied existence. We are created by God as embodied creatures. And our sexuality—to exist as male or female—belongs to our embodied status. Genesis 1:27 declares, "male and female he created them." There is simply no other way to be a created human, to exist as a human being, except as an embodied person. And embodiment means existence as a sexual being, as male or female.

This close relationship between embodied existence and being male or female is in keeping with the discovery of modern psychology that identity formation is closely connected with our sexuality. We simply see ourselves as male or female, and our fundamental sexuality becomes the primary and deepest aspect of our existence in the quest to determine who we are.

The doctrine of the resurrection indicates that the foundational role played by sexuality in determining identity is not destroyed in eternity. Resurrection means that our entire person, including our body, passes through transformation. But because existence as an embodied person means existence as male or female, our sexuality must participate in the event of resurrection as well. Our sexuality participates by necessity, for it is a part of the total person who undergoes transformation.

3. Objections to the Essential Nature of Sexuality

As has been mentioned, an alternative tradition has been present in Christian history, maintaining that sexuality is external to the essential nature of humanity. From this tradition arise certain objections to the assertion that sexuality is an aspect of our essential personhood.

First, it could be argued that our sexuality does not belong to our personhood, because we are complete persons apart from our maleness or femaleness. The strength of this position is found in the claim that each human being, as a human person, participates in the image of God, and this apart from any distinctions among people, including those of gender. Two texts stand out as the most prominent in support of this position. The Old Testament law puts forth a strong injunction against murder, the basis of which lay in the creation of humans in the divine image. The Torah places the genesis of this prohibition in the covenant God made with Noah:

> "Whoever sheds man's blood,
> By man his blood shall be shed,
> For in the image of God
> He made man." (Gen. 9:6 NASB)

The sole New Testament reference to the universality of the image of God in humanity comes in the context of a warning concerning the destructive power of the human tongue: "With the tongue we praise our Lord and Father, and with it we curse men, who have been made in God's likeness" (James 3:9).

There is, of course, a sense in which each person as an individual is the image of God, albeit in the sense that to be in the image of God is the divine intention or goal shared by all. Nevertheless, we ought not to surmise from this theological conclusion nor from these two biblical statements that we are complete beings as individual selves. To do so would run counter to the tenor of the Bible as a whole. The biblical anthropology is quite clear that we are not complete in ourselves. On the contrary, we are created for and destined for life in community. We find true fulfillment in community, ultimately in the eschatological community of the people of God characterized by fellowship among the human family, harmony with creation, and fellowship with God.

The two texts cited above may readily be understood in this context. Neither actually asserts that each individual now possesses the image of God. On the contrary, corporate or generic language is employed in both. Although the eschatological perspective is not specifically present in either text, neither categorically denies this perspective, but both may readily be read within it. Finally, the main emphasis must be placed on the intent of each of the two texts, which lies in the moral injunction each carries. To support the commands they enjoin, the texts appeal to a widely held premise, the universal participation of humanity in the divine intent for creation. No indication is given in either text as to how humans actually participate in this divine ideal.

A second argument against the assertion that sexuality is essential to humanity appeals to a common human essence. All persons share in humanness, it is maintained. The strength of this position is found in its link to the assertion of the unity of humanity, which is both a theological dictum and a biological reality. Theologically, this assertion declares that all persons, regardless of sex, are members of the one human family. In terms of biology, we are all linked genetically.

The declaration of the fundamental unity of all human beings is a crucial theological assertion that carries important implications. And the existence of a common genetic pool is a significant biological discovery.

Nevertheless, neither of these statements leads to the conclusion that there is a common human essence which, because it transcends our sexual distinctions, makes them nonessential to our existence and identity as human beings. On the contrary, we are human only as male or female; there is no other way for each of us to exist except as this embodied, and therefore sexual, human person.

A third argument moves in a quite different direction from the other two. It readily admits that our sexuality—our existence as male or female—is a central aspect in determining who we are. But it denies that sexuality is uniquely determinative of personal identity. Our basic maleness or femaleness is a factor in who we are, how we perceive ourselves, how we think, how others perceive us, how we relate to others. Other factors—such as race, for example—play an equally important role in the process of identity formation, it is argued.

Although undeniably important, racial differences and other factors do not loom as foundational in personal and social identity as do those distinctions which arise out of the fact that we are sexual beings. The first aspect noticed at birth is not race, but sex. And we carry with us throughout our lives the tendency to see our maleness or femaleness as the fundamental demarcation among ourselves. It is interesting to note the presence of this human tendency in the early biblical stories of human origins. Racial distinction is not presented in Genesis as arising from creation itself, as is the case with sex distinctions. Rather, the races first emerge after the Flood.

4. Embodiment in Christian Theology and in Secularism

Contrary to what we might at first surmise, the emphasis of the human person as an embodied and therefore a sexual being is more pronounced in the Christian understanding than in the basically secular anthropology widespread in Western culture today. The biblical doctrines of creation and resurrection imply that our sexuality is basic to our sense of self and foundational to our understanding of who we are as God's creatures. God intends that we be embodied beings who are either male or female.

Further, because our sexuality is the product of God's creative intention, it constitutes an essential aspect of the way we stand before God. As God's creatures, humans are responsible before God to be stewards of all they are. This responsibility extends to our sexuality as well, for our existence as male or female is essential to our being. The Christian, therefore, must take the Pauline admonition seriously.

> Do you not know that your body is a temple of the Holy Spirit, who is in you, whom you have received from God? You are not your own; you were bought at a price. Therefore honor God with your body. (1 Cor. 6:19–20)

The secular anthropology, in contrast, tends to view sexuality largely as an activity, not as a constitutive aspect of our being. Sexual expression becomes thereby something in which the self engages. When viewed in this manner, as an activity in which the acting subject engages rather than an essential aspect of who a person is, sexuality is more readily separated from the self. Similar to the Gnostics of the New Testament era, the secularist differentiates between "who I am" and "what I do," seeing "what I do" as external to "who I am," that is, to my personhood.

This attitude toward human sexuality in general and the sex act in particular is readily linked with the modern understanding of the basic nature of the human person. A fundamental shift in thought has emerged since the

Enlightenment. In contrast to the more socially oriented viewpoint character-istic of much of Christian tradition, there has been a growing tendency in the modern era toward a fully individualistic understanding of human nature. The human person, the modern view maintains, is an independent self, whose essence is to make choices in freedom. The self is fundamentally a free deci-sion maker, and this fundamental nature of the self characterizes all persons regardless of whatever distinctions (such as sex) differentiate one human self from another. In the choosing self, modern anthropology claims to find the transcendent human essence lying beyond all observable differences.

As an outworking of this anthropology, the sex act is viewed as one vehi-cle for the expression of the freely choosing self. Sex is a means whereby the human person as a free agent of action actualizes personal freedom. In keep-ing with this understanding the code words of the modern sexual revolution in-clude *self-expression* and *self-actualization*. The 1960s phase of this revolution declared that the modern outlook ought to be applied not only to the male do-main, as was the case in prior decades, but to females as well. Thus, it called for freedom of sexual expression not only for men but also for women.

The Christian viewpoint differs radically from the modern, secularized al-ternative. Because of our view of the human person as a unified being, we sim-ply cannot follow those voices which assert that the body can be indulged with-out affecting the essential person. Because we are created as embodied persons, we cannot relegate the sexual dimension of our existence to the realm of the nonsignificant, as having no bearing on our relation to God. Further, we refuse to view our fundamental identity as human beings in terms of freedom. The human person is not primarily the freely choosing self. Nor can our exis-tence as male or female be set aside as external to our essential nature. Because of this mistaken understanding of sexuality, therefore, the sexual freedom es-poused by the sexual revolution, despite whatever positive gains it may have brought, in the words of Vance Packard, "seems to be a dubious goal."[30]

According to the biblical documents, we are not primarily and essentially souls and secondarily and consequently bodies. Rather, from original creation to the new creation we are embodied beings. Our personhood is tied together with the fact that we are "flesh and blood." But to be embodied, to be flesh and blood, entails being male or female. There is simply no other way to ex-ist except as this particular female or this particular male. We are indeed es-sentially sexual beings.

Male and Female

2

Humankind as a Sexual Creation

Human beings are sexual creatures. The individual dimension of our fundamental sexuality is part of normal living, for we are continually made aware of the fact that humankind is divided into two sexually determined groups, male and female. The previous chapter offered the first step in the attempt to provide a Christian perspective on the phenomenon of human existence as male and female, which can serve as a beginning point for the task of developing a Christian response to the ethical issues surrounding human sexuality. That chapter looked at the individual side of the thesis that humans are a sexual creation, viewing the human *person* as a sexual being.

Less obvious than the individual dimension, but no less real, is the corporate dimension of human sexuality. We are not sexual beings in isolation from each other. Rather, our individual sexual nature is closely linked to our situation as social beings. In short, sexuality is significant for community. This chapter develops the theme of the corporate or social dynamic of human sexuality, asking the theological question, what does the Creator intend in constituting us as sexually determined beings?

The Social Purpose of Our
Creation as Sexual Beings

The quest for an understanding of the social dimension of our sexuality is closely connected with an awareness of the purpose of this aspect of our essential nature. The concept of purpose can be formulated in terms of a question: What can be discovered concerning the role that our essential sexuality plays in our total existence? This question seeks to understand the social outworking of individual sexuality, in order thereby to discover the goal the Creator had in view in creating us as sexual beings.

1. Bonding—the Basic Purpose

The basic purpose of our existence as sexual creatures is related to the dynamic of bonding. There is a close relationship between human sexuality and the bonding process, so much so that sexuality forms the fundamental drive that leads to this human phenomenon. The close relationship between bonding and sexuality is borne out by the biblical documents. However, the two Testaments find the central expression of the dynamic of bonding in two different institutions, the family and the church.

The Old Testament: the family bond. Human sexuality and the drive toward bonding play an important role in the Old Testament. Perhaps the most powerful statement of the relationship between sexuality and bonding is presented in the second creation story. This connection lies behind the narrative of the formation of the woman in Genesis 2.

The creative act that brought the first woman into existence is presented in Genesis 2 as the outworking of the divine intent: "I will make a helper suitable for him," called forth by the divine observation of the situation of the first human, "It is not good for the man to be alone" (Gen. 2:18). Although the human enjoyed a relationship with the animals, none of them was an appropriate bonding partner for him: "But for Adam no suitable helper was found" (v. 20). The Hebrew term *helper* ought not to be interpreted in the sense of serving as an assistant. The Hebrew word, *'ēzer,* derived from the verb *'āzar,* which means "other" or "helper," also refers to one who saves or delivers. Apart from this verse it is only used with reference to God in relationship to Israel (Deut. 33:7; Ps. 32:20; 115:9). God's desire, therefore, was to create another human being who would deliver Adam from his solitude by being a suitable bonding partner for him, not merely sexually, but in all dimensions of existence.[1] At this point God creates the woman. In contrast to his response to the animals, Adam immediately senses a bond with her. He bursts forth in joyous declaration: She is "bone of my bones and flesh of my flesh" (v. 23).

The Genesis narrative indicates that the sexual nature of the human person forms the impulse that drives an individual beyond the self to seek bonding with others. Adam's solitude arose from a void that could not be filled by his companionship with the animals nor, interestingly enough, even by the presence of the solitary Adam before God. The appropriate antidote for this situation was the creation not merely of a counterpart, but more specifically of a female counterpart. This indicates the sexual nature both of Adam's solitude and of his awareness of solitude. The void in his existence was sexually based, for he was fundamentally incomplete. And his sense of incompleteness gave birth to the cry of joy, when he was introduced to his sexual counterpart.

The narrator concludes the episode with the application of his story to the phenomenon of male-female bonding expressed in the marriage relationship: "For this reason a man will leave his father and mother and be united to his wife, and they will become one flesh" (v. 24). The meaning of the phrase, "and they will become one flesh," is lost if it is interpreted to refer only to the begetting of offspring. It is rather a further statement of the previous clause, "a man . . . will be united to his wife." Thus, it moves beyond procreative unity to encompass the entire bond enjoyed in the marriage relationship. Hence, the narrator's comment presents the awareness of a fundamental personal incompleteness ("for this cause") as the dynamic lying behind the phenomenon of the two actions, "leaving" and "cleaving." This awareness, in other words, results in the drive for the bonding expressed in the relationship of husband and wife.

The Old Testament finds a further outworking of the relationship between sexuality and bonding. The bonding that transpires through the union of male and female, although completed in the marriage relationship, does not end with husband and wife as an isolated union. Rather, this intimate bond becomes a first step toward the establishment of the broader human community.

This too is evident already in Genesis. The fellowship between man and woman formed in the marriage relationship is presented in the Genesis creation narrative as the primal human community. But arising naturally out of this union is the expansion of community into the family unit that occurs as Eve bears children. And the primal human community expands beyond the family as the generations multiply, resulting in the establishment of cities (Gen. 4:17) and even entire societies characterized by a division of labor (4:21–22).

In this way sexually based bonding forms the basis for the Old Testament view concerning human community in general.[2] For the ancient Hebrews, the primary social unit was the extended family, headed generally by a male patriarch and including his wife/wives, offspring, and household. As a result, there arose in Israel a strong emphasis on the importance of bearing children, especially sons. The emphasis on progeny, in turn, provided the context for the ancient understanding of the development of the wider social order. Patriarchalism produced the sense of tribal identity, for a person's participation in the tribe as a wider expression of social relationships was determined by lineage as derived from male ancestors.

The centrality that tribal identity enjoyed among the ancient Hebrews was never lost within Israel. Despite attempts by the Davidic monarchy to develop a sense of nationalism to displace tribalism among the twelve tribes, the nationalistic impulse was never able to overcome the primacy of the tribal consciousness. In fact, tribalism remained a dominant aspect in determining the sense of community identity and participation in the social order in Israel into the New Testament era.

In the Old Testament, however, the family remained the primary focus for the experience of human community. The primacy of the family is highlighted in various ways in the Old Testament. The Ten Commandments enjoin honor to father and mother, as carrying great significance as "the first commandment carrying a promise." The family is likewise presented as the first focal point for religious instruction. Through the family the traditions of the tribe are to be passed from generation to generation (e.g., Deut. 4:9; 6:1–9; Ps. 78:5–6).

The basic relationship between sexuality and bonding, leading to community set forth in the Old Testament, continues to carry importance into the modern era. As in the ancient world, sexuality functions today as the primary drive toward bonding and community. Despite what one might conclude from the rise of divorce in Western society, most people continue to view marriage as the most enduring and stable bond formed during a human lifetime. The conclusion of the Genesis narrator remains appropriate: "For this cause a man shall leave his father and his mother, and shall cleave to his wife" (NASB). And stable marriages that provide the context in which children can gain a sense of personal identity continue to function as the backbone of societal stability.

The Genesis 2 narrative carries significant implications for a contemporary understanding of sexuality. Because we are sexual beings, as isolated individuals we are fundamentally incomplete. Our sexuality not only participates in, and in part is the cause of our incompleteness; it also allows us to sense this incompleteness, an incompleteness that in turn moves us to seek community through bonding.[3] For many, the primary place of community becomes marriage and the family, both of which arise out of our basic sexuality. But as will be developed in chapters 9 and 10, even in the case of unmarried persons, the drive to community, while not specifically oriented toward genital expression, is nevertheless based in the sense of the incompleteness of the human individual apart from community.

The drive for community has powerful theological implications as well. Our sexually based sense of incompleteness forms the dynamic lying behind the search for truth, a search which ultimately becomes the search for God. We long to have our incompleteness fulfilled, and this longing gives rise to the religious dimension of life. The message of the Bible, beginning already in the Old Testament book of Genesis, claims that in the final analysis, the source of this completeness is found in the community that focuses on fellowship with the Creator.

The theological interpretation of the quest for community has been given expression in various ways in the Christian tradition. Augustine, for example, described it in terms of the restlessness of the human heart until it finds rest in God.[4] Likewise, medieval mysticism arose as a response to the same impulse to find completeness in union with God. The emphasis on the new birth characteristic of pietism and of contemporary evangelicalism is similarly motivated by the desire for fellowship, specifically fellowship with God and with the people of God.

The drive for completeness and for completion in fellowship with God is not surprising, because it is in keeping with the theological assertion that we are created in God's image. Just as God is the community of the trinitarian persons, so also God has created us for the sake of community, namely, to find completion in community with each other and together in community with our Maker.

The New Testament: the bonded community. The Christian understanding of community finds its roots in the New Testament. The early church moved beyond the ancient Hebrews by offering a new understanding of the nature of the primal human community. In the Old Testament era, the sense of community was primarily associated with one's immediate family, extended patriarchal family, and tribe. Only subsequently and secondarily did the individual sense an identity with the nation of Israel as constituting one people and a specifically religious people.

In the New Testament era, however, an important change occurs. Now the primary community is no longer presented as the physical family, entrance to which occurs through natural familial heritage. Rather, the central community is the fellowship of Christ. More important than physical ancestry—who one's parents are—is one's spiritual ancestry—who one's heavenly Father is (e.g., Luke 3:7–8; John 8:31–59). The highest loyalty is now directed to God through community with Jesus Christ. And the primary bond is that which binds the disciple to the Master and to the community of disciples.

This change in outlook was inaugurated by Jesus himself. It is embodied in his demanding challenge to discipleship, summarized in his admonition:

> "Anyone who loves his father or mother more than me is not worthy of me; anyone who loves his son or daughter more than me is not worthy of me." (Matt. 10:37)

At the same time he promises to the loyal disciple a larger, spiritual family to compensate for the loss entailed in leaving one's natural family for the sake of discipleship:

> "I tell you the truth, . . . no one who has left home or brothers or sisters or mother or father or children or fields for me and the gospel will fail to receive a hundred times as much in this present age . . . and in the age to come, eternal life." (Mark. 10:29–30)

But what Jesus demanded of his followers, he required of himself. He too forsook family for the sake of the cause of the kingdom of God. Rather than attaching himself to his physical mother and siblings, he counted as his true family "whoever does the will of my Father in heaven . . ." (Matt. 12:50).

Jesus' view was carried over into the early church. The Jerusalem believers, for example, looked to the community of discipleship as their primary focus of fellowship and loyalty. They were bonded to each other, and as a result they held even their material possessions in common (Acts 4:32–35).

As the gospel made inroads in the Hellenistic world, the view of the church as the believers' primary community expanded with it. So keen was this sense of community, apparently some thought that their new status as members of the Christian fellowship severed all previous social bonds, including the marital. To combat this dangerous tendency, Paul and others found it necessary to forge a middle position. Membership in the community of believers was to be primary. In fact, once a person joined this fellowship he or she ought not to form additional social bonds, at least not outside the community (2 Cor. 6:14).

But the believer nevertheless ought not to instigate action with the goal of severing one's previous bonds, as Paul's advice to believers who were married to unbelievers indicates (1 Cor. 7:13). For Paul, the basic rule was "each one should retain the place in life that the Lord assigned to him and to which God has called him" (v. 17). In fact, such previously formed bonds could serve to advance the kingdom of God, for they are to be used as occasions for the spread of the gospel (e.g., 1 Cor. 7:14; 1 Peter 3:1–2).

The Genesis narrative indicates that God created us as sexual beings. Our sexuality has a purpose, for sexuality is a primary force that places in us the drive toward bonding. This drive leads to the development of social communities, beginning with marriage, family, tribe, and finally larger societies. For the Christian, however, this drive is fulfilled ultimately only through fellowship as part of the society of disciples who have been redeemed and therefore enjoy fellowship with God. The New Testament offers as the highest location of community the corporate community of believers in Christ.

2. Gender Roles

The understanding of the basic purpose of our sexuality outlined here forms a context in which to offer a theological perspective on gender roles. A discussion of this topic is important in this context because of the important relationship that exists between sexuality and the roles we fulfill as male or female. It was argued in the previous chapter that human sexuality lies deeper in the individual than physical sex. That means that our existence as sexual beings encompasses more than how we function in the biological process of reproduction. This deeper dimension of sexuality forms a basis for the social dimension of human interaction we refer to as "gender roles."

In part as a result of the impact of the feminist movement, gender roles both in marriage and in society have become an explosive issue. Much of the discussion focuses on the relationship between biology and sociology: Do differing functions in the reproductive process dictate specific roles for male and female in social relationships? Advocates of hierarchical models of male-female relationships often appeal to the Bible in support of the claim that biological differences do indeed determine social roles. Despite the attempts by some to reduce the issue to a simple matter of God's truth versus human rebellion, this is actually a complex question that has several dimensions.

a. The rise of differing roles. A first dimension raises the question as to the historical (or prehistorical) genesis of the phenomenon of role distinctions between men and women. This question has been the subject of much anthropological research.

Perhaps the most widely held theory today maintains that male/female roles developed in the prehistoric hunting and gathering societies. They were supposedly based on the need for women to be protected during pregnancy, a state which typified the greater portion of their lives.[5] The weaker position of the female while carrying and then nursing offspring was paralleled by the relatively greater physical strength of the male, and this situation led to male dominance. Even in the New Testament, written long after Mediterranean society had moved beyond the prehistoric stage, women are referred to as "the weaker partner" (1 Peter 3:7).

The prehistoric situation indicated by this theory as the genesis of role distinctions is obviously no longer operative in Western culture. Women are not pregnant or nursing offspring for the greater part of their lives. Nor is a pregnant woman dependent on the physical strength of her husband for protection and sustenance. In the same way, brute strength has lost the importance for survival that it once had. The significance of this change ought not to be overlooked. As roles in procreation and nurturing of offspring lost their determinative influence over the wider social roles assumed by males and females, the door was opened to the assumption of new social functions for the sexes, especially for females, which in turn placed the traditional gender roles under great strain.

b. Changing views on gender roles. The awareness of the changed situation of women and men in modern society has ignited a discussion of the second dimension of the question of gender roles, namely, the dispute as to whether any inherent gender differences necessitate set roles. Recent years have witnessed a marked fluidity concerning this issue. In a sense, the current situation forms the third of a series of social-developmental stages.

The first stage: traditionalism. In the first stage of the modern era, what are now considered traditional gender roles were put in place, formed by adapting the roles assigned to the sexes in the older gathering and hunting societies to Western culture. In this situation, the husband was viewed as the "breadwinner" and the head of the home, with the wife subservient and domestically oriented. Differences between the sexes were considered great, with men viewed as rational and dispassionate, whereas women were seen as emotional. The outcome of these differences was the advocacy of a hierarchical model of male-female relationship, with men retaining the dominant status they enjoyed in prior eras.

The second stage: androgyny. A second stage arose under the pressure of the various women's movements, bolstered by early twentieth-century anthropological findings. Now the theory was put forth that apart from the obvious difference in reproductive organs no fundamental distinctions exist between males and females. Whatever distinctions may be present were seen as not sufficient enough to warrant the assigning of gender roles (except the specific role of the woman in giving birth). This position obviously constituted a major shift in understanding away from the traditional model of male-female relationships that envisioned definite and fixed gender roles. In its most radical form, it called for the eradication of all gender-based distinctions in roles.[6]

The newer view concerning gender roles corresponded to a shift away from a male-female anthropology to an androgynous viewpoint, one that maintains that our sexuality is external to our essential being. Maleness and femaleness, this understanding asserted, are external characteristics which have no bearing on the fundamental humanness that forms the true essence of all persons regardless of sex.

Although the androgyny model provided a much-needed corrective to the traditional view concerning gender roles, its own foundational flaw soon emerged. At its basis lies a denial of all sexually based distinctions.[7] But as has been argued earlier, this violates the emphasis on embodiment, for it posits some ultimate humanness beyond existence as male and female. Because we can exist as human beings only as male and female and because this distinction is deeper than mere physical features related to reproduction, there are indeed certain basic differences between the sexes.[8] The androgynous ideal is likewise theologically questionable, because it is based on an erroneous view of sin. It sees sin primarily as sensuous in nature and ascribes our sexual polarity to the fallen human condition.[9]

Recent thinking: sex-based differences. The assertion that certain basic distinctions, beyond functions in the reproductive process, do exist between the sexes has gained support through recent anthropological research. One widely held view characterizes men as being more linear and rational,[10] whereas women are oriented to a network of relationships embedded within the social context. Carol Gilligan, for example, has declared that women tend to define their identity through relationships of intimacy and care, rather than through assertion and aggression.[11] Janet Spence and Robert Helmreich offered a similar description of this distinction, suggesting that the core properties of femininity can be conceptualized as a "sense of communion" and those of masculinity as a "sense of agency."[12] (Like Jung, however, they find both traits present to varying degrees in all males and females.)

In a textbook intended for use in university social science courses, Diamond and Karlen succinctly summarized other distinctions noted by contemporary researchers:

> It is fact, not social stereotype, that men virtually everywhere are sexually more active and aggressive than women, and that if either sex is to have more than one sexual partner, it is likely to be men.

And in all known societies, men have greater authority than women both inside and outside the home. Images of power and success as masculine seem deeply rooted in the minds of both men and women, in our society and probably in virtually all others.

It is also fact that in most animal species, including most primates, the male must be more dominant than the female before she will allow copulation.[13]

Despite earlier attempts to minimize the importance of our different procreative capacities, it now appears that the differing functions of male and female in this process do affect to some extent the distinctive outlook of each of the sexes toward the world. Take, for example, the differences noted by anthropologists, for several of these distinctions may readily be linked to our differing roles in childbearing. Only the female has the capacity to nurture developing life within herself, whereas the male must always nurture externally. Perhaps this internal nurturing capacity contributes to the greater tendency toward networking found among females.

According to recent research in the human sciences, the basic difference between the sexes goes beyond the reproductive dimension of life. Current discussions in neuropsychology, for example, focus on the theory that men and women also think differently, even dream differently,[14] and this difference in the way of thinking is due to the differing stages of brain development in boys as compared with girls.[15] Women, it is purported, are more readily able to employ both "left brain" (i.e., verbal, logical, and analytical) and "right brain" (emotional, intuitive, creative, and holistic) functions simultaneously.[16] As a result, women are apparently more capable of holistic reasoning, whereas men tend to be more analytical.[17]

It is probable that both the distinctions in physical structure and in brain development, noted by research in the human sciences, have a common source, namely, the hormones that control our physical development and functioning. This common basis of both types of sexual differences points to the foundational formative nature of our sexuality, our existence as male or female. Not surprisingly, some distinction in roles between men and women arises.[18] Lisa Sowle Cahill offered a helpful summary of the relationship between sex-specific physiological differences and gender roles:

> It appears that different physical characteristics, deriving at least in part from their reproductive roles, may create in men and women a tendency toward certain emotional (nurturing, aggressive) or cognitive (verbal, visual) capacities, which may in turn influence the ways they fulfill various social relationships. This is not to say, however, that emotional and cognitive traits vary greatly between the sexes or are manifested in comparable degrees by every member of each sex; or that the fact that males and females may fulfill

certain roles somewhat differently implies that each sex can fulfill only a certain set of social roles, much less the devaluing of one sort of role or set of roles, and the subordination of it to that of the opposite sex.[19]

These various findings not only indicate certain fundamental differences between the sexes; they also serve as an indication that our basic sexuality is part of our essential being. We exist as male or female, and this fundamental way of being human influences our basic orientation to the world, others, and ourselves.

To maintain that biological differences may indeed color the differing ways that males and females view the world is not to deny the significance of the socialization process in establishing gender identity in young children and thereby subsequently in determining roles in social relationships. Recent research seems to indicate that both biological and sociopsychological influences must be viewed together as accounting for the basic orientation toward the world, others, and oneself that characterizes the human person as a male or female.[20]

The third stage: role flexibility. The rediscovery of sexual differences, as focused as they may be, has placed contemporary Western society on the boundary of yet a third stage in the discussion of gender roles in society. Whereas stage one was characterized by fixed and static roles and stage two emphasized the total fluidity of roles, stage three promises to move between these two. This new understanding acknowledges differences between the sexes. But at the same time it declares that society must provide more flexibility for both individuals and the sexes in general in the area of roles.[21]

Based on biological findings, Milton Diamond offered this advice: "A goal for our culture might be to recognize and accept that generalities can exist simultaneously with allowable deviation from the typical."[22] In the light of contemporary thinking, the admonition of Emil Brunner earlier in this century appears more in keeping with current attitudes than with the viewpoints of his time:

> The criterion of the genuine emancipation movement must always be this, that sex difference—in the broadest sense of the word—is not removed but is fully emphasized. For this is the effect of all spiritual development: that it intensifies the individuality and does not remove it.[23]

c. Traditional hierarchy and Genesis. For many Christians, a move from traditionalism to flexibility is neither easy nor completely possible. Some continue to find in any suggestion of inherent gender distinctions a basis for setting forth a hierarchical model for relationships between male and female. Their apologetic often brings together anthropological findings and certain biblical materials, in the attempt to make a case for the assertion that gender roles are based in the divine order of creation. An example of this approach among evangelicals is found in the formation of the Council on Biblical Manhood and Womanhood and the drafting of its Danvers Statement in December 1987. Among other points, this statement affirmed that "distinctions in masculine and feminine roles are ordained by God as part of the created order, and should find an echo in every human heart." More specifically, "Adam's headship in marriage was established by God before the Fall, and was not a result of sin."[24]

Closer inspection, however, yields the conclusion that the grounding of gender roles in our creation as sexual beings does not necessitate the advocacy of a hierarchy of men over women.[25] The creation story of Genesis 2 offers an appropriate point of departure for a discussion of this issue.

Defenders of the traditional hierarchical view often find in the order of creation—Adam first, followed by Eve—an inherent hierarchy. This exegesis is seen as confirmed by the Pauline comment concerning the creation of the woman: "For man did not come from woman, but woman from man; neither was man created for woman, but woman for man" (1 Cor. 11:8–9). The intent of Paul's reference in this context is a complex exegetical question. In any case the suggestion that the order of creation constitutes a hierarchy of male over female as part of the created order is quite foreign to the intent of the Genesis narrator.[26]

In contrast to the exegesis that is used to support traditional roles, there are several features of the story that could conceivably indicate that the woman may actually be the more important of the two characters. For example, some contemporary exegetes argue that if the principle governing the first chapter is applied to the second—namely, the ascending order of creation—then being created second would place the woman above, not below, the man.[27] This argument, however, is invalid, for it fails to take into consideration the great difference in intent between the two creation narratives. In contrast to the first story which indeed employs the principle of an ascending order of creation, the second narrative focuses on human solitude. The central figure in Genesis 2 is clearly the man. And the alleviation of his solitude forms the basic motif generating major divine actions of the chapter, the bringing of the animals to Adam, and the creation of the woman. Despite its faulty importation of considerations from the first chapter into the second, the egalitarian exegesis is helpful, in that it points out that in so far as the function of the woman in the text is to serve as savior of the man from his loneliness she becomes indeed the crown of creation.[28]

Other observations, however, are more significant. It is notable that in the conclusion to the second creation story the narrator speaks of the man as the one who leaves family and cleaves to his wife, not the reverse, as one might expect in a patriarchal context in which the male holds the dominant position in a sexually determined hierarchy. Further, in the story of the Fall (Genesis 3) the woman appears as the dominant figure. The serpent comes to her and reasons with her. She sins on her own, whereas the man follows his wife into sin. Finally, as noted earlier, the creation of woman "for man " (1 Cor. 11:9) or as his "helper" (Genesis 2) is understood in Genesis in terms of being the one who rescues him from his solitude. This casts the woman in a role exactly opposite of the subservient position one might expect, for she is elevated to the status of being an agent in God's saving design.

Advocates of the male-domination, hierarchical model correctly point out that in the Genesis narrative a male/female hierarchy is present. But they fail to see that it is introduced only after the Fall. The hierarchy of male over female is presented in the text as a direct consequence of the sin of the first human pair. For this reason the statement of hierarchy given to the woman, "'Your desire will be for your husband, and he will rule over you'" (Gen. 3:16), is to be interpreted as a curse, not a command. Rather than being a prescription of what is morally binding on all subsequent relationships, it is a description of the present reality of life after the Fall, of what is likely to be the situation in marriage. The woman's desire will be for her husband; the husband will rule over the wife.

A clue as to why the Fall led to male, rather than female, dominance is found in the curse spoken to Adam:

> "Cursed is the ground because of you; through painful toil you will eat of it all the days of your life. It will produce thorns and thistles for you, and you will eat the plants of the fields. By the sweat of your brow you will eat your food. . . ." (Gen. 3:17–19)

The anthropological research of Peggy Reeves Sanday indicates that in addition to biological sexual distinctions, the nature of the environment in which a society is found has a bearing on the relationships between the sexes. A hostile environment readily leads to male domination, whereas relative equality between the sexes is most frequently found when the environment is beneficent.[29] In the light of her conclusions it is instructive to note that the biblical narrative of creation and Fall views the curse which resulted from human sin as giving rise both to a hostile environment and male dominance.

Because the hierarchy of male dominating female is a curse and not a morally binding injunction, a result of the Fall and not of creation, this is to be changed in the New Creation. That this curse is indeed overcome through the coming of Christ is evident in the New Testament. The radically new situation of the new era is evidenced in Peter's declaration that women are coheirs of salvation with men (1 Peter 3:7). As an outworking of Christ's conquering of sin, one would expect to find in the church the proleptic experience, a foretaste, of the egalitarianism of the kingdom of God envisioned by the apostle. Such ecclesiological egalitarianism is articulated in Galatians: "There is neither Jew nor Greek, slave nor free, male nor female, for you are all one in Christ Jesus" (Gal. 3:28). And it is enjoined in Ephesians 5:21—"Submit to one another out of reverence for Christ"—where it is presented as the overarching principle that is to govern social relations involving Christians (husband-wife, master-slave, father-child).

An important apparent counterexample to the position outlined above is the crucial New Testament commentary on Genesis 2—3 found in 1 Timothy 2:11–15. Women are not to teach or have authority over men, the writer declares, "For Adam was formed first, then Eve. And Adam was not the one deceived; it was the woman who was deceived and became a sinner" (vv. 13, 14). Rather, the woman will be saved through childbirth.

A central exegetical issue is whether the author appeals to two arguments or one. Some exegetes see two arguments for the injunction concerning women—Eve was created second, and Eve sinned first. This interpretation, however, runs the risk of setting the text against the Genesis story, which does not base the hierarchy of male over female on the creation order (Adam first, then Eve), but on the Fall. To find two arguments in 1 Timothy is to conclude that the New Testament text takes a crucial and far-reaching step beyond, and perhaps even in contradiction to Genesis.

An alternative is to view 1 Timothy 2:13 as offering only one argument. The author's point, it should be noted, is not based on seeing the creation of the first two humans and the order of their fall as two isolated events, as would be the case if the verse were setting forth two arguments. Rather, for the apostle it is the relation between the two orders (creation and Fall) that is important. Specifically, he notes the *reversal* in order between creation and Fall, that the one who was second in creation became the first in sin. Thus, the point of the verse is that the female, who was given by God in order to complete the creation of humanity as the deliverer of Adam from his solitude, rather than fulfilling this intended function, actually became the agent of the opposite result. She led him into the bondage that brought a deeper alienation—a severing of the relationship with God, with each other, and with the environment.

But the author cannot leave this pronouncement of human sin as the final word. He immediately speaks of a new role that God has for Eve in the process of salvation, her role in procreation. The best interpretation of verse 15 sees in the statement another allusion to the Genesis narrative of creation and Fall, specifically to the *protoevangelium* in Genesis 3:15.

Understood in this way, the point of the text is the same as that found in Genesis 3. The hierarchy between the sexes is a product of the Fall, in that Eve fell into sin first. The final creation of God is the first to transgress and therefore now will be ruled by the one who followed her into sin. But only with Adam's transgression is the fall of humankind complete. Cahill offered an appropriate summary of the import of the curse as it relates to the two sexes:

> It is ironically appropriate that the more passive sinner, the man,
> who took and ate, now is condemned to the exertion of laboring

to wrest human sustenance from a resistant environment; the more active sinner, the woman, who debated with the serpent and led her husband, is condemned not only to subordination to the man, but also to helpless submission to the inexorable pain of childbirth. But what is the sum effect of the judgment? It is to condemn equally pride as active self-assertion and pride as passive complacency.[30]

To this statement of curse, however, must be added the promise of salvation inherent in Genesis 3 and explicit in the New Testament. According to 1 Timothy 2, the toil of the woman will bring salvation, for through the process of giving birth, the Savior comes. And the role of Adam in the completion of the human fall into sin offers Paul the basis for this appropriate employment of this act in Romans as the basis for a typology between the willing transgression of the first Adam and the chosen obedience of the Second Adam, Christ (Rom. 5:18).

With the coming of the Savior, the curse of the Fall can be lifted. This redemption includes liberation from hierarchy as the way in which the sexes relate. Because in Christ there is neither male nor female (Gal. 3:28), hierarchy can give place to a new model of relationship, mutual submission (Eph. 5:21). This new pattern for the establishment of male-female community as a whole forms the overarching principle not only for the church, but also for the particular expression of this community in marriage. In this context mutual submission calls husbands to love their wives after the pattern of Christ's love for the church and calls wives to respect and submit to their husbands in the Lord (Eph. 5:22–32).

The Theological Significance of Our Creation of Sexual Beings

The Bible and empirical evidence agree that we are created both individually and corporately as sexual beings. Sexuality is an essential feature of each human person and is a central aspect contributing to the identity of each as a person. At the same time, this essential feature of our being constitutes a basic factor leading to the drive toward bonding and eventually toward the establishment of human community. But the biblical understanding of humanity as created in God's image invites the search for further meaning to our sexuality. Our creation in the divine image indicates that there is theological meaning to our sexuality as well. Because we are created in the image of God and our creation includes being formed as sexual beings, the sexual dimension of our existence must in some way reflect the divine reality. As a result, our sexuality offers insight into the nature of the Creator.

1. Sexuality and the Nature of God

The primary statement concerning the creation of humankind in the divine image is given in Genesis 1:26–27:

> Then God said, "Let us make man in our image, in our likeness, and let them rule over the fish of the sea and the birds of the air, over the livestock, over all the earth, and over all the creatures that move along the ground." So God created man in his own image, in the image of God he created him; male and female he created them.

The Genesis declaration that humankind is created in God's image is found in the same context as a reference to humans as existing as male and female. This raises the question as to whether maleness and femaleness is significant for creation in God's image. Is the division of humankind into male and female related to the image of God? If so, in what sense is this to be understood? What could humankind as created male and female suggest about the nature of God?

a. Sexuality and the gender of God. A well-established tenet of Christian theology is that God is beyond sexual distinctions. Since biblical times, masculine pronouns have been traditionally used to refer to God: yet, these are not intended to declare that God is essentially sexually oriented, specifically, being male and not female. The biblical documents simply will not be pressed into such anthropomorphisms. In fact, one significant point of difference between the Old Testament and the religions of the surrounding nations lies in the Hebrew desacralizing of sexuality. Yahweh is not a male god who has a goddess at his side, as in other ancient religions, for he alone is God.[31]

Despite this amazing secularization of sex in the Old Testament, it is not without significance that in both Genesis narratives when God chooses to create what would mirror the divine being, he creates male and female. This aspect of the Genesis stories indicates that our sexuality and human sexual distinctions are somehow grounded in the divine reality and that the existence of two sexes is important for our understanding of God.

On this basis, the Christian doctrine that God is beyond sexual distinctions, although correct, must not be understood in an oversimplified manner. God is beyond sexuality not in that God is nonsexual, but in that God encompasses what to us are the sexual distinctions of male and female. What we perceive as feminine and masculine characteristics are present in and derive their significance from the divine reality.

b. Masculine and feminine motifs in the Bible. In speaking of the divine reality, the Bible repeatedly employs motifs that are related to gender-based traits. Of these, masculine-oriented references predominate. The primary names for God found both in the Bible and in theological history reveal this. Names with an Old Testament source include the Lord of the universe, the King over all the earth, the Father of humankind,[32] and the Husband of Israel, a theme explored in the next chapter.

In addition to the use of specific names for God, God is pictured in a masculine manner through the activities ascribed to him, which center largely on the action of an agent presented as external or transcendent to the world. Thus, in creation God speaks the universe into existence; in redemption God sends his Son into the world; and in salvation God places the Holy Spirit into the hearts of people.[33] This basically masculine orientation lies behind the consistent use of male pronouns to refer to God.

Despite the predominance of the masculine in the Bible, it would be a mistake to conclude that the ancient Hebrews perceived of God in strictly masculine terms. Feminine allusions are prevalent as well. Not only is God the transcendent one who like a monarch exercises sovereign power, God is also the imminent one who nurtures from within creation.

The nurturing motif is present in various ways in the Old Testament. For example, it is evident in the first creation account. At the foundation of the world the Spirit of God hovers over the primeval waters (Gen. 1:2b).

One feminine motif is foreign to the Bible, however. In contrast to masculine metaphors that speak of Yahweh as husband to Israel, the imagery of God as wife is never employed. Instead, feminine relational metaphors focus on the mother-offspring relationship. God is presented as one who like a mother protects, cares for, and nurtures her offspring.

In the Old Testament the mother bird was used as a specially apt picture for the divine care enjoyed by the people of God. God's care for Israel was likened to "an eagle that stirs up its nest and hovers over its young, that spreads its wings to catch them and carries them on its pinions" (Deut. 32:11). In keeping with this imagery, the Hebrew poets repeatedly spoke of the refuge available "in the shadow of your wings" (Ps. 17:8. See also Pss. 36:7; 57:1; 61:4; 63:7; 91:4). This Old Testament background adds poignancy to Jesus' lament over Jerusalem: "how often I have longed to gather your children together, as a hen gathers her chicks under her wings, but you were not willing" (Matt. 23:37).

At times the metaphor of maternal nurture is also used to convey the divine compassion on the people who have forsaken their God. Isaiah, for example, who presents God as lamenting, "'I reared children and brought them up, but they have rebelled against me'" (Isa. 1:2), declares "for the Lord comforts his people and will have [motherly] compassion on his afflicted ones" (Isa. 49:13). The maternal allusion is evident in the Lord's subsequent exclamation: "'Can a mother forget the baby at her breast and have no compassion on the child she was borne? Though she may forget, I will not forget you!'" (v. 15).

The parental heart of God, especially in its maternal aspect, forms an important imagery in Hosea as well:

"When Israel was a child, I loved him, and out of Egypt I called my son. . . . It was I who taught Ephraim to walk, taking them by the arms; . . . I led them with cords of human kindness, with ties of love; I lifted the yoke from their neck and bent down to feed them." (Hos. 11:1–4).

Maternal and conjugal imagery unite in the opening chapters of the prophecy. The child of the prophet's unfaithful wife is Lo-Ruhamah, which Samuel Terrien claims means "the one for whom there is no motherly love."[34] In contrast to this unloved state, according to the prophet's vision, in the renewal God will extend motherly compassion to Lo-Ruhamah (2:23).

Terrien notes that the Hebrew term *compassion* was etymologically linked to *womb* and that the word for *grace* originally meant "maternal yearning." One must be careful not to put too much stock in such conclusions from word rootage. But we are surely correct in seeing at least a parental, if not a specifically maternal aspect of the Hebrew understanding of God at work in the Old Testament reflections on experiences of God's gracious compassion. (Even Paul, who could never have experienced the maternal dimension of parenting, could not avoid entirely speaking of his relationship to his converts in terms reminiscent of the Old Testament image of the divine maternal care of God's people: "but we were gentle among you, like a mother caring for her little children" [1 Thess. 2:7]).

The ancient Hebrews rose above the blatant equation of sexuality with the divine that characterized the religious orientation of the surrounding peoples. Yahweh was not simply a male deity for whom there existed a female counterpart, for he alone is God. Despite Israel's cautionary stance with regard to ascribing sexuality to the deity, the Bible is not reticent to employ sexually based terminology and allusions to speak of the divine nature. God is not to be thought of as either male or female, but as encompassing and serving as the ground for both. For this reason, imagery based on human sexuality is appropriate.

2. Sexuality and the Plurality of God

Because sexuality is a characteristic of God's highest creation, it would not be surprising to find a foundational sexuality in the divine nature which forms the ground for human sexuality. Similarly, because a plurality of sexes is essential to God's highest creation, it would not be surprising to find a foundational plurality in the divine being as well. In fact, the creation narratives in Genesis 1 and 2 provide a hint that the plurality of humanity as male and female is to be viewed as an expression of a foundational plurality within the unity of the divine reality.

In the creation statement of Genesis 1:26–27 the plurality of human sexes is explicitly linked to a plurality found in the divine self-references. God expresses the creative intent with the declaration, "Let us make man in our image." Although the use of the plural forms ought not to be interpreted as indicating that the writer was prototrinitarian (as many exegetes since Tertulian have erroneously argued), at the very least they suggest, in the words of Derrick Bailey,

> that he envisaged God as associating others with himself in some mysterious way as patterns in the act of creation, and that he regarded Man as constituted in some sense after the pattern of a plurality of supernatural beings.[35]

The fuller divine self-disclosure of the New Testament allows us, however, to see in these words in Genesis a more profound meaning. "They express," continues Bailey, "the Creator's resolve to crown his works by making a creature in whom, subject to the limitations of finitude, his own nature should be mirrored." The plural self-reference, therefore, finds its outworking in the creation of humankind as male and female, that is, as a plural sexual creation.

A fuller presentation of this idea is reflected in the story of the formation of Eve from Adam. The bond formed between the man and the woman in the Genesis narrative arises out of a dialectic of sameness and difference. The man sees in the woman a creature like himself, in contrast to the animals who are unlike him. For this reason bonding can occur. At the same time, the two are different, for he is male and she is female.

The narrator is keenly aware of both aspects of this unique relationship; they are the same, yet different. In the application, the narrator draws from the interaction of sameness and difference in explaining the mystery of the bonding which leads two to become "one flesh." Male and female form a dialectic of sameness and difference. The result of this dialectic is mutuality. The two are alike and different, and on this basis supplement each other. The mutuality of the sexes is the result of the attraction (*eros*) experienced between the male and the female, beings who are fundamentally both alike and different. In this way the dialectic of difference and similarity forms the genius lying behind human bonding, which from the beginning has taken as its primary form the marital bond with its attendant production of offspring.

The creation of humankind as male and female comes in response to the divine self-declaration, "Let us make man in our image." This suggests that the same principle of mutuality that forms the genius of the human social dynamic is present in a prior way in the divine being. The assertion of just such a supplementarity within the one divine reality constitutes the unique understanding of God that lies at the heart of the Christian tradition, namely, the doctrine of the Trinity. God, Christians declare, is three persons in one essence. In other words, God is the divine community.

3. Sexuality and the Community of God

The importance of community to our understanding of God and God's program in the world is everywhere evident in Christian theology. For example, it is central to the doctrine of creation. God's will to community lies at the heart of our understanding of God's design for all creation, but especially for the creation of humankind. This theme is evident in the creation narratives. God creates the first human pair in order that humans may enjoy community with each other. More specifically, the creation of the woman is designed to deliver the man from his isolation. This primal community of male and female then becomes expansive. It produces the offspring that arise from the sexual union of husband and wife and eventually gives rise to the development of societies.

God's design as directed to the formation of community may be pursued from another theological direction as well, for it is evident in the biblical concept of the kingdom of God. Ultimately God's reign carries an eschatological orientation point, in that it refers to the completion of God's program at the end of the historical process. The reign of God finds its consummation in the eschatological New Creation promised by God. This future reality will be characterized by full communion between God and creation. The seer in Revelation envisions this even in terms of God coming to dwell with humankind:

> And I heard a loud voice from the throne saying, "Now the dwelling of God is with men, and he will live with them. They will be his people, and God himself will be with them and be their God." (Rev. 21:3)

The vision of the Bible is that of a coming kingdom of God which will consist of a redeemed humanity populating a renewed universe. The final goal of God's salvific activities, then, is community—a human society enjoying perfect fellowship with the created world and with the Creator.

The community dynamic is likewise visible in New Testament ecclesiology. The church is presented as the eschatological community, the fellowship of those who seek to reflect in the present the future reality of the reign of God. The church is the primary expression of this community in the New Testament, replacing the Old Testament emphasis on family and tribe.

It is not surprising that the concept of community emerges as the focal point of our understanding of the program of God. Community is an expression of the nature of the Creator. As the doctrine of the Trinity seeks to express, throughout all eternity the divine reality is the community of Father, Son, and Holy Spirit who comprise the triune God.

The concept of trinitarian community is closely related to the divine attribute of love. Throughout the Bible God is presented as the loving one. In fact, John put forth love as the central divine attribute (e.g., 1 John 4:16). This assertion suggests that the community that comprises the Godhead is likewise best characterized by reference to the concept of love. The doctrine of the Trinity—the affirmation of one God in three persons—allows this idea to be taken a step further. It indicates that the bonding that characterizes the divine life is similar to the dialectic of sameness and difference found in human sexuality. The persons of the Trinity share in the one divine essence, for there is but one God. Yet they differ from one another, for each is a distinct person and cannot simply be equated with the others.

The presence of this dialectic within the bonding inherent in the Godhead may be seen by recalling a further aspect of the doctrine of the Trinity. In the Western tradition, the Father-Son relationship has been viewed as forming the basis of the divine reality. Like the divine nature itself, this is a relationship characterized by love, a bonding between the Father and the Son. The foundational bond between the first and second persons of the Trinity is characteristic of the divine nature as a whole but also emerges as a separate hypostasis in the third person, the Holy Spirit, who is the spirit of the relationship between the Father and the Son. In this way, the love generated by the relationship of the Father and the Son in their difference from each other means that they likewise share the sameness of the divine nature, which is love. This sameness is the Holy Spirit, who nevertheless is neither the Son nor the Father, and therefore differs from both.

On the basis of the creation of humanity in the divine image it has been asserted that the dialectic of sameness and difference characteristic of human bonding is analogous to the dynamic within the divine Trinity. This suggestion, however, ought not to be seen as indicating that the true reflection of the image of God is only found in the marital union of male and female.[36] As noted earlier, there is a sense in which the biblical tradition presents each person as related to the image of God, albeit within the context of community which in the New Testament focuses on the community of Christ as the foretaste of the eschatological renewed community.

The New Testament link between the image of God and the church as an expression of the future human community lies in three theological considerations. Two of these have been described: God's intent in creation and God's eschatological purpose for creation. The third arises from the metaphor of the church as Christ's body and Christ as the head of the church. According to the New Testament, Christ is the image of God (2 Cor. 4:4; Col. 1:15; Heb. 1:3). As Christ's body, however, the church shares in Christ's relationship to God. For example, the community of Christ is invited to utilize the address the earthly Jesus preferred in speaking to the Father, namely, the term *abba,* with its deep relational meaning. In the same way, by extension the church shares in Christ's calling as the image of God. Through its connection with Christ, it has been given the responsibility and privilege of reflecting the very nature of the triune God. And as a result of this connection, the Pauline literature speaks of believers, the members of the church, as now being transformed into the image of God in Christ (1 Cor. 15:49; 2 Cor. 3:18; Col. 3:10).

In the final analysis, then, the "image of God" is a community concept. It refers to humans as being-in-fellowship. This conclusion completes the circle of our discussion. Human sexuality forms the basis of the drive toward human community. True community, community in accordance with the divine design, gives rise to the primal male-female relationship, the bond of marriage. But community is given expression preeminently in the community of Christ which is to be expressed by the church, for ideally the church is the highest form of human community in this age. As we live in love, as we live in true community, we reflect the love which characterizes the divine essence. Not only in marriage, but in every expression of community, this living-in-love is an outworking of our sense of personal incompleteness. At the foundation of this recognition of incompleteness lies our sexuality, our existence as male or female with its fundamental need for relationship. Because of its function as the basis for the drive toward the bonding of community, sexuality is foundational not only for the bond of marriage, but also for the forming of the highest human community, the community of those who enjoy fellowship with each other through their corporate fellowship with Christ.

Sexuality and the Dynamic
of Creation and Fall

Christian anthropology summarizes the human situation by two assertions. We are the good creation of God, designed to be the image of God, to reflect the divine nature. But we are fallen. Our present existence is not fully in keeping with God's design. Instead, we fail to actualize the divine intention. This contradiction between being the image of God and yet being tainted by sin characterizes all aspects of human existence.

A Christian understanding of sexuality must therefore take into consideration this fundamental understanding of human existence. Like all aspects of the present human reality, our sexuality, our existence as sexual beings, must be viewed under the dual dynamic of creation and Fall.

1. Sexuality Viewed under
the Dynamic of Creation

Humans are the creation of God, the Bible maintains. Indicative of the basic anthropology of the Bible as a whole, the creation narrative of Genesis 2 depicts the first human as an animated earthly being. This indicates that we are the creation of God in all aspects of our existence, including the material or bodily dimensions. As a result, we are God's creation as sexual beings.

Viewing our sexuality under the dynamic of creation leads to two related assertions. First, our sexuality is given by God. Existing as male or female—as this particular male or female human being—is willed by God. Second, not only is our sexuality given by God, it is affirmed by God. It is an aspect of our being pronounced *good* by the Creator. Thus, our sexuality is a positive dimension of who we are as God's creatures. It is foundational to our existence in God's image and can be a means for reflecting the character and nature of God.

Because God gives and affirms our sexuality, we also are to acknowledge and accept our existence as male or female. We are who we are because God has created us so and wills us to be this male or female human person. Our sexuality is not to be displaced, replaced, or denied. Rather, we are to see ourselves as sexual beings by divine design.

Likewise, because God gives our sexuality, we are to be stewards of this dimension of our existence. Repeatedly the New Testament issues a call to responsible stewardship of our bodies (e.g., 1 Cor. 6:20; 10:31), and such injunctions are often placed in the context of issues relating to sexual ethics or conduct. Our stewardship, however, moves beyond the negative, beyond mere avoidance of sexual sin, to include the positive aspect as well, for we are to glorify God in our bodies (1 Cor. 6:20). By extension this Pauline admonition means that we are to employ our sexuality to fulfill God's intention, namely, that as sexual creatures we actualize the divine design, reflect the nature of God, and thereby bring glory to the Creator.

2. Human Sexuality Viewed under the Dynamic of the Fall

Christian anthropology asserts that we are God's good creation. At the same time, however, the Bible teaches that we are fallen creatures. The Reformation emphasized the radical effects of the Fall through the doctrine of total depravity. Simply stated, this doctrine declares that because of the Fall, sin extends to every area of human existence. There is no aspect of our being that escapes the crippling effects or influence of sin. As a result of the Fall our sexuality lies under the domain of sin as well. Our fundamental fallenness, which raises its ugly head in so many ways, is also expressed through our sexuality.

The Reformation emphasis on total depravity forms a stark contrast to much current thinking. Contemporary popular media, for example, often present human sexual expression in a romanticized manner. Sex is depicted as a dimension of human life that is pure, divine, or wholly ecstatic. It is the last refuge for fulfillment and self-expression untainted by evil and corruption.

The contemporary romantic portrayal, however, is simply unwarranted.

As the doctrine of total depravity indicates, sin is given expression through every dimension of our being. There is no area of human existence, not even the sexual, to which we can escape and thereby find a haven of wholeness and freedom from the downward pull of sin. Rather than being a last vestige of primal innocence amidst an otherwise fallen world, sex is an area of great vulnerability. As a result of the all-pervasive presence of sin, our sexuality, which was intended to be a vehicle for expressing the nature of God, can easily be twisted. Sexual passion, designed as the foundation for the bonding that leads to community, can be misdirected and expressed in unhealthy and damaging ways.

The twisting of sexuality is depicted in the narrative of the Fall in Genesis 3, which presents the effects of sin in the area of sex roles. The man and the woman were created in order to supplement each other. But after the Fall, mutuality digressed into competition. Now the desire of the woman is directed toward her husband, but he exercises rulership over her. Sex roles, which were given by God in view of the procreative and nurturing functions, are now incomplete expressions of God's design and lie under bondage.

Like all dimensions of human existence, therefore, sexuality lies under the dynamic of creation and Fall. It is ambiguous, sharing both in the dynamic divine intent for humanity, that is, in the divine will directed toward the establishment of the community of male and female, and in the uncanny human capacity for selfish exploitation of others. Jersild and Johnson rightly concluded:

> As sexual beings we are capable of establishing beautiful relationships of mutual dependence and respect, but we are also capable of reducing another person to an extension of ourselves, creating excessive dependence because we need to control. It is precisely as sexual beings that we are most vulnerable to the desire to possess another person and to reduce him or her to the object of our desire.[37]

The good news of the gospel, however, speaks to human beings living in the midst of the tension between creation and Fall. The gospel declares that despite human sin and in the midst of human fallenness divine grace remains evident. Although humankind is expelled from the paradise garden, God nevertheless offers guidance for the proper channelling of our sexuality. The Creator even employs our sexuality, despite its participation in the Fall, in the service of the attaining of the divine redemptive goal. God's employment of human sexuality in bringing about the divine intention—including the coming of the Redeemer as the seed of the woman and the coming into being of the community of God's people through the human drive toward bonding—forms the foundation for expressions of the divine design in the present, fallen world.

The following chapters explore two alternative contents for the expression of human sexuality within the overarching divine will to community. First, attention is given to the community of male and female within the marriage bond as an expression of human sexuality. In the present era this life choice is the more widely followed. In Part 3 an alternative life situation comes into view, singleness within the community of the people of God as a context for expressing human sexuality. While not as prevalent in our day as the option of marriage, singleness is the chosen or de facto status of a growing number of Christians.

PART 2

MARRIAGE

AS AN EXPRESSION

OF HUMAN

SEXUALITY

3 Marriage in a Christian Perspective

Human beings are sexual creatures. According to the Bible we are created with the purpose of reflecting God's image. These two statements are related, for our sexuality—our existence as male or female—is an integral part of the way in which we reflect the divine nature. Human sexuality plays a role in the reflection of the divine image and fulfills the divine intention, in so far as it forms the basis for the drive toward bonding that leads to community. Despite the Fall, the Creator uses our sexuality in the service of attaining the divine goal for creation. God's employment of human sexuality in bringing about the divine intention forms the foundation for the expression of human sexuality in the present fallen world.

Actually, there are alternative expressions of human sexuality within the context of the divine will to community, the fellowship of male and female within the marriage bond and singleness within the fellowship of the people of God. This section explores the first of these options, whereas its alternative is the subject of Part 3. The goal here is to develop a Christian view of marriage, the sex act, and the boundaries for this expression of our sexuality. This, in turn, provides a basis for interaction with the significant ethical issues related to human sexuality that we face today.

The opening chapters of the book of Genesis indicate that marriage has been a part of human exercises from the beginning. And anthropological studies confirm that marriage in some form is present in all societies.[1] Marriage, therefore, is not a specifically Christian institution, even though by including it among the sacraments the Roman Catholic Church has given to it a special Christian status.[2] Despite its presence among the orders of creation, to use Luther's phrase—despite its nature as a general human institution—marriage does take on special significance in Christianity, for it wins a special understanding within the Christian faith.

The Meaning of Marriage

In Matthew 19 Jesus offers a radical interpretation of the Genesis narratives of the creation of man and woman. He asserts that according to the design of the

Creator marriage consists of the monogamous union of a male and a female in a lifelong commitment to one another which is to be characterized by fidelity. This view of the marital union, he declares, summarizes what has been the essence of the divine intent from the beginning. Jesus then articulates a far-reaching assertion concerning the depth of this bond: "'So they are no longer two, but one. Therefore, what God has joined together, let man not separate'" (Matt. 19:6).

Christians maintain that this radical teaching of Jesus forms the heart of the biblical understanding of marriage and as such constitutes the ideal in all eras. But how is this central teaching concerning the marital relationship to be understood? In order to draw from Jesus' declaration a basis for the development of a Christian perspective on marriage, we must place this saying within the context of two significant biblical emphases, *community* as God's ultimate intention for humanity and *the marital bond* as a metaphor for deeper theological truth. Then we can offer some concluding comments concerning the implications of marriage for our understanding of the triune God.

1. Marriage in the Context of God's Ultimate Intent

The primary consideration in developing an understanding of the marital relationship must be God's intent in instituting marriage. As has been noted, God's ultimate goal can be described as the desire to enter into covenantal fellowship with human beings who thereby enjoy community with each other and with the Creator. This intent will find its highest fulfillment in the consummation, when the community that will characterize the reign of God arrives in its fullness.

Yet, in history there are foreshadowings or precursory experiences of this eschatological enjoyment of community. Certain of these earthly experiences are integral to the divine activity which brings about the establishment of the community that will characterize God's reign. Biblical history gives an indication of this.

a. The primary expression of God's intent: the Old and the New. As was indicated in the previous chapter, in the Old Testament, family and tribe were the primary focal points of community. The primacy of the marital bond in the Old Testament is already visible in the creation narratives. Genesis 1:27 offers a hint concerning the role of marriage as an expression of community:

> So God created man in his own image,
> in the image of God he created him;
> male and female he created them.

What is only implicit in Genesis 1 is made explicit in chapter 2. The description of the creation of the first human pair indicates that the husband-wife relationship is to be seen as the primary expression of the God-given human drive to bonding and thus to community. The creation of the man and the woman as similar and yet different is intended to be viewed as a step in the direction of the establishment of community. The narrator indicates that God's desire is that a natural fellowship arise between Adam and Eve in the garden, a fellowship which God as the Creator would likewise enjoy.

After the Fall (Genesis 3) the divine intention for sexuality in the establishment of community takes on added significance. Human sexuality, with its procreative ability, now is shown to be the means God will utilize in the establishment of a redeemed humanity. The Redeemer will be the Child of the woman.

The New Testament asserts that this Old Testament expectation is fulfilled in Jesus of Nazareth. In this way the story of Jesus marks the true interpretation and confirmation of the Genesis *protoevangelium*. A fitting climax to this New Testament commentary on Genesis 3:15 comes in the book of Revelation. The promise of God that the offspring of the woman would crush the head of the serpent forms the background for the imagery of the birth of the Child in Revelation 12:1–9.

On the basis of the fulfillment of God's promise concerning the coming of the Child of the woman, the New Testament, in contrast to the Old, maintains that the greatest earthly expression of the divine will to community is now the community of Christ, not the family. For the Christian, therefore, the fellowship of believers is intended to be the primary locus of the experience of community and the primary orientation point for personal identity. This is evident, for example, in Jesus' declaration that those who do the will of the Father are his true family (Matt. 12:50) and in Paul's emphasis that the primacy of service to the Lord be the chief consideration in decisions concerning entering into marriage (1 Cor. 7:29–35).

b. The role of marriage in the New Testament. Although the New Testament maintains that after the coming of the Child the church replaces family and tribe as the central expression of the establishment of community, marriage is not for this reason rejected. Nor is it afforded an unimportant status. On the contrary, it retains a vital, albeit different role in the light of God's saving work. Specifically, marriage continues to be important for the ongoing development and expansion of the divine community as it is focused in the church. This role, however, is no longer to be understood in terms of bringing the community of God into the world, as in the Old Testament era. Rather, it is now to be viewed from within the context of that community. Marriage is an expression of the expansive nature and outreach mandate of the church, and it functions quite naturally as a vehicle of that mission.

The New Testament speaks of this new role for marriage as operative in two directions. First, marriage serves as an agent for the expansion of the church through the influence of the believer in the home. Such influence may come in the form of the witness of a believing spouse. This dynamic motivates the admonition to wives in 1 Peter 3:1–6. Peter maintains that through a holy lifestyle, the believing partner (in the first century, generally the wife) may be able to win her spouse:

> Wives, in the same way be submissive to your husbands so that, if any of them do not believe the word, they may be won over without talk by the behavior of their wives, when they see the purity and reverence of your lives. (1 Peter 3:1–2)

The same possibility forms the background for Paul's admonition that a believer not separate from an unbelieving spouse so long as the latter is willing to maintain the marriage (1 Cor. 7:12–16). The presence of a believer in a marriage entails a special occasion for the working of the gospel in the life of the spouse, as the unbeliever is able to see the embodiment of allegiance to Christ in the believing partner.

In addition to the influence of the gospel within the marriage itself, the New Testament speaks of the influence of godly parents on children. This understanding may in part lie behind Paul's somewhat obscure assertion that children of marriages in which one spouse is a believer are "holy," not "unclean" (1 Cor. 7:14b). This remark ought not to be interpreted as suggesting that such offspring are automatically members of the believing community. Recent exegesis finds the background for the statement in the postexilic problem of unholy marriages involving the returning Jews and their pagan neighbors.[3]

At the same time, Paul may have in view the special working of the gospel that is present in the lives of such children because of the embodiment of the gospel in the believing parent. If this is the case, then the text bears resemblance to the admonition to fathers in the Ephesian epistle. Reminiscent of the Old Testament understanding of the home as the focus of religious training, they are commanded to rear their children "in the training and instruction of the Lord" (Eph. 6:4). In short, the faith of parents is to exercise a positive influence on the children, disposing them to subsequent membership in the believing community.

Second, the New Testament speaks of marriage as a vehicle for the outreach mission of the church. This occurs through the influence of godly families in the wider society. Repeatedly in the New Testament era the homes of Christians became bases for the launching of the church in specific locations. The Philippian congregation, for example, began with the baptism of the households of Lydia and the jailor (cf. Acts 16:11–15, 25–34, 40). Further, families often offered their homes to provide facilities for house churches (e.g., Philemon 2). Priscilla and Aquila comprise the most vivid example of the influence of a married couple for the cause of the church. These two believers are mentioned several times in the New Testament documents, and on each occasion indication is given that they were working together through their home to advance the gospel (Acts 18:2–3, 26; Rom. 16:3; 1 Cor. 16:19).

Whether within the family relationship or in moving from the home into society, marriage performs a significant role within the context of God's intent for the expansion of the community of believers. Within the marriage relationship this expansion moves from person to person, as marriage becomes the vehicle for the incarnation of the gospel in the life of a spouse so that the believer's partner is drawn into the fellowship. This expansion likewise moves from generation to generation. Marriage becomes an important vehicle for this, as the family forms the context for the training of the next generation, so that children eventually express the same faith as their parents. The expansion of the gospel also moves from the family outward, as the marriage itself and the home that the marriage partners establish serve as the foundation for ministry beyond their boundaries.

2. The Metaphorical Meaning of Marriage

Marriage derives its meaning from its role in the divine program for the establishment of the community of the people of God. The Bible also employs the marriage bond as a metaphor of certain aspects of the spiritual relationship between God and God's people. Like the first, this theme is also presented in both Testaments.

a. Marriage as metaphor in the Old Testament: Yahweh's relationship to Israel. An interesting description of the relationship between God and his people is developed by the Old Testament prophets. In the prophetic movement, marriage came to be viewed as a metaphor for Yahweh's relationship to the nation Israel. The plot of the story they told through this metaphor consists of three acts.

Act one describes the betrothal of Israel to Yahweh. The prophets utilize the experience of engagement and becoming married to picture the special covenantal relationship that Yahweh intended for Israel as his people. The introduction of the marriage metaphor added the idea of love and willing fidelity to the concept of covenant that in the ancient world originally carried the connotations of a contract between a king and his vassals. God's relationship to his people was to be more than legal contract: it was to be a relationship of mutual love. The link between love and covenant is aptly portrayed through the picture of marriage. The marriage metaphor is likewise significant in that it could reflect the idea of the permanence of the relationship. The intention of Yahweh was that Israel be like a virgin bride who gives herself willingly, continually, and exclusively to her husband (Jer. 2:2) and thereby becomes his delight (Isa. 62:5).

But in act two, Israel shows herself to be an unfaithful spouse, forsaking

Yahweh for other gods. Jeremiah is an important example of the prophets who employed imagery of adultery to speak of the idolatry of Israel and Judah:

> During the reign of King Josiah, the Lord said to me, "Have you seen what faithless Israel has done? She has gone up on every high hill and under every spreading tree and has committed adultery there. . . . Yet I saw that her unfaithful sister Judah had no fear; she also went out and committed adultery." (Jer. 3:6, 8)

The prophet finds in adultery and divorce an appropriate metaphor for the apostasy and divine judgment of the northern kingdom. He declared that Yahweh "gave faithless Israel her certificate of divorce and sent her away because of all her adulteries" (v. 8), a fate which he sees as threatening Judah as well.

The most heart-rending use of this theme, however, is found in the prophecy of Hosea, whose own marriage paralleled the sad tale of the relationship of Yahweh to Israel:

> "Rebuke your mother, rebuke her, for she is not my wife, and I am not her husband. Let her remove the adulterous look from her face and the unfaithfulness from between her breasts. . . . I will not show my love to her children, because they are the children of adultery. Their mother has been unfaithful and has conceived them in disgrace." (Hos. 2:2, 4–5)

Nevertheless, the story does not end on this negative note, for act three follows. Despite Israel's "adultery" Yahweh has remained faithful. And this faithfulness of Israel's husband forms the basis for the future restoration envisioned by the prophets. They hold out the hope that God will bring about a renewal of the relationship some day in the future. In the words of Hosea, "'I will show my love to the one I called "Not my loved one." I will say to those called "Not my people," "You are my people"; and they will say, "You are my God"'" (2:23).

In this way, then, in the prophetic community marriage serves as a metaphor of the covenant faithfulness of Yahweh to his people. But this theme does not lose its poignancy with the completion of the Old Testament. Paul quotes verbatim the promise in Hosea in reference to the church (see Rom. 9:25), and in speaking of the community of believers Peter employs a mixture of metaphors from the Old Testament, including allusions to the marriage theme (see 1 Peter 2:9–10).

b. Marriage as metaphor in the New Testament: Christ's union with the church. Not only does the New Testament understand marriage within the context of the expansion of the church, but, following the example of the Old Testament, it also finds theological significance in the marriage bond. Marriage was used as a metaphor to speak of Christ and the church. This idea comes forth in two basic ways in the New Testament documents.

The first employment of the relationship of male and female in marriage as a metaphor depicting the relationship of Christ and the church is found in Ephesians 5. The author develops a reciprocal connection between the spiritual and the marital aspects. Thus, the bond between husband and wife serves as a metaphor of that between Christ and his people. But the analogy moves in the other direction as well. The roles fulfilled by the Lord and the church in their relationship provide a model for husbands and wives.

The context out of which the discussion of marriage emerges in this text is the general admonition concerning all relationships within the church: "Submit to one another out of reverence for Christ" (Eph. 5:21). Within the context of the general principle of mutual submission, Paul cites marriage as a specific case. The husband-wife relationship, he asserts, is to follow the pattern of the relationship between Christ and the church, becoming thereby an object lesson of that deeper spiritual reality.

This means, on the one hand, that wives are to respect and submit to their husbands, as the church responds to Christ. Husbands, on the other hand, are to love their wives after the pattern of Christ. Christ's self-sacrificing and cherishing love for the church becomes the model for a husband's care for his wife. Husbands, Paul adds, should care for their wives, just as they care for their own bodies. Again he draws analogy from Christ who cares for us as members of his body. The discussion climaxes with a quotation of Genesis 2:24. Paul, however, moves beyond the original application to marriage of the "leaving and cleaving" (in the Old Testament text), declaring that the mystery involved is in reference to Christ and the church (v. 32).

This text is significant because of the parallel it draws between the primal focal point of human community—the community of male and female in marriage, which is given elevated status in the Old Testament—and the primary focus of the New Testament, namely, the church as the body of Christ. In so doing, Paul sets the order of marriage, which according to the Old Testament has been central to human fellowship since creation, within a broader and far-reaching theological context, namely, salvation history as it comes to light in the church. This situating of marriage within the dynamic of Christ's relationship to the church gives to the male-female bond a special status as a metaphor of the gospel. This bond must not be treated lightly. On the contrary it is to be viewed with all seriousness, because of the theological truth it is able to convey. As the primal human bond, marriage points to the spiritual bond that God desires to enjoy with humankind, a bond created proleptically by Christ's bond with the church.

As a man and a woman enter into and then maintain the marital union, they offer a picture of the great mystery of salvation—the union of Christ and the believing community. In so far as the marriage partners relate to each other properly, through mutual submission (the submission of the wife to the husband and the love of the husband for the wife), they portray the mystery of Christ's self-sacrifice for the church and the church's submission to Christ.

As is developed in subsequent chapters, the metaphorical significance of the marriage relationship is an important dimension in marital faithfulness. Unfaithfulness is a serious matter, because it destroys the metaphor and mars the picture that marriage is intended to provide.

The metaphor, of course, ought not to be pushed too far. Marriage is a picture of a significant spiritual reality, but the marital bond does not portray every dimension of Christ's relationship to the church. The most obvious aspect not found in marriage is the sanctifying function that belongs to the self-sacrifice of Christ (Eph. 5:21–27), which finds no parallel in the husband's love for his wife. Nevertheless, to the extent that this human institution can function as a picture of a divine reality central to God's saving design, marriage is an apt metaphor, offering a visible representation of the spiritual bond between Christ and the community of faith.

Related to the theme of the mystery of Christ's relationship to the church is a second, the imagery of the bridegroom and the bride. This imagery is implicitly present in Ephesians 5, where Christ appears in the role of the bridegroom, even though he is never referred to as such. Veiled references to Jesus as the bridegroom are found in several places in the Gospels. In his final address, John the Baptist refers metaphorically to his relationship to Jesus in terms of that between the friend and the bridegroom: "The bride belongs to the bridegroom. The friend who attends the bridegroom waits and listens for him, and is full of joy when he hears the bridegroom's voice. That joy is mine, and it is now complete" (John 3:29). Likewise, Jesus uses this terminology in responding to those who criticize his disciples for not fasting: "'How can the guests of the bridegroom fast while he is with them?'" His reference to himself is made obvious as he continues, "'the time will come when the bridegroom will be taken from them, and on that day they will fast'" (Mark 2:19–20).

At the climax to the book of Revelation this theme is most pronounced and most explicitly employed. Reference to Jesus as the bridegroom first appears in Revelation 19 where the great multitude shouts forth praise to God, "'for the wedding of the lamb has come, and his bride has made herself ready'" (19:7). Later an angel shows to the seer "'the bride, the wife of the lamb'" (21:9), namely, "the Holy City, Jerusalem, coming down out of heaven from God" (21:10, cf. 21:2). This bride is the new city of God, in which complete fellowship between God and humankind is enjoyed. In other words, the bride of the lamb is the consummated new society of redeemed humans, the bringing into being of which is the goal of the work of the incarnate Christ.

The significance of this metaphor is unmistakable. The marital bond as the pristine focus of human fellowship is thereby linked metaphorically to the eschatological bond between God and humankind. The fellowship which God intended from the beginning in the divine creative act is consummated in the new society at the end of salvation history.

Viewed in this light, marriage stands as a symbol of that consummated reality and thereby gains an eschatological orientation point. As a male and a female enter into the matrimonial bond and maintain that bond in all fidelity, they offer a picture of the fellowship of the eschatological redeemed humanity with the Creator. Marriage is an apt symbol of this because of the dialectic of sameness and difference that this bond entails. The man and the woman come together as persons who are alike ("bone of my bone"), yet different (male/female). This dialectic forms the basis for the bonding that occurs in marriage. In a metaphorical way the fellowship in the reign of God is likewise characterized by a dialectic of sameness and difference. Individual redeemed persons are brought together in the redeemed society and thereby form a unity of diversity. And they enjoy fellowship with the One who created them as beings who are different from God, but who nevertheless are able to reflect the divine image. Marriage is an apt symbol of the eschatological new society, likewise, because the community of this male and this female is a foretaste and sign on a small scale of the great future community God is bringing to pass.

3. Marriage and the
Triune Nature of God

The meaning of marriage arises out of the place of this institution within the purposes of the Creator. This meaning is enhanced by the biblical use of marriage as a metaphor of God and God's people. However, there remains yet a further dynamic, one which brings together the Old and New Testament uses of the male-female bond. Both in itself and in its relationship to the church, marriage can be a fitting symbol or metaphor of the triune nature of God.

As was noted earlier, the divine community is a dialectic between sameness and difference. God is a unity of three persons who share the one divine nature but who are distinct from each other. This aspect of the trinitarian life of God is reflected in marriage itself. When God determines to create what would reflect the divine nature, he forms as the divine image bearer humankind—as male and female—and through marriage he joins the two together. This dimension arises out of the Old Testament presentation of marriage as the primal form of intimate human bonding. The marital bond is able to reflect the intimacy of the relationship that is present within the Godhead among the trinitarian persons.

God's program to bring into existence the divine image bearer does not end with the institution of the male-female bond in the Garden of Eden. Rather, the divine design reaches completion only in the human community, the society of redeemed persons who through fellowship with Christ enjoy community with one another and thereby experience fellowship with the Creator who is likewise their Savior. This dimension is most closely tied to the church, the body of Christ, which according to the New Testament constitutes the highest form of human fellowship in this age and most closely approximates the consummated fellowship of the future reign of God.

The coming of the church does not mark the end of the meaning of marriage in the divine program, however. Even within the fellowship of believers the primal human bond found in marriage plays a role, for it symbolizes the relationship between the Redeemer and the redeemed community, the church. Because of this twofold importance of marriage, this institution belongs both to the order of creation and to the order of salvation.[4]

The Purpose of Marriage

Marriage is a significant institution because it arises out of the divine program for humanity, is a metaphor of deeper spiritual realities, and is intended to mirror the intertrinitarian relationship. This understanding of the meaning of marriage provides a context in which to view a related issue, the purpose of marriage. Despite the phenomenal rise in divorce during the last decades, marriage continues to be popular in our society. In fact, people have high expectations for the marital relationship.

There are today several competing suggestions concerning the central goal of marriage. Vance Packard, for example, concluded that marriage has taken on enhanced importance, as a way of meeting the needs for the warmth arising from attachment to another, for personal identity, and for a sense of stability in an uncertain world.[5] Christian ethicists, however, have offered four main purposes for marriage.

1. Marriage as the Context
for Sexual Expression

The Bible provides the basis for a first suggestion concerning the purpose of marriage. In 1 Corinthians 7, Paul indicates that marriage provides the proper context in which to direct the human sex urge. His advice arose largely out of concern that the Corinthian believers not become involved in the loose moral practices for which their city was famous. Thus, he offers a general principle: "But since there is so much immorality, each man should have his own wife, and each woman her own husband" (1 Cor. 7:2). On the basis of this principle, he advises the unmarried and widows, "It is good for them to stay unmarried, as I am. But if they cannot control themselves, they should marry, for it is better to marry than to burn with passion" (vv. 8–9).

Paul is not alone in seeing marriage in this light. The position of the biblical writers is that marriage is the proper context for the sex act and forms the boundary within which the sex drive is to be exercised. The Old Testament law codified this view. And Jesus and the New Testament reaffirmed it.

We must acknowledge the importance of marriage as the context for the expression of the sex drive. The drive for expression through sex, to use the phrase preferred by Lester A. Kirkendall,[6] is undeniably strong. And its unbounded employment has been rightly viewed by every culture as dangerous to human communal life. For this reason marriage has become a nearly universal phenomenon, and most societies have viewed the marriage relationship as in some sense a sacred or inviolate bond.[7]

Despite its biblical sanction, this understanding cannot be put forth as the only, nor the highest purpose of marriage. There are other aspects of the male-female bond, beyond its serving as the outlet for the human sex drive. In many cases, the marital bond remains strong even after the sex drive has weakened or in situations where for physical or psychological reasons one or the other partner is unable to engage in the sex act. This phenomenon indicates that other dimensions of marriage are equally important.[8] Even more significantly, viewing it solely as the context for the expression of the sex drive robs marriage of its theological meaning described previously.

2. Marriage as Directed Toward Procreation and Child-Rearing

Augustine spoke of marriage as encompassing three dimensions, the fidelity of the spouses, the procreation and rearing of children, and a holy sacrament. Building on the thinking of the patristic era, the Roman Catholic Church has long viewed the second of these dimensions as the chief purpose of marriage.[9] In Catholic thinking this emphasis has been taken a step further, for the sex act has often been affirmed solely in terms of its role in procreation. Church teaching generally declares that the possibility of or openness to procreation forms the only context in which sexual intercourse is legitimate.

The centrality of procreation to marriage was given renewed expression in the 1987 Vatican statement on human reproduction, *Donum vitae,* which applies contemporary Roman Catholic understandings of the nature of the human person and marriage to several crucial ethical issues surrounding human reproduction.[10] The primary purpose of the document was to maintain the mystery of human procreation in the face of the unchallenged intrusion of technology into human life. The burden of the argument presented by the magisterium rests on the meaning of the sex act within the context of marriage. It insists that the "unitive meaning" of the act, which the document acknowledges, cannot be separated from the "procreative meaning." In so doing the magisterium in essence reaffirmed the traditional Roman Catholic understanding that elevates procreation as the central meaning both of sexual activity and of marriage itself, despite the changes in outlook that we have developed in the church in the twentieth century.[11]

As in the case of the first proposal, we ought to affirm the viewpoint that sees marriage as designed for procreation and child-rearing. The validity of this view is confirmed by studies that indicate the importance of stable marriages to the development of children. Children mature best when good role models of both sexes are present in the home, most specifically in the form of parents who share together the marital bond.[12]

This viewpoint also carries biblical precedence. The ancient Hebrews clearly emphasized the importance of having and raising children. In fact, to be "barren" constituted a source of shame, even a "reproach" for a Hebrew wife. The Hebrews considered children to be a gift or blessing from Yahweh and valued them as such (Ps. 127:3). Parents, and especially fathers, were therefore commanded to train their children in the fear of Yahweh (cf. Deuteronomy 6:6–9). Although the family is not elevated to the same degree in the New Testament, the command to train children is repeated in Ephesians 6:1–2.

Nevertheless, procreation and child-rearing, while important to marriage, cannot be elevated to its central meaning. Two arguments substantiate this conclusion. The first relates to the permanence of the marital bond beyond the child-rearing function. During the early years of marriage, procreation and the raising of children occupy a crucial position within the marriage. But, with the increase of life expectancy characteristic of our era, a couple can expect to live together nearly as many years after the "nest is empty" as they did with children in the home. The completion of the child-rearing function, then, does not signal the end of the marriage bond.

Secondly, procreation and child-rearing do not represent the sole nor the central meaning of marriage, in that they fail to embody the theological understanding of the marital bond described earlier. As the primal expression of the drive toward bonding, marriage constitutes a picture of the divine plan of fellowship in community. Procreation and the rearing of children serve this intention, rather than being served by it. And although the presence of children as the fruit of the marital union gives added expression to this primary intent, the intent is ultimately found in the marital bond itself, and therefore it is present even when no children are produced. It is instructive to note in this context that the longest presentation of the beauty of marital love found in the Bible, the Song of Songs, makes no mention of procreation in its celebration of sexual relations.

3. Marriage as the Focus of Companionship

Western society in general has adopted a third understanding of the meaning of marriage, namely, companionship. The ideal marriage is now pictured as that in which the husband and the wife become for each other closest friends. According to current thinking, the truly happy marriage partners are those who experience intimacy, who enjoy being together, and who share in the interests, goals, and dreams of their spouses.

The predominance of this understanding of the meaning of marriage is partially due to the influence of nineteenth-century Romanticism. But its roots go deeper, including the Protestantism which has played such an important role in shaping the understandings of the Western world.

Companionship as the central meaning of marriage can also be defended by appeal to the social sciences. Psychology emphasizes the importance of stable primary bondings for the release of the full personhood of the individual. The marital bond can be a fruitful relationship as husband and wife are freed from the need to compete with others and to prove themselves to each other. As they live in an atmosphere of complete acceptance and mutual companionship, they are able to express themselves freely, leading to a wholeness of existence. And the companionship of marriage provides a source of identity and intimacy in an otherwise impersonal society.[13]

This viewpoint can appeal to the biblical materials for support as well. The story of the creation of the female in Genesis 2 provides an important foundation for seeing marriage primarily in terms of companionship. The creation of the woman was precipitated by God's desire to provide a suitable companion for the man. We can almost hear Adam's expression of joy reverberate through the garden when he met his partner: "'This is now bone of my bones and flesh of my flesh; she shall be called "woman," for she was taken out of man'" (Gen. 2:23).

The same theme is implicitly present in the stories of the Hebrew patriarchs. The narrator gives the sense that the relationships between the spouses in these marriages were characterized by intense companionship. Examples include Abraham and Sarah, Isaac and Rebekah, and Jacob and Rachel, as well as the tender love story of Ruth and Boaz.

Although perhaps not as pronounced, the New Testament likewise implicitly presents the theme of marital companionship. Peter's wife apparently accompanied him on his missionary journeys (1 Cor. 9:5). Priscilla and Aquila shared together in the ministry which radiated from their home. Above all, the injunctions to spouses given in Ephesians 5:21–33 would be best facilitated by, and even quite naturally lead to, a relationship of companionship within the marital bond.

While this understanding is likewise crucial to the marital bond, it is not without dangers. As Diana and David Garland have noted, in contemporary Western society the companionship model can easily fall prey to "the overemphasis in our society on the you-me relationship and issues of intimacy in marriage," which runs the risk of "turning marriage into a self-centered system that mirrors the individualistic, self-actualizing goals of our society."[14]

Dangers such as these have led some Christians to look to other models for the primary purpose for marriage. The Garlands, for example, have called for a movement beyond companionship to a partnership model, with focuses on "the purpose and calling of the relationship, the task of husband and wife to make their relationship meaningful in the context of God's will."[15]

Attempts to find new models for the purpose of marriage are surely correct. The considerations offered in this chapter indicate that the spiritual metaphor which marriage is designed to be forms a basis from which to develop such a purpose. Understanding marriage as a picture of the overarching intent of God to fashion the community of male and female within creation for the sake of the reflection of the divine reality offers a perspective which can bring the various dimensions of the marital relationship together. Sexual activity, procreation, and companionship are all important as expressions of the primary intent of marriage, namely, to express the divine will to community.

4. Marriage as a Spiritual Metaphor

These considerations lead to the conclusion that the primary meaning of marriage is found in its function as a spiritual metaphor. As has been described above, this metaphor moves in two directions, both of which are related to the divine design of community. First, marriage forms a picture of the community which is present in a prior way within the triune God—the community of Father, Son, and Spirit. Just as the Trinity is a community of love, so also the marital relationship is to be characterized by love, thereby revealing the love inherent in God. Marriage accomplishes this in that the bonding that brings man and woman together incorporates a dialectic of sameness and difference not totally dissimilar to the dialectic present in the Trinity. One specific dimension of the divine love, its exclusiveness, is to be reflected in marriage. The exclusive relationship of love found within the Trinity (there is no other God, but the Triune One) and the exclusive, holy nature of God's love for creation are to be reflected in the exclusive love shared by husband and wife.

Secondly, marriage is intended to be a picture of the divine will to community among humankind and between humanity and God. As the primary expression of the drive toward bonding, marriage is closely related to, even instrumental in, the bringing to pass of the corporate fellowship God intends for humans. In this context marriage becomes a picture of the mystery of redemption, the love of God expressed through Christ, which gives rise to the church.

Here again marriage has a divinely given role as an instrument to bring about what it symbolizes. Historically, it was through the fruit of the marital bond—the procreative function—that the Christ Child came into the world. But until the consummation of the age, marriage continues to serve as a vehicle for the expansion of the church from person to person and from generation to generation. And the husband-wife relationship is intended to function in every era as a picture of certain aspects of the relationship between Christ and the church.

This being the case, marriage is to stand as a constant symbol of these spiritual realities. The forming of the marital bond and the birth of children ought to serve as reminders that God chose marriage as the context in which to work the miracle of the coming of the Son into the world. The establishment of a home must occur within the realization that this union is to be a vehicle for the expansion of the fellowship of believers as a dimension of the divine design for bringing about human community. And as husbands and wives live together in the marital relationship, they should be conscious that their life together is intended to be an important picture both of the mystery of Christ and the church and of the mystery of the divine love. Marriage, in short, is to be viewed with high regard, because the divine intent is that it function as a picture of great spiritual realities.

Within this context—marriage as a picture of the divine will to community—the bond between husband and wife can indeed become in the present an experience of community, the community of male and female. Lewis Smedes indicated the depth of relationship that comprises genuine community:

> The trick is to find a real community, not an insider's club. Not a group that makes believe it is a community just because everyone recites the same creed. But a community where people care enough to give each other permission to be strugglers, wounded strugglers, who are hanging on to their commitments by their fingernails. A community that cares enough to permit people to fail helps people dare to reveal their own struggles, including their failures as well as successes.[16]

The development of this depth of community ought to be the goal of husband and wife.

What Constitutes Marriage?

Marriage was instituted by the Creator and therefore has been endowed with a purpose in the context of the divine intention for humankind. To this point, our discussion has focused on marriage in general. No thought has been given to what may appear to be a prior issue, namely, that of the inception of the marriage relationship. Now we must ask: When are a man and a woman married? What is required for a bona fide marriage? And what actually constitutes the marital bond?

1. The Constitutive Elements of Marriage

In the Old Testament era, a well-ordered pattern developed for the establishment of marriages.[17] Finding a suitable marriage partner was accomplished either by the prospective groom himself or by his family (e.g., the selection of Rebekah to be the wife of Isaac, Gen. 24). The wedding was a festive occasion that could last a week or longer (Judg. 14:12; Gen. 29:28). The wedding night carried two sociolegal functions. As the occasion for the consummation of the marriage through intercourse, it sealed the marital contract between the two families. The bloodstained bedsheets passed among the guests and set aside for possible future reference (Deut. 22:13–21) proved that the bride's father and family had fulfilled their duty to preserve her integrity.

For the ancient Hebrews the formation of the marital bond was a relatively straightforward matter: Marriage consisted of a family contract plus its consummation in intercourse, all of which transpired within the context of the interested community. Changing cultural patterns, changing values on matters such as virginity prior to marriage, and a heightened sense of individualism prevalent in Western society have altered this ordered pattern greatly. As a result an important question has been left unclarified. At what point are a man and a woman married?[18]

a. Contemporary options. The movement away from ancient emphases, understandings, and customs concerning marriage has resulted in changing viewpoints concerning the constitutive elements in a bona fide marriage. In contemporary society, three basic elements in various combinations emerge as the most generally acknowledged ingredients.

A first proposal elevates the private, inward commitment of the two consenting parties. This idea, more than any alternative, reflects the modern understanding, which views marriage as the bond entered by the free and personal choice of two people. This understanding shapes our dating and courtship customs. And it often becomes the foundational principle to which appeal is made in the face of various related ethical questions, such as premarital sex, adultery, and divorce. The contemporary emphasis on marriage as constituted by inward commitment sets our world apart from ancient Hebrew society, in which not only sexual intercourse but also love itself was seen as following, not preceding, marriage.

Second, the public ceremony continues to play a major role next to inward commitment as an important element in the forming of the marital bond. Despite the sexual revolution of the 1960s, "living together" has not made the public ceremony obsolete. Most people continue to look to the wedding, whether it be a large gathering or merely a small ceremony, as an important occasion and as necessary if a couple would be truly married.

The continued acceptance of the wedding ceremony, while differing greatly from the weddings of biblical times, nevertheless forges a link between the ancient world and ours. The public nature of the wedding offers a modern affirmation of the public aspect of marriage. This institution is not merely a private affair, a matter between two consenting adults. Rather, there is a sense in which the wider society also has an interest in the forming of this intimate bond.

Less widely followed today but more closely connected to the ancient Hebrew outlook is a third element in the forging of the marital bond, namely, its consummation in sexual intercourse. Some would maintain that the marriage is not yet fully inaugurated until the sex act. This understanding forms part of the basis for the Roman Catholic practice of granting marriage annulments in certain circumstances.

b. The essence of marriage: inward commitment expressed in outward act. Despite the dangers inherent in its abuse, the modern movement toward viewing the essential element of marriage as being the inward commitment of the two persons must be hailed as a positive development. Rather than being a falling away from the biblical view of the marital bond, the emphasis on inward commitment actually comprises a movement back to the understanding of marriage presented in the stories of creation in Genesis 2 and of the marriages of the patriarchs in subsequent chapters. These stories give the impression that these early marriages, although generally arranged by the respective families, were constituted above all by the love and devotion of the spouses for each other.

Of course, it would be correct to argue that romantic love as we view it today is not an essential element in marriage.[19] This understanding of love, which we take for granted, has actually gained wide acceptance only in recent times and only in westernized societies. Therefore, while romantic love may form a dimension of the inward commitment that constitutes marriage, this commitment must also take other forms in addition to romantic love. But what other forms are necessary to constitute marriage?

Many Christians look to *agape,* defined as the unconditional giving of oneself to the other and unconditional acceptance of the other, as the essence of inward commitment.[20] While *agape* is without a doubt the New Testament ideal for all relationships and specifically for marriage, it always remains an unachieved ideal. Therefore, while the ideal ought never to be lost, *agape* alone is too lofty a concept to serve as the actual basis for marriage. There have been many lasting marriages in which neither this nor romantic love has characterized the marriage partners' relationship. What depth of inward commitment is present in such marriages? What minimum commitment is necessary to constitute a marital bond in the absence of the ideal? At the very least, marriage requires some rudimentary commitment on the part of each spouse to the other person and to the marriage itself. This commitment must include the willingness of the husband and wife to continue in the marriage state and contribute what he or she can in order to foster a successful life together. When this degree of commitment is present, marriage can become a reality.

Inward commitment forms the basis of marriage. But by its own nature such commitment calls forth outward acts in some form. Lying behind this assertion is a principle that is operative in various dimensions of human life, namely, that the inward life must come to outward expression. The Epistle of James, for example, applies this principle to the area of faith: "In the same way, faith by itself, if it is not accompanied by action, is dead. . . . Show me your faith without deeds, and I will show you my faith by what I do" (James 2:17–18). John echoes this same idea with respect to love: "This is how we know what love is: Jesus Christ laid down his life for us. And we ought to lay down our lives for our brothers. . . . Dear children, let us not love with words or tongue but with actions and in truth" (1 John 3:16, 18). In the same way, the commitment that two persons sense inwardly to each other leading to the bond of male and female calls forth outward expression.

The inward commitment of male and female that leads to the sealing of the most intimate human bond, marriage, finds outward expression in many ways. Yet, two actions are so foundational so as to lie at the heart of the others. The first, the declaration of covenant in the presence of witnesses, is the outward act that constitutes the actual beginning point of the marital bond, for it comprises the public formalization of that bond. The second act, which will be discussed in greater depth in the next chapter, is the physical expression of personal commitment in the sex act. This act forms the repeated reenactment of the covenant felt between the two partners and formalized in the wedding ceremony. These two outward acts, the wedding vow and sexual intercourse, form the most symbolic outward expressions of the inward marital commitment.

c. The significance of the wedding ceremony. During the sexual revolution of the 1960s many couples raised the question concerning the importance of the wedding ceremony. "Of what value is a piece of paper?" was the repeated cry. Since those turbulent years, many people have gained a renewed appreciation for the marriage license. This rediscovery of the public declaration of vows is significant.

As has been indicated above, essential to marriage is the inward commitment of the partners to each other and to the marriage bond. But the marriage license and the wedding ceremony are reminders that marriage entails more than the purely personal. It is not merely a private covenant between two persons. As all societies in all eras have known, marriage has a social or public dimension. The wedding ceremony, with its publicly witnessed reciting of vows and its legally signed marriage certificate, functions in our society as the social recognition of the married status of the new husband and wife. The relationship between the inward and the outward, or the private and the public dimensions, was aptly summarized by Kari Jenson's conclusions from her observations of various long-term nonmarital relationships:

> In fact, the promise of marriage is anything but private. As marriage is the most profound commitment between two persons, so its public declaration is the most profound action we can perform in the world of men. The public promise to love is the remarkable merging of the private with the public, of the individual with the universal, of the world of thought with the world of action. For in the public sphere, actions rule, in the private, thought. To assume that one can promise love in private is seriously to misunderstand the nature of promise. Promise is action and therefore an *essentially* public undertaking.[21]

In addition to the social dimension implicit in the wedding ceremony, there is for the Christian understanding another aspect of the importance of the public act. A public vow solidifies an inward commitment. This principle operates in at least two ways.

First, a public declaration of commitment before witnesses assists the individual in determining whether or not that inward commitment is actually present. To stand in public and recite a wedding vow means that two persons have advanced in their relationship with each other to the point where they are ready to commit themselves to lifelong growth together. The declaration of such a vow in the presence of witnesses calls the two persons to determine if they indeed mean what they now are asserting and what they likely have already spoken to each other in private.

Second, the public declaration of commitment to another person and to the marriage relationship, coming as it generally does after a time of preparation and planning and occurring within the context of a celebration, offers the couple an event to remember. When the difficult times arise and the temptation to bail out of the marriage haunts them, the marriage partners can mentally return to their wedding day and remind themselves of the vow they spoke in the presence of witnesses. Such a bold reminder can provide a source of renewed strength to continue to be faithful to the covenant they share.

In each of these aspects, the wedding ceremony operates in a way analogous to baptism. Baptism, too, is a public affirmation of an inward faith and commitment, faith and commitment to Jesus as Lord. As such it is a solidification of that commitment and can become a day to remember for the baptized believer.

The wedding and baptism are analogous in a further way as well. Ultimately faith, not baptism, is what taps into the resources of God's grace and opens the door to salvation. As the apostle declared, "For it is by grace you have been saved, through faith" (Eph. 2:8). Nevertheless, without baptism as its divinely ordained outward expression inward faith remains incomplete and tentative. So also with marriage. Ultimately the commitment of two people to each other forms the primal human bond. Yet, this inward commitment remains incomplete and tentative without its corresponding outward expression, the marriage ceremony, whatever form that ceremony may take.

2. Is the Marriage Ceremony a Matter for Church or State?

A question that carries importance in current ecumenical discussions of marriage concerns the governing order that has primary interest and responsibility in the inauguration of the marriage bond. Are the wedding ceremony and the acknowledgment of married status under the jurisdiction of the civil or the ecclesiastical government? In the United States and Canada there is no practical problem associated with this issue, for in church weddings officiating clergy function not only as representatives of the church but also as agents on behalf of the civil magistrate. Because of this dual role of the clergy, civil and church ceremonies occur simultaneously.

The situation is quite different in certain European countries. There a civil ceremony, which marks the point at which a couple is legally married, is required in addition to whatever church wedding they may have planned. This situation poses a problem for the Roman Catholic Church because of its tradition of viewing marriage as a sacrament and therefore as coming under the jurisdiction of the church.[22]

The considerations put forth in this chapter suggest that marriage is a matter of interest to both the civil and the ecclesiastical spheres, for it crosses whatever boundaries exist between church and state. First, the marriage bond is both a social and legal contract and a spiritual union. The civil sphere has been delegated authority to govern in the affairs of the wider society. The contractual nature of marriage means that the state is entitled to stipulate the legal and social dimensions of the entrance and continuance of marriage, in so far as these matters affect society as a whole. The church, however, is interested in the spiritual union that marriage is intended to mark.

Second, marriage is related to both the civil and the ecclesiastical realms, because it crosses the boundary between creation and salvation history. Throughout its history, the church has maintained in one form or another the assertion that both the civil and the ecclesiastical authorities are expressions of the rulership of God. The state carries jurisdiction under God over all persons within its domain, and thus it is related more closely to what all persons share by virtue of their creation by God. The church, in contrast, is the product of, and the witness to the salvific work of God in Christ. Its authority and interest, therefore, is more closely connected to the believing community, which comprises its membership. As has been developed previously, marriage belongs to both orders—creation and salvation. It is divinely instituted for humankind in general, but because it has a special purpose within the context of salvation history, it carries a special meaning for Christians. The general and special aspects of marriage indicate that both state and church share an interest in this institution.

The marriage ceremony, therefore, is an act of the state and of the church, yet each with differing interests and emphases. The civil authority is involved in the forming of the marriage bond in terms of its status as a civil, legal contract. At the same time, the ecclesiastical authority is involved as well. The church is active in the wedding in view of the status of marriage as a spiritual metaphor. In addition, the church seeks to act in the interest of the marriage partners. The goal of the church's action is that the husband and wife experience the blessing and grace of God, so that they may enjoy community with one another—a community of male and female—and may form a home which can serve as the basis for the expansion of the community of God in the world.

The Sex Act within the Context of Marriage

We, as created sexual beings, may fulfill the divine intent and reflect the divine image in the community of male and female constituted by the marriage bond. This foundational affirmation calls forth the development of a Christian view of marriage, which, in turn, can provide a basis for interaction with contemporary ethical issues related to human sexuality. Such a view maintains that ideally marriage is inaugurated by means of the private, inward commitment of the two consenting parties as it is expressed in the outward act of the wedding vows, that is, in the declaration of covenant in the presence of witnesses. This forms the context for the consummation of the marital union in the sex act. Marriage is maintained through the steadfastness of that inward commitment, as each spouse remains faithful to the other and to the marriage itself.

Related to, but not required for the establishment and continuation of marriage is a second outward act, the physical expression of personal commitment in sexual intercourse. This act forms the repeated reenactment of the covenant between the two partners as formalized in the wedding ceremony. Therefore, just as marriage is significant as a central expression of the drive toward bonding that characterizes us as sexual beings, so also within marriage the sex act serves as a primary means of expressing not only our fundamental sexuality but also the mutual commitment of the marriage partners. The act, therefore, must likewise be understood in the context of Christian theology.

The Sex Act and Meaning

The sexual revolution has raised anew the question concerning the meaning of the sex act. The wake of the changes of the 1960s has splashed on the shore of sexual ethics, offering attempts to provide a theoretical rationale for the more permissive attitude toward sexual exploration. In their intent to sanction a broadening of sexual expression beyond the boundaries of marriage, such proposals often articulate outlooks toward the sex act that ultimately only serve to reduce the meaning of intercourse. The Christian understanding of human sexuality, however, cannot condone any reduction of the meaning of sexual intercourse. Rather, this act must be viewed in terms of its deep meaning within the context of marriage as intended by the Creator in accordance with the divine purpose.

1. The Sex Act and Anthropology

Current proposals which attempt to provide a foundation for more openness toward sexual expression beyond the context of marriage tend to accomplish this goal by offering some alternative understanding of the meaning of the sex act. Such alternative understandings often draw from aspects of Christian doctrine. But in effect they truncate the full meaning given to the act as an expression of the whole person, a meaning that must be emphasized in any truly Christian sex ethic.

At times the newer openness is defended by appeal to the sex act as a vehicle for self-expression or self-actualization. Episcopal priest Raymond Lawrence, for example, articulating a position he termed "the principle of Jephthah's daughter," claimed that "sexual self-actualization is a value superior to the values of 'innocence' and 'purity.'"[1]

Others defend a more open practice by reducing the act to the purely bodily sphere, suggesting that sexual intercourse is to be viewed solely as a function of the body that can be satisfied without involving the real person.[2] As a purely bodily act, intercourse carries no meaning beyond being an expression of the needs of the body, it is argued.

This outlook has been put forth repeatedly in the history of Western thought and often with two quite opposite ethical conclusions drawn from it. On the one hand, some have argued from this premise that all sexual expression should be avoided. Such a view apparently had infiltrated the first-century church in Corinth, set forth with the slogan, "It is good for a man not to touch a woman" (1 Cor. 7:1 NASB).[3] Today the opposite conclusion is far more likely to emerge, namely, that a person may engage in sex freely and with few restraints, should one so desire, for sexual intercourse is of no consequence for the acting agent. Others state the matter even more strongly, declaring that in the interest of personal well-being we ought to give expression to our human sexual needs.

However defended, the contemporary indulgent attitude toward sexual expression is simply incompatible with the view of sexuality that arises from the Christian understanding of the nature of the human person. Regardless of the claims of its proponents to the contrary, it is ultimately based on a dualistic anthropology that divides the human person into two parts, body and soul, puts forth the soul as the focus of the "real" person, and reduces the body to being at best the vehicle for the expression of the "true" person. Dualisms of this type are quite foreign to the basically holistic or unitary anthropology developed by the ancient Hebrews, as reflected in the Old Testament and assumed by the writers of the New Testament. In fact, it was this type of dualistic view that several New Testament epistles seek to combat.

Not only did the church in Corinth harbor an ascetic party, as noted above. There may likewise have been teachers who, on the basis of the mistaken idea that what a person's body does has no effect on one's spirituality, argued that they could simply indulge the body without restraint. In response, Paul admonishes the Corinthian Christians to honor God with their bodies, for the body belongs to the Lord. He applies this general principle specifically to the sexual area. On the basis of Genesis 2:24, Paul concludes that the sex act is more than an insignificant and inconsequential bodily function. In some way it actually is able to effect a personal union between the partners (1 Cor. 6:12–20). Paul insists that at the very least this act be viewed as highly meaningful.

The conclusion that the sex act is meaningful, and not merely a function of the body, is gaining a hearing within the human sciences. An increasing number of psychologists, for example, now maintain that sex without "commitment" is dehumanizing. As Richard Hettlinger concluded, "there can be no question that recreational sex is always in danger of treating people as merely convenient objects for pleasure."[4] Such a use, or misuse, of another person's body is a blatant denial of his or her humanity as an embodied being.

2. The Sex Act and the Nature of Meaning

Christian theology, with growing agreement from the human sciences, asserts that the sex act is meaningful and cannot be dismissed as a "mere" bodily function devoid of meaning. But a full Christian understanding must probe deeper concerning the meaning of the act. Is the significance, whatever it may be, intrinsic to the act? That is, does the act carry its meaning within itself? Or if not, from what does sexual intercourse derive its meaning?

A helpful point of departure lies in a contemporary understanding of meaning itself and of how meaning arises, which relates to an understanding of the nature of history and historical events in general.

Basically, this view maintains that events carry meaning as they form a part of a larger context. No event carries its significance simply within itself. There are no "brute facts" of history, for every event always transpires within a context. By extension, the meanings of human actions are always dependent on the context in which they transpire. No act carries its own meaning within itself. No meaning is conveyed by a solitary "brute" act. Rather, all acts occur within a context and are dependent on their context in order to be meaningful. Further, this context is closely related to the intent of the actor in performing the action. Meaning, therefore, is the product of the union of two elements, the physical action itself and the context in which it occurs, which is related to the intent of the actor.

This theory concerning the nature of meaning has important ramifications for the question of the meaning of the sex act. The meaning of any participation in sexual intercourse is dependent on the context in which it occurs and on the intent of the persons involved. The participants pour meaning into the sex act by the intent that motivates them and by the context they create when they engage in the act. Abraham Maslow, himself no committed proponent of traditional sex ethics, nevertheless confirmed this view in declaring,

> It would appear that no single sexual act can per se be called abnormal or perverted. It is only abnormal or perverted individuals who can commit abnormal or perverted acts. That is, the dynamic meaning of the act is far more important than the act itself.[5]

As a result of this relationship of act, context, and intent, the sex act cannot be separated from the entire human being who engages in it. Sex is not something that happens "out there," at a distance from the person who participates in the act. Rather, like human actions in general, the sex act is an expression of the intent of the actor who creates a context for the action, from which, in turn, the act derives its meaning. Just as there is no "brute fact of history" and thus no "brute act," so there is no sex act apart from the context in which it transpires. To attempt to separate the sex act from the personhood of the participant, then, is doomed to failure. Instead, the participants must engage in the act cognizant of what this specific act of sex is intended to declare.

The general meaning of the sex act is that it is an expression of our existence as sexual beings. The Christian asserts, however, that this act as an expression of human sexuality carries even greater significance. Similar to every action the Christian performs, sex is to be understood within the context of the Christian life as a whole. Like every dimension of life, sexual expression must be placed under the parameters of our fundamental commitment to the lordship of Christ. As a result, the Christian seeks to understand the sex act theologically, that is, in terms of what is being said thereby about the self, the nature of life, and ultimately about God.

The Christian ethic maintains that the fundamental meaning of the sex act is derived from its setting within the marriage relationship. Its meaning is constituted by its practice within a proper context, marriage, and with a proper intent, an expression of covenantal love under the lordship of Jesus Christ.

The Sex Act within
the Marital Bond

The context of the sex act is crucial in giving to it the meaning it is intended to carry. According to the Christian understanding, this act denotes a variety of negative meanings when it is practiced within improper contexts.

When engaged in improperly, sexual intercourse is no longer the positively meaningful, beautiful act it is designed to be, but becomes instead an expression of self-gratification, adultery, infidelity, or exploitation. The divinely intended, positive meaning of this act is found only when it is enjoyed within its divinely given, proper context, namely, marriage. This assertion, however, raises the question concerning the relationship of the sex act to the marital bond. What is the meaning of the act within the context of marriage?[6]

1. The Sex Act as the Sacrament of Marriage

The positive meaning of sexual intercourse is related to its employment as an act of marital union. When practiced within this content, the act can become a beautiful statement of the total bond and covenant between husband and wife. The enjoyment of sex within the marital bond can become the reenactment, reaffirmation, and symbolic embodiment of the marriage vow. This dimension of the meaning of sexual intercourse within marriage suggests that the sex act may be termed the sacrament of marriage.[7]

a. The meaning of the term.   The phrase, "the sacrament of marriage," is intended to build from the patristic understanding of the nature of the Christian sacraments. Since at least the time of Augustine, a sacrament has been defined as an outward, visible sign of an inward, invisible grace. That is, a sacrament is a physical act that seeks to give visible expression to a spiritual reality. As an outward sign, however, a sacrament does not merely depict the inward dimension; it also seals in a symbolic way the spiritual reality of which it serves as a sign.

This understanding of the relationship between the rites of the church and the underlying spiritual reality of union with Christ, which the sacraments signify, forms a basis for understanding the relationship between the sex act and marriage. The physical act of sexual intercourse can become a visible expression and symbolic sealing of the marriage bond uniting husband and wife.

The symbolic dimension of the sex act has become a topic of interest among psychologists in recent years. One scholar, J. Richard Udry, even claimed that "failure to understand the symbolic functions of sex in the marital relationship is a failure to understand the human sexual relationship at all." He found in the sex act "a symbolic affirmation of the exclusiveness, privacy, and psychological intimacy of the husband-wife relationship." And it serves to reaffirm both the male and female difference and complementarity.[8]

In affirming the symbolic or sacramental nature of the sex act within marriage, two cautions are in order, however. First, to use the term *sacrament* is not to affirm that marriage itself is a sacrament,[9] that is, a means of grace. Through a process that began in the patristic era and came to a climax in the Middle

Ages, the Roman Catholic Church erroneously elevated marriage to a sacrament and at the Council of Trent codified its status as such.[10]

The Christian tradition knows a threefold criterion for bona fide sacraments. A sacrament is an act that was ordained by the Lord, was practiced as such by the early church, and is so closely bound up with the gospel so as to be a vivid picture of the gospel story. When judged according to this traditional criterion, marriage simply cannot be considered a sacrament of the church.

The second caution is equally important. The sex act likewise ought not to be viewed as a sacrament. That is, the act itself is not a means of grace. Sexual intercourse is not a sacred act, understood in terms of being linked with the worship of God or with the reception of grace in some magical way, nor ought it to be seen as holy in some mystical fashion.

This assertion stands in contrast to certain ancient religions, which viewed sexual intercourse as a religious act linked to religious fertility rites. In these religions, "sacred" sexual relations were established and nonmarital intercourse condoned. The biblical documents from the patriarchs to Paul, however, repeatedly reject the deification of sex. In fact, one of the definitive characteristics that was to separate the Hebrews from the surrounding peoples was the assertion of one God who as the only God was beyond the sexual activity other ancient religions ascribed to the deities.[11]

Nor ought the sex act be viewed as a "means of grace" understood in terms of the marriage itself. As important as it is to the ongoing functioning of a good marriage, sex alone cannot infuse vitality into an ailing relationship, nor can sex be the "glue" which holds a marriage together, as some people today mistakenly believe.

The assertion that the sex act is the sacrament of marriage is to be understood in a metaphorical sense. It is a way of describing the relationship between the act and the underlying marital bond. And it serves as a way of characterizing the meaning of the act within that bond. Within the marriage relationship, sexual intercourse functions in a manner analogous to the Christian understanding of sacramental acts. The rites of baptism and the Lord's Supper signify and seal the covenant of believers with each other and with God. In a somewhat analogous way, the sex act is meaningful as it signifies and seals the marriage covenant. More specifically, analogous to participation at the Lord's table which reaffirms the covenant made in baptism, participation in the sex act is a reenactment of the wedding vow.

b. The basis of the relationship between the sex act and marriage.
This understanding of the relationship between the sex act and the marital bond has a twofold source. It arises out of the nature of the triune God as the primary community of love and out of the divine intention that marriage as the community of male and female serve as one means of actualizing the creation of humankind in the image of God.

As has been argued earlier, God is the primary community of love. Throughout all eternity the triune God—as Father, Son, and Holy Spirit—forms the perfect community, for the three trinitarian persons are bonded together eternally through love. Further, classical trinitarian theology asserts that the relationship of Father and Son, as the dialectic of sameness and difference, forms the basis for the trinitarian distinctions in the Godhead.

Because God created humankind in the divine image, by God's grace humans can reflect the divine nature and being. We express the central aspect of the divine nature—being the community of love—in various ways. According to the Genesis creation accounts, the primal reflection of the divine essence is the community of male and female which we call marriage, the bonding of two people to form a unity.

The sex act is intended to be an expression of the bonding of male and female in the community of love. In fact, it comprises the most intimate and meaningful act embodying the deep union of husband and wife that lies at the basis of marriage. But not only does it express that bond, the sex act also serves to solidify the unity of male and female in marriage. As the unity of husband and wife is formed and expressed—that community of male and female which God intends to serve as a reflection of the divine nature—a picture is presented of the higher unity of the divine life.

On this basis, the sex act may be seen as the sacrament of the marriage covenant. It is an outward act which signifies an inward commitment and also seals that inward commitment. Something changes when a couple engages in sexual intercourse. The act has altered their relationship. They have become one in body and therefore have symbolized their becoming a unity of persons, as Paul indicates to the Corinthians (1 Cor. 6:15–16), building from Genesis 2:24. When practiced within the context of the covenant of marriage, engaging in the act has deepened the commitment of the partners to each other and to their life together. They have in this act truly become one.

c. Aspects of the relationship between the sex act and marriage.

The unity of marriage which constitutes the community of male and female is designed by God to be an expression of the divine community of love. Within marriage the sex act can become a reenactment, reaffirmation, and symbolic embodiment of the marriage vow. In this context, it may be viewed in terms of being the sacrament of marriage. The sacramental meaning carried by the sex act within marriage arises in two major ways.

(1) First, the sex act receives meaning from its context within marriage as it becomes a visible expression of the marital covenant between husband and wife. Whenever the couple engages in sexual intercourse they are reaffirming the pledge made on their wedding day and are giving visual representation of the content of that vow. This may be seen by looking at the nature of the marital covenant and then by viewing the sex act as an enactment of that covenant.

The marital covenant has many dimensions. But in each of these dimensions the intent of the covenant is to produce in marriage a foundational community in which male and female live together in fellowship. To this end, the covenant includes a commitment on the part of the covenant partners to give and receive freely. Ideally the marital state is one in which the free exchange of the partners can transpire in daily life together.

Further, the covenant includes a commitment to transparency. The human sciences have documented the importance of such personal openness as a means to the fostering of healthy relationships. In forming the marriage bond the partners commit themselves to seek to be transparent to each other, sharing with each other their deepest needs, dreams, and goals.

Likewise, the marriage covenant includes a commitment to total and unconditional acceptance. This, too, is crucial to a good marriage and is a sign of genuine community. In forming the marriage bond the partners covenant together to move toward full acceptance of each other.

A commitment to this goal helps to release the marriage partners from the performance orientation characteristic of contemporary society, that is, from the need to live up to the expectations of another in order to gain for oneself the acceptance of the other. Rather, acceptance by one's spouse forms the context in which each marriage partner is free to act. Within this context of acceptance both partners are able to function according to their gifts, responsibilities, and abilities. In this way, the human community of marriage becomes a reflection of the divine nature, which includes God's unconditional acceptance of us despite our finitude and God's perfect forgiveness of our sin in the midst of our fallenness. Just as God justifies the sinner by grace apart from works, so also marital commitment is based upon unconditional acceptance apart from the "performance" of one's spouse.

The sex act is a visible enactment of these various dimensions of the marriage covenant. In sexual intercourse intimacy is freely given and received. The commitment to give of oneself freely and to receive from the other in freedom is visually and physically enacted through this intimate sexual relation. As this occurs the sex act points to the various ways in which the partners give to and receive from each other in day-to-day life together. And by this act the partners renew their commitment to the task of giving and receiving freely, which they expressed in their marriage vows.

Further, sexual intercourse is an act of physical transparency. This act forms a return, as it were, to the transparency of the Garden of Eden, for husband and wife are "naked and not ashamed." Physically they are fully transparent to each other, for in the nakedness of the sex act the most private aspects of one's physical being are no longer hidden from the partner. This physical transparency symbolizes the deeper transparency between the marriage partners, to which they have committed themselves in the marriage covenant. And through physical transparency the partners commit themselves anew to the development of the full transparency they promised to one another in the marriage vow.

Likewise, sexual intercourse is an act of total acceptance. This moves in two directions. On the one hand, it includes acceptance of oneself and of one's own sexuality. In coming to this self-acceptance a marriage partner is often assisted by one's spouse. This is especially important in situations in which a person has been conditioned, whether by upbringing or through some traumatic experience, to deny or be embarrassed by one's sexuality. As one's spouse accepts the partner's sexuality, however, the partner is moved in the direction of self-acceptance and self-affirmation as this embodied, sexual being.

On the other hand, in the physical sex act a partner acknowledges and accepts the other for the person he or she is. And each affirms the maleness or femaleness of the other.[12] In so doing, through the physical act of mutual acceptance the marriage partners reaffirm the commitment they made in their marriage vow to accept each other in all areas of life.

The acceptance aspect of the meaning of the sex act within the context of marriage is of special importance in the postsexual revolution era in which we live. In contemporary society, sexual intercourse has increasingly become oriented toward preconceived standards of performance. In an age of multiple and ever-changing partners, persons are forced into a performance mentality. Each actor is continually conscious of the need to maintain his or her performance rating. A sexual partner not only competes with oneself, but with the previous partners of one's "lover" and with all potential rivals for the affections of that "lover."

When the sex act is viewed in the context of the marriage covenant, however, this performance mentality is dissipated in the grand solvent of mutual love. The commitment that binds husband and wife is directed toward permanence and full, unconditional acceptance. Within this context each partner in the sex act is released from being absorbed by concerns about measuring up to expectations and is released to seek in freedom to please one's lover. The desire to please one's spouse in the sex act, in turn, opens the door to the second aspect of the sacramental meaning of the sexual intercourse within marriage, pleasure.

(2) The sex act within marriage carries sacramental meaning as an act of pleasure. Recent research has confirmed what many people have known for some time: the sex act can be uniquely and intensely pleasurable.[13] The pleasure of sexual intercourse arises in part from its physical dimension, for we have been designed biologically to derive pleasure from this act. This biological design is not limited to the male, as is sometimes suggested, but includes the female as well. In fact, as Letha Scanzoni pointed out, drawing on the work of Masters and Johnson, "only women have a sexual structure that has absolutely no other function than to provide sexual delight."[14]

The pleasurable aspect of sexual intercourse is enhanced when the act is intertwined with love. For this reason, marriage, as the bond of love uniting male and female, can provide the context for the most fulfilling enjoyment of the act. Practiced within this context, sexual intercourse can become a physical act carrying deep significance. For it can declare that true pleasure is a by-product of relationship or covenant.

In contrast to popular misconceptions, the Bible presents a pleasure-affirming, not a pleasure-denying, message. The biblical authors maintain that God's concern is not to eliminate this dimension of embodied existence, but to direct it properly in the interest of the enjoyment of true pleasure. In the same way the pleasures of sex are celebrated in the Bible.

Although there are hints of this celebrative dimension repeatedly in the Bible, the most explicit affirmations of sexual pleasure are found in the wisdom literature of the Old Testament. Several of the Proverbs, for example, are devoted to the theme of finding true sexual pleasure. This theme is expressed both through warnings against seeking sexual fulfillment outside of marriage and through assertions concerning the delight that the married person should find in one's spouse.

Above all, however, the Song of Songs is significant in this regard. Despite attempts throughout both its Jewish and its Christian exegetical history to view it as an allegory of God and God's people, the book is best seen as an extended description of the celebrative dimension of sexuality.[15] This literature is erotic in the positive sense of the term. It celebrates sexual pleasure and *eros,* the attractiveness that a lover finds in the beloved.

As a declaration that pleasure arises from commitment within relationship (the concept of covenant), marriage as a covenantal bond brings together the two aspects of love, *agape* and *eros.* Within the context of marriage the sex act declares that the desire for the other, the physical attraction that two persons may sense toward each other (so central to *eros*), can truly be fulfilled only in the total giving of one to the other and the unconditional acceptance of the other (*agape*).[16] As the love of the other characterized by desire for the other (*eros*) merges with the love of the other characterized by self-giving (*agape*), love in its highest form emerges. Sexual intercourse constitutes a visible object lesson of this reality.

Similarly, sexual intercourse is the celebration of the marital bond. It is an act of joyous pleasure in which the partners delight in one another and in their relationship of love. This aspect of love between spouses is likewise emphasized in the wisdom literature of the ancient Hebrews. The Song of Songs provides an extended commentary on the beauty of the sex act within the context of marriage. This same beauty forms the basis of the admonition of the Preacher to his son to find in his own spouse a continual source of celebrative sexual relations and thereby to avoid seeking such fulfillment in other women (Prov. 5:15–19).

Here again *agape* and *eros* are joined in the sex act by means of the desire to give and receive. This occurs in the deep sense of mutual pleasure that comes in fulfilling one's partner (*agape*) while having one's own desire (*eros*) fulfilled.

2. The Sex Act as an
Expression of Mutual Submission

The sex act is the "sacrament" of marriage, the reenactment, reaffirmation, and symbolic embodiment of the marriage vow. Closely related to this meaning is a second. Sexual intercourse is likewise a meaningful expression of the commitment of the partners to the principle of mutual submission.

The concept of mutual submission within the marriage relationship is put forth most explicitly in Ephesians 5:21–33. There the ideal of mutual submission is evident in two ways. First, the statement of this principle found immediately prior to the author's presentation concerning the roles of husband and wife forms the context for his discussion of marital relationships. The preceding verses (5:18–21) speak of being filled with the Spirit, one hallmark of which is mutual submission. Thus, the apostle declares, "Submit to one another out of reverence for Christ" (Eph. 5:21). Mutual submission, therefore, is to be the guiding principle in all interpersonal relationships in the church. The roles of husband and wife, in turn, are to be viewed in the context of, and comprise a specific application of this principle. However understood, therefore, these roles cannot be seen as contradicting the principle of mutual submission which forms their context.

Second, although the command of submission is specifically given only to wives in the text, the love command directed to husbands actually moves in the same direction. Husbands are enjoined to love their wives in accordance with the model given by the self-sacrificial love of Christ for the church. This kind of love quite obviously includes one dynamic central to submission. For submission is in the final analysis giving deference to the other or setting aside one's own prerogatives for the sake of the other. Precisely this constitutes the kind of attitude that Christ put into action.

Another text applies the principle of mutual submission directly to the area of sexual intercourse in marriage: "The husband should fulfill his marital duty to his wife, and likewise the wife to her husband. The wife's body does not belong to her alone but also to her husband. In the same way, the husband's body does not belong to him alone but also to his wife" (1 Cor. 7:3–4). Paul's admonition rings as radical today as it must have in first-century Corinth. In contrast to both the self-possessive attitude of the "me-generation" and to the widely held double standard that elevates the male, he declares that the body of each marriage partner belongs to the other and therefore that each should fulfill one's marital duty to the other. The radicality of his statement is enhanced in that Paul specifically addresses not only wives, but husbands as well, declaring that the husband's body belongs to his wife. Not only is the wife to be submissive to her husband in sexual matters, which would be the situation if submission were her role alone, but the husband is to submit to his wife as well. Here is a clear example of the outworking of the principle of mutual submission in marriage.

As Paul's admonition indicates, the sex act is a physical, visible expression of mutual submission. It symbolizes in a vivid manner the desire of each of the marriage partners to give freely and completely for the sake of fulfilling the other. In this way it pictures what is to be true of the marriage relationship as a whole. Marriage is intended to be a most intimate human fellowship—the community of male and female—in which each person gives freely for the sake of the other.

The giving of self for the sake of the good of the other is to be expressed in the mundane aspects of daily life together. But the highest symbol of this aspect of the fellowship within marriage, the most expressive symbol of the willingness to give of self freely and totally for the sake of the pleasure and well-being of the spouse, is the sex act. In this act a person gives fully and unashamedly and becomes fully vulnerable and open to the other.[17]

As an expression of the giving of self for the other, the sex act also becomes a physical embodiment of the meaning of marriage as a spiritual metaphor. Like the relationship to which it is intimately tied, this act is a vivid reminder of the self-giving love of Christ for the church, which is described by analogy to marriage in Ephesians 5:22–33. The sex act, as a sign of the desire to give completely for the sake of the other, which desire is to characterize the marriage relationship as a whole, is an appropriate reminder of the spiritual truth that Jesus has given himself completely for his church. The coming together of the marriage partners with the intent to please and satisfy each other in this intensely intimate act speaks of Jesus' act of total self-giving in living and dying for others. As a person's first desire in the sexual act should be to please the other, so also Jesus sought to meet the ultimate human need for spiritual intimacy with God.

3. The Sex Act as an Expression of Openness

Within the context of the sex act as the embodiment of the marriage covenant and as an expression of self-giving in the marriage relationship, yet another meaning to sexual intercourse arises. This further dimension is derived from the link between intercourse and procreation. Because of this connection, the sex act is an expression of the openness of the spouses individually and jointly to new life as a possible outworking of the marriage bond.[18] This openness, in turn, may readily be extended beyond the child as the product of marriage to other dimensions of marital life.

Of course, sexual relations do not always result in pregnancy and childbirth.

This is especially true in contemporary Western society, which has increasingly separated the sex act from procreation both physically and psychologically. And even in marriages in which the couples are open to pregnancy, procreation results from sexual intercourse only on a few occasions, if at all.

Nevertheless, the relationship between the sex act and procreation is never completely erased. Sexual intercourse continues to be the most common means whereby children are procreated. And even when intercourse does not lead to pregnancy, the lovers cannot escape the realization that precisely in this way procreation is normally accomplished. This enduring relationship between the sex act and procreation endows this act with an additional meaning, namely, its function as a sign of the couple's willingness to open their relationship beyond themselves.

a. The sex act and openness to others.

One important aspect of the marital union is the openness for the expansion of the love of the spouses beyond themselves. The beginning point for this openness arises as the marriage partners become open to expand the marital bond into a family bond, as they include within their horizon the offspring who are the product of the love dynamic they share together. This expansion of the horizon of the marriage bond is most readily depicted in sexual intercourse, for this act is the means that effects procreation and through procreation brings new life into the marriage relationship as its product.

Sexual intercourse symbolizes the love of the spouses for each other. At the same time, through this expression their mutual love is expanded, for it is the sex act that procreates the child produced by their union. The joining of these two dimensions in the sex act makes it an apt and beautiful picture of expansive love. But precisely in this way, as a symbol of the openness of the marriage partners to new life, sexual intercourse, through its link to procreation, constitutes an apt human analogy to the expansive love of God, which likewise creates the other as its product. The sex act offers an analogy to the divine expansive love both in a general and in a specific way. Each act of intercourse constitutes a picture of a truth concerning the nature of marital love in general. It declares that through this act of mutual love, the love between spouses is expanded to include the new life of the child formed through this act. By analogy this picture of marital love in general depicts as well God's expansive love. In the context of the statement it makes concerning the marital union in general, the sex act then becomes an affirmation of the specific role of this marital couple in God's design for marriage in general. Sexual intercourse becomes a declaration of the will of the couple to allow their love to be expansive, to overflow the limits of their two lives and flow out to others.

The sex act functions in this manner even when pregnancy cannot or does not follow. In the case of a childless couple, for example, sexual intercourse remains a statement concerning their will to allow their love to include what would be the product of that love. Their will to expansive love could take other practical forms, such as adoption. Hence, their expression of the will toward creative, expansive love is not dependent on the ability of the act to become procreative. The same is true for the continued practice of sexual intercourse even after the family is complete. In such cases, the act serves as a reminder and reaffirmation of the will toward expansive love that earlier resulted in the birth of children to the marital union. Through this act the couple is reminded likewise of the parental responsibilities that the procreative dimension of the sex act has brought to them.

b. Procreation as the central meaning of the act? But do these considerations mean that procreation is either a necessary or at least the central meaning of the sex act? The Roman Catholic Church, for example, has traditionally emphasized the procreative dimension of the sex act, recognizing that as the central meaning of sexual intercourse. This position was affirmed anew in the 1987 Vatican statement, *Donum vitae*. While acknowledging other meanings of the sex act, specifically its "unitive" meaning, the document places all such meanings within the context of the procreative meaning, asserting the "inseparable connection . . . between the two meanings of the conjugal act: the unitive meaning and the procreative meaning."[19]

To elevate procreation as the central meaning of the sex act, however, results in a truncated and therefore potentially damaging understanding of its meaning within marriage. The 1987 Vatican statement serves as a case in point. By insisting that the "unitive meaning" cannot be separated from the "procreative meaning," the magisterium is maintaining virtually unaltered the unacceptable traditional understanding of the church that works to limit sexual activity to procreation.

Such a reduction of the meaning of intercourse to the procreative function is truncated, for within the marriage bond sexual activity can carry other equally significant meanings, as noted above. These other aspects of the meaning of the sex act may all exist apart from the procreative intent. In fact, rather than the procreative meaning being determinative for the unitive meaning, as is implied in *Donum vitae,* these other aspects of the sex act form the context for procreation. It is because self-giving love is creative that the giving of oneself in the marriage act can be procreative within the context of the marital covenant. And because covenant faithfulness releases the creativity of the covenant partners the reaffirmation of the marriage covenant in the sex act forms the context for the acceptance of the creative fruit of that act.

The elevation of procreation as the sole or at least central meaning of the sex act, as in the Vatican document, is also dangerous. By maintaining the inseparability of the unitive and procreative meanings of the act, it fails to see that the latter properly belongs in the context of the other, more profound meanings. The outworking of the position of *Donum vitae* is an unwholesome, tacit condemnation of marital sexual relations where no "openness to procreation" is possible or intended. By extension this works to preclude the enjoyment of sex for a great many married couples, including those who are seeking to practice responsible family planning or are beyond the childbearing years. The end result of such a position is the reintroduction in a slightly altered form of the asceticism of an earlier era.

In contrast, however, the Bible does not promote sexual asceticism. The wisdom literature celebrates the expression of human sexuality in the sex act. And even Paul, for whom celibacy was the personal choice, never discourages the practice of sexual relations within marriage. In combating the Corinthian ascetics, he offers only one concession, abstinence for a short period of time for the purpose of concentrated prayer (1 Cor. 7:3–5).[20] Procreation, therefore, is an important dimension of marital sexual relations. But it certainly is neither the only nor the central dimension.

4. The Relative Value of the Sex Act

The sex act has been described in these pages as a meaningful and therefore valuable symbolic act within the context of the marital union. Nevertheless, a cautionary word is needed. We must continually keep in mind that sexual intercourse is not the "end all" of marriage. This conclusion arises from several related considerations.

First, marriage does not exist merely for the enjoyment of sexual intercourse. Rather, the sex act gains its meaning from marriage as its sacrament, as an expression of mutual submission, and as the normal means for the expansion of marital love in the form of the procreation of children.

Likewise, marriage is not dependent on the sex act for its well-being. The marriage bond can remain strong even without sexual intercourse. It is especially important to keep this in view when debilitating physical problems arise in one or the other partner due to illness, accident, or the aging process. This consideration also gains importance when normal sexual relations are temporarily disrupted, because the marriage partners are separated for a length of time.

Further, there is more to the marriage relationship than the sex act. Marriage has other dimensions as well as this specific sexual expression. In fact, the major tasks of marriage, apart from procreation (which is but the beginning of parental responsibility), lie fully outside this dimension. And as the relationship between the spouses grows, the dynamic and importance of sexual intercourse changes, even deepens. Through the deepening relationship that emerges through the journey of life together, coming together in the sex act comes to be less important in cementing the marriage bond and becomes instead the deepest act of celebration of that bond.

5. The Enjoyment of the Sex Act to the End of Married Life

In the past it was thought that sexual intercourse was to be enjoyed only by younger married persons. Consequently, sexual relations among middle-aged couples and especially the elderly were considered an aberration and were therefore discouraged. Fortunately, these old stereotypes are slowly being discarded. We are coming to realize that although sexual relations may change with the aging process, couples at most any age may still both desire and find enjoyment in the sex act.

a. Sexuality and aging. Recent studies indicate both a much higher physical possibility and a much keener personal interest in sex among older persons than was formerly thought. The research of William Masters, for example, indicated that no biological limitation normally arises in the aging woman and that the changes in the male do not substantially diminish the potential for sexual satisfaction in men. A Duke University study found that there were individuals who had remained sexually active in every decade of the human lifespan up to age 100.[21] While the interest in, and the capacity for sexual intercourse remain present, the ways of expression of human sexuality may change with the coming of older age; the presence of one's lover and his or her gentle touch become more important when the passion of youth subsides.[22] Even in this dimension of sexual expression, we remain sexual beings throughout life.

b. Sex and the older couple. The continuing presence of both the capability and desire for sexual expression suggests that the sex act can be an enjoyable part of the marriage relationship at all stages of adult life. Although its frequency will likely diminish, sexual intercourse remains pleasurable.

To older couples sexual intercourse can continue to be a meaningful act. In fact, it may take on meanings not associated with the act in younger years. In terming it "the second language of sex," Butler and Lewis stated several such possible meanings.[23] Sex can be a means of affirming one's body and its continuing capability of functioning and providing pleasure or of feeling in charge of one's life despite the experience of physical and social decline. Likewise, it may provide a way of feeling masculine or feminine and therefore of being valued as a person. Finally, sexual activity can be a way of protest, of defying stereotypes of the process of aging.

Apart from the possible addition of meanings such as these, sexual intercourse can continue to express the significance it carried earlier in life. Actually, its significance could intensify for the couple that has enjoyed a lifelong partnership within the marriage bond. Now the sex act becomes an affirmation of a lifetime bond, the community of male and female that has weathered the storms and enjoyed the beauty of life together.

The Public Dimension of the Sex Act

It has been argued in these pages that the sex act carries a multidimensional meaning. Above all, it is the sacrament of marriage, a reenactment of the wedding vow which signifies and seals the covenant between husband and wife. Further, it is an expression of the principle of mutual submission within the marital relationship. And it is a declaration of the married couple's openness to receive new life, to widen the marriage bond by forming a family bond. At first glance this understanding appears to emphasize the private nature of the sex act. Do these meanings of sexual intercourse, therefore, make that act solely private, appropriately viewed only in terms of its hiddenness within the secret confines of individual decision?

During the 1960s the declaration that sex is a private matter was touted as a first principle of the new religion of sexual freedom. "What occurs between two consenting adults in the privacy of the bedroom is nobody's business," declared one popular slogan of the sexual revolution. In recent years, however, there has arisen a growing uneasiness with the complete privatization of sex. As a result of various influences and concerns, not the least of which is the surge in cases of sexually transmitted diseases, a movement is developing in Western society away from free sexual expression under the banner of the right to privacy. Now the call is to social responsibility in sexual expression.

The new mood in society makes this an appropriate setting in which to reaffirm that there is a public dimension to this intimate expression of human sexuality. But the question arises concerning the basis of such an assertion. What gives rise to the public aspect of the sex act? And what are the implications of its public dimension?

1. The Case for a
Public Dimension of the Sex Act

The previous chapter affirmed that marriage entails a public dimension. This public aspect is seen, for example, in the wedding ceremony as a public event. The wedding declares that the joining together of two persons is not merely a private affair, a matter between two consenting adults. It has a social or public dimension as well, for the wider society also has an interest in the forming of this intimate bond. Marriage is not merely a private covenant between two persons, but is a private covenant made within the context of the social community. All societies in all eras have expressed the public interest in this private covenant through the social regulation of marriage. If in addition to the private aspect a public dimension is inherent in marriage, it would seem quite natural to anticipate as well a public aspect of the sex act, in addition to its very private nature. Of course, such a public character does not overshadow, but nevertheless augments its personal, private aspect. Several considerations support this conclusion.

First, the public nature of the sex act arises from the public contractual nature of marriage. In addition to being a covenant between two lovers, marriage is a legal contract. To the ancient Hebrews the marital contract went beyond the bride and groom to encompass the families of the wedding couple. The sex act served as a ratification of the contract between the families of the couple.

Western societies have moved away from the emphasis on the familial nature of the contract. From the legal perspective marriage is now defined solely in terms of a contract between two independent individuals. Likewise, in our society sexual intercourse is neither legally nor socially tied to the marriage contract as in former times. Despite such changes, however, the wider social dimension of the legal contract and of sexual intercourse as somehow linked to that contract have not been totally lost. The sex act still retains some status as the expression of the marital contract, and it therefore continues to retain some aspect of the public dimension associated with this status.

The public dimension of the sex act as associated with marriage as a contract is especially evident when extramarital sexual intercourse threatens a marriage. In this situation the sex act indeed becomes a public matter, because the breakup of a marriage in the form of divorce always has public implications. The wider society expresses its interest in such cases in the form of court settlement of matters relating to property and child custody.

Second, the relationship of the sex act to procreation gives rise to a public dimension of the act. Sexual intercourse remains the way in which procreation generally occurs. Because this act has the potential of creating a new life, it carries implications for the society in which it is practiced and thereby gives rise to a public interest in its practice. Raymond J. Lawrence offered this terse summarization of the matter:

> What happens in any bedroom is always potentially the business of the whole human family. Whoever decides to have a child in some way or another affects the community because they bring into being and they shape another member of the community with whom the community must relate.[24]

Thirdly, the public dimension of the sex act arises from its connection with morality. If there are both proper and improper contexts for the exercise of sexual intercourse, then this act is a moral act. Morals, however, are always to some extent a public concern. The contexts in which its members practice sexual intercourse eventually affect the morals of the wider society.

2. Implications of the
Public Nature of the Sex Act

The public dimension of the sex act indicates that society has an interest in the practice of sexual intercourse among its members. This public concern is given expression by all societies, in that they not only regulate marriage, but also set some limitations on the practice of the sex act. Such regulation comes in various forms, ranging from taboos and informal social customs to actual civil laws. But at the heart of all regulation is the importance of marriage and the special sexual privileges and obligations associated with this institution. As Frank A. Beach concluded, "There is not and can never have been, a true society without sexual rules."[25]

The public dimension inherent within the sex act indicates that there is a legitimate social interest in its practice. If Beach's thesis that a "true society" requires sex rules is correct, then some regulation of sexuality is always necessary, even in a permissive society such as ours. Of course, proponents of the new morality will continue to agitate for sexual freedom. And a great latitude in sexual matters will in all likelihood continue, so long as the emphasis on personal choice remains indicative of Western society. The defense of the principle of choice is, of course, right and necessary. Nevertheless, as our society is now coming to see, individual choice must always be tempered with responsibility, for freedom is always subject to abuse. This is as true in sexual matters as in any other aspect of human life together.

The current situation indicates that the development of sexual mores that can balance freedom and responsibility for the sake of social well-being stands as one of the pressing challenges of contemporary Western society. In this matter, the church must take the lead by serving as a model. Our challenge is to show to the broader society what it means to articulate in word and practice an understanding of marriage that views this institution as a community of male and female, a means to reflect the divine image, and therefore as the sole context in which the sex act can be fully and truly meaningful.

Marriage is a divinely designed and divinely sanctioned institution. Together with the sex act practiced within its context, marriage overflows salvation history to encompass the order of creation itself. At the same time, however, there remains a specifically Christian understanding of marriage and of the sex act as the sign of the marital bond. In the context of Christian faith, marriage and sexual intercourse undergo a deepening of meaning, as the marital bond comes to be viewed as a dimension of the saving work of God in history and as the sex act comes to be seen as the sign and seal of that special bond.

Living with one's spouse as persons of faith, therefore, is important for the establishment of a marriage that probes the depths of the divine design for this expression of human sexuality. But this does not mean that personal faith and presence within the Christian community in and of themselves insure a care-free, happy marriage. On the contrary, as Emil Brunner so perceptively noted,

> Even the marriage of the best of Christians is not the renewal of Paradise; here, too, there is sorrow, conflict, pitiful sinking of heart, shortsightedness, and inadequacy. Indeed, the happy marriage in particular contains special hidden dangers, the danger of being cut off from others, the danger of a wrong kind of self-sufficiency, and of a Pharisaical denial of solidarity with suffering, erring, curse-laden humanity.[26]

Thus, while marriage contains a particular grace of creation it also contains a particular need for redemption. With this in view, we must now turn to the negative side of the marriage relationship that is experienced when the solemn covenant is violated.

The Marital Bond

5

Fidelity versus Adultery

We are created by God as sexual beings. This fundamental dimension of our existence is expressed in many ways. Yet the most intimate expression of our sexuality is sexual intercourse. When practiced within the context of the marital bond this act conveys its intended meaning. Within marriage the sex act can be a joyous celebration of the marital covenant, for it can serve as a symbol and seal of that bond, as a declaration of mutual submission, and as an expression of the partners' openness to new life.

In our fallen world, however, sexual intercourse often occurs outside the context of marriage. In such situations it no longer signifies the marital bond that unites husband and wife in the community of male and female. According to the Christian sex ethic, when the sex act is practiced by a married person with someone other than one's spouse, the act becomes the symbol of the violation of the marriage covenant. But this ethic has come under attack in recent decades. Sexual activity outside of marriage is not always viewed as the violation of the marital bond, for some voices argue that marriage does not necessarily require a commitment to exclusiveness in sexual activity.

This newer concept of marriage raises anew certain important questions, several of which will be explored in this chapter and the next. The first issue concerns the boundaries of sexual expression. Ought sexual intercourse be limited to the marital bond, or are there legitimate contexts for its practice outside of marriage? On the basis of a response to this foundational question, we will discuss adultery as the breaking of the marriage convenant, followed by a delineation of the deeper theological implications of fidelity and infidelity. Finally, in chapter 6 we will focus on the issue of divorce as the ultimate severing of marriage.

The Boundaries of
Sexual Expression

Viewed from what many see as the traditional Christian perspective, the question of the legitimate context for the sex act can yield only one conclusion. The proper context is the permanent, monogamous relationship called marriage. This perspective is the basic teaching of the Bible in both Old and New Testaments. The biblical writers do not present this sexual ethic without reason. On the contrary, as the findings of the human sciences confirm, permanent commitment plays a vital role in providing the boundaries and thus the context for the practice of the sex act.

1. Boundaries and the Biblical Sex Ethic

From Genesis onward, the Bible elevates a specific sex ethic as the ideal for humankind, even though because of human sin it presents the ideal in a realistic fashion. Repeatedly the biblical writers either explicitly enjoin or implicitly assume that the institution of marriage joins together a man and a woman in what is intended to be a permanent, monogamous union.

According to the second creation story (Genesis 2) this ideal was part of the original intent of creation. Jesus reaffirmed the ideal as reflecting the original intent of the Creator (Matt. 19:4–6). The early Christian community continued the practice (e.g., 1 Cor. 7:2; 1 Thess. 4:3–6;[1] 1 Tim. 3:2). And it formed the model for the divine-human fellowship found in the apocalyptic vision of the eschatological renewal (Rev. 21:2, 9–10).

Despite the emphasis on the ideal of permanent, monogamous marriage, two concessions to the human fallen situation are likewise reflected in the Bible. Neither monogamy nor permanence was strictly followed by all members of the ancient Hebrew society. This situational reality called forth a realistic response from the biblical authors.

One concession related to the failure of the society to live up to the ideal of monogamy. Among the ancient Hebrews, the principle of monogamy was set aside through the incorporation of polygamy and prostitution into the social fabric. Polygamy gained entrance into the community quite early. It is present among the patriarchs (although neither Abraham nor Isaac were polygamists). The story of Jacob, for example, presents his marriages to Leah and Rachel plus his begetting of children by concubinage as a matter of course. No explicit condemnation of these practices is found in the text, only indication that his polygamy originated through the trickery of Laban and resulted in jealousy between his two wives. By the era of the monarchy, polygamy is viewed as an accepted practice, at least among royalty and the wealthy.

The monogamous ideal was also violated by the tolerance of prostitution within Hebrew society. As with polygamy, the presence of this practice dates to the patriarchs, as is indicated by the story of Judah and Tamar (Gen. 38). In contrast to polygamy, however, prostitution never came to be an accepted, sanctioned dimension of the community, but was always relegated to the fringe of societal life and even became the object of legal stricture (e.g., Lev. 19:29).

Despite the presence of polygamy and prostitution within Hebrew society, neither ought to be viewed as a positive development. On the contrary, when evaluated from the perspective of the New Testament, each must be judged as forming a blight on the commitment of the ancient Hebrews to the ideal of monogamy.

The presence of these practices among the ancient people of God was due to certain cultural factors in the ancient societies. Specifically, both were related to the relative positions of male and female in community life. Polygamy and prostitution found their way into society as attempts to respond to the generally lower status of women in the economic and social order and woman's more fragile situation in the community.[2]

The position of a woman in society was generally a function of her place in the household of a man, whether the man be her father, husband, or a male member of her extended family.[3] In this context, polygamy served a useful function. It was a way of providing sufficient marriage opportunities or marital households for the women of the community, so that there would be a minimum number of unattached women. Prostitution, on the other hand, formed a type of economic safety net, for it was one of the sole available means of livelihood for women who had no fixed position in a male household or who, for whatever reasons, had lost their status within their former households.

The presence of these two practices in the biblical stories ought not to be interpreted as a divine sanction on them. As the prohibition in the Mosaic law indicates, prostitution constituted a violation of God's intent, even for the ancient Hebrew society. As for polygamy, a movement toward monogamy developed already in the Old Testament era and had become the norm prior to the writing of the New Testament. This development indicates that even though polygamy met a specific need in the ancient society, it was never intended to become a permanent pattern.

The second concession to the reality of ancient Hebrew society as deviating from the biblical marriage ideal came in the form of divorce. The presence of this practice indicates that the ancient people compromised the ideal of the permanence of marriage. According to the narrative of Genesis 2, the Creator intended from the beginning that marriage be an inviolate bond. However, in ancient Hebrew society, as in ours, this bond was not always permanent. At times it was severed, a reality that was codified and institutionalized in the regulations concerning divorce found in the Mosaic law.

As Jesus' discussion of this subject with the scribes and Pharisees indicates, the Mosaic allowance for divorce came about as a concession to the sinful reality of human life, not as an expression of the divine intent. Rather than giving sanction to, or confirming the right to divorce, the Mosaic concession ought to be seen as an attempt to regulate a practice already present in Hebrew society. The purpose of such regulation was not to make divorce easy or to elevate it to an accepted practice, but to make the situation more humane for the divorced woman by demanding that her status be clearly spelled out by the man who was putting her out of his household.

Polygamy, prostitution, and divorce indicate that exceptions to the marital ideal arose even among the ancient Hebrews. The development of these exceptions, however, does not serve to deny that a marriage ethic did indeed provide the basis for life in the Old and New Testament communities. On the contrary, these violations of the norm and concessions to human sin actually highlight the commitment of the biblical documents as a whole to the ideal of the permanent, monogamous relationship between male and female as the foundational context for the expression of human sexuality.

2. The Importance of Permanency

As has been noted above, the biblical sex ethic elevates marriage as the central context for human sexual relations and views marriage ideally as a permanent, monogamous relationship. Although in recent years proponents of the sexual revolution have waged a relentless attack on this ethic, even in the contemporary situation the traditional viewpoint retains its importance.

The wisdom of the biblical ethic of marital permanence has been confirmed by anthropological studies. Margaret Mead, for example, asserted, "No known society has ever invented a form of marriage strong enough to stick that did not contain the 'till-death-do-us-part' assumption."[4] With its emphasis on permanency of relationship between one man and one woman, the Christian sex ethic carries continuing validity, because it offers the most constructive means for developing relationships between male and female.

a. Permanency and freedom. The constructive nature of the biblical sex ethic may be seen through consideration of the link between permanency of relationship and personal freedom. The biblical emphasis on marriage as a permanent commitment is helpful, in that the permanency it enjoins provides freedom to the marriage partners to develop true community. As was discussed in the previous chapter, permanency frees us from the syndrome of needing to perform and compete. In so doing the marital bond provides the context in which true fellowship between the partners can arise.

The assertion that commitment to permanence brings freedom applies to many areas of the male-female relationship. But it is especially evident in the dimension of the sex act. In the wake of the sexual revolution, increasing importance has been placed on sexual performance. This has often brought the opposite of the freedom its proponents promise. Anxiety concerning personal abilities and concern over being compared with other partners has a debilitating effect, for it destroys true sexual freedom.

A marriage characterized by commitment on the part of both partners to the exclusiveness and permanence of the marital bond, in contrast, provides freedom in the sexual dimension of the relationship. The commitment to permanence offers a context of full acceptance of the marital partner. In this context we are free to fail, learn, develop, and relax. This freedom allows for the development of a beautiful and fulfilling sexual relationship between the marriage partners. From the findings of Clark and Wallin, Vance Packard concluded,

> Unless there is the day-to-day warmth and love, sex is a matter of mechanics. There is no evidence that an adequate, tension-releasing relationship in bed will sustain a good marriage; but there is an abundance of evidence that if there is a good personal relationship, the in-bed aspect of marriage will improve with the years.[5]

The importance of freedom for sexual performance has been confirmed by modern psychology. This human science indicates that full acceptance by another, acceptance in which an individual is free to fail and to learn, forms the very context in which fulfilling sexual expression can occur. As a result of such freedom, the sexual partners are free to enjoy sexual community in the fullest sense. In his eloquent treatment of the significance of marital love as fidelity, freedom, and conjugality, Eric Fuchs touched the depth of the relationship between permanence and sexual freedom:

> Thus the experience of being a couple allows each of the conjoined to know the freedom which is discovered through a liberating trust in each other. Here again, sexuality can express this trust which frees the other from his fears and his anguish, and allows him to express joy and tenderness, pleasure and play, even by means of his body.[6]

b. Permanency and celebration.   The constructive nature of the biblical sex ethic may be seen likewise by viewing the relationship between permanency of relationship and sexual celebration. The previous chapter presented the sex act as the vivid portrayal of the bond of community between male and female. In this way sexual intercourse becomes a festive celebration of that bond. But if celebration is the proper meaning of the sex act, then it follows that permanency of relationship is required for the conveyance of this meaning. The true celebration of the bond between male and female, which the sex act is intended to be, can only occur within the context of a permanent relationship. Only as an expression of the permanent marital bond can the sex act become the celebration of the covenantal relationship. In the words of Sidney Callahan, "the Yes to the mate is built upon and strengthened by the No to everyone else."[7]

In summary, the monogamous, permanent marriage relationship between male and female is often attacked as an antiquated sex ethic which stifles individual development and sexual expression. This attack, however, is misdirected. It simply cannot be leveled against the ideal presented in the Bible. On the contrary, this ideal is important to human well-being. It offers the best context for the development of the sex partners and of the sex act as a true celebration of the intended meaning of the sex act. As Emil Brunner noted:

Genuine love is single-minded—indeed that is its power. Genuine love—still apart from all ethical demands—always feels: "it is with this particular person that I wish to live alone and for always."[8]

Adultery as the Violation of the Marital Covenant

Given this understanding of the permanent, monogamous marital relationship as the proper context for the sex act viewed as an expression of human sexuality, the rejection of adultery as a violation of the marital covenant follows. The rejection of adultery has likewise come under attack in recent decades by proponents of the sexual revolution. In spite of this stance by certain segments of contemporary culture, the traditional viewpoint concerning extramarital sexual relations carries lasting value and therefore is worthy of reaffirmation.[9]

1. Fidelity in an Era of "Open Marriage"

Contemporary critics of the biblical sexual ethic generally do not maintain that the institution of marriage itself should be discarded. Rather, their call is for more flexibility of sexual expression beyond the context of marriage. Raymond J. Lawrence, for example, articulated this position:

> The issue of sexual exclusiveness is one of the most intractable problems for any form of pair bonding. No other issue so powerfully threatens committed relationships. The threat comes from two sides, from the anxiety stirred up when sexual exclusiveness is loosened, and from the burden of oppression experienced when exclusiveness is rigidly adhered to. Recent literature increasingly supports the viability of pair bonding that is not absolutely exclusive sexually.[10]

Lawrence called for what he terms "flexible monogamy," which replaces the exclusive genital sexual relationship characteristic of traditional monogamy with a "primary genital sexual relationship."[11] Despite its apparent positive evaluation of marriage, this proposal offers a radical challenge to the view of marriage as an inviolate bond.

a. Extramarital sex and the health of the marriage bond. As Lawrence's statement indicates, the intent of many proponents of a more open attitude on sexual matters is positive. They are not necessarily seeking to undermine marriage, but often are motivated by concern for its continued vibrancy as an institution and for the enhancement of the relationship between the marriage partners.[12] Although these contemporary voices desire to attain the same goal as proponents of the traditional ethic, they differ radically as to the ways to best insure good marriages. Within this context, the question concerning the actual effect of extramarital relations is highly significant. Are sexual relations outside marriage destructive or helpful for the marriage bond? This question forms the crux of the difference of opinion between proponents of the traditional ethic and advocates of the newer openness.

The contemporary outlook declares that the future of marriage as an institution and the well-being of the marriage partners is best served by an ethic that is at least open to sexual relations beyond the marriage bond. Nena and George O'Neill popularized this view in terms of fostering an "open marriage." Proponents of this concept work from the premise that no individual can hope completely to fulfill all the various needs of one's spouse. Therefore, we ought not look to marriage as the only focus of fulfillment of physical, emotional, and even sexual needs. In fact, it is argued, those marriage partners who realize this and therefore agree together to allow each other to find certain dimensions of fulfillment outside the marital bond enjoy more stable and wholesome marriages. This premise, however, is then extended to the sexual sphere. Proponents of the "open marriage" position advocate sacrificing sexual exclusiveness within marriage for the sake of marital permanence, for, it is assumed, both cannot be maintained together. This position calls for an evaluation encompassing several points.

(1) Positive features of the open marriage concept.

The concept of "open marriage" is correct in one point. It rightly reminds us that marriage was never intended as the vehicle of individual fulfillment. The romantic view of marriage, which is a relatively recent development, actually places undue expectations on this institution. By expecting marriage to be the instrument of the fulfillment of the spouses, we doom it to certain failure. We ought not to look to the marriage relationship as the sole source of personal fulfillment. In so far as it serves as a reminder of this, the concept of open marriage offers an important critique of the romantic view that sees in the marital bond the ideal of interpersonal relationships.

In contrast to the modern romantic view, the Bible and the entire Christian tradition redirect the search for ultimate personal fulfillment from other humans to God as the wellspring of fullness of life. No one person can ever hope to be the source of total fulfillment for another, for only God is our final resting place. As Augustine declared, a restlessness remains in the human heart until it finds rest in God.

In addition, the fulfillment that each person seeks is in the final analysis an eschatological reality. A foretaste may be experienced in the present, but its fullest enjoyment lies in the future, when the reign of God is consummated and God's dwelling is with humankind (e.g., Rev. 21:3).

The fulfillment offered in the marital relationship must be understood in light of this eschatological divine fulfillment. Husband and wife ought to find within their marriage a fulfilling relationship, a community of male and female. Yet even the best marriage can offer only a partial reflection of the glorious future state. And marriage serves the goal of human fulfillment only as one means in reflecting and advancing the interpersonal relationships that will characterize the society of humankind in God's eschatological reign.

While not discounting the marital bond, the New Testament puts forth another community, the church in so far as it fosters community with Christ, as the primary sign of the future human fulfillment. In fact, as has been noted previously, the New Testament places primary emphasis on the fellowship of the people of God in the church, not on the marriage bond, as the focal point of human community in this age. As a result, the Christian spouse should find in marriage a source and means toward a partial experience of the eschatological fulfillment which is ultimately derived from God. But beyond the marriage bond, the community of Christ is to form an even more primary community of fulfillment and identity for all believers, whether married or single.

(2) Shortcomings of the open marriage concept.

Despite the important critique that the open marriage proposal offers of the romantic conception of marriage, in the final analysis it too must be rejected. As generally articulated by its proponents, the new openness builds a faulty position on faulty presuppositions.[13]

First, the proposal is often human- and person-centered. It tends to be human-centered in that it generally eliminates the divine dimension and looks instead solely to humans as the source of personal fulfillment. It becomes person-centered whenever it looks to personal fulfillment as the highest good.

In contrast, the biblical ethic places human involvement in the process of fulfillment within the context of God as the ultimate source of human well-being. Further, this ethic refuses to see the individual as the highest good. Rather, it places individual fulfillment within the context of a corporate, social fulfillment. And it understands the corporate in terms of the final glory of God found in the consummation of history in the reign of God.

Second, the concept of open marriage may be faulted as being too pessimistic concerning marriage. It declares that the marital relationship cannot enjoy both permanence and sexual exclusiveness. This presupposition of the newer openness has been called into question by a host of good marriages that have brought together these supposedly mutually exclusive characteristics. It is simply not true that a healthy marriage, in which both partners are seeking to give of self for the other and in which the purpose of marriage within the context of God's work in history is understood and advanced, needs adultery to survive. Nor is it true that such a marriage could be enhanced by the introduction of extramarital sexual relations. Such a marriage is already functioning in basic accordance with its divine design.

(3) The potential harm of the open marriage concept.

In contrast to the claims of proponents of the "open marriage" model, it must be concluded that extramarital relations are harmful to the marriage bond. Basically, this destructive influence is due to the fact that such relations are detrimental to the fellowship or community which is to characterize marriage. The marital bond is intended to foster a deep sense of community between male and female. This task, however, is made more difficult whenever the marriage bond is violated. It is simply the case that extramarital sexual relations undermine the fellowship of the marriage bond.

First, extramarital sexual relations undermine marital fellowship because they are often devastating to the sense of self-worth of either or both partners. This devastation is obvious in the case of the partner who has not engaged in an extramarital affair. Knowledge that one's partner is looking outside the marriage relationship for sexual fulfillment deals a blow to personal self-esteem, a blow which is difficult to overcome. The destruction of the spouse's self-esteem comes as a result of the inclusion of a third party into the relationship. Nonexclusiveness implies the willingness of a married person to share the deep intimacies of sexual intercourse with someone other than one's spouse, which carries the implicit suggestion that the spouse is no longer as important as he or she once was. But an affair can also injure the self-esteem of the adulterous partner as well, when that person comes to grips with the motivation and consequences of the affair. As a result of the introduction of a third party, therefore, the security of the marriage relationship is diminished both in fact and in the perceptions of all three persons.

Second, extramarital relationships are harmful to marital fellowship in that an affair produces feelings of guilt. Here again both marriage partners are affected. The situation of the partner who entered into an affair is readily seen. The affair leads to a sense of having violated the marriage bond and one's marital partner. But a deep sense of guilt can arise in the faithful partner also, who may be plagued by anguished questions: Did I drive my mate into an extramarital affair? What part of the blame is mine!

This person's guilt feelings may even grow to be deeper than those of his or her spouse. The one who has engaged in an affair may be able to overcome the matter by means of asking for and receiving forgiveness. But the injured partner cannot deal with the violation of the marital bond in such a decisive manner. This person may be plagued for some time with nagging doubts and fears concerning his or her own complicity in the affair of the spouse and concerning the uncertain future of the marriage.

Third, extramarital sex is detrimental to marital fellowship in that it undercuts trust and openness between the marital partners. This is quite obviously the case during the life of the affair. Generally such relationships must be carried out in secrecy, often by means of covert action and duplicity; a less than honest atmosphere is required in order to maintain the marriage and the affair simultaneously. The O'Neills rightly put forth trust as "the most important quality two partners can share in a marriage."[14] Yet, trust and the openness required for true community are often the first casualities of extramarital relations.

Contrary to the claims of its proponents, open marriages are difficult to maintain in the long run. A person may indeed contract together with another that he or she will be the primary, but not the exclusive sexual partner for the other. But these contracts are difficult to keep intact. Recent psychological research indicates that such marriages simply lack the basis in commitment to fidelity necessary to the building of a lasting bond. And in the end, as Joseph Allen rightly concluded, "It would be a rare marriage in which the couple's agreeing to sexual nonexclusiveness were not a sign of weakness in the marriage and a harbinger of its further deterioration."[15]

b. The basis of ethical decision making. The contemporary call for a more open understanding of marriage raises a second ethical question, that of situational versus universal ethics. Are personal sexual acts to be determined situationally or is there some universal norm which is applicable? This issue probes deeper than the specific question of the impact of extramarital relations to the well-being of marriage, for it asks concerning the basis on which ethical decisions themselves are to be made.

The situational approach was popularized in the 1960s especially through Joseph Fletcher's explosive book, *Situation Ethics*.[16] Fletcher maintained that no norms can be devised which cover all cases of interpersonal relationships.[17] Rather than rules, Fletcher argued that love is the sole good and therefore the sole norm.[18] This means that no norms can govern all cases of male-female relations either. Rather, decisions concerning sexual expression between persons must be decided in each situation in accordance with the single norm of love—what is the most loving act in the specific situation. The "most loving act" in a specific situation could conceivably include adultery. Fletcher stated, "But if people do not believe it is wrong to have sex relations outside marriage, it isn't, unless they hurt themselves, their partners, or others."[19]

It must be admitted that Fletcher rightly appealed to certain strands in the Christian, especially the Protestant, ethical tradition. His viewpoint has unfortunately suffered misunderstanding. Proponents have taken it beyond the bounds he intended and opponents too casually have dismissed the case he established. Yet despite Fletcher's argument to the contrary, throughout much of Christian history the Christian sex ethic has been nonsituational—or, at least, situational only within the context of certain rules. Until recent years Christian ethicists have generally agreed that certain universal principles are to govern human sexual expression. These principles have emphasized permanent, monogamous marriage and have rejected adultery in any form.

Christian tradition has been wise in its rejection of the pure situational approach to sex ethics. It is true that ethical decisions are made in the individual situations of life and that as a result ethical laws cannot be devised that will cover every conceivable situation. But nevertheless, certain principles can be stated which serve to guide ethical decisions in most cases.

Pure situational approaches, in contrast, not only disavow the attempt to devise ethical rules for action, they also reject the attempt to set forth ethical principles that could offer parameters for decision making. In the case of Fletcher's situational ethic, one dictum is put forth as a governing principle— love. He is surely correct in elevating the ethic of love, for it is in keeping with the teaching of Jesus. Yet, Fletcher's proposal remains too nebulous. In contrast to Jesus' teaching, it lacks concrete guidelines as to what constitutes the loving response in the situations of life. Such guidelines are crucial, because all humans, even conscientious believers, remain tainted by sin. Because of sin, we are all too easily led astray by less than loving motives. Because of sin we are susceptible to mistaken motives, and we too readily become blinded to our actual less-than-altruistic motivations for our actions. Ethical guidelines, while not an end in themselves, serve a useful function. They indicate to us where the boundaries lie within which loving conduct can be truly found.

The application of this understanding to marriage and adultery is obvious. The Christian sex ethic offers guidelines for married persons concerning loving conduct. The traditional ethic declares that love for spouse cannot be expressed through extramarital affairs. The Christian ought indeed to ask in each situation what is the most loving act, and to seek in every situation to act in the most loving manner, as Fletcher pointed out. But the Christian ethic declares that the most loving action in any situation cannot be an act of adultery. To commit adultery in the name of love is simply to be deceived or deceptive.

c. The purported inconsistency of the Bible.
The traditional Christian rejection of adultery in favor of fidelity within a permanent, monogamous marital bond claims to derive its principles from the Bible. The biblical documents, Christians traditionally maintain, present marriage as forming the boundary for the sexual act. Proponents of the newer openness, however, often point to a perceived internal inconsistency within the biblical documents themselves, which they believe undercuts the Christian position.

The charge of inconsistency generally focuses on the claim that the people of God practiced a double standard, at least in the Old Testament era. Hebrew males, among them certain patriarchs and other prominent biblical figures, readily engaged in extramarital relations, whereas women are strictly forbidden from such practices. Even the injunction against adultery in the Old Testament, critics argue, did not arise as an attempt to offer a just sex ethic. Rather, the law was motivated by a social situation in which women were viewed as the property of males. Adultery, then, was not condemned because it was a violation of the woman, but because this act constituted a violation of the property rights of another male.[20]

This presentation of the Old Testament material, as unflattering as it may be, is to a certain extent valid. Such attitudes are indeed reflected in the documents, although they are not necessarily condoned by the writers. Nevertheless, the presence of unwholesome attitudes within Hebrew society does not invalidate the stand of the Bible against adultery and the importance of this biblical ethic. Several considerations point in this direction.

First, the critique of the biblical ethic fails to differentiate what arose in the ancient society and what the Old Testament presents as the intention of the Creator. Here the Genesis creation narratives must be given central emphasis as offering the understanding of the community concerning the intent of God and as providing a critique of societal practices, even among the Hebrews. Laws designed to govern sexual conduct, in contrast, do not present the ideal, but are attempts to mitigate the evil, unjust effects of human failure to follow that ideal.

Second, the New Testament, as reflecting and expanding the sexual ethic of the Old, must be given priority over the practices of the ancient society. Whether or not they reflected Hebrew attitudes, the double standard and the injunction against adultery as solely based in male property rights is clearly not the position of the New Testament community. Rather, beginning with Jesus, the community appealed to the meaning of Genesis 2 to develop an ethic which called for a return to the intent of the Creator.

This ethic elevated fidelity within the monogamous marriage bond as the standard for both partners. It viewed women as coheirs with men of "the gracious gift of life," to use the words of Peter (1 Peter 3:7). And it viewed adultery in any form—whether with another married person or with a prostitute of either gender—within the context of that divine intent. For this reason, the early church, following the teaching of Jesus, spoke of adultery as the violation of God's design.

The biblical outlook concerning marriage and sexual relations, therefore, is quite different from the "open marriage" advocated by some persons today. It is undeniable that the biblical writers did not condone extramarital sex in any form or for any reason, however noble. At the same time, the Bible reflects the actual conditions within the ancient societies. The marital ideal presented as the divine intent was discarded and violated by people then as it is now. The failure of the people of God in the past to live up to the divine ideal does not, however, negate that ideal. Rather, it offers a context in which to attempt to biblical evaluation of all such failures.

2. The Meaning of Adultery

The biblical sex ethic with its emphasis on the original intent of the Creator offers a vantage point from which to view the practice of sexual intercourse beyond the boundaries of marriage. Simply stated, such activity constitutes the violation of the marital bond. The understanding of adultery developed here will build from conclusions reached in previous discussions. The most foundational of these is the assertion that *the context of the sex act is determinative of its meaning*.

It was argued earlier that acts are dependent on their context in order to establish their meaning. Applied to the sex act, this principle suggests that the act is intended to be a highly symbolic and meaningful expression. The meaning the sex act carries is, however, dependent on the context in which persons engage in it.

When the sex act is enjoyed within the context of marriage, it has been argued, it carries its divinely intended meaning. Within this context sexual intercourse constitutes a reaffirmation of the vow and covenant into which the marriage partners entered on their wedding day. Further, the sex act within marriage becomes a beautiful celebration of the marital relationship enjoyed by the marriage partners as well as an expression of their openness to the new life that may arise from their bond.

Whereas the sex act enjoyed within the context of marriage can carry these important meanings, outside of marriage the meaning of the act is radically altered. On the one hand, the adulterous sexual relation cannot carry the meanings indicated above. It cannot symbolize the marriage covenant nor be a reaffirmation of the marriage vow, for no such covenant unites the adulterous pair. It cannot be the joyful celebration of the relationship of fellowship and community between two persons who have bonded themselves together, for no explicit commitment to each other has been made. On the contrary, such a commitment was made by at least one of the two persons to another person, who is now physically absent.

No adulterous relationship can state what the sex act is intended to declare when practiced within the marriage relationship. On the other hand, the adulterous sex act is not for that reason devoid of meaning. Within the context of an extramarital relationship the act can carry several specific meanings.

Ultimately the act is a declaration of the violation of the marriage bond. This violation is stated by both partners in the act. Through it the unfaithful spouse is declaring the will to violate the marriage covenant made at an earlier time. The adulterous act symbolizes the actor's personal disregard for the prior commitment made to one's spouse. The one who engages in the sex act with a married person is likewise acting in contempt of the marriage bond. Both parties thereby violate the personhood of the married person's spouse, to whom the pledge to form the community of male and female was made.

In addition to carrying this primary meaning, namely, disregard for the prior marriage commitment, the adulterous sex act symbolizes the fallenness of the marriage community and of the actors. Through this act the married person proclaims the fallen nature of his or her marriage relationship. Adultery declares that a relationship that was intended to be an embodiment of the community of male and female and stand as a witness to the will of God toward the establishment of community has actually failed to reflect the ideal.

Adultery symbolizes as well the hopeless abandonment on the part of a spouse of the marriage relationship. It declares that one marriage partner has concluded that true community cannot be found within the marriage bond or with his or her marriage partner, for such community is now being sought beyond the marriage relationship and with another person who is not the spouse. In this act a married person is voicing an unwillingness, or at least a hesitancy, to work at restoring the fallen marriage.

Within the context of adultery the sex act likewise speaks about a marriage partner's fallen relationship to one's spouse. In the context of marriage the act symbolizes the desire of the spouses to give and receive fulfillment simultaneously. In the context of adultery the act symbolizes the desire of one spouse to seek personal sexual fulfillment apart from the spouse and apart from the desire to fulfill one's spouse. In short, with respect to the spouse, adultery declares the triumph of *eros* over *agape,* as personal desire for another outside the marriage relationship is placed above the desire to accept unconditionally and to fulfill the needs of the other with whom he or she has previously entered into covenant.

Through adultery the married adulterous person proclaims the fallenness of the marriage situation. The one who engages in sex with a married person declares thereby personal willingness to participate in that fallen situation. Further, through this act, this person proclaims personal complacency concerning the adulterous partner's disregard and abandonment of the marriage covenant. In this way both parties share together in the sin of the act.

Fidelity and Promiscuity
in a Theological Context

The discussion of marriage and adultery can be viewed from another vantage point as well. These two choices may be located within a theological context by means of a consideration of the related concepts of fidelity and infidelity. These, too, carry theological significance.

1. The Nature of Promiscuity

The contemporary rejection of the traditional Christian ethic by the architects of the sexual revolution has often sought to endow promiscuity with the social respectability afforded chastity and fidelity in the past. Already in 1963 Rollo May criticized this situation, terming it somewhat erroneously "a new Puritanism":

In our new Puritanism bad health is equated with sin. Sin used to be "to give in to one's sexual desires"; now it is "not to have full sexual expression." It is immoral not to express your libido. A woman used to be guilty if she went to bed with a man; now she feels vaguely guilty if after two or three dates she still refrains from going to bed; and the partner, who is always completely enlightened (or at least plays the role) refuses to allay her guilt by getting overtly angry at her sin of "morbid repression," refusing to "give." And this, of course, makes her "no" all the more guilt-producing for her.[21]

The perspective developed in these pages forms a basis for evaluating the contemporary elevation of promiscuity. The new view is faulty at three points.

First, as developed earlier, rather than being an expression of the new freedom, promiscuity, with its tendency to separate "what I do" from "who I am," is in actuality an expression of the new dualism.[22] The biblical sexual ethic, in contrast, is the outworking of a holistic anthropology. According to the biblical understanding, the human person is created by God as a whole, a unified entity. Therefore, the acts of the body cannot be separated from the acts of the person. In keeping with this understanding, biblical writers such as Paul maintain that sexual intercourse is an act of the person as a whole. It cannot be relegated to the status of being merely an act of the body apart from and having no affect on the person.

In the new emphasis on promiscuity, however, the body is often seen as a type of tool or vehicle for the use of the person. It is a means to personal "experience" and pleasure. Such an understanding has more affinity with the ancient Greek view, which gave rise to Gnostic theories of bodily indulgence, than to the holistic view of the body as integral to the self, found in the Bible. The dualism and externalization of sexual expression characteristic of this outlook are epitomized in the jargon that refers to sexual relations as "having sex." From the perspective of a unitary anthropology, however, "sex" is not something one can "have." Rather, sexual expression is an act of the entire person.

Second, the new promiscuity undercuts the building of community between male and female. This community is destroyed in many ways. Promiscuity encourages viewing others as sex objects and not as persons with worth and value. In a promiscuous framework, value comes to be viewed in terms of external beauty and the potential for affording sexual pleasure. The breakdown of community is found even in the sex act itself and even within the context of marriage, as the new emphasis on promiscuity and infidelity gives rise to a performance orientation in sexual relations. Sex partners must continually seek to measure up to the sexual expectations of the other. Fellowship is further threatened by the sense of competition; partners must be concerned about being compared with others.

Third, the new promiscuity claims to have destroyed the double standard and liberated women as well as men to engage in the sex act. Of course, the old double standard is unworthy of defense and ought to have been laid aside long ago. Yet, the claims of the new outlook are an illusion. Rather than being the liberation of women, the move toward female promiscuity actually constitutes a victory for dualism. As James Nelson aptly stated:

> Yet, if women are . . . to learn a casual and physical orientation toward sexual expression, if they are encouraged to take up the quest for orgasmic experience divorced from the integrity of the person, then the mind-body alienation will continue.[23]

And rather than being a victory *over* the double standard, female promiscuity is actually the triumph *of* the double standard. As many women have come to realize, the emphasis on sexual liberation has worked on behalf of male promiscuity. "Freeing" women from their former "bondage" to chastity before marriage and fidelity within it serves the interest of the promiscuous male, for it merely increases the pool of available, willing females.

2. Fidelity vs. Infidelity: the Deeper Implications

Apart from these matters concerning adultery and promiscuity, the question of fidelity versus infidelity carries deeper implications. Each of these terms speaks not only of personal choice and lifestyle, but also symbolizes a personal outlook concerning the nature of the human order and even of ultimate reality. Each is an enactment of fundamental theological beliefs.

a. Fidelity and personal theology.   A person's attitudes and actions in the area of sexual expression are related to one's personal theology. They reflect in a vivid way certain fundamental outlooks concerning ultimate reality. Two important aspects of personal theology are revealed through the choice of fidelity or infidelity.

First, a lifestyle of fidelity or infidelity reveals a person's fundamental belief concerning the nature of humankind. To practice or even condone infidelity and promiscuity is to declare that the solitary ego constitutes the final human reality. To engage in promiscuous sexual practices is to set out on the path to sexual solitude. Sex without long-term commitment readily leads to a reduction of one's sexual partners, and thus, of others in general, to objects that move in and out of one's life. In the end, other persons easily come to be perceived as objects to be used for fulfilling the perceived needs of the ego-self.

Sexual fidelity, in contrast, affirms the significance of community as fundamental to the human reality. To practice fidelity is to declare that community, not the solitary ego, is the ultimate dimension of humankind, that is, that community is more primary than the solitary individual. Fidelity likewise emphasizes the importance of reciprocal relations among humans and the coincidence of give and take. It asserts that fulfilling the other while being fulfilled by the other lies at the heart of human existence. To be human, then, means fundamentally to be human in community.

Second, fidelity and infidelity are related to a person's understanding concerning the nature of the divine reality. To practice or condone infidelity or promiscuity is to imply that ultimate reality—whatever one perceives as standing behind the world or merely the world in its totality—is in the final analysis capricious. Infidelity asserts that the universe (or whatever powers are thought to be at work in the world) is characterized fundamentally by unfaithfulness and that despite the seeming order in the world, the world is ultimately disorderly and untrustworthy. In short, promiscuity declares that God either does not enter into covenant with humankind or lacks faithfulness to this covenant.

This connection between sexual infidelity and personal perceptions of the nature of ultimate reality is reflected in the link made in the biblical materials between idolatry and sexual unfaithfulness. The Old Testament prophets developed the theme of the marital relationship between Yahweh and Israel. Yahweh, the prophets declared, remained a faithful spouse, but Israel committed adultery through idolatry, that is, through the worship of other gods. The metaphorical use of sexual language was appropriate, in that the idolatry against which the prophets warned was generally some form of fertility religion which often incorporated sexual acts within worship.

The New Testament authors employ the theme of sexual fidelity to encourage holy living within the Christian community. Paul, for example, argues that because the body of the Christian belongs to the Lord, sexual immorality must be avoided (1 Cor. 6:18–20). The author of the Epistle to the Hebrews understands keeping the marriage bed holy to be an important dimension of the disciple's larger fidelity to the Lord (Heb. 13:4).

In contrast to promiscuity, sexual fidelity affirms the eternal faithfulness of God. For this reason the covenant between male and female in the fellowship of marriage constitutes a fitting analogy of the relationship between Christ and the church (Eph. 5:22–33). Faithfulness between the spouses within that covenant proclaims their faith in the faithfulness of the divine covenant partner to his people. As a result, to practice fidelity is to offer a profound declaration of the fundamental faithfulness of God.

b. The social implications.   In addition to being assertions of theological meaning, attitudes and actions in the dimension of sexual practice carry social implications. Sexual practices form the wider outworkings of a person's theology, that is, of one's understanding of the human person and the nature of ultimate reality. Such practices carry social implications, because personal actions are never merely isolated, but affect others and eventually even extend to the broader society of which one is a part.

Stated broadly, personal sexual practices affect the general well-being of society. Fidelity between spouses and stable marriage relationships are crucial to fidelity in society and for this reason to social well-being. Promiscuity and infidelity, in contrast, work to undermine social stability and well-being.

Important in this context is the broader social outworking of the opposing theological commitments reflected by fidelity and infidelity. Christians affirm that God designed us for existence in community and that God is a faithful covenant-maker. These affirmations ought naturally to affect our attitude toward society and our role in it. They ought to lead to personal involvement in the wider human society that is characterized by the same emphasis on commitment and the same presupposition of the underlying dependability of reality expressed in marital faithfulness.

Sexual infidelity, in contrast, expresses other basic understandings of reality. Foremost among them are the ultimacy of the individual ego to the exclusion of the fellowship of persons in community and the ultimate unfaithfulness of reality. These convictions likewise work their way out in the wider social dimensions of life. They dispose a person to deemphasize constructive involvement in society. And they readily foster a pessimism not only about sexual relationships but also about social relationships on many levels. In the end, social breakdown and anarchy form the ultimate expressions of the conviction that reality is fundamentally unfaithful, as depicted by promiscuity.

Two further, practical considerations also come into play. First, a crucial relationship between marital faithfulness and social well-being. This relationship arises out of the crucial importance of marriage for the development of social bonding in the experience of most people. Marriage forms the foundational, interpersonal community for the majority of citizens of the nation. As a result, marriage and family life readily become a microcosm of the larger society and the attitudes and patterns of relationship found there.

The manner in which one relates to one's spouse in this primary field of community life will quite naturally shape and mold the way a person relates to others in the wider social life beyond marriage. Faithfulness to another, learned by practicing faithfulness on the deep level of sexual fidelity within the marital bond, assists the individual in learning and practicing faithfulness in the various levels of life with others in society. On the other hand, if a person develops a pattern of infidelity in the primary social relationship of the marriage bond, he or she may likewise practice unfaithfulness in other areas of social life. Marital infidelity, therefore, can carry an unwholesome outworking in the broader social context.

Second, the relationship between social well-being and fidelity arises out of the role of the marital relationship in the rearing of children. In our society, the family remains the primary training ground for the future citizens of the land, who are the future participants in the society. Children learn primary attitudes about fidelity and relationship from their parents, specifically from the way in which their parents treat each other. The human sciences have indicated the crucial role played by parents in the formation of attitudes in their children. Marital fidelity is crucial for healthy child development. Erik Erikson, through his widely known concept of "basic trust," set forth the thesis that a covenantal relationship is necessary for the development of a sense of self in the child. A relationship of trust, however, must exist between father and mother before it moves between parent and child.[24]

Further, children first learn their fundamental attitudes toward relationships in the home from their parents. For this reason, the choice of sexual fidelity or infidelity by spouses has a profound effect on the children. Children carry the basic attitudes they develop from observing their parents into their own social contexts. It is no wonder that even secular authors such as Vance Packard have called for a return to faithful monogamy:

> Extramarital affairs, if widely tolerated, would threaten the family, especially during the child-rearing phase, and this in turn would threaten society. If we accept the highly suggestive evidence of anthropologists, we can assume that in permitting monogamy to be optional we might well be undermining the advance of Western civilization.[25]

Marriage is a covenant, an agreement on the part of husband and wife to create, as far as possible in a fallen world, a community of male and female. The sex act is an intimate expression of their intent and therefore finds its proper context only within the marital bond. When a married person engages in sexual intercourse with someone other than one's spouse, the marital covenant is violated and the marriage bond is threatened. The importance of sexual faithfulness of spouses is aptly summarized by Joseph Allen:

> If a husband and wife are seeking to build a good marriage, and if they desire to be faithful to each other in the most fundamental marital sense, they will find that the way to do so lies in affirming each other with all possible loyalty and patience and resourcefulness in a sexually exclusive relationship. This is true not simply because it is traditional; rather, at this point the tradition has grasped the reality of the matter. In such mutual self-limitation is true marital freedom found—the freedom to be themselves with each other, confident that each is unconditionally and dependably affirmed by the other as spouse.[26]

Divorce

6

The Ultimate Severing of the Marital Bond

The divine will is directed toward the establishment of the community of male and female. The intent of God for humans as sexual beings is that male and female live together in fellowship with each other and with the Creator. Marriage constitutes one divinely ordained context in which to express this community. It is therefore natural that persons give expression to the divine intention by forming communities of one male and one female in the marriage relationship.

Its connection with the divine intent means that marriage is more than a formal, legal contract. It also carries theological significance. For as the covenant and bond between man and woman, marriage is intended to reflect certain dimensions of the nature of God. Because of the theological importance of marriage, the divine ideal is that this expression of the community of male and female, the marital bond, be characterized by permanence and fidelity. In God's ideal, the marital bond in turn forms the context for the sex act, which is to be the celebration of the marital relationship.

Any discussion of the divine intent for human community in terms of the ideal for marriage cannot avoid the reality of the impact of human fallenness and sin. Not all married persons experience the divine ideal of permanence and fidelity. Many marriages do not reflect the community of male and female intended by the Creator. The outworking of fallenness sometimes grows so great that the partners terminate their marriage. In fact, even the concept of the permanency of marriage is increasingly on the defensive in contemporary Western society. As the divorce rate continues its unrelenting upward trend, marital breakup is not only becoming increasingly viewed as totally acceptable—increasingly people anticipate that it will be the inevitable outcome of most marriages.

The presence of unsuccessful marriages and the explosion of divorce, even among Christians, raises a crucial issue. How can a Christian sex ethic come to terms with the brokenness of community that arises in the midst of marriage? How can we understand divorce within the perspective of the Christian ethic?

Divorce as a Modern Phenomenon

A widespread breakup of marriages has come to characterize life in Western society. As a result, we must place this modern phenomenon of divorce within the context of a theological perspective of marriage.

1. Historical Overview

The divorce explosion in contemporary society is a recent phenomenon, unparalleled in human history.

The Old Testament documents include the establishment of laws concerning divorce. These indicate that the practice was present to an extent sufficient to warrant its regulation. But divorce nevertheless remained the exceptional situation in the ancient Semitic world.

In the patriarchal society of the Hebrews, divorce was primarily an option for the husband, so that the possibility of a woman instigating divorce was virtually unheard of. And divorce, although carrying legal sanction, never enjoyed widespread acceptance within the community itself.

By contrast, divorce was frequent in the Greek and Roman societies of the late ancient period.[1] Yet, the practice was largely an indulgence of the attitudes of the upper classes and apparently did not become common among the masses. Many people viewed marriage and family stability as very important. Further, although women did at times divorce their husbands, the general tendency paralleled that of the Hebrews, with divorce largely a male prerogative.

The early Christian community formed a stark contrast to the wider society of the Roman Empire.[2] The church taught a high view of marriage, and divorce was rare among Christians. This attitude was carried over into the wider society when Christianity came to be the dominant cultural influence. During the Middle Ages and even into the Reformation era, ecclesiastical strictures against divorce were paralleled by civil laws and social sanctions in European society as a whole. Not until the Enlightenment did divorce reemerge in Western culture. And only in the twentieth century have popular attitudes concerning the practice begun to change.

2. Reasons for the Modern Phenomenon

The rise in divorce in the contemporary world is a curious phenomenon. There are many theories as to why divorce has suddenly become so prevalent. Donna Schaper, for example, found the proposed causes "as numerous as the breakfast cereals on the supermarket shelf." Those she cited include extended adolescence, women's liberation, masculine shortcomings, economic issues, genetics, lack of commitment, the rise in sexual expectation, apocalyptic attitudes, peer pressure, and escape/avoidance.[3] Several factors, all of which are characteristic of modern society, warrant further elaboration.

a. Lengthened life expectancy. A first factor contributing to the rise in divorce in the modern world is the phenomenal increase in the length of the human life span. In 1850, for example, the average life expectancy for people in the United States was less than forty years. By 1900 it had only risen to about fifty years for whites, whereas the life expectancy for nonwhites was still less than thirty-five years. A baby born in 1986, in contrast, could expect to attain the age of seventy-five years. Equally significant, a person who was forty years old in 1985 (and thus may have already been married ten to twenty years) could anticipate living at least another thirty-seven years.[4]

The fact that people simply live longer means that people who are committed to permanency in marriage must now look to being married longer than in past eras. In early twentieth-century America, for example, the average marriage lasted a mere fifteen years before being cut short by death, often the death of the wife. Now, however, when two people say their wedding vows they can anticipate a half-century of life together. Given the fast pace of technological and social change, a fifty-year commitment will need to carry with it a sufficient supply of flexibility, if it is to maintain the bond throughout the multitude of changes the couple will witness. Further, the greater possible length of marriages today also increases the length of time during which marital tensions may lead to divorce.

On the basis of this new phenomenon of the great lengthening of life expectancy, some have argued that marriage never was intended to last fifty years. Therefore, they argue that a twenty-year marriage followed by divorce and remarriage ought to be viewed as normal and expected.

b. Contemporary demands on marriage. A second contributing factor in the modern increase in divorce is the modern view of marriage. Demands now placed on the marital bond are quite different than in previous eras. These demands are sometimes too great for the relationship to bear, especially over the length of years that marriages can conceivably now last. This consideration led sociologist Talcott Parsons to deny that high divorce rates mark a decline in the importance of marriage. Rather, "divorce is an index of the severity of the burden placed on the marriage relationship in modern society, and back of that, of the importance of its functions."[5]

(1) Companionship. One heightened demand placed on marriage in the contemporary world is the expectation that spouses be companions. In previous eras, marriage was largely oriented toward economic goals. In agricultural societies these goals were related to the maintenance of farm or agrarian life. The rise of industrialization shifted the focus from farm to factory, but the basically economic orientation of marriage remained intact. In both cases marriage

was intended to provide workers—spouse and children—who could shoulder responsibilities and thereby assist in providing economic stability for the family, both in the present and in the future. The twentieth century, however, has altered the role of the family from that of being the foundational unit of economic production to that of being the unit of economic consumption.

Prior to the contemporary era, companionship was generally found in relationships beyond the marital bond. The social structure was more static; people were less mobile. As a result, stable relationships with other persons in the social structure, including members of a large extended family close at hand, fulfilled the need for companionship.

In contemporary Western society, however, families are highly mobile. Friendships are made, only to be interrupted by the relocation of the nuclear family. As a result of this mobility we now place a greater emphasis on marriage and the nuclear family as the source of abiding companionship. In this social context, the marriage bond becomes the chief relationship, and a spouse looks to his or her mate as the chief companion. At the same time, in a mobile environment divorce is easier because the couple is likely living away from friends and family whose concern would strengthen a faltering marriage.[6] Further, the goal of family bonding is less likely to be based on common involvement in the family economic enterprise. Spouses no longer see each other as economic partners; they are expected to fulfill each other's emotional and psychological needs.

(2) Sexual satisfaction. Coinciding with the emphasis on companionship has been an emphasis on the fulfillment of sexual needs. Contemporary society has become increasingly oriented toward sex. People now tend to define sex in terms of determining what constitutes "sexiness," and they answer this question in terms of youthful vigor and appearance. As a result, married persons look to their spouses to be partners who will provide sexual fulfillment, and spouses increasingly sense that they are in competition with a fantasy idealization presented in the media.[7]

Expectations such as these place increased pressure on the marital bond. Spouses today sense a burden of responsibilities and desires quite different from those shouldered in past eras. These pressures, added to the longer life spans, contribute to the breakdown of marriage characteristic of our society.

c. Orientation away from life-long relationships. A third factor contributing to the contemporary rise in divorce is a new understanding of relationships and commitment. The general orientation today in all areas of life is away from permanency and toward the short and intermediate term. Social mobility has rendered lifetime friendships, a common experience in the past, at best difficult to maintain and for many persons even obsolete. In this environment, virtually all personal relationships and commitments are now viewed as short-term contracts.

At the same time, a fundamental shift in the focal point of personal identity has occurred. Whereas in the past, identity was derived from a person's role and participation in a wider social network, today emphasis is placed on the autonomous individual and the quest for self-actualization. As a result, people do not approach relationships from the perspective of their role in identity formation, but in terms of how they enhance the individual person who willfully enters into them.

These changing attitudes obviously affect perceptions of the marital bond. Marriage is often viewed as an example of the relationships entered for the convenience of the short or intermediate term, rather than as a permanent commitment designed for the enhancement of both spouses, the rearing of children, and the betterment of society. This outlook deemphasizes the values associated with permanency, such as "sticking with it" during difficult times. When the marriage is no longer meeting the needs of the contractual parties, it is often assumed, the relationship is to be terminated.

d. Lack of positive role models.   Divorce breeds divorce. With the increase in marital breakup, fewer positive, permanent marriages are available as role models for others. In fact, our society has created a new type of role model, the media celebrity. These "stars" rarely exemplify any semblance of marital commitment, but generally practice serial monogamy, entering into marriage on the basis of the personal and professional advantages the relationship offers at the time.

The creation of media celebrities as the new role models may be viewed in part as an expression of the bias in society against the elderly. In contrast to past eras, older persons are no longer revered, but marginalized and set aside. It is the elderly, however, who are more likely to have lived many years with one spouse, thereby offering positive role models of the permanency of marriage.

e. Changes in societal attitudes toward women.   Finally, the changed attitudes toward women in general have contributed to the increase of divorce. The women's movement has produced a more accepting attitude toward the presence of women in realms that were traditionally seen as belonging to the male domain. Great changes have also occurred in the economic status of women. Although they have yet to attain parity with men in certain areas, women are more independent economically than they were in the past. Recent years have witnessed the rise of a more accepting attitude toward divorce itself as well. Thus, the divorced person, especially the divorced woman, is no longer viewed in the negative light to the degree that predominated earlier. Nor is she as economically dependent, as was the case in previous eras.

The results of these changed attitudes and statuses have been phenomenal. Women are now less likely to remain in abusive situations or in marriages in which their needs are not being met. The divorce rate, therefore, may not be simply an indication that marriage as an institution is in decline. The increase in divorce may also indicate that women are now able to take action when they perceive their marriage to be unfulfilling, a prerogative that in the past was largely reserved for men.

3. The Effects of Divorce

Although present in many societies and in many eras, divorce is largely a modern, Western phenomenon. Many of the factors which have given rise to this phenomenon are understandable and indicative of contemporary society as a whole. To state these factors, however, does not mitigate against the fact that even in the contemporary world divorce carries a deeply felt negative impact, an impact which ought not, therefore, to be glossed over.

Divorce inevitably affects the spouses involved. Even in a difficult marriage situation, the breaking of the marital bond comes only with pain. Living with another always entails the development of a pattern of life, a pattern that is disrupted when the other person is suddenly absent. More significant than the pain of lifestyle change, however, is the pain associated with the loss of innocence and the dashing of dreams that comes with divorce. The marital partners, who had entered the relationship with such high expectations of self, spouse, and the marriage itself, now are forced to admit defeat. No wonder, as the Garlands noted, "Many couples who go through divorce find it more painful than the death of a partner."[8]

Divorce likewise carries a negative impact on the children of the broken marriage. In fact, recent studies indicate that the burden children bear may even outweigh that of the divorcing spouses. Craig A. Everett reached this chilling conclusion:

> There is little question that the children in divorcing families carry the greatest vulnerability and often sustain the greatest pain and anguish during and after the divorce process. In fact it is the adjustment crisis that the children of divorce experience which may linger well into adulthood. Disillusionment, anger and fear may shape their own adult mate selection processes as well as the parenting and interactional patterns of the next generation.[9]

Full awareness of the long-lasting effects of divorce on children is only slowly emerging.[10]

Divorce also affects society. This effect is in part legal, for divorce generally includes legal ramifications. Being the disruption of a legal contract, each divorce carries a judicial cost and potentially an added burden on the law enforcement agencies responsible for insuring compliance with the divorce settlement. But more significant is the wider toll in social well-being brought about by divorce. Divorce is never a merely private matter between two individuals, but brings about a social disruption in family, neighborhood, career, and the like. And each divorce constitutes a negative model for those who observe the marital breakup.

Divorce as the Breakup of Marriage

Regardless of the context in which it occurs, divorce remains, in the final analysis, the breakup of a relationship that carries theological importance. For this reason, Christian ethics cannot avoid speaking to the issue. The following discussion will move from two central biblical texts to the development of a theological understanding of divorce, followed by an attempt to offer certain principles for decision making.

1. The Biblical Data

Divorce as it is currently known is a modern phenomenon. Nevertheless, it is not without rootage in ancient societies. Its presence in the ancient world gave rise to interaction with the practice by the authors of the biblical documents.

a. The Old Testament: the regulation of divorce.   The discussion of divorce in the Old Testament centers around two basic assertions. On the one hand, the foundation for the way in which the Hebrew community came to deal with divorce lay in the Genesis creation narratives. These stories express the intent of God in terms of the permanent relationship between husband and wife. Beginning with Genesis, the Old Testament clearly articulates a marital ideal, and this ideal includes neither unfaithfulness nor divorce. On the contrary, unfaithfulness and its climax in divorce serve as a metaphorical expression of the unfaithfulness of Israel to Yahweh found in Israel's idolatry.

On the other hand, in addition to the ideal, the Torah includes the practical, the legalization of divorce. Divorce was a reality among the ancient Hebrews. Its presence required that the religious leaders deal with the problem. As a result divorce was institutionalized and codified in the law. Yet, as Jesus' encounter with the scribes indicates, the legalization of divorce ought not to be interpreted as a sanctioning of the practice. Rather, it was an attempt to assist women, whose status in the patriarchal society was jeopardized by the loose way in which divorce was practiced.[11] Divorce, then, came under legal structure, which required that the former husband give formal acknowledgment of a divorced woman's status.

b. The New Testament: the intended permanency of marriage.   The New Testament was written in the context of an era in which divorce was readily practiced. In contrast to the attitudes widespread in the Greco-Roman world, however, the early church emphasized the permanency of marriage and viewed divorce as being contrary to the divine will. Two texts stand out as most significant in forming the basis of the position of the early church.

(1) Jesus' view of divorce (Matthew 19:1–9 and parallels, cf. Matthew 5:31–32). The most explicit Gospel text concerning Jesus' view of divorce is Matthew 19:1–9. His statement occurs in the midst of a discussion of the subject with the Jewish religious leaders, who themselves may have been divided on the issue as to what constituted the proper grounds for divorce.[12] Three features of Jesus' response are significant.

First, Jesus placed the discussion of divorce within the context of Genesis 2. In keeping with the creation story, he reaffirmed that the divine intention entails the permanency of marriage. By placing the discussion in this context Jesus refused to become involved in the debate concerning legalisms which characterized the discussions of the Pharisees. Rather than siding with either of the two options advocated by his rabbinical contemporaries, he avoided sanctioning divorce under any circumstances. Jesus elevated God's ideal, indicating thereby that divorce always and in all circumstances constitutes a departure from that ideal.

Second, in contrast to the parallel text in Mark and in keeping with the statement in the Sermon on the Mount, the Matthew account includes what appears to be one acceptable basis for divorce, namely adultery. This addition has led some exegetes to assert that Jesus (or the early church) put forth adultery as proper grounds for terminating a marriage. This conclusion will be addressed later.

Third, the intent of Jesus' teaching on divorce does offer a marked break with Jewish thought at one significant point. He overturned the double standard. Jesus set forth the same requirements for both sexes, placing men and women equally under the double law of love and thereby affirming the fidelity of both husband and wife. Divorce, therefore, was equally treacherous, whether at the hand of wife or husband (Mark 10:11–12). In this egalitarianism, however, Jesus saw himself as merely reaffirming the implicit teaching of the second creation account and the insights of Deuteronomy.

(2) Paul on divorce (1 Cor. 7). Paul shared with Jesus an abhorrence for divorce as being contrary to the divine intent. His discussion of the subject, however, moves in a more pragmatic direction. In the text as a whole the apostle's chief goal is to encourage Christians to remain in whatever social situation they find themselves (v. 17). As an outworking of this principle, the married should remain married, and the unmarried should consider remaining single.

To this general rule, however, Paul offers one exception. If because of the religious difference between them introduced by the conversion of one partner a Christian's unbelieving spouse is not willing to continue the marriage, then the believer is not bound to remain in this social situation, i.e., in the married state. Paul's statement has been interpreted as allowing for what is known as "the Pauline privilege," that is, as viewing desertion as a grounds for divorce.

2. A Theological Understanding of Divorce

The Bible in both the Old and New Testaments views divorce as contrary to the divine intent. These biblical considerations together with the conclusions of the previous chapters provide the basis for the development of a theological understanding of divorce.

a. The context in human sexuality. Divorce cannot be understood in a vacuum. Rather, the context for the development of a theological understanding of divorce must be the understanding of human sexuality delineated previously.

We are created sexual beings, and our sexuality forms the basis for the drive toward human bonding, one expression of which is marriage. Thus, marriage is an outworking of human sexuality understood as the drive to form a community of male and female. The marriage bond is formed by covenant, namely, the covenant between husband and wife, which therefore lies at the foundation of the marital union. As a result, the drive toward bonding implicit in human sexuality carries theological importance. God's intent for marriage is connected with the divine will to establish community with humans and among humans. The human community God intends to be established in marriage is to be characterized by a permanent bond and by covenant fidelity. In this way, marriage serves as a reflection of an important aspect of the divine reality, namely, the exclusive nature of the relationship God seeks to establish with human beings.

b. The divine intent and the violation of the marital bond. This understanding of the divine intent for marriage as a reflection of the divine reality forms the context in which to understand the violation of the marital covenant. In the previous chapter the gravity of the violation of the bond through adultery was discussed. Adultery constitutes an open breach of the marital bond, and as such it marks the highest act in the violation of that bond. For this reason adultery must be treated with seriousness.

Adultery—overt sexual unfaithfulness—is not the only violation of the marriage bond, however. There are other breaches as well. In fact, all attitudes and actions on the part of the spouses that undermine or destroy the community that marriage is designed to fulfill contribute to the fissuring of the covenant. These violations include even the seemingly harmless attitudes readily found in marriage, such as taking one's marriage and one's spouse for granted. Left unchecked, such attitudes easily translate into hurtful words and harmful actions. The most blatant of these are abusive language and, ultimately, physical abuse.

A marriage, therefore, is not only undermined by adultery, but by a host of what may appear to be more minor offenses. A spouse may practice sexual fidelity and yet be violating the marriage covenant. For the covenant that lies at the foundation of marriage is the pledge to create a community of male and female, of husband and wife, through which the divine reality may be reflected.

c. Divorce as the final declaration of the violation of the marital bond. Viewed in this context, divorce is not an abrupt termination of a marriage. Rather, it is but the final statement concerning the process whereby the marital bond has been violated over time. As such, it is a declaration about the broken state of a marriage and the status of the marital partners vis-a-vis their marriage relationship. This declaration moves in several directions.

First, divorce is a declaration that through a series of actions or displays of attitudes a marital bond has been irreparably broken. The final parting of ways constituted by divorce confirms that the community of male and female this marital bond was intended to form has been effaced and destroyed to the point that whatever community may have been present in the past simply no longer exists.

Second, divorce is a declaration that one spouse (or both) now views the situation as beyond repair. The spouse who has initiated divorce proceedings thereby declares that he or she has given up hope for the marriage and therefore is simply no longer willing to expend any further energy in seeking to maintain some semblance of community or to reestablish the community that has been lost.

Thus, third, divorce is the declaration of failure and sin. The sin involved in divorce is multifaceted. One focus lies with the marital partners. It is, of course, possible that the greater responsibility for the breakup of the marriage must be laid at the feet of one spouse. He or she has failed the other by violating the marriage bond to the extent that the community of male and female the marriage was designed to be has been irreparably marred. More likely, however, both partners share in the responsibility for the destruction of the marriage.

In addition to being a sin against one's partner, divorce is ultimately a declaration of sin against God. Of course, any sin against another human is at the same time against God. But the sin acknowledged by divorce goes beyond this dimension. It marks the failure and sin not only of the individual covenant partners, but of this specific community of male and female that the two marriage partners set out to establish. Divorce is the final declaration of the failure of this marriage to mirror the divine reality. The permanent separation of the marriage partners is a confession that their marriage has failed to fulfill the divine intention, namely, that the community of this male and this female reflect the exclusive love of God and the divine will to community.

d. "No-fault divorce." These considerations form a context in which to view the concept of no-fault divorce. No-fault divorce has arisen as a response to the earlier approach to the legal aspect of divorce in which it was necessary to affix blame for the marital breakup on one or the other of the marriage partners. No-fault divorce, in contrast, asserts that no single party was responsible for the situation.

The intent lying behind no-fault divorce carries a certain degree of validity. There are situations, of course, in which the greater responsibility for the marital demise can be placed without question at the feet of one of the marriage partners. In such situations it is valid to speak of the "innocent partner," for one spouse may indeed have made every reasonable attempt to maintain the marriage, even at great personal sacrifice. In many cases, however, the destruction of community in marriage is more complicated. Mistakes are generally made by both partners, and both are often involved in the sin and failure that in the end led to the final breakdown of the marriage. In such situations, it is both unhelpful and dishonest to attribute the marital breakup to one partner. No-fault divorce is an attempt to give legal recognition to this reality.

Viewed from the theological vantage point outlined above, however, the idea of no-fault divorce is a misnomer. The name implies that no one is at fault, no one must bear the responsibility for the breakup of the marriage. But this is never the case. There simply is no situation in which divorce comes at the fault of no one, for divorce is always the declaration of failure. The term "no-fault" conveys the impression that the divorce simply "happened," that it was inevitable, that the marriage itself was the problem rather than the attitudes and actions of the marital partners. Of course, it is conceivable that such a situation could arise, that a marriage could have been doomed from the beginning. Yet such situations are rare. Most generally the marriage itself is not the problem that leads to divorce; nor is the institution of marriage to be blamed. Rather, divorce occurs because the marital partners fail to live up to the commitments they made in covenanting together to create a community of male and female.

Related to the theological difficulty, is a more "secular" one. The concept of no-fault divorce is questionable from a social perspective. It constitutes a denial of the interest of society in the maintenance of marriage and family. Ellen Wilson Fielding stated this problem well. Concerning no-fault divorce she wrote,

> Without even a pro forma announcement that one or both parties are doing something blameworthy, there is nothing to demonstrate society's recognition that something is at stake when marriages fail.[13]

The development of the term "no-fault divorce" is in keeping with an unfortunate mood of contemporary society. People today have a tendency to deny personal responsibility for their own failures, choosing instead to point to someone else, society as a whole, or social institutions as the culprit. Some other designation, such as "mutual-fault divorce," might better serve us. Generally a divorce is the climax of a process in which a marriage is dismantled by the actions of both partners. In such situations, both spouses share mutually in the blame acknowledged by the divorce.

e. Divorce as a possibility. God's ideal is that those who enter in the marriage covenant create a permanent community of male and female and thereby reflect a significant aspect of the divine reality. Yet, the setting forth of this ideal and the conclusion that each breakup of a marriage constitutes a failure to actualize the ideal do not mean that divorce is never an option. Openness to the possibility of divorce within the context of a sex ethic that affirms the divine ideal arises from a consideration of the relation of the ideal of marital permanence to God's overarching intent. God's design for human community includes the inviolability of marriage. But this inviolability is not an end in itself. The permanence of the marital bond is but the means to a higher goal, the establishment of a community of male and female that is able to reflect the divine reality.

In certain situations in which the divine intent has been effaced by sin and failure, the principle of marital inviolability may need to be balanced by other principles. This is especially the case when the continuation of normal marital arrangements endangers spouse or children. Situations arise in which God's ideal for marriage is being effaced and human failure and sin are causing great suffering—even to the point of endangering human life. Such situations could reach a stage in which continuation of the relationship would actually bring great harm to the persons involved. At this stage, the principle of God's compassionate concern for the persons involved, God's intent to establish *shalom* or human wholeness, must take precedence over the concern to maintain the inviolability of marriage.[14]

Yet, even in these seemingly hopeless situations, the awfulness of divorce must not be overlooked. Divorce must never be initiated lightly; it must always be viewed as the last resort, employed only when all other methods and attempts have been of no avail. Likewise, divorce must never be greeted as a positive act. In such situations it may be a liberating act, freeing a spouse from a tyrannizing relationship. Yet even then, divorce is nothing less than the declaration that a marriage has failed, that the attempt to create a community of male and female with the purpose of reflecting the divine reality has ended.

3. The Nonlegalism of the New Testament

The Christian must always elevate the inviolability of marriage as the divine ideal and oppose any casual approach to divorce. At the same time, however, Christian ethics must avoid constructing a new legalism to replace that of the scribes and Pharisees.[15] The New Testament documents undermine any attempt to construct a new Christian legalism. This may be seen by looking again at the two major texts that deal with divorce.[16]

a. The antilegalism of Jesus' statements. The tenor of the New Testament is evident in Jesus' response to the query about divorce brought to him by his enemies. Several aspects of his statement indicate that his intent was to replace the legalism of the Pharisees with a deeper nonlegalistic understanding. Rather than being a source of appeal for a new Christian legalism, therefore, Jesus' statement in actuality carries an antilegalistic tone.

The antilegalism of the Master is evidenced in Jesus' refusal to become involved in the legalistic debate of his opponents. The stricter school of Pharisees limited divorce to adultery, whereas a more liberal school allowed a man to divorce his wife for virtually any reason. Rather than joining this debate, Jesus returned the discussion to the question of the original intent of the Creator. In contrast to the shared presupposition of both positions, namely, that Moses gave to husbands the right to divorce their wives (albeit under certain circumstances), divorce for Jesus is never in keeping with the will of God. It never carries the sanction of divine law. According to Jesus, divorce is always a tragic sign of human sin.

The antilegalistic stance of Jesus is evidenced by the absence of the adultery clause in Mark. This raises the question of the authenticity of its insertion in Matthew (does the statement reflect Jesus' own intention, or is it Matthew's addition?). Regardless of the answer, the absence of the clause in Mark indicates that Jesus' intent in answering the Pharisees is not to set down a new legalism, but to place the question of divorce within its proper theological context—God's design for marriage. Any violation of the marriage bond is a breach of this design, Jesus asserts. In this way he stands opposed to the scribes' position. They maintained that in certain circumstances the marital bond could be, or perhaps even should be legally broken. In such cases, they claimed, divorce was not a violation of the divine will—it was not sin—for the act carried the sanction of divine law. Not so, Jesus declares. Divorce is always a concession to, and declaration of, human failure.

The significance of the omission in Mark forms the basis for understanding the presence of the adultery clause in Matthew. The Matthew text ought not to be interpreted in a manner that would bring it into conflict with Mark. The adultery statement, therefore, must not be interpreted as Jesus' authorization of a new legalism.

This assertion runs counter to the exegesis of those who see in Matthew 19 the institution of a Christian legalistic approach to divorce. In the case of adultery, it is sometimes argued, divorce is permissible; it is not to be viewed as a violation of the intent of God, because it is allowed by Jesus.[17] Such an understanding, however, contradicts the tenor of the Jesus-word in the text. God's design is for permanency in marriage. Even in the case of adultery, therefore, the divine intention has been violated when the couple divorces. Even in adulterous situations divorce remains a declaration of sin. It might occur, as a declaration of the irreparable destruction of the marital bond, but divorce can never be viewed as sanctioned by divine law, whether that be the law of Moses or the law of Jesus.[18]

In his reply as a whole, Jesus is arguing for a reinstitution of the high regard for the marital bond given in the design of the Creator. This means that the marital partners (in a first-century context, especially the husband) should be committed to working out the problems of the relationship. Divorce should always be viewed as a last resort and always in recognition that the divine design has not been actualized.

What, then, is the significance of the divorce clause inserted in Matthew? Perhaps two meanings emerge. The central point of the clause appears to move in the direction of indicating the new situation that adultery introduces into a difficult marital relationship. It is meant to indicate as well that the adulterer must shoulder the greater personal responsibility for the failure of the marriage.

The inclusion of the adultery clause asserts that the dissolution of a marital bond is raised to a new level, whenever adultery is introduced. Unfaithfulness constitutes the ultimate breach of marital trust. In the face of adultery it becomes much more difficult to stop the deterioration of the community of male and female which was to characterize the relationship. The adultery clause, therefore, adds a pessimistic note to the reply of Jesus. As a grave breach of the marital bond, adultery compounds the problem. It does not make divorce inevitable. But it increases the risk.

As a result, including the adultery clause indicates as well that the adulterer carries the greater blame for the marital failure. Jesus' statement introduces the concept of the so-called "innocent party," or better stated, the "more innocent party." Both spouses may carry responsibility for the marital demise, for each may have sinned against the other and failed in the attempt to establish community. Yet, the adultery of one partner increases the difficulty of reconciliation in a troubled marriage. For this reason, the unfaithful spouse, who introduced this additional burden into the relationship, must assume the greater burden for the divorce.

The inclusion of the adultery clause adds an individualist tone to the process that climaxes in divorce. Yet we must not lose sight of the other dimension. Divorce always carries the corporate dimension as well as the individual. It remains a declaration of the failure of the community of the married partners to reflect the divine reality. One or the other partner might carry the greater responsibility, but in the end divorce marks the final statement that husband and wife were not able to establish a community of male and female. Rather than setting forth a new legalism to give sanction to divorce cases, then, Jesus' statement emphasizes the violation of the divine design which is inherent in every divorce.

b. The antilegalism of the Pauline privilege.   The other major New Testament text permitting divorce, the so-called Pauline privilege found in 1 Corinthians 7, shares the tone of the Jesus-word in Matthew.

The goal of the Pauline statement concerning divorce differs from that of Jesus' discussion. The Gospels indicate the attempt by God's messenger to reestablish the original design of the Creator against the scribal legalization of divorce. Paul's goal, in contrast, is not that of returning the discussion to "first principles." His task is to apply the gospel pragmatically, to work out the implications of those "first principles" to a specific situation.

The situation Paul sought to address arose in the Gentile churches. As one or the other marriage partners left the old religions to join the Christian community, a two-sided problem emerged. One side was the problem of the desertion of a believing spouse by an unbelieving partner. The other was the question as to whether a new believer ought to remain with an unbelieving partner.

Both problems are understandable, given the new situation that a change of religious adherence introduced into first-century marriages. Because of conversion to Christianity, the believing spouse came to view the marriage from the perspective of a new understanding of the nature of the marital bond, which the unbelieving spouse did not share. Such "religious incompatibility" apparently encouraged many unbelievers to terminate their marriages or tempted believing spouses to find no compulsion to maintain their marital status.

Paul's application of the Christian marital ethic to this situation comes in two parts. First, the believing spouse was to live out the Christian understanding of marriage within the context of the marital bond, he maintained. The Christian spouse was to view marriage, and therefore his or her marriage, as a permanent commitment. As a result, the believing partner was to remain with the unbeliever, so long as the unbeliever was willing to stay married. In short, Paul cautioned against the believing spouse appealing to religious incompatibility as a reason for ending the relationship, even though the believer had a higher view of the nature of marriage.

Second, however, should the unbeliever choose to terminate the marriage, the situation changed radically, Paul argued. Then the believing spouse had no alternative but to grant the divorce, even though it constituted a violation of the marital bond as the believer had come to view it. In such cases the principle of the Christian's calling to peace, Paul indicated, took precedence over the inviolability of marriage.

In this response to a specific situation, Paul refused to institute a new Christian legalism. Rather, he followed a path similar to the one Jesus took in his discussion of divorce. When possible, Paul in essence argued, the divine ideal of permanency in marriage is to be actualized, and the believing spouse is to stay in the marriage. Yet, situations arise in which human sin (here the unwillingness of the unbelieving partner to maintain the ideal) undermined the community of male and female that marriage is to establish. In such cases, divorce indeed occurs, forming thereby but the definitive statement that community has been destroyed.

Like the Jesus-word, the statement of Paul must not be read as bestowing on divorce the sanction of divine law, in this case the law of Paul, for Paul is not a law-giver. Divorce, even in the case of desertion, does not carry divine sanction. Even then it remains a testimony to the reality of human sin. While not condoning divorce in this case, Paul, again in harmony with Jesus, gives place to divorce as a reality of the fallen human situation.

4. Principles for Christian Decision Making

The permanence of the marriage bond is the divine ideal. Yet, sin and failure climaxing in divorce are realities of human existence. Christian ethics responds to the contemporary casual approach to divorce by demanding that this reality be taken seriously. On the basis of the conclusions outlined above, several principles for approaching situations of life can now be offered. These principles are an attempt to incorporate what the New Testament texts say on the issue of divorce within the entire biblical context of the nature of marriage.

(1) The inviolability of the marriage bond as intended by God. The foundational principle operative in both Old and New Testaments relates to God's intention as the designer and instigator of marriage. As the Genesis creation story asserts and Jesus confirms, God intends that marriage be a permanent bond of fidelity through which husband and wife establish a community of male and female.

As a result, divorce is always a breach of God's ultimate intention, and no conditions may be seen as carrying divine sanction of divorce. It is a product of human sin and human failure to actualize the divine intent and is always the final declaration that a community of male and female has not been established. Therefore, divorce should never be celebrated as a victory, but should always be viewed with sadness and a sense of tragedy. Likewise, any movement in the direction of divorce and all reflection on the completion of a divorce should be accompanied by humility and repentance, as well as gratitude for God's forgiveness of sin and failure.

(2) The nonultimate status of marriage. God's design for marriage is that the marital relationship be characterized by permanence and faithfulness. The principle of the inviolability of marriage, however, ought not to be made absolute. It must not be interpreted as conveying to marriage the status of being the highest good. Nor does the principle of the inviolability of marriage mean that a marital relationship is to be maintained at all cost. Although divorce is always a declaration of human sin and failure, in certain situations it could loom as a better course of action than any available alternative.

This principle is operative in the Pauline specific, desertion. Paul's advice to the deserted spouse carries an important implication: If one partner has terminated the marriage in an irrevocable fashion, the marriage is terminated, despite the desire of the other to continue the bond and to view it as inviolable. In short, it takes two to be married.

Likewise, it must be admitted that divorce is at times but the formal declaration of the actual state of affairs. In certain circumstances it is but the final owning of the fact that the community of male and female has been destroyed, the bond has been violated, and the marriage is a failure, for it no longer reflects the divine reality it was intended to mirror.

This principle is perhaps reflected in the addition of the adultery clause in Matthew's account of Jesus' discussion with the teachers of the law. Adultery is to be viewed here as the intentional (and perhaps repeated) breach of the marital bond and its attendant violation of marriage as the reflection of the divine reality.

Even when divorce would be but the formal declaration of the actual situation, however, this act must never be undertaken lightly. Even when it is but a formalization of the brokenness of a marriage, divorce does alter the situation. It carries a finality that is lacking in the maintenance of the status quo. It has the effect of making permanent the marital breach which may have de facto characterized the relationship for some time. For so long as the legal contract of marriage has not been dissolved, there remains a faint hope of healing and reconciliation, even in the midst of the sickest marriages. Once divorce has been finalized, however, the breach has in all likelihood been made permanent as well.

(3) Considerations for Christians facing difficult marital situations. Two considerations follow from this discussion for Christians living in the midst of deteriorating marriages. First, the believer must remain committed to the divine ideal, which includes that marriage is intended to be a permanent community of male and female. Such a commitment will mean on the one hand that the Christian seek to do whatever possible to maintain the relationship. The believer, in other words, will "fight" for one's marriage, rather than give up easily.

In this context it should be noted that the termination of a marriage through divorce is rarely an unavoidable necessity, so long as one's spouse does not end the relationship. Even in the face of the violation of the marital bond by his or her spouse through adultery or abuse, the violated partner is not required to seek divorce. Generally speaking, then, the believer will not be the party initiating divorce proceedings. And a Christian ought never to view divorce as an easy solution to marital problems. Rather, in the midst of a difficult marriage the Christian looks first for workable options which are less permanent than divorce. Even situations of adultery or abuse could be opportunities for the Christian spouse to seek to demonstrate Christlike forgiveness and endurance, within the limits imposed by concern for all persons affected by the conduct of one's spouse.[19]

The advantages of separation as an alternative to divorce ought not to be overlooked. In abuse situations, for example, separation provides an opportunity for a spouse to remove herself (or himself) and endangered children from an abusive situation without ending all hope of healing and reconciliation. Separation allows a believer to take defensive action while continuing to express personal commitment to the inviolability of the marital bond. This step, however, ought to be viewed as an interim measure and not as the permanent solution to marital difficulties. Separation provides an opportunity to gain time for the sake of the restoration of the relationship. It allows occasion for counseling and evaluation of the situation, and, one could hope, for the beginning of the process of healing.

Second, the Christian must always pursue the path of peace.[20] Paul's admonition to the Romans, "as far as it depends on you, live at peace with everyone" (Rom. 12:18), finds practical application in 1 Corinthians. Paul's advice sets forth a principle. In the case of a partner who is no longer willing to remain in the marriage relationship the pursuit of peace may mean that the spouse becomes resigned to divorce as a last resort, for when all else has failed it is the only possible route to follow. This principle continues to apply even beyond the finalization of a divorce. In subsequent relations to a former spouse, the path of peace must always be followed, as far as is possible.

Divorce and Remarriage

Divorce constitutes the final declaration that the attempts of husband and wife to establish a community of male and female have ended in failure. While it is the end of the marriage, divorce is not the end for the former spouses as individuals. The good news of the gospel is that God loves us despite our failure and sin. There is, therefore, life after divorce.

Life after divorce, however, raises certain important questions. Each person who goes through divorce must face the basic existential question: What now? What lies beyond divorce for me? Although for a divorced person this may be the most crucial personal question, Christian ethics must deal with the issue concerning the possibility of remarriage after divorce. We may confront this issue through two related questions.

1. Does Divorce Entail Freedom to Remarry?

The possibility of remarriage after divorce is dependent on a positive response to the question as to whether or not divorced persons are *free* to remarry. Although mainline churches readily answer this question in the affirmative, Roman Catholics and conservative Protestants are generally more cautious. The Roman Catholic stance is related to the sacramental understanding of marriage, and therefore a crucial question in this tradition is whether the remarriage of a divorced person can carry sacramental status.[21] Conservative Protestants rarely frame the question in these terms, finding it instead purely a matter of biblical interpretation.

a. Central texts.   The debate in evangelical circles largely centers on the interpretation of the two texts discussed above, Matthew 19 (together with Matthew 5) and 1 Corinthians 7. Evangelicals often view these texts as providing a basis for determining under what circumstances a divorce may be considered "proper" and thus permissive of remarriage. Although there are differing positions concerning what the texts actually present as proper divorces, all such views approach the issue by constructing some type of "new legalism" to replace the old legalism of the Pharisees.

(1) The textual basis for the "legalistic" approach concerning remarriage. Perhaps the dominant position among evangelicals finds in the two texts clear teaching that in two and only two situations, adultery and desertion, divorce entails the right to remarry.[22]

The first text is Jesus' teaching on divorce and remarriage (Matt. 19:1–9). Jesus' response to the Pharisees, it is argued, closes the door to remarriage in divorce situations with one exception, marital unfaithfulness on the part of one's spouse. Proponents maintain that this saying gives warrant for a differentiation between the guilty and the innocent parties, giving the right of remarriage to the faithful partner, but denying it to the unfaithful spouse.

The second case in which remarriage comes as a right arises from the Pauline privilege (1 Cor. 7:12–17). According to Paul if a believing spouse is deserted by an unbeliever, the believer "is not bound." This is interpreted to mean that the deserted believer is free from the constraints of the marital bond, and thus free to remarry.

This understanding of the proper grounds for remarriage, while widespread in conservative Protestant circles, is not universally held. Some conservatives reject this view as too loose. They offer a narrower interpretation of the texts, claiming that Jesus and Paul allow for separation or divorce but not remarriage. As a result they envision virtually no situation in which a divorced Christian could freely remarry. Rather, regardless of the circumstances, once one's marriage has ended, the only options are remaining single or being reconciled to one's former spouse.[23] Others, however, criticize this view as too restrictive. Based on their reading of these two texts and others, they argue for a greater openness to remarriage after divorce, so long as certain criteria are met.

(2) Evaluation. As will be seen subsequently, it is surely proper to conclude that in both cases mentioned above remarriage is an option. When the marriage bond has been broken through adultery or desertion, the divorce

has forced the faithful partner to return to the unmarried situation. In this light, the interpretation that allows remarriage under such circumstances is indeed correct. Further, this position may offer certain advantages in pastoral situations. It casts a seemingly charitable light on the situations of faithful partners who find themselves the victims of divorce, while taking seriously the actions of the guilty party.

Apart from such positive considerations, however, all forms of the legalistic approach to this question—even the position that allows for remarriage in cases of adultery or desertion—are not without problems. A first difficulty is exegetical. All such approaches move directly counter to the intent of Jesus' remark to the Pharisees. As noted earlier, the Master's goal was not to set up a new legalism, but to return the understanding of marriage to the level of the original design of its Creator. With this in view, it is simply contrary to the spirit of the text to derive from it a new set of stipulations, whatever that set be, by means of which to judge whether or not a divorced person is entitled to remarry.

That Jesus' goal is to combat any loose view of the permanence of the marital bond may be seen in the way he framed his response. He appealed to the creation stories which state the high intent of the Creator. Then he commented on the situation in which a person divorces one's spouse with the intent of marrying another. The one who treats this matter lightly, the one who divorces one's spouse and remarries, commits adultery, he declared. There is no discussion of the "innocent partner" and no comment concerning the possibility of divorce for the sake of remaining single. Jesus' concern was directed solely toward combating the loose regard of the marital bond he perceived as motivating the question posed to him.

The same conclusion arises from the Pauline text. Paul's main purpose was to admonish his audience not to think that becoming a Christian altered their social relationships. The married, therefore, were to remain married and to carry out normal marital relationships. In other words, all were to remain in whatever relationships they were in when they became believers. "The Pauline privilege" arose from the cases in which this basic admonition could not be followed, due to the fact that the unbelieving spouse was unwilling to maintain the marital relationship. Paul's intent, therefore, is not to act as a new law-giver and establish the grounds for a proper divorce with the attendant right of remarriage, but to deal with an exceptional case in which a believer's social relationship had been altered by another.

The second difficulty of any legalistic approach to this issue is pastoral. Such viewpoints are helpful only in situations of blatant disregard of the marital vow by only one partner. These situations do arise, of course. However, many cases faced in pastoral ministry are not so simple.

More often, divorce is but the final stage of a lengthy process that has included mistakes, sins, and failure on the part of both spouses. Legalistic approaches, therefore, run the danger of viewing complex marital problems too simplistically. A legalistic structure seeks to force the situation into categories of "guilty partner" versus "innocent partner" which simply may not fit the case at hand. The determination of the "innocent partner" in many cases of marital breakup is difficult, if not impossible. It may well be that both partners share in the guilt.

b. Principles concerning divorce and remarriage.

b. Principles concerning divorce and remarriage.   The attempts to draw from the New Testament parameters for divorce and remarriage are significant in that they arise out of a desire to take both this issue and the biblical teaching seriously. For this reason they are not to be disdained. Nevertheless, it seems that an approach more in keeping with the spirit of Jesus and Paul would delineate from the Bible guidelines for use in situations of marital breakup. Such principles cannot determine in advance what circumstances entail a proper divorce and the right to remarriage. These questions must be answered in the midst of the situations of life, in which divorce is never "proper." Rather, they provide the foundational considerations for the decision-making process. Two such principles are central.

(1) Reconciliation. The first principle to be considered in each situation focuses on what should be the primary goal of all action, the reconciliation of the two persons. This principle is in keeping with the fundamental Christian commitment to the inviolable nature of marriage. God never sanctions divorce. As a result, the chief concern of a believer experiencing the trauma of marital breakup ought to focus on the continuing possibility of reconciliation with one's spouse.

In practice this principle would mean that proposed actions are to be evaluated according to their possible effect on the reconciliation process. How will my taking this step affect the possibility of reconciliation? Will this act further jeopardize reconciliation? Obviously, a believer would hesitate to enter into a new marriage, so long as there remains both the possibility and the hope that the breach could be mended and the relationship between the two persons could be restored.

(2) Peace. Despite the best and most sincere attempts, hope for renewal of the marriage may eventually fade. When this occurs the principle of peace (*shalom*) must temper the search for actual marital restoration and define the nature of the reconciliation that must now be pursued. This quest for peace must move in several directions.

First, attempts must be directed toward the establishment of peace between the two marriage partners. This peace includes the honest recognition and acknowledgment that they cannot live together as husband and wife, as painful as this recognition may be. Peace by necessity includes a peaceful parting and a resolution of lingering responsibilities of their marriage, including a fair division of material goods and a just arrangement for providing for the children. Finally, interpersonal peace must work toward a normalization of their relationship as two separate persons, including the cessation of whatever hostilities the marriage breakup may have engendered.

Second, attempts must be directed toward the establishment of peace in the heart of each former marriage partner. A believing partner would seek to uphold the former spouse in prayer and to maintain a credible Christian witness in all contacts with him or her. Important as well is the establishment of a peaceable attitude toward the former marriage and its demise. While not sidestepping personal responsibility nor denying the evil that each divorce actually is, a divorced believer who has repented of personal wrongdoing and truly sought reconciliation must come to the quiet assurance that despite all personal efforts no return to the marriage is now possible.

The door to reconciliation may have been permanently blocked by the remarriage of the former spouse. Such a step introduces a new factor into the situation. Restoration of the marriage could come only through the dissolution of another marriage, one which, however formed, is now to be viewed as inviolate.

Third, attempts must be directed toward the establishment of peace in terms of the wholeness and well-being of all persons affected by the marital dissolution—one's former spouse, one's children, and oneself. This concern may include the possibility of remarriage, if the establishment of a new relationship would contribute to the *shalom* of all persons concerned.

c. Implications.   Seen in the light of these principles, allowing remarriage only in cases of adultery and desertion fails to reflect the intent of the New Testament to uphold the inviolability of marriage and the concern for personal well-being. On the one hand, viewing adultery or desertion as biblical grounds for divorce and remarriage could serve to encourage the "innocent party" into a hasty divorce and even a premature remarriage. This person may think that he or she had been wronged by the former mate and therefore is entitled to break the marital bond and enter into a new relationship, even though her or his spouse has experienced a genuine change of heart and as a result senses a desire to repair the damage and restore the broken marriage.

On the other hand, limiting remarriage to cases of adultery or desertion may disallow a person suffering in a marriage that has in fact ended from seeking a new life with a new spouse. A person's spouse may have lost all interest in establishing the community of male and female that marriage is designed to be, but may not have violated the bond through either adultery or desertion. Despite sexual fidelity, the marriage may have died through years of neglect, open hostility, or even abuse. A legalistic approach would limit the alternatives of the believing spouse to maintenance of the status quo or separation until such a time as the other partner commits adultery, files for divorce, or dies.

Although the believing partner ought to be cautioned against entering too hastily into divorce and another marriage, such steps must not be categorically ruled out. It may be that God's concern for the well-being of both persons in this marriage, not to mention the children, could include the remarriage of the believing spouse to another who is indeed committed to the building of a truly God-centered marriage.

2. Should a Divorced Christian Remarry?

To this point the discussion has focused on the question concerning the possibility of remarriage after divorce. Yet to be mentioned, however, is the issue as to whether a divorced person should remarry.

a. Biblical principles.   The Bible does not directly address the question as to whether a divorced person should remarry. Some exegetes explain this silence as an obvious result of what they perceive to be a New Testament ban on the remarriage of divorced persons. This position, however, is an oversimplification of the biblical outlook. The question for Jesus and Paul is not whether divorced persons have the right to marry again, but whether divorce is condoned by God.

A more helpful approach to this silence is afforded by consideration of the similarity between being divorced and being widowed. Both divorce and the death of one's spouse return a formerly married person to the single life. Both carry similar difficulties, such as raising children as a single parent and dealing with the changed dynamics of personal sexual expression. These similarities suggest that the principles offered by the New Testament to those who have lost their spouses through death apply to divorced believers as well, even though it must be kept in mind that the circumstances surrounding their return to singleness are different.

Widowhood is addressed in two Pauline epistles, which set forth two basic principles. Neither comes in the form of a command, but appear as guidelines or considerations for those facing the return to the single life.

First, Paul offers for consideration his own preference for singleness as a permanent lifestyle (1 Cor. 7:8). He argues that the single life allows for single-minded attention to the work of the Lord (vv. 32–35). Widows are happier if they too remain single (v. 40), he declared, although they are free to remarry, if each marries a believer.

By extension, this advice is applicable to divorced believers as well. Any decision about entering into a new marriage ought to be preceded by considerations of the Pauline advice. The crucial question arising from Paul's discussion is whether the proposed marriage or a continuation of the single life provides to the persons involved greater benefit for ministry and for the development of personal well-being.

This consideration is tempered in the Pauline literature by a second, the importance of providing a proper context for sexual expression. Paul states this concern in a somewhat negative fashion: "But if they cannot control themselves, they should marry" (1 Cor. 7:9). A similar outlook appears to motivate the injunction in 1 Timothy that the younger widows marry again (1 Tim. 5:14).

Again by extension these considerations apply to divorced believers. They must come to terms with their own calling within the kingdom of God, whether it entails the married or the single life. For those not called to celibacy, marriage should be looked to as the alternative. But, as Paul adds, the new mate must "belong to the Lord" (1 Cor. 7:39); only marriage to a believer is advised.

b. The special situation of the divorced. The similarities between a return to the single life by the loss of one's spouse through death or through divorce suggest that certain principles that apply to the widowed are appropriate for the divorced as well. Nevertheless, divorce and widow(er)hood are not entirely parallel. This realization ought to form an important consideration in any discussion of whether the divorced should remarry.

The obvious difference between the two situations is the means by which the individual reentered the single life. In widow(er)hood, the loss of the spouse came through death, whereas for the divorced person it arose through a process that climaxed in the legal breakup of the marital bond. Each situation involves pain, but the pain of each is of a different sort. The pain of the widow(er) is the grief experienced in the face of death, whereas the pain of the divorced is the grief of a relationship which ended in failure.

This difference can work a profound and lasting effect on the psychological state of the now single person. A widowed person often carries few scars from the now-ended marriage, for that relationship, though not perfect, did stand the test of time and did include the fulfillment, as partial as it may have been, of the marriage vow of commitment "till death do us part." For this reason the widowed person faces the future with a high value of marriage and a high sense of personal integrity. Nevertheless, these positive feelings toward the first marriage do introduce certain adjustment difficulties for remarriage.[24]

The divorced person leaves marital life under different circumstances. Regardless of how healthy it once was, the marriage ended in failure. The process that eventually led to divorce probably has taken a toll and left deep scars in the psyche of the divorced person.[25] The situation is often compounded by a lingering sense of guilt and even of abandonment. The divorced person might have a somewhat negative view of marriage based on his or her bad experiences.

The difference between them at this fundamental point means that an added consideration applies to any contemplated marriage involving a divorced person. Whether consciously or unconsciously, a divorced person will bring into any subsequent marriage a certain amount of "baggage" from the failed relationship. Residual guilt, mistrust of the other sex, and low self-image readily raise their heads in the new marriage, becoming thereby additional factors requiring understanding and attention, if the new relationship is to succeed.

Divorce, in other words, is a traumatic experience. A broken marriage always wounds its victims. The trauma of adjusting to a new marriage is compounded by these wounds. And often they are not limited to one of the marriage partners. Rather, the remarriage might be that of two wounded people entering into a new marital relationship.

A further complicating factor is added whenever the new family unit produced by a marriage of formerly married persons includes children of the previous marriage(s). They, too, must adjust to the loss of one parent and the entrance of a new authority figure. Where this situation has arisen because of divorce rather than death, the children have also experienced the unique trauma of marital and family breakup. Their wounds add additional strains to the new marriage.

Remarriage, then, is not to be entered into lightly. It can be God's gracious provision for the well-being of those who have gone through the deep waters of divorce. At the same time, the divorce(s) the partners bring into a new marriage can affect their relationship for many years.[26] For such marriages to be successful—to bring about the establishment of a true community of male and female—requires an additional measure of sensitivity and commitment of all affected persons—husband, wife, and children.

Divorce and the Church

Divorce is a growing phenomenon. For this reason there is increasing need for the church to deal with the problems associated with it. In fact, the church is no longer being afforded the luxury of ignoring the phenomenon as a problem found only in the world. Rather, the number of divorced people in the church is steadily increasing. The great commission bestows on the people of God an important responsibility to minister in divorce situations and to divorced persons. More specifically, when viewed from the perspective of Christian ethics, the phenomenal rise of divorce in modern culture poses a twofold challenge to the church.

1. Developing a Redemptive Outlook
Toward Divorced Persons

In the attempt to respond to the current situation and to fulfill its responsibility, the church often senses that it is caught in a dilemma. How can the people of God unequivocally maintain God's ideal if the inviolability of the marriage bond and remain compassionate toward those who have experienced the trauma of marital breakup? To deal with this perceived dilemma, the church must develop a redemptive outlook toward divorced persons.[27]

For some churches, the development of such an outlook would necessitate a move beyond current understandings. Sometimes church policies focus on the question as to when divorce could receive sanction. This focus is characteristic both of more restrictive and of more tolerant approaches. More restrictive approaches are prevalent among conservative Protestants and Roman Catholics, who focus on the issues of what circumstances constitute proper grounds for divorce and who are the innocent partners who then can enjoy the right of remarriage. More tolerant approaches are often found in mainline Protestant bodies. Both approaches, however, often move from the same foundational question, namely, in what circumstances may divorce be sanctioned, differing only concerning the conclusions they reach.

The redemptive approach offers a helpful alternative to that often currently followed. Its goal is not that of determining when divorce can be sanctioned nor which marital partner is right and which is in the wrong. Rather, it elevates to central concern the question as to how relationships and individuals can be redeemed, how they can be restored to wholeness and peace.[28]

Focusing on redeeming relationships and persons does not mean that divorce is taken lightly. Actually the more legalistic approaches are the ones that fail to consider the full gravity of divorce. In this sense, both the restrictive and the more tolerant attitudes prevalent in the church are similar, for both seek to define the conditions under which divorce is proper. As has been argued earlier, to take divorce seriously means that no divorce can ever be sanctioned. Divorce is always an offense against the divine ideal for marriage, and therefore it is always sin.

Despite the sinfulness connected with any divorce, the church is called to be a community that meets all people where they are, even in their sin, with the message of the grace of God. The proclamation of the church, therefore, following the example of Jesus, emphasizes God's forgiveness of the sin and failure of the past, God's available power for genuine change in the present, and hope for the future. Although it is a declaration of God's grace freely given, this proclamation is not a message of cheap grace. It never simply condones sin and failure. Rather, it is the declaration that forgiveness and new life are available for those who repent of their past and desire a new start.

The church, then, ought never to excuse divorce. Each dissolution of the marital bond must be dealt with radically. For this reason divorces may not be categorized according to those which are proper and those which are improper. Instead, the church seeks to minister in the midst of the reality of divorce to persons who are in need of reconciliation and healing. Focusing attention on this ministry must become a crucial task of the church if it is to meet the challenge of the divorce explosion in our society.

2. Delineating the Role
of Divorced Persons in the Church

A related task facing the church is that of delineating the role of the divorced within the life of the church. This ticklish issue has at least two dimensions: It must be resolved both in terms of church life in general and in terms of the participation of the divorced in the office structures of the church.

a. Divorce and the general life of the church.   It has been argued that the church is to take seriously every instance of divorce and thereby to refuse to condone divorce in any form. But does this mean that all divorced people are to be doomed to second-class status in the church?

This has been the case in many churches in the past. There has been a tendency among Christians to be less compassionate when responding to persons who have experienced the trauma of divorce or who have fallen into sexual offenses than when responding to offenders in other areas. In fact, a convict who is gloriously converted in prison is often more welcome and may more readily rise to leadership and influence in the church than a divorced person. This tendency is not without foundation. The violation of the marriage bond is a serious matter, because, as has been noted earlier, it mars a divinely given picture of the divine reality and the metaphor of the relation of Christ and the church.

The seriousness of divorce, however, offers the church, as the redemptive community, opportunity to model the compassion of the God of new beginnings. The church's ranks include not only "respectable people" but believers whose former lifestyles involved many types of sin, including sexual sins (e.g., 1 Cor. 6:9–11). Therefore, the task of the church is not that of dividing the former sinners within its membership into categories. Rather, the goal of its ministry is to bring about the full inclusion of all believers, regardless of past failures, into the life of the congregation.

b. Divorce and church offices.   The ultimate expression of the acceptance of the divorced and of an openness to their participation in the church's life comes as they are welcomed to serve as leaders within the church. And the most difficult question the church must wrestle with is that of the inclusion in or barring from ordained offices of such believers. As in the case of other issues, a proper response must move within the creative tension of the church's commitment to the divine ideal for marriage and its mandate to be a redemptive, ministering community of pardoned sinners.

Congregations have sought to resolve the issue as to whether or not divorce disqualifies a believer from certain church offices in various ways. At the opposite ends of the continuum are (1) the position that sees divorce as permanently debarring a person from any church office and (2) the view that finds a person's divorced status irrelevant as a criterion for church office. Between these poles lie a variety of alternatives. These tend to differentiate among the possible offices in which divorced persons may serve or among the circumstances which determine whether divorce debars one from such service. Thus, one alternative would allow divorced persons to function in less authoritative church offices, but not, for example, as ordained clergy. Another position would limit ordination to persons who were divorced prior to conversion or perhaps to the "innocent party" in a divorce. The considerations outlined in this chapter lead to a position between the extremes, one which incorporates two principles. A circumstance such as divorce may indeed bar a believer from holding church office for a period of time. Nevertheless, divorce in and of itself ought not permanently to disqualify anyone from any office, even from ordained offices.[29]

(1) No permanent disqualification. The question of permanent disqualification of a believer through divorce should be viewed first. The conclusion that divorce ought not to lead to permanent disqualification from any office is consistent with the New Testament understanding of the nature of the church and its outlook about who may serve as a church officer. First, the church is a fellowship of redeemed sinners, persons who have been liberated from all types of sin. The past of every believer is marred by sin and failure. There are no righteous ones in the church. The disqualification of a believer from an office solely because a divorce is found in that person's past elevates this one expression of sin and failure to a status of sinfulness beyond all others. Although given in a different context, James's declaration nevertheless decries any such construction of a hierarchy of sin:

> For whoever keeps the whole law and yet stumbles at just one
> point is guilty of breaking all of it. (James 2:10)

Second, this conclusion follows from the New Testament outlook toward church offices. The general tenor of the New Testament views officers as providing leadership to the congregations for the purpose of corporate fulfillment of the common mandate. In keeping with this, the texts that set down guidelines for the selection of officers focus on three basic prerequisites—giftedness for leadership, spirituality and character, and public reputation (e.g., 1 Tim. 3:1–13). While the history of the candidate is a component in this, these criteria give central emphasis to the importance of one's present life of faith. This emphasis on the present arises out of the firm belief that qualifying a believer for service and leadership is the prerogative of the Spirit and therefore is a function of the individual's walk in the Spirit. The past becomes important only in the third area, that of public reputation. Only in this context do the sins of the past have any bearing on fitness for service. Neither in the ancient nor in the contemporary world, however, does divorce by necessity permanently mar one's public reputation.

(2) No hasty selection. Divorce should not itself constitute a permanent

impediment to service within church office structures. Nevertheless, divorce does entail a temporary disqualification, following from three considerations.

First, any divorce is a traumatic experience which leaves hurt and scars that require healing. This healing process is often protracted and extracts energy and concerted action from the individual who must go through it. For this reason, it is simply in the best interests of the persons involved that they progress through the time of readjustment free from the demands that leadership roles in the church require. Second, this conclusion is in keeping with the New Testament emphasis that persons in church leadership enjoy a good reputation both in the church and in the wider society. A temporary period of inactivity in the church gives opportunity for the healing of whatever interpersonal scars the divorce process has produced. Third, the presence of divorce, while not a permanent disqualification, ought nevertheless to be a consideration in any church leadership position, especially in ordained offices. This follows from the concern of the church to preserve the future integrity of its offices.

The Pastoral Epistles offer helpful advice in warning the church against hasty ordination (1 Tim. 5:22). The injunction is intended to insure a proper testing of potential officers so that possible future problems can be avoided (1 Tim. 3:10). Because church officers carry pastoral care responsibilities, it is important that they be proved worthy of the trust of the congregation. While applicable in every situation, this principle is especially important for candidates whose past is marred by sexual offenses. In all cases, a time of service in other capacities prior to holding church leadership positions or ordination is crucial.

Divorce is never to be taken lightly. Regardless of the circumstances, it is always a declaration of the failure of a marriage. The community of male and female desired by God has been marred. While being a declaration of failure, divorce is not a declaration of the boundaries of divine grace. God's forgiveness and healing meet fallen human beings where they are. As a result the people of God are called to do likewise, to minister to the victims of divorce for the sake of their inclusion in the higher community of male and female—the church.

Technology and the Prevention of Pregnancy

7

Many of the most controversial ethical dilemmas we face in contemporary society focus on human sexuality. Among these, few are more difficult than those related to procreation. In this area scientific advances have allowed human beings to relegate to ourselves capabilities and prerogatives hitherto seen as belonging solely to the divine domain. We are, to use the hackneyed phrase, in a position to "play God."

The current situation raises acute questions for Christians, who desire to be open to the benefits of modern technological advances while sensing the dangers that lurk among the blessings technology brings. A step forward for concerned Christians is to place the technological dimensions of procreation within the context of a Christian sex ethic. What does the understanding of marriage and the sex act within marriage say about the use of technological means either to diminish or enhance the chances of procreation? In this chapter and the next, the issue of the use of technology is viewed in connection with various dimensions of the procreative process.

The Ethics of Birth Control

One dimension of the procreative process which technology has invaded is the area of the prevention of conception. This intrusion of technology to inhibit the process of human reproduction is neither new nor unique to modern society. Some form of birth control has been practiced in nearly every age and culture. Nor is the attempt to grapple with the ethics of birth control unique to contemporary ethicists. Christians have interacted with the ethical validity of various means of birth control since the early centuries of church history.

At the same time, the current situation is in a sense new, or at least quite different from past eras. This new situation has been produced by the introduction of artificial or technological processes which greatly reduce the chances of pregnancy occurring through normal sexual relations. Only a few options were available to couples in past generations, and these were largely "natural"—that is, they did not interfere with normal bodily functioning. Today, however, a variety of measures are available, several of which thwart the process of conception by disrupting the natural functioning of either the male or the female. As a result, the question of birth control has taken on new meaning in our day and the problem of birth control has become acute.

In discussing the ethical questions concerning birth control, we must keep in mind that they relate to two quite different situations. As a result, two basic questions emerge, the propriety of the use of such measures within the context of marriage and their use outside the marriage. Here we will limit the discussion to the first general situation, the use of such measures by married persons. Is it proper for a married couple to employ technological methods in an attempt to prevent conception while engaging in normal sexual relations?

1. Birth Control and the Churches

Christians today are divided concerning the propriety of the use of birth control in marriage. The official position of the Roman Catholic Church, for example, allows certain "natural" birth control practices (such as the "rhythm method"), but rejects as sinful the use of artificial contraceptives. This stance prohibits church members from using any artificial means that would prevent conception (although many Catholics in the United States do not adhere to this prohibition). A somewhat similar viewpoint is put forth by certain contemporary sectarian groups, who for theological reasons require that their members not only refrain from using artificial contraceptives, but also disavow most medical treatments.

Most Protestants, in contrast, display a general openness to the use of contraceptives within the marriage relationship, finding no overriding theological reason to ban all such birth control methods. This divergence of viewpoint among Christians on the question of the propriety of birth control is rooted in theological history.

a. The rejection of contraceptives. The strict rejection of artificial birth control on the part of the Roman Catholic Church has its roots in the patristic era. In his essay *De bono coniugali* (The Good of Marriage), written in 401 A.D., Augustine articulated the theological basis for the subsequent rejection of birth control. In this work the influential church father set forth procreation as the legitimate purpose of the sex act[1] and termed all other incidences of sexual intercourse within marriage, including intercourse for the purpose of satisfying concupiscence, a venial sin.[2] Although he himself did not treat the question of birth control in this essay, Augustine's understanding of the sex act offered a theological basis for the prohibition of artificial birth control developed by the church.

The position of Augustine formed the foundation for the discussion of the subject in the fourteenth century by the "angelic doctor of the church,"

Thomas Aquinas. Like Augustine, Thomas asserted that the sex act is not sinful when connected to procreation, which is the proper goal of intercourse.[3] Lust, on the other hand, "consists in seeking venereal pleasure not in accordance with right reason," he declared. This sin could even be present in marriage, whenever a couple engages in the sex act in a way that is inconsistent with the goal of the act (procreation): "Every venereal act from which generation cannot follow" entails a "vice against nature."[4]

As in the case of Augustine's essay, Thomas's *Summa Theologica* does not specifically address the question of birth control. Yet, his understanding of the connection between the sex act and procreation as its only proper goal, like the position of his forebear, calls birth control into question. The use of contraceptives quite obviously indicates that a couple is intending to do what the doctor of the church prohibits, namely, to enjoy sexual intercourse while reducing the possibility of conception that normally accompanies the act.

What is implicit in the writings of Augustine and Thomas has been the explicit teaching of the Roman Catholic Church to the present day. Even within the context of marriage, the goal of the sex act is procreation, from which the "unitive" meaning of the act ought never to be separated. On the basis of this understanding the church rejects artificial birth control, because it separates the sex act from its intended goal.

In the twentieth century the church has reaffirmed the traditional position in several official statements. The papal encyclical *Casti connubii* (1930), for example, declared artificial contraception to be "criminal abuse" and "shameful and intrinsically vicious."[5] Even the reform-minded church leaders at the Second Vatican Council were unwilling to move much beyond the older teaching, for they affirmed that marriage and conjugal love are ordained for the procreation and education of children.[6] The same view was elaborated in 1987 in the controversial Vatican statement on human reproduction, *Donum vitae.*[7] Although acknowledging that there are "two meanings of the conjugal act: the unitive meaning and the procreative meaning," the document declared that there must be an "inseparable connection" between the two. As a result, the magisterium again voiced condemnation of artificial birth control, arguing that through such methods the sex act can occur without "respect for its openness to creation."

b. The acceptance of contraceptives. In contrast to the total rejection of artificial birth control on the part of the Roman Catholic Church most Protestants today are open to the use of such means within the context of marriage. The roots of this more open stance lie within the Reformation itself, for this movement served to introduce two principles which have had a great impact on subsequent understandings of the purpose of marriage and of the sex act within marriage. These principles led to an altering of the close connection between sexual intercourse and procreation characteristic of medieval thinking.

First, Protestant theologians, most of whom were themselves married, differed with the Augustinian-Thomist tradition concerning the value of marriage. Augustine articulated the good of marriage in terms of fidelity (*fides*), offspring (*proles*), and sacrament (*sacramentum*). The Reformers rejected the sacramental significance of marriage, at least as it had come to be developed in medieval theology. At the same time, they offered a heightened view of the importance of the marital relationship as a source of companionship and pleasure. This opened the way for a broader understanding of the role of the sex act in marriage. No longer was its use tied exclusively to the goal of procreation. Rather, sexual intercourse could also be viewed as a dimension of the companionship enjoyed by the marriage partners.

Second, the Reformation spawned a movement in the direction of greater individualism. Although the social dimension of life was not discarded, emphasis came to be placed on the individual and on the responsibility of each human being in the various aspects of existence. As a result, sexual relations within marriage came to be seen as a private matter, best decided by the marriage partners themselves.

Despite the introduction of these principles, the Reformers themselves did not automatically or wholeheartedly welcome the use of contraceptives. Luther, for example, had a high regard for procreation. In commenting on Genesis 3, he suggested that the general limitation of one child each year is a result of the Fall: "If the human race had continued to remain in innocence, the fertility of the women would have been far greater," for "if there were no sin women would have given birth to a much more numerous offspring."[8] This regard for conception forms the basis for Luther's one-sentence disparagement of contraceptives, abortion, and childlessness. While commenting on Genesis 25:1–4, he wrote:

> How great, therefore, the wickedness of human nature is! How many girls there are who prevent conception and kill and expel tender fetuses, although procreation is the work of God! Indeed, some spouses who marry and live together in a respectable manner have various ends in mind, but rarely children.[9]

Rather than being a direct consequence of the Reformation, the openness to birth control widespread today is a relatively recent phenomenon. In the United States its rise was enhanced by developments such as the women's suffrage movement and the medical advancements of the nineteenth and early twentieth centuries. These in turn led to legislation in the 1930s allowing the sale of contraceptives.[10]

2. The Debate Concerning Birth Control

In addition to these considerations, several specific issues have often been raised concerning the use of birth control methods of any type. These must be looked at before developing a positive apologetic for the employment of such practices within the marriage relationship.

a. Objections to birth control. The various objections that have been raised regarding the use of birth control center on three areas: biblical texts, theological understandings, and practical considerations.

Biblical arguments against birth control arise largely from the Old Testament. Christians who oppose the use of all birth control methods, including such "natural" means as coitus interruptus, point to the one situation in the Bible in which a man employed this method, the story of Onan (Genesis 38). After the death of his brother this second son of the patriarch Judah was instructed to engage in sexual intercourse with Tamar, his brother's widow, in order to fulfill his duty as her brother-in-law to produce offspring in his brother's stead. The narrator declares, "But Onan knew that the offspring would not be his; so whenever he lay with his brother's wife, he spilled his seed on the ground to keep from producing offspring . . ." (v. 9). This, the narrator concludes, "was wicked in the Lord's sight," and as a result Onan died (v. 10).

God's judgment on Onan is interpreted by opponents of birth control as expressing divine displeasure of all birth control practices. However, the issue in the text is not birth control as such. The narrator intends to condemn Onan's unwillingness to follow the social code that required that he fulfill his obligations to the wife of his deceased brother. The exact means by which Onan violated the social code is irrelevant.

The Old Testament emphasis on the importance of children forms the basis for another objection to birth control. The Hebrew attitude toward progeny is reflected in the declaration of the psalmist, "Sons are a heritage from the Lord, children a reward from him" (Ps. 127:3). This same attitude is revealed in the creation narrative, as God commanded the first humans, "'Be fruitful and increase in number; fill the earth and subdue it'" (Gen. 1:28a). This emphasis on the importance of children extends beyond the boundaries of the Old Testament, for Jesus himself blessed the children (e.g., Matt. 19:13–15).

Yet, acceptance of the importance of children does not in itself necessitate a rejection of birth control, nor dies it imply a total ban on the use of all forms. What it does demand is an openness on the part of married couples to the coming of children into their relationship. To this attitude of openness other considerations must be added, when a couple is facing the decision concerning the conception of offspring.[11]

In addition to biblical objections such as these, some opponents argue from theological considerations. One objection is based on an understanding of the origin of the soul put forth already in the patristic era by the Greek church father, Origen.[12] A modern reformulation of the theory is an important tenet of the belief system of the Mormons. According to Mormon theology, at the beginning God formed many human souls out of preexistent matter, and these souls exist in heaven until bodies are procreated for them through human intercourse.[13] Birth control, therefore, ought not to be used, for it inhibits the process of bringing these souls into the world, which is the task of married couples. This position, however, has never gained wide adherence in the church.

More significant is another theological argument. Some Christians object to birth control, because its use constitutes human interference with the procreative process which is solely the divine prerogative. The argument goes this way: Because God is the one who blesses a couple with children, attempts to upset the procreative process through birth control run the risk of thwarting God's intentions.

In response, two considerations ought to be mentioned. First, this argument could be (and has been) used to reject human action in nearly every area of life. Death, for example, also belongs to the divine prerogative, and therefore by extension of this argument all attempts to heal sickness or forestall death would constitute meddling in matters which belong to God. Second, in many areas of life God has given to human beings certain powers of decision and the responsibility to make decisions wisely. One area of human responsibility is procreation, over which each person does indeed exercise some degree of control. Virtually all human beings have some say in their involvement in sexual intercourse. Further, most persons decide whether or not to marry, and married couples decide the time and frequency of sexual intercourse. Likewise, single persons choose whether or not to remain abstinent. Decisions made in these areas entail a certain degree of birth control. Medical science has only added to the degree of decision and to the responsibility each human being is called to exercise in the matter of procreation.

A third type of argument against birth control arises from practical concerns. Here the objection is not based on biblical or theological considerations, but on concern for the welfare of either the couple or one of the spouses. Birth control techniques, it is argued, can be harmful to those who use them. This harm might be either physical or psychological. In both dimensions the woman is especially at risk. Certain contraceptives could involve damaging side effects that could affect her health or reduce her future chances of pregnancy. Negative psychological effects include the possible emotional changes caused by certain contraceptives or the personal or social stigma she might sense at the prospect of remaining childless.

While these dangers are not to be discounted, they do not form a compelling case against birth control in general, but rather offer a caution concerning the use of certain methods. Although physical risk remains, advances in medical science have increased the options for those couples who desire to practice family planning. A variety of contraceptives are now available, many of which have been proven to be medically safe, posing little or no risk to those who use them. The social stigma connected with being married but still childless has been on the wane in recent years. Today it appears to be more closely connected to individual family traditions than to widespread societal attitudes.

b. The validity of using birth control. As has been argued above, most persons do exercise some power of decision in the area of procreation, regardless of conscious use of specific birth control methods. Most people, therefore, already practice birth control, albeit for some not as a result of conscious deliberations. What remains, however, is the development of a basis for the conscious employment of such means on the part of Christian married couples. This basis is found in two considerations.

The first opens the way for the use of birth control practices, insofar as such practices do not destroy the meaning of the sex act. This conclusion arises from an understanding of the sex act within the context of marriage which views intercourse as signifying more than procreation. Such an understanding runs contrary to the traditional Roman Catholic viewpoint which maintains that there can be no separation of the unitive and procreative meanings of the sex act.

In chapter 5, an explanation of three meanings of the sex act led to an alternative understanding of sexual intercourse within the context of marriage. Within marriage, sexual intercourse can be a beautiful statement of the covenant between husband and wife, becoming thereby the "sacrament" of the marital bond. Further, this act can serve as an expression of the mutual submission of the marriage partners. Finally, sexual intercourse may be an expression of openness beyond the marital bond. Only in this third dimension does a close connection between the sex act and the procreative possibilities entailed in it become visible.

Because sexual intercourse includes these several meanings, it is too much to demand that the unitive and procreative meanings always be kept together, which demand forms the basis of the major religious objection to birth control. Within marriage the sex act retains its meaning even when no possibility of pregnancy is present. The connection between the act and its procreative potential is most important to the third meaning of sexual intercourse, the sex act as an expression of the openness of the marriage partners to the expansion of their love beyond themselves. Nevertheless, even this meaning remains intact, when for various reasons, including because the couple is using some method of birth control, the specific act of intercourse cannot result in procreation.

The other meanings of the sex act are less closely bound to its procreative potential. Therefore, their significance is not destroyed when the possibility of procreation is lacking, such as through the use of birth control techniques. Regardless of whether or not pregnancy is feasible, therefore, sexual intercourse remains a reenactment of the marriage covenant, as well as an exchange of giving and receiving on the part of the mutually submissive partners.

The second consideration moves beyond the possibility of the use of birth control methods to suggest that under certain circumstances their employment may actually be desirable. Birth control is a valid option for married couples on the basis of the importance of responsible family planning in the midst of the contemporary situation. In a world in which the population is increasing rapidly and the cost of providing for children is escalating, it is not surprising that many couples are deciding to limit the size of their families. Birth control is an important way in which they can continue to give expression to their covenant, to mutual submission, and to their openness to new life, while seeking to accept responsibility in the matter of family size.

3. Specific Methods of Birth Control

The wider meanings of the sex act developed previously suggest that the use of birth control is not unethical, for it does not violate the significance of intercourse. The importance of responsible family planning may encourage some couples to use birth control. Nevertheless, the judgment that birth control is a proper ethical choice and the suggestion that in some circumstances birth control may actually be advisable, do not necessarily imply that all currently available methods are acceptable. Each means of reducing the chance of pregnancy must be tested individually in accordance with other ethical considerations. There are several basic types of birth control methods.[14] These may, however, be grouped under three headings.

a. "Natural" birth control methods.   Generally two methods of birth control have been termed natural, the "rhythm" method and coitus interruptus. The rhythm method follows the woman's monthly cycle, with the couple avoiding intercourse during those days in which the chances of pregnancy are high. In coitus interruptus the male withdraws the penis from the female's vagina prior to ejaculation.

The term "natural" is not adopted because the methods are natural ways of engaging in intercourse. In fact, both are in a sense quite unnatural. The rhythm method prohibits normal sexual relations during at least half of each month and introduces an element of calculating pregnancy risk into the relationship. Coitus interruptus is unnatural for it demands that ejaculation occur outside the wife's body. These methods are called natural in that they do not introduce any artificial or technological agent into the act of intercourse.

It would seem that neither of the natural methods constitutes an ethically questionable means of birth control. Objections to their use could not arise from any actual harm arising from the techniques employed but only from the *unnatural* nature of their utilization within the marital relationship. Of the two, coitus interruptus appears the more problematic, in that its use on a regular basis could run the risk of precluding the couple from giving full expression to the meanings intended by the sex act. At the same time, using the two meth-ods together—full intercourse practiced on "safe" days and coitus interruptus whenever sex occurs other times during the month—may be a viable way of practicing natural birth control.

It must be noted, however, that these two methods do not provide the de-gree of protection against pregnancy offered by artificial means. Coitus inter-ruptus demands a great degree of will power, and the possibility of some sperm being deposited in the vagina before withdrawal is always present. The uncertainties surrounding a woman's monthly cycle and the monitoring it re-quires make the rhythm method somewhat unreliable. Some couples, how-ever, may find that the uncertainties involved in these methods make them a preferable birth control plan, for their use emphasizes the openness to new life that unites the sex act with the procreation process bound to it.

b. Contraceptives.   Perhaps more widely utilized than the traditional natural means of birth control are the artificial contraceptives developed by modern medical research. Narrowly defined, contraceptives are preconcep-tive; they seek to reduce the risk of pregnancy by preventing conception, by reducing the chances of sperm and egg coming together.

Older contraceptives include devices such as condoms and diaphragms, which place a barrier between the penis and the vagina. Other techniques, such as foams, attempt to kill the sperm after being deposited. A widely ac-claimed breakthrough was the development of a birth control pill, which pre-vents conception by disrupting a woman's reproductive cycle. Newer research has been directed toward the development of corresponding pills for men, which curtail sperm production.

Of these various techniques, "the pill" has been both the most successful in preventing pregnancy—and the most controversial. The other devices have been found problematic in that they introduce an unnatural element into the sex act (e.g., foreplay must be interrupted in order to put the device in place), while offering only a limited degree of protection. None of these difficulties, however, lies in the realm of ethics.

The pill, in contrast, does introduce certain ethical dimensions, two of which are most crucial. Some ethicists object to the use of birth control pills, in that it moves birth control beyond the realm of natural or mechanical means of preventing conception. Its use is not external, but internal to the body, in that contraception is avoided by actually interfering with normal body func-tioning. Others reject the use of such means because of the risks of harmful side effects.

It would seem that the second of these two objections is the more impor-tant. The argument against the pill on the basis of interference with normal body functioning is not to be lightly discounted. Nevertheless, this assertion would by extension eliminate many procedures of medical science. While it may indeed be true that natural health care ought to be given more consideration, procedures that seek to regulate or alter body functioning for medical reasons ought not to be eliminated categorically. The risks of the pill, however, do indeed raise ethical concerns, and as a result some Christian couples have turned to other means. Anyone who opts for the use of this method, therefore, ought to be aware of the risks in order to balance them against the positive benefits the pill offers in comparison to other devices.

c. Postconceptive methods. The desire to provide effective alternatives to the pill, which do not carry the risks of harmful side effects, led to the development of certain other means of birth control. Rather than preventing conception itself, these devices seek to prevent pregnancy after conception has occurred. For this reason such methods have been quite controversial.

One popular means is the intrauterine device (IUD). Although medical scientists are not completely sure exactly how the IUD acts as a birth control device, many suggest that it somehow prevents a fertilized egg from attaching itself to the wall of the uterus. If this is the case, then the IUD causes artificially what the female body often accomplishes on its own, for as many as 50–75 percent of all fertilized eggs fail to implant themselves and are naturally "washed out" of the body. Apart from the difficult question of side effects, which are generally less than with the pill, the ethical question posed by the IUD is related to its probable classification as a postconceptive device. Those Christians who believe that life begins at conception would likely find the use of the IUD inappropriate. If on the other hand implantation is the point at which life is truly present in the womb, then the IUD may be judged a viable means of birth control. The ethical propriety of this device, therefore, is tied to the question of the beginning of life, discussed in the next section.

Less widely used are certain "morning after" pills. In contrast to the IUD which may be postconceptive in function, but which must be inserted prior to engaging in sexual intercourse, these pills are postconceptive in the sense that they are taken after intercourse. They prevent pregnancy by destroying the fertilized egg. The morning after pill, therefore, is basically an abortive device.

From a Christian point of view, the most drastic and questionable means of birth control is abortion. Because this issue has been so divisive in the United States and because it is so significant for the entire question of technological procreation it must be treated separately.

The Ethics of Abortion

Many capabilities and practices gained widespread use in the second half of the twentieth century which empowered human beings to take responsibility over the results of their sexual behavior. Of these technological innovations, none has become as emotionally charged and divisive as the practice of abortion and certain capabilities which the availability of abortion unleashes. This issue in the United States raises not only practical concerns, but also theological questions of great magnitude, world-view questions concerning our understanding of what it means to be alive, what it means to be human, and who we are in relationship to others, to the unborn, and even to God.

1. The Abortion Debate

Since the landmark 1973 Supreme Court decision, *Roe v. Wade,* and continuing through the aftermath of the 1989 decision, *Webster v. Reproductive Health Services*[15] abortion has remained a divisive issue.[16] Two diametrically opposite positions have been vying for public support. The absolutist position holds that abortion is always wrong, except when the life of the mother is threatened. The permissivist position claims that because the question of the "interruption of a pregnancy" can only be answered by the pregnant woman herself, abortion ought to be permitted for nearly any cause the woman herself deems as warranting the act. Between the two is the vast middle ground of opinion which would allow abortion under certain circumstances and until the attainment of a some specific stage of fetal development. The broad middle, therefore, although including differences of opinion concerning exact circumstances and stages of pregnancy that would allow abortion, is united in rejecting absolutist legislation that would prohibit virtually all abortions, while desiring to place some limits on the practice.

A moderate solution was given legal sanction by the Supreme Court in the notable *Roe v. Wade* decision, which declared unconstitutional a Texas law prohibiting abortion during the first six months of pregnancy. This decision stood for over a decade, despite heated and vocal opposition from those who saw the decision as going too far in allowing abortions. In 1989 the Court reopened this explosive issue.

a. Major arguments in the debate. Many arguments have been articulated both pro and contra in the abortion debate. Several of these have been persistently presented.

(1) Arguments favoring abortion on demand. Three basic types of arguments have generally been put forth in favor of liberalized abortion laws. First, abortion on demand is said to be a means toward certain humanitarian goals, serving for example as an important method in the fight against overpopulation and against severe genetic retardation. Similarly, abortion is praised as a way to minimize the effects of pregnancies resulting from criminal acts such as rape and incest, for it prevents the additional injustice of requiring the victim of a sexual crime to give birth to the product of forced intercourse.

Second, abortion on demand is said to be warranted by proper consideration for women. Liberalization, it is argued, replaces illegal, dangerous abortions with safer, legal abortions. Proper consideration for the total health of women would allow for the abortion option not only when life itself, but also when psychological well-being is threatened by continued pregnancy. It is argued further that a mother has a fundamental right to a private decision as to whether or not to bear her child.

A third type of argument appeals to equal justice for all. Strict abortion laws, it is asserted, discriminate against the poor and minorities, who are less likely to have the resources needed to obtain access to abortion should they elect that option. The rich will always have an option; the poor will not.

(2) Arguments against abortion. The various arguments raised in favor of strict abortion laws fall into four basic categories. First, it is suggested that due consideration for the mother naturally leads to strict laws, in that abortion always carries inherent physical and psychological dangers. Second, abortion is seen to be at best an inferior means of attaining worthy humanitarian goals, when compared with other options such as adoption of the unwanted and adequate care for the handicapped. Third, a direct relationship is posited between abortion and morality, for this practice promotes promiscuity, threatening thereby stable family life; and it sets a dangerous precedent for other issues, such as euthanasia and infanticide. And fourth, antiabortionists appeal to a concern for the unborn, stating that abortion constitutes murder of the innocent.

b. The fetus and personhood. The fourth argument set forth by opponents of abortion, that abortion constitutes murder, is of added significance, in that the legal controversy has often centered around its validity. In response to what appears to be a strong claim on the part of antiabortionists, proponents of abortion repeatedly declare that abortion need not constitute murder because the fetus is not a person with full legal rights. In this way, the question of abortion has introduced a deeper question, that of the fetus and personhood: When does the fetus become a person? This issue has been the subject of debate within several academic disciplines.[17]

For philosophers and theologians the issue is traditionally articulated in terms of the soul: When does the fetus possess a soul? One tradition, which perhaps could be traced to Aristotle, claims that the human "soul" is received through a process that climaxes with the presence of the "rational" soul at quickening (the point at which the fetus makes its first independent movements within the womb), which possibly leads to the conclusion that a fetus is a person only after this stage has been attained. The opposite conclusion flows from another longstanding tradition, which dates as early as the time of Tertullian. This view asserts that the reception of the soul is not a process at all, but that human persons beget human persons in their entirety, so that the soul is present already at conception.

In keeping with the modern elevation of natural science as the source of answers to life's crucial questions, many look to biology for a definitive answer to the question of the fetus and personhood. They seek to understand this issue in terms of the point which marks the beginning of biological human life. Some biologists suggest that *birth* constitutes the advent of life, for at this point all biological functions, including respiration, are present. Others point to some earlier stage of fetal development—*viability, quickening, the beginning of brain activity,* or *implantation* (which marks the point at which final, irreversible individualization has been achieved).[18] Many biologists, however, see human life as beginning already at conception, for the genetic code is finalized as soon as fertilization occurs.

The question of the fetus and personhood is discussed by sociologists as well, who state it in terms of the fetus and society: When is the fetus a member of the moral community? Some concentrate on determining what characteristics, in addition to human parentage, must be present for membership in the community. Others raise the question as to whether personhood is intrinsic or bestowed by the society.

The academic debate has produced no consensus concerning the status of the fetus. Some proabortionists even dismiss that debate as irrelevant. Even if the fetus were a person and abortion therefore were in some sense murder, the act would still not be wrong in every situation, they argue. Most ethicists agree that taking human life is justifiable in self-defense, under duress of circumstances, and when killing is the only way to avoid a greater evil; proabortionists would classify abortion within these categories.

Other proabortionists appeal to the principle of double effect. Abortion, it is argued, is not necessarily wrong when the death of the fetus is not the primary goal of the act, but rather is an indirect result of the attempt to produce a greater good than that death, namely, the resultant benefit to the mother.

c. Abortion and civil rights.   In recent years some opponents of abortion have augmented the claim that the fetus is a person and that abortion is murder with a new focus—individual civil rights. The fetus possesses a fundamental right to life, they argue, which right is violated by abortion. This challenge, however, has been countered by proabortionists with an alternative emphasis on rights, the fundamental right of a woman to her own body, which they see as necessitating abortion on demand.

Christians have not remained aloof from the debate over fetal vs. maternal rights. Their involvement, however, is unfortunate, for this way of framing the issue of abortion focuses attention in the wrong direction. The rights controversy is debating the wrong question, because all participants in the discussion are arguing on the basis of the same individualistic world view and accepting the same fundamental presupposition, the ultimacy of individual rights. Proabortionists often argue on the basis of the principle that each person has the right to fulfill one's private destiny relatively unhindered. The right-to-life position is equally individualistic. It also presupposes that society is an aggregate of individuals who possess intrinsic rights, and that the unborn are to be included. Because the unborn are not yet in a position to defend their own rights, the movement views itself as a champion of the outcast, engaged in the last, and perhaps greatest civil rights protest movement in United States history.

2. A Christian View of Abortion

Rather than acquiescing to arguments derived from the Enlightenment emphasis on personal rights, Christians do well to become aware of the worldview issue underlying the abortion debate. Their response must concern itself with action that flows out of a distinctively Christian understanding of reality, at the heart of which is the fundamental tenet of a world under God. The Christian posits the reality of the Sovereign Lord over all creation and from whom all value and meaning flow. For this reason, value and meaning are not intrinsic to any person or thing, but neither is reality devoid of meaning and value. Rather these are bestowed on all creatures by God as a gift in accordance with the coming reign of God, which is the fundamental value and meaning of all reality. God calls society and each member of society to recognize the value and meaning which God has given to each creature.

Human life comes under the sovereignty of God in a special sense, for human beings have a special value, because they are the special objects of God's salvific love and have a special place in God's purposes as potential participants in God's recreated, eschatological community. The special meaning of human life must be protected, because it is just that life which will be transformed in the New Creation.

Because of the world view of cosmos under God, the Christian is not in a position to argue intrinsic rights, whether they be the rights of the unborn or of the mother. Rather, a believer can only speak concerning servanthood, love, and self-sacrifice in the attempt to cooperate with God's program of bringing potential participation in God's new society into actual participation. In this, it is ultimately irrelevant "when life begins," for at every stage fetal life is potential human life. Christians, therefore, can never take abortion lightly or view it as an easy solution to social problems. On the contrary, their appeal is to the teaching and example of Jesus, who calls on the "strong" to sacrifice personal "rights" for the sake of the weak. In the case of abortion this means that a mother be willing to sacrifice her "rights" for the sake of the one who is developing in her womb.

The principle of appealing to the strong is applicable even to the difficult "boundary" situations so often debated today. Although crimes such as rape and incest are heinous acts, the abuse they represent should not be used as an excuse to add a further injury when such acts result in pregnancy, namely, by taking the life of the person developing in the womb. Such a situation could offer an opportunity to one who has been victimized to extend the gift of concern motivated by self-sacrifice to the new life whose procreation, though unintended, nevertheless is now a reality.

For the same reason, however, Christian concern cannot cease with the unborn. Rather, it must encompass pregnant women in unique situations. Often the Christian community has been perceived as being concerned for the unborn but not for those bearing unwanted children; it has been tragically guilty of casting shame on the victims of sexual crime or on young girls who have sought affection by selling themselves. Such an attitude stands in stark contrast to Jesus' response to the adulterous woman (John 8:1–11). The Christian community ought to minister God's acceptance and healing to mothers in distress, counseling them toward nonabortion options, if these are feasible, within an atmosphere of understanding, but standing beside them no matter what decisions they ultimately make.

Further, the Christian's concern must extend to the unwanted child and the handicapped. Yet all too often the Christian community has rightfully been perceived as championing the unborn but snubbing the outcast—the abused, the handicapped, the children of the poor. In contrast, Christians ought to be ministers of God's acceptance and care, standing ready with open hearts to receive the unwanted. In short, the Christian's concern must encompass all humanity, for each one, regardless of his or her stage in the process of life—old, middle-aged, young, child, or yet in the womb—is a potential participant in the coming community of God.

3. Eugenics, or Selective Birth Control

The dream (or nightmare) of improving the human race through a combination of selective breeding and selective birth control has been articulated since ancient times. Although he was unaware of the role of genetic material in the inheritance of characteristics, Plato was one of the early voices calling for the improvement of humankind through manipulation of the genes. In the *Republic* he advocated bringing together persons with good traits in order to produce children with such characteristics, and for limiting intercourse among those of inferior stock.[19]

The modern rebirth of Plato's dream may be traced to Francis Galton, who introduced the term *eugenics*. Building on the theories of his cousin Charles Darwin, he proposed the improvement of human populations by decreasing the reproduction of defective individuals and increasing the reproduction of better ones.[20] In America, Herman Muller advocated that society take purposeful control of the human evolutionary process.[21] Although the public outcry over Nazi breeding experiments caused a temporary setback, the advent of modern abortion procedures has made the idea technologically feasible.

The attempt to manipulate genetic material of living organisms carries the general name of genetic engineering. Such manipulation by humans in the animal and plant world has become commonplace in modern Western society and has apparently brought certain positive results, including stronger varieties of grains which have increased food production.

In the wake of the discovery that certain diseases are related to genetic defects, scientists have proposed applying manipulative techniques to the human species as well, with the goal of improving the genetic makeup of humankind. This eugenic endeavor has already given rise to new practices, many of which raise ethical problems. It is beyond the scope of this book to provide a full treatment of the topic. Certain dimensions of the program of eugenics, however, are more closely bound up with questions surrounding abortion and birth control and therefore demand some comment.

a. Eugenics and abortion. Of the various practices directed toward the improvement of the human genetic pool, two are related to abortion.

(1) Genetic counseling. One means to improve the human genetic pool, sometimes called "negative eugenics," seeks to prevent individuals with known genetic defects from passing them on to their children. This process may include several steps.

A first step is preconceptive, as medical counselors inform such individuals of their genetic makeup and of the risks they will encounter if they choose to have offspring. Once aware of their situation, prospective parents are entrusted with the determination as to whether the risks warrant choosing not to produce offspring. Viewed from the ethical perspective, this practice is laudable. When offered without coercion, it encourages informed, responsible decision making on the part of the people who will be primarily affected by the results of the decision. The couple can then choose whether or not to open their marriage to the new life their relationship could produce, knowing that the choice to have a child could possibly entail additional pain for them and their offspring.

Once pregnancy has occurred, a second step is also possible. A couple could elect to use a process such as amniocentesis to detect the presence of certain genetic disorders in the developing fetus. Should abnormalities be present, the couple would be faced with the option of either carrying the child to birth or seeking an abortion.

Although the use of amniocentesis itself is not ethically problematic, the knowledge it mediates could place a pregnant woman in an ethical dilemma, namely, that of bearing an abnormal child or employing a questionable birth control method. If the knowledge of the presence of an abnormal child in the womb would lead to such a dilemma, it is perhaps best to avoid using the procedure. If on the other hand the couple is committed to bearing the child regardless of the findings of amniocentesis, then knowledge at an early stage of their child's disorder could assist them in making preparations for the birth and care of their baby.

(2) Sex selection. The development of amniocentesis and abortion procedures have introduced another dimension of eugenics, that of sex selection. By means of amniocentesis it is often possible to determine the sex of the developing fetus. Persons who for various reasons have a strong preference for either a boy or a girl may then abort, if the fetus is of the undesired sex. From the point of view of ethics, it is impossible to condone such a practice. The openness to expand the marital bond to include the new life produced by the love of husband and wife that is symbolized in the sex act ought to welcome that new life regardless of its sex.

b. Other techniques of eugenics. Genetic counseling and sex selection raise the question of abortion. Other dimensions of the enterprise of eugenics, however, are not necessarily related to this practice.

One possibility which has yet to gain sufficient technological precision to be viable is fetal therapy. Scientists hope that one day they will be able to apply treatment in the womb to babies with known genetic defects. Should such capability arise, great caution will need to be exercised lest technicians take to themselves too much power to decide which traits indeed require treatment. Nevertheless, advances in this area hold out the promise of developing a welcomed way of improving the quality of life for persons who otherwise would suffer from severe abnormalities.

Other techniques currently being developed involve in vitro fertilization. We will reserve comment on them for chapter 8, in the discussion of artificial pregnancy enhancement.

Technology and Pregnancy Enhancement

8

In previous centuries the debate over technology and procreation focused largely on birth control. Today, however, another dimension of the relationship between technology and procreation is becoming increasingly important, namely, technological assistance for the process of conception. Is it proper to seek to enhance the chances of a pregnancy through technological means? In recent years several dramatic cases have been reported about single women who have been impregnated by artificial means. Although these situations raise significant ethical questions, more important in the context of this chapter is the use of technological means among married couples.

Technology and Infertility

Few problems faced by married couples are as heart-wrenching as infertility. In a world in which unwanted pregnancies end in abortion and unwanted children are abused, battered, and abandoned, the unfulfilled desire of a couple to have a child of their own to love and nurture seems so unfair. Estimates put the number of married couples in the United States who are touched by problems of infertility at 10 to 15 percent, and the number is rising.[1]

In attempting to come to terms with their situation, infertile couples often experience a host of emotions—loneliness, hurt, crushed expectations, despair, doubt, anger, frustration. They receive much well-meaning but ignorant advice. They endure the trauma of visits to doctors and bear the financial costs involved.

Infertile couples are increasingly turning to technology to improve their chances of pregnancy. Given the traditional Christian openness to new life and emphasis on children as a "heritage from the Lord," what Christian would not desire that such couples be enabled to experience the joy of giving birth? In keeping with this desire, many Christians readily welcome medical advancements that hold out the promise of overcoming infertility. Yet such advances are not without ethical considerations.

1. The Causes of Infertility

The inability to conceive is not a new problem. Even the ancient Hebrews wrestled with this phenomenon. The Old Testament relates the stories of wives who suffered reproach because their wombs were "barren." Such stories then celebrate the joy that was felt when the Lord would hear their prayers and "open the womb." In fact, some of the significant heroes of the Bible—including Isaac, Samuel, and John the Baptist—were conceived by previously infertile women.

Despite its presence in ancient times, infertility is becoming more acute in contemporary Western society. Between 1964 and 1984 the incidence of infertility rose almost 300 percent, and the trend has not abated. The increase has been so dramatic that one medical doctor has termed it an epidemic.[2] And there is no reason to be hopeful that the number of infertile couples will diminish in the foreseeable future.

Doctors cite several factors as responsible for the increase of infertility.[3] Barrenness in women is often the result of blockage of the fallopian tubes or scarring of the tissue of the ovaries or uterus. These conditions are often the result of genital infections. In fact, estimates suggest that 75 percent of these cases arise from two venereal diseases, chlamydia and gonorrhea. By placing women at risk, liberalized sexual practices have contributed to the incidence of infertility.

The sharp increase in infertility is likewise caused by the trend toward postponing pregnancy until the mid- to late-thirties, for generally the ability to conceive has decreased at this stage. The emphasis on fitness is also a contributing factor, in that athletic women sometimes experience temporary infertility, if their body fat falls below the level needed to produce estrogen.

Infertility among men is generally due either to low sperm count or to blocked sperm ducts. It is now suggested that certain chemicals, including insecticides, can also reduce sperm production.

Not to be overlooked in the case of both men and women is the role of stress in the rise of infertility. The pace and demands of contemporary life have produced a degree of stress unparalleled in the past. The presence of stress among couples in their prime child-bearing years is compounded by the rise in the number of two-career marriages. According to Robert R. Bell, studies found that "working wives had higher incidence of fecundity impairments than those who did not work."[4] Of course, it remains an open question as to whether or not stress interferes directly with the reproductive process and thereby is a direct cause of infertility. Stress and the fast pace of life today might only indirectly contribute to infertility; modern couples simply find less time for each other. However, whether its impact is direct or indirect, stress cannot be ruled out as a contributing factor.

While such factors are partially responsible for the rise in infertility to epidemic status, it must be remembered that in some specific situations, none of these may actually be the culprit. Sterility continues to be caused as well by personal biological problems unrelated to any of these factors associated with modern life.

2. Technological Assistance and the Christian

In the second half of the twentieth century medical science has responded to the problem of infertility with several technological procedures aimed at enhancing the prospects of conception for barren couples. Yet each procedure developed in recent years has been the object of heated debate not only in society as a whole but also within the church. Before looking at several of these procedures a more basic question must be addressed: the propriety of employing any technological means to enhance possibilities of pregnancy.

a. The rejection of all technological assistance. Opposition in principle to all technological procedures in the area of procreation has been voiced from diverse sources within the Christian community.

The most often cited of these objections focus on the relationship between sexual intercourse and procreation. Some critics argue that technological procedures ought not to be employed, because through such means human beings—e.g., doctors and the married couple—take to themselves God's prerogative in conception. Others claim that these procedures constitute an unwarranted intrusion of science into the realm of nature. But the most basic formulation of the argument reasons that such processes separate sexual intercourse and procreation, the joining of which are the intent of the Creator.

Perhaps the most lucid assertion of this argument has been offered by the Roman Catholic Church. The Catholic position on the latest technological advancements was outlined in the 1987 Vatican statement on human reproduction, *Donum vitae.*[5] Although the document's specific subject is artificial insemination, the catholic magisterium in effect spoke against any type of technological assistance in the procreative process.

Foundational to the rejection of the technological means is the statement's reaffirmation of the traditional church position concerning the goal-directedness of the sex act as demanding an "inseparable connection . . . between the two meanings of the conjugal act: the unitive meaning and the procreative meaning." Technological fertilization undermines the origin of the human person as the result of "an act of giving," the fruit of the parents' love; it results in the child being "an object of scientific technology." In short, "such fertilization entrusts the life and identity of the embryo into the power of doctors and biologists and establishes the domination of technology over the origin and destiny of the human race."

b. The case of openness to technological assistance. The understanding already set forth in this volume concerning marriage and the sex act within the context of the marital relationship leads to a conclusion quite different from that presented in the Vatican statement. As in the case of birth control, this wider understanding of the meaning of the sex act within marriage suggests that the magisterium's objection to technological assistance in the procreative process is unwarranted. All Christians ought to applaud the Roman hierarchy for launching a commendable attempt to maintain the mystery of human procreation in the face of the unchallenged intrusion of technology into human life. Yet, the wholesale rejection of all types of technological assistance in the natural human drive to produce offspring is unfortunate.

As is readily evident from the discussion in earlier chapters, the rejection voiced by *Donum vitae* reflects a truncated and therefore damaging understanding of the meaning of the sex act within marriage. By insisting that the "unitive meaning" of the sex act cannot be separated from the "procreative meaning," the magisterium is maintaining virtually unaltered the Augustinian-Thomist understanding that works to limit sexual activity to procreation.

The document's understanding of the meaning of the sex act is truncated, for within the marriage bond sexual activity can carry other equally significant meanings. Several of these have been presented in chapter 4. The sex act may serve as an expression of the marriage covenant the partners share, and thereby as the "sacrament" of the marriage covenant, an outward act which repeatedly seals and signifies their inward commitment. It can be an illustration of the mutual submission that is to characterize marriage, thereby forming a spiritual metaphor, a beautiful reminder of the self-giving love of Christ. These aspects of the meaning of the sex act may exist apart from the procreative intent. In fact, rather than the procreative meaning being central for the unitive meaning, as is implied in the Vatican statement, the other aspects of the sex act are what form the context for procreation. As self-giving love is creative, so the giving of oneself in the marriage act can be procreative within the context of the marital covenant. Even the meaning most closely bound to the procreative process, namely, the couple's openness to the broadening of their love beyond the marital bond, remains when there is no possibility that pregnancy will result from the sex act.

In contrast to the position of *Donum vitae,* therefore, it would seem that a fuller understanding of the meaning of the sex act within the marital bond would welcome as God's gift, rather than discourage, technological assistance in procreation, so long as the process is not objectionable on other moral grounds.

Technological assistance as such, therefore, is not ethically questionable. Rather than a wholesale rejection of technological assistance *in toto,* such assistance, within certain limitations, in the process of pregnancy can be a great benefit to childless couples and therefore ought to be welcomed. The ethical issue, in other words, does not lie with the idea of assistance from medical science. Rather, each specific means must be ethically tested.

3. Alternatives to Technological Procreation

Of course, the availability of technological assistance does not mean that conscientious childless couples ought to sense a compulsion to resort to it. The Vatican document goes too far in asserting that infertile couples are called to find in their situation "an opportunity for sharing in a particular way in the Lord's cross. . . ." Nevertheless, the suggestion that this be a valid attitude is surely correct. In addition to turning to technological assistance, two other options are worthy of consideration by couples touched by infertility: adoption and remaining "child free" for the sake of service to Christ.[6]

a. Adoption. Adoption ranks as the preferred option for couples who cannot have children through natural means. This practice carries biblical precedence. Moses, for example, was adopted. And the implication of the doctrine of the virgin birth is that Jesus was adopted as well (by Joseph). Further, the adoption of a child who for some reason is given up by his or her natural parents becomes a gracious act, for therein a couple extends a home to a homeless little one. In this way the act can serve as a reflection of the gracious compassion of God, who provides home for the homeless. Finally, adoption can also serve as a metaphor of God's adoption of human beings into the divine family.

Because of the picture of spiritual truth that it offers, adoption is a viable option. As John and Sylvia Van Regenmorter aptly declare, "For the Christian infertile couple adoption is not 'second best.' It is simply the way that God in his wisdom can choose for us to be parents. Whether one becomes a parent biologically or through adoption, the fact is that children are not a right but a gift from God."[7]

Nevertheless, adoption is not without its difficulties.[8]

One major problem is that of completing the adoption process. The availability of abortion and the trend toward single mothers electing to keep their babies has reduced the number of adoptable babies in the United States. As a result, waiting periods have lengthened from two to, at times, eight years. Many couples find the length of the wait, which draws out the adoption process, simply too great an obstacle to overcome. An alternative to which many have turned is the adoption of children from impoverished countries. Others have been willing to take into their homes children who are either physically or mentally disadvantaged or rejected from some other reason.[9] Such an act requires great fortitude, but also becomes an example of great love.

A second difficulty focuses on the expense surrounding the adoption process. Although some institutions may offer their services at little charge, the costs of adoption through other agencies can be high. These expenses often come after a couple have already spent a large sum of money on infertility treatment.

Finally, adoption brings a certain amount of trauma not associated with biological birthing. An adopting couple will need to cope with the implications of their pursuance of adoption, for thereby they are acknowledging that their efforts to give birth have been unsuccessful. Family and friends might find it difficult to accept the adopted child, adding to the stress of the adjustment. And in later years the family will need to assist the adopted child in coping with the knowledge that the biological parents gave the child for adoption.[10] Despite these difficulties, adoption can be a laudable expression of the openness of the marriage partners to broaden their bond in order to welcome new life in their midst.

b. Remaining child free.   Another alternative for the infertile couple is that of remaining child free. The ancient Hebrews viewed childlessness as an unfortunate, even a reproachful situation. A similar viewpoint was widespread in American culture until recently, in that children were viewed as crucial to the economic well-being of the family. But as the focus of the nature of the family shifted from production to consumption, attitudes toward childlessness began to change as well. On the heels of such changes, this option has become more acceptable and more commonplace.

Viewed from a Christian perspective, a case could be made for choosing to remain child free. A New Testament foundation for this option arises by extending Paul's argument regarding the single life (1 Cor. 7:25–40) to the already married who are contemplating having children. Just as marriage can distract a person from full service to the Lord (the point Paul raised), so also parenting is a time consuming, potentially distracting occupation. Consideration of this principle could motivate a couple to remain child free for the purpose of devoting more energy to the Lord's work, just as a single person may choose to forego marriage for the same reason.[11]

It must be added, however, that just as it is not to be assumed from 1 Corinthians 7 that all Christians are to choose to remain single, so also being child free is not the norm for Christian couples. It may well be that many couples will conclude that having children in fact enhances their ministry in the Lord's work. At the same time, the choice of remaining child free for the sake of devotion to the Lord does offer an opportunity to infertile couples to see their situation as the vehicle to what for them may be greater service in the fellowship of Christ.

As in the case of adoption, the option of remaining child free is not without difficulties. First, the couple will need to cope with lingering negative attitudes from both family and society toward such a decision. It is often assumed that all couples have children and that those who do not are motivated only by selfishness. Child free couples will need to learn to pass off rude and unloving comments by others, which reflect such judgmental attitudes.

A second danger is that of falling into the temptation to live only for oneself or for one's spouse. Without the cares and financial burdens involved in raising a family, child free couples can get caught in the trap of focusing on themselves. Therefore, they might need to make a conscious effort to open their relationship beyond themselves by discovering ways of giving of themselves to others. Children who for various reasons are in need of the support and love of replacement "parents" or adult friendship and guidance offer one important means to this end. By ministering to such children, a couple with no children in the home can both extend a type of parental love to children and experience in a unique way the joys of being "parent."

Both adoption and remaining child free for the sake of devoting greater time, money, and energy to the Lord's work are worthy options for the infertile couple and therefore ought to be given careful consideration. Nevertheless, they must not be cited as the only options. For some infertile couples the desire to experience the joy of being partners with God in the mystery of procreation is a divinely given impulse that ought to be facilitated, so long as it is morally proper and technologically feasible. By developing the means to accomplish this, modern medical technology now offers hope to many infertile couples that this joy may be realized.

Methods of Technologically Assisted Conception

The battle against infertility has produced several technological means of assisting in the process of procreation.[12] These offer to many otherwise childless couples the hope of experiencing the joy of procreation and parenting.

1. Representative Methods

Medical technology has advanced at an astounding rate. Although new possibilities seem to emerge almost constantly, several basic procedures are now widely accepted.

a. Artificial insemination. Several causes of infertility, including the situation in which the sperm count in the husband's semen is insufficiently high to bring about pregnancy, can at times be rectified through artificial insemination. This process involves the injection of sperm by artificial means rather than by normal intercourse either into the vagina or into the uterus. (Intrauterine insemination is used when the sperm are unable to survive in the wife's cervical mucus.) A semen specimen is collected during masturbation and either brought directly to the doctor for insertion or stored first in a sperm bank. At times methods may be introduced to enhance the sperm count of the fluid that is employed in the process.

There are actually two types of artificial insemination currently in practice. The difference between them lies in the source of the sperm used to impregnate the wife—whether that of the husband (AIH) or that of a "donor" other than the husband (AID).

b. In vitro fertilization (IVF). Infertility may be caused by certain difficulties in the woman's reproductive system, such as blocked fallopian tubes. In these situations an egg can be drawn out of the woman's ovary and placed in a solution of sperm. In this way, fertilization occurs external to the woman's body, in a petri dish, hence, in vitro (in glass). After two or three days the developing embryo is placed in the uterus, and the pregnancy is established.

To increase the chances of pregnancy, drugs are generally administered to the woman to induce the production of more than one egg in the given month. Multiple fertilizations are attempted in vitro, so that preferably three embryos may be placed in the uterus. Current technology also allows for the freezing of embryos for possible implantation at a later time.

A variation of this technique allows for fertilization to occur in the fallopian tubes. Rather than placing the withdrawn eggs in a glass dish, eggs and sperm are squirted into the fallopian tubes, where fertilization is to occur. This procedure is known as gamete intrafallopian transfer (GIFT). In a third related procedure, zygote intrafallopian transfer (ZIFT), an embryo created in a petri dish is placed in the fallopian tube.

c. Embryo transfer and surrogacy. Two related procedures have been developed in response to an assortment of other problems surrounding conception and pregnancy. In embryo transfer, embryos conceived in one woman are removed and transplanted in the uterus of another. Through this procedure, a woman who cannot conceive in her body can nevertheless give birth to a baby she has carried in her womb. Women who have the opposite difficulty, who are able to provide an egg for conception but for a variety of reasons cannot carry a fetus, can elect to employ a surrogate mother. If the genetic mother has functional ovaries but no functional uterus, embryo transfer can be employed in order to move the fetus from her to the surrogate. Or the surrogate's egg is inseminated by the husband's sperm, whether in vitro or through GIFT.

These various procedures open the door to multiple parenting situations. Perhaps the most complicated arrangement imaginable is the situation in which the sperm from a male donor fertilizes an egg from a female donor, which is then placed in a surrogate mother, all on behalf of a married couple consisting of a husband with a low sperm count and a wife who has neither functioning ovaries nor uterus.

2. Ethical Considerations

In a sense, technological procedures such as those described above are blind to ethical considerations. The process of assisting in the combining of sperm and egg inside a woman's womb or in a laboratory, for example, is oblivious to the source of the material being brought together and to the relationship between the donors of that material. But the purported biological neutrality of such procedures does not necessarily make them ethically neutral. Nor does a theoretical openness to the efforts of modern medicine in assisting infertile couples in these ways require that Christians conclude that all such techniques are ethically acceptable.

The mere fact that medical research has made a process possible does not mean that it is morally justifiable. Whereas medical technicians may on occasion find ethical considerations irrelevant to their task, the Christian dare not. The methods put forth by the medical community must be tested not only by whether they are able to assist in the process of conception, but by whether or not they maintain Christian ethical standards.

a. Technological procreation within the marriage bond. For many, artificial insemination and IVF/GIFT loom as the gateway to the strange world of technological procreation. In a sense this perception is valid, for when viewed from an ethical perspective, they stand on the border between technological assistance that remains strictly within the bond of marriage and that which moves beyond this bond.

The boundary characteristic of the process arises from the ethical importance of the source of the sperm and egg brought together in these procedures. Viewed from the technical dimension, of course, the source of the elements sperm and egg is irrelevant. From the ethical perspective, however, this factor is more significant than the technological differences among the various procedures, because they employ sperm derived from different sources (for example, AIH and AID are distinct acts). AID introduces sperm from a third party, with the result that the genetic makeup of the offspring is the product of the combination of the genes of a woman and those of someone other than her husband. In AIH, only the husband's sperm is used to impregnate the wife, thereby maintaining the closed nature of the marital relationship in the procreative process. In the same way, practices such as IVF and GIFT carry differing implications depending on whose sperm is being united with whose egg.

Some ethicists have rejected all these procedures on the basis that they employ masturbation in the process. This objection, however, is not warranted. The ethical problem with masturbation does not lie in the act itself, but in the dangers that surround the practice, such as the risk of developing into a self-gratifying habit, dependent on pornography to maintain. The act of masturbation that provides sperm for procedures such as artificial insemination, however, generally does not carry these dangers. The potential problems with these procedures lie elsewhere.

Unless there are other complicating factors, procedures that use a wife's egg and a husband's sperm are gaining widespread acceptance.

Of these, AIH is the simplest, and it generally engenders no grave concerns for Christian ethicists.[13] The use of the husband's sperm maintains the integrity of both the marriage relationship and of the genetic inheritance of the off-spring produced by the process. In fact, when utilized within the covenant of marriage, AIH ought to be greeted as a helpful means that assists in the formation of new life—the natural offspring of the marital union—giving expression to the creative love present in the union of that husband and wife.

Whenever it uses only the wife's egg and the husband's sperm, GIFT could also gain wide acceptance among Christians. In vitro fertilization (IVF) may likewise serve as a helpful way of bringing together the elements from an otherwise infertile married couple. But it introduces certain other complications that increase the potential for ethical problems. These will be discussed later.

b. The introduction of a third party into the marriage bond. Although many Christians find AIH relatively uncomplicated in its ethical implications, the situation with other practices, beginning with AID and including IVF and surrogacy, is somewhat more complicated.

Some ethicists argue that these various practices produce an adulterous situation, in that the sperm of the husband is not combined with the egg of the wife. Although there is a sense in which this suggestion poses an important ethical question, the charge of adultery as generally proposed offers an oversimplified prognosis of the ethical problem involved. The technological combining of sperm and egg, regardless of their source, does not entail adultery simply because neither the intent to be unfaithful to one's marital vows nor the act of intercourse is present.

On another level, however, the charge of adultery does raise a difficulty inherent in all technological processes that employ sperm or egg from someone other than the marital partners. Each of these methods introduces a third party not directly into the marriage bond itself (as in adultery), but into the procreative process. Does this introduction of another person in the procreative process constitute a violation of the marital convenant? An affirmative response to this question was succinctly articulated by the 1987 Vatican statement: "The fidelity of the spouses in the unity of marriage involves reciprocal respect of their right to become a father and a mother only through each other."

The perspective offered by Judeo-Christian history on this issue is not totally unambiguous. The ancient Hebrews were characterized by a double standard. They viewed marriage as giving to the husband exclusive rights to his wife in this regard, but the exclusiveness was not reciprocated. Polygamy was practiced in the Old Testament era, but not polyandry. The church, however, has rejected this double standard. By appeal to various sources, not the least of which is the creation story in Genesis 2, it has consistently championed the practice of monogamy. In Christian history, it became simply assumed that the marriage covenant means that each of the spouses may become father or mother only through the other.

Yet, the witness of history does not confirm the Vatican statement without further consideration, for there is a sense in which the contemporary situation lacks historical precedence. Once the church came to adopt monogamy, the only way in which a married person could become a parent apart from one's spouse was through adultery. This link to adultery, perhaps more than any other consideration, led to the viewpoint reflected in *Donum vitae*. Now, however, procreation can occur within the context of marriage yet apart from the union of the sperm and egg from the marriage partners without thereby introducing either the intent or the act of adultery. The only way to find technological procreation to be adulterous is to define adultery not as the willful violation of the covenant of sexual faithfulness, but as the violation of the assumed right of each spouse to become parent only through the other.

Contrary to the language of the Vatican statement, however, the New Testament does not emphasize rights. Instead, its speaks of the willingness to give up one's rights for the sake of another. This viewpoint appeals to the example of Jesus who put aside his divine prerogatives in order to fulfill his mission and die on the cross (Phil. 2:7, 8). On the basis of this example and the New Testament emphasis, a case be made for practices involving donor sperm or egg within the context of marriage.

Modern technological capabilities allow a married person, motivated by the desire to facilitate the wish of one's spouse to give birth to biological offspring, to choose willingly to set aside his or her "right" to be the sole means whereby the spouse is able to become a parent. And this can be done without introducing the physical act of adultery into the marital relationship. Thus, a husband could choose to allow the technological introduction of the sperm of another male so that his wife may become the biological mother of the child they welcome into their marriage. Or a wife might consent to the introduction of the egg from another woman, for the sake of allowing her husband to be the biological father of their child. This decision need not be viewed as consent to an intrinsically unethical act, for the introduction of the sperm or egg of another occurred apart both from any intended or actual physical act of marital unfaithfulness. It is the absence of both intent and act that sets the technological process apart from situations in which actual sexual intercourse involving a third party is employed to bring about conception.

The technological introduction of a third person into the procreation process is not unethical, insofar as it does not constitute a violation of the marital bond. Nevertheless, other difficulties potentially arise from the procedure. These ought to be considered by any couple contemplating the use of such methods of technological procreation.

Several potential difficulties are psychological in nature. The knowledge that the new life was produced by neither their physical nor genetic union may make it difficult for one or the other of the spouses to extend full acceptance to the child. Similarly, the fact that one partner, but not the other, was able to be involved in the procreative process could result in feelings of guilt or incompetency[14] that potentially place undue and lasting strain on the marriage relationship.

The potential for legal complications is likewise present. For example, the question of progenitorship could become a factor should the trauma of the experience eventually lead to marital breakdown and divorce. In such a situation would each spouse continue to view the child as his or her own? And how would the attitude of each of the parties affect the divorce settlement? Likewise, the introduction of other persons into the procreative process introduces questions concerning the legal status of all such persons, which could conceivably trigger litigation. Recent court cases have indicated the legal muddle that can occur when the prerogatives of each of the partners, the donor(s), or a surrogate mother must be juggled. The potential exists as well for legal entanglements in the more distant future, if the anonymity of the other person(s) involved is challenged because of the child's need to know his or her full genetic heritage for medical reasons or in order to insure against an unintentional incestuous union.

A third area of possible difficulties is the trauma which the child conceived through such means will face. This trauma arises from the fact that not only is a third party introduced into the marital relationship, but a third "parent" is added into the horizon of the child. This difficulty could be nothing more than the need to deal with the questions the child might raise concerning his or her genetic inheritance. Yet, the child's interest could develop beyond the natural inquisitiveness motivated by the desire to know about oneself and one's biological background. The couple might eventually need to deal with the issues surrounding very practical situations in which genetic history is crucial to the health or well-being of the child.

The addition of a third party into the procreative process potentially brings a third parent into the child's life. This could occur through the initiative of the child, who sets out to discover his or her genetic father or mother. But it could also arise should the genetic parent later seek to establish contact with the child.[15]

While none of these potential problems is inherently insurmountable, each ought to be considered seriously by any couple contemplating the use of these technological means.

c. Problematic dimensions of technological practices themselves.

When contemplating the possible use of donors, a couple will want to give consideration to the weighty complications cited above. In addition to these, several other more technologically oriented factors add to the problems inherent in certain procedures.

(1) Problems of IVF. Apart from the potential for difficulties within the marriage and family relationships, the process of in vitro fertilization intro-

duces several ethical problems.[16] One of the most perplexing of these is the question of "waste," which arises in several different ways. The problem of waste can emerge through the inefficiency of the process. Whereas in natural reproduction as few as 25 percent of the embryos produced actually become implanted in the uterus of the mother, the failure rate of IVF is even higher. As many as fifteen eggs may be required for a successful implantation.[17]

A more widely known waste problem is that of disposing of the multiple conceptions that regularly occur outside the woman through IVF. In the United States all of the embryos produced in vitro are generally placed in the uterus (which introduces the risk of a multiple pregnancy); however, the possibility is always present that some embryos may be destroyed.

Third, the problem of waste is potentially present each time human embryos are frozen for future disposal or use. Several recent court cases have involved the bizarre problems of the rights of various parties to determine what is to be done with the products of IVF which have been placed in storage.[18]

These various dimensions of the question of waste raise foundational issues, such as when life begins as well as the intrinsic worth and rights of embryos.[19] Does life begin at conception? Is a human embryo to be treated with the full respect due to a human being? And do embryos have the right to be placed in the womb so that they can possibly develop and be born? William and Priscilla Neaves offered a succinct summary of the relationship of IVF to these issues:

> If the intrinsic worth of an early human embryo is no less than that of a newborn infant, IVF cannot be rationally justified. On the other hand, if the principal value of a human embryo derives from its ability to become a baby, IVF may be seen as a moral way of awakening this potential where it would not otherwise exist.[20]

The issue of waste requires that certain minimum guidelines be followed in all IVF situations. The practice of placing in the womb all the embryos so produced is surely correct. Thereby all embryos are given opportunity to implant and develop. Beyond this step, great caution must be exercised in placing embryos in storage for future use.[21]

Although certain cautions ought to be used as a general practice whenever IVF is used, it would be ill-advised to argue against the procedure solely on the basis of the high percentage of embryos placed in the womb that do not finally attain implantation. Even in natural reproduction a great number of embryos are wasted. It seems that even God is willing to risk the loss of embryos in the process of bringing new life into the world.

(2) Problems of technological procreation in general. One crucial question must be raised concerning all procedures involving third parties: Is it ethical to use a person's reproductive capacities apart from procreating offspring within the context of marriage?

Here the issue of personal motivation arises. It is conceivable that a donor or a surrogate could be motivated purely by altruism, by the desire to assist a childless couple in having a baby. Nevertheless, it is questionable if such pure motives actually govern any such action. Technological procedures introduce the temptation of allowing less laudable motivations to surface and offer the heinous possibility that the process of procreation could be commercialized, as donors sell their wares and surrogates rent their bodies.

Steps in this direction are already visible. Donors, for example, are often students who sell sperm for economic reward. Many past donors have apparently later undergone a change of attitude, sensing both a greater responsibility for and a greater interest in their AID children.[22] Regardless of the actual motivation of the donor, the child conceived by such means may never be able to overcome his or her negative feelings toward the donor parent. As one AID child who undertook a search for her genetic father asked, "Didn't he feel any sort of responsibility for the life he was creating?"[23]

A further issue raised by technological conception in general is that of final outcome: Where will it lead? Current capabilities are already producing radical changes in societal attitudes and outlooks. Sperm banks, for example, are already a reality. Will their acceptance, together with the use of technological procedures, lead to a complete separation of procreation and childbearing from the traditional context of the inviolate bond between husband and wife that is so crucial for the psychological and spiritual development of children? Already single women and lesbian partners have sought children by AID. If such practices increase dramatically, they will call into question widely held, traditional understandings of the basis of parenthood and the nature of the marital union. Is our society prepared to deal with such changes?

Other changes are also on the horizon. Practices such as IVF and embryo transfer that provide "waste products" open the door to experimentation with embryos on the basis that they will be discarded anyway. Experimentation has already indicated the potential of fetal parts in the fight against certain diseases. Will we eventually create a society in which embryos are produced for the purpose of providing for the medical well-being of the living?[24]

Technology also holds the possibility of increased interest in eugenics. Current procedures already enable some degree of gene selection. One sperm bank was established specifically for the purpose of collecting sperm from persons of high intelligence. Future possibilities are mind boggling. For example, by combining IVF and gene-splicing procedures, technicians could attempt to eliminate genes that are considered undesirable.[25]

Some scientists are beginning to advise caution concerning the possibilities that loom in the not-too-distant future. Oxford University zoologist William D. Hamilton for example, after contemplating the current trend of "unnatural human reproduction," concluded at the 1987 Nobel Conference at Gustavus Adolphus College, "I would like to see sex kept not only for our recreation but also, for a long while, let it retain its old freedom and danger, still used for its old purposes."[26]

3. Conclusion

The consideration of these various matters leads to two conclusions. First, procedures that technologically introduce a third party into the procreative process may not constitute a violation of the marriage covenant. Therefore, they are not for that reason ethically suspect. At the same time, however, the variety of problems that potentially arise from such procedures indicates that the good they might bring simply does not outweigh the risks they involve. Janet Dickey McDowell aptly summarized the matter in terms of the genetic confusion that arises: "Such deliberate scrambling of lineage seems to serve only the purpose of allowing a couple to experience pregnancy and birth—a purpose that does not seem sufficiently important to warrant the possible confusion."[27]

Second, procedures that bring together only the sperm of the husband and the egg of the wife ought to be welcomed. Although they are not free from all potential difficulties, they can serve as a means of assisting an infertile couple in producing a child that is in every respect truly their offspring. Properly limited in this manner, technological assistance need not be dangerous, but could become a God-given means of assisting happily married couples to enjoy the blessings of parenthood.

PART 3

SINGLENESS AS AN EXPRESSION OF HUMAN SEXUALITY

The Single Life

The divine design for humanity includes the development of the community of male and female as an outgrowth of our creation as sexual beings. The previous chapters viewed marriage as a central, divinely ordained context for the expression of human sexuality. As such, marriage can be a reflection of God's nature and of God's design for human community. Marriage, therefore, is one expression of the divine will to community. But not all people are married. Does this understanding of marriage as the reflection of the divine will to community mean that single persons do not share in the image of God, that they are merely second-class citizens of the kingdom of God, or that they are not living in accordance with the will of God?[1]

The thesis of this section is that there is another expression of the divine will to community, singleness. At first glance it may be questionable as to how the single life could be related to human community. In fact, the emphasis on marriage presented in the previous chapters may be interpreted as raising the question of the role of the single life and of the single person in the divine economy. Closer inspection, however, reveals that singleness is indeed an expression of the divine will, for it too can be a means for the realization of the human destiny as the community of male and female and thereby a reflection of the divine nature.

This chapter seeks to interact with the role of the single person and the single life. It attempts to develop a theological understanding of singleness, which in turn can provide a basis for interacting with several ethical issues that relate largely to the single life.

Singleness, Marriage, and God's Design

Most persons are married. Yet, a significant percentage of people are single. In fact, the number of single persons is growing. Statistics gathered by the United States Bureau of the Census indicate that the 1970s was a decade of phenomenal growth in the number of single persons in the U.S.A. As a result, by 1980 persons living alone constituted 23 percent of all households.[2] And the number keeps rising.

The phenomenal upsurge in the number of single persons is due to several factors. The emphasis of earlier generations on marriage as virtually the sole option for everyone except "old maids" is on the wane in contemporary society. Increasing proportions of the population are postponing marriage or never marrying. As a result, singleness is becoming increasingly accepted as a valid lifestyle. But not only are more people choosing the single life, the ranks of singles are being swelled by the formerly married, a trend fueled by the ever-expanding number of broken marriages.

In this context of an upsurge in the ranks of single persons the question concerning the design of God emerges in full force. The attitude of the recent past maintained that God's intent was that nearly all marry. Is this indeed the case? Is God's will for all persons the same, namely, that they marry and raise a family? Is the single life an option, but only for a select few, and then only as a lesser choice of lifestyle? Or ought singleness to be afforded a place alongside marriage as equally belonging to God's purposes?

1. Varieties of Single Existence

Before looking more specifically at the issue of the place of the single life in God's design, we must clarify what is meant by singleness. In actuality several quite different situations of life may be grouped together under the term. Four of these are representative.

a. Youth/early adult singleness. A first state of singleness is that experienced in one's "growing-up" years, that is, before one is even eligible for marriage. All of us enter the world as single persons and remain single for several years. This singleness almost always extends beyond adolescence, thereby including the first several years of our potential child-bearing state. The current trend of postponing marriage until a person has reached the mid- to late-twenties means that for many, singleness likewise includes several years of one's adult life.

This stage of life is crucial to personal development. These years offer opportunity for the individual to discover one's identity, develop one's potential, and prepare for one's future role in society. Except perhaps for the final years of this stage, its characteristic singleness is not so much chosen as it is a de facto reality. People at this point in life are single simply because they have not yet chosen to marry, rather than because they have made a conscious determination to be single.

The de facto nature of the single life of youth forms the context for the attitudes toward singleness often found at this stage. Singleness, in the view of this young generation, is not an end in itself, but the prelude to a married life that might loom in the future. Further, although this stage is often characterized by sexual inactivity, the young single person is likely to view this inactivity, like the single state itself, not as a personal commitment to celibacy, but as a temporary abstinence that will give way to genital sexual activity at a later stage in life.

b. Unchosen singleness. Singleness can likewise refer to a second stage of life, ongoing unmarried existence. In some respects this stage could be rightly viewed as merely the extension into adulthood of the singleness of youth. It can arise as the continuation of the unmarried state beyond the normal marrying age.

For many people, the continuance of the single state of existence that characterized their youth is not based on a willful decision in favor of the single life. Rather, like the singleness of childhood and youth it often emerges in a de facto manner. Because of several different reasons, the single person simply did not get married. Perhaps no opportunity of marriage emerged. Or, more likely, he or she rejected the opportunities that did come. Maybe "the right person" never appeared, or commitments to parents or to personal goals preoccupied the individual during the prime marrying years. In any case, the older single did not explicitly will or positively choose the life of singleness as such. Rather, this situation slowly emerged as the result of other factors.

The unchosen nature of this state of existence influences the attitude toward singleness that comes to characterize the person. As in the case of the singleness of youth, the single young adult often does not view the unmarried state as an end in itself. In fact, the person's attitude toward marriage might not have changed significantly over the years. He or she might not have given up the desire to be married, but only the hope of becoming married in the foreseeable future.

Likewise, the unchosen nature of this state can influence one's outlook toward sexual relations. Often the individual does not sense a commitment to celibacy as such. If he or she is practicing sexual abstinence, such abstinence is likely not a positively chosen way of life. It might be a "forced abstinence" resulting from the unavailability of sexual partners. Even those who choose abstinence are often motivated by moral considerations, such as the commitment to the principle that sexual relations are to be reserved for marriage (which they may anticipate for some future time), and not by a commitment to celibacy as a chosen lifestyle.

Some unmarried persons, however, come to terms with the "unwilled" dimension of their existence by affirming their singleness. In so doing, they begin to will an existence that first arose in a de facto, unintended manner. When this occurs, singleness becomes for them an end in itself, a chosen lifestyle. But even such an affirmation of one's singleness does not necessarily include a commitment to celibacy. Some who come to terms with their singleness by transforming it into a chosen lifestyle are actually sexually active or wish to be active. And even those who practice abstinence as a definite choice are sometimes motivated by a commitment to a specific sex ethic, rather than by a commitment to celibacy as a personal calling.

An individual can, however, move beyond the choice of the single life and likewise affirm abstinence as a means to a higher end. When this willful choice is made on the basis of a personal commitment to celibacy as a means to the fulfillment of one's calling, a new type of single existence arises.

c. *Willed celibate singleness.*

Some men and women are both single and celibate, because they have chosen this life. They have at one point in life made a transition from de facto singleness to celibate singleness as a volitional decision. For some, the transition is made during childhood or youth, opening the way to a lifetime of celibacy. Others come to this decision later in life. In either case, this transition includes setting aside marriage as a personal option for the intermediate future, if not for the remainder of one's lifetime.

The choice of celibacy can arise as the outworking of several different factors.[3] The decision may be motivated by the belief that celibacy is the best means to accomplish certain life goals. Often these goals are religious, or perhaps altruistic in nature. Examples of religious goals include service to the church in clergy or missionary roles. The Roman Catholic Church, for example, continues the tradition of celibate clergy established formally at the First Lateran Council in 1123.[4]

Although celibacy is not a requirement among Protestant groups, many celibate persons have served well in various aspects of church endeavors. Altruistic goals could include dedication to providing service to underprivileged people. The choice of the celibate lifestyle, however, might also be motivated by less lofty goals, such as the desire to devote oneself entirely to occupation or the quest for fame or monetary wealth.

Some people choose celibacy in the belief that it affords them a way to offer an important statement or because it embodies an important truth. For example, they might see celibacy as a means to speak out against some aspect of modern Western society, such as the so-called middle class values and life—the nuclear family of husband, wife, and two children forming the basic unit of consumption—perceived to be dominating our society. Others choose celibacy in order to express a theological truth. This dimension will be developed subsequently.

d. *Postmarriage singleness.*

A final situation subsumed under the term *singleness* is the unmarried existence that follows when one's marriage has ended. This situation shares certain characteristics with the others. With the exception of those cases in which a person files for divorce simply because of a personal desire to return to the single life, postmarriage singleness, like youth and unchosen singleness, is generally entered involuntarily or arises de facto.

Despite similarities and affinities with the other situations, however, post-marriage singleness differs from them in that this existence follows marriage, rather than either precedes or sets it aside. Because of this important difference, postmarriage singleness is characterized by several unique attitudes and requires certain unique adjustments.

The most significant dimension that affects the attitudes and adjustments that mark postmarriage singleness is that men and women in this state of existence bring to the single life firsthand experience of marriage. Their experiences as married persons vary—from being generally positive, which is more likely the case for widows and widowers to being highly negative, as can readily be the case for those whose marriage ended in divorce. In either case, however, perceptions of the nature of married life gained through personal experiences greatly affect one's perceptions of the single state as a viable alternative. And one's outlook toward singleness is likewise affected, being seen either as a permanent, chosen way of life or a temporary condition to be endured during the quest for another spouse.

The above discussion does not exhaust the varieties of single existence. It does, however, indicate that singleness ought not to be viewed in an oversimplified manner. The term encompasses several quite different situations of life, each of which entails unique attitudes toward marriage and sexual activity. The remainder of this chapter focuses on three situations of adult singleness. Adolescence and youth come into closer view in the next chapter. This division of the material follows the basic traditional Christian sex ethic concerning the single life, which treats adult singleness, however entered, as a unit and views adolescent singleness as a separate category.

2. The Alternatives of Marriage and Singleness

Foundational to the issue of singleness in general is the assertion that God's intent is that not all partners marry; there is a place for singleness in the divine program. Lying at the foundation of this assertion, which appears almost self-evident, is a specific understanding of marriage and singleness which requires exploration.

a. Marriage and singleness as alternative expressions of human sexuality. Lying behind the declaration that singleness stands next to marriage as a valid expression of the divine intent is an understanding of the complementarity of these two ways of life. Marriage and singleness constitute two equal and reciprocal options for expressing our identity as sexual beings.

A theological view of marriage and singleness which sees them as alternative ways of life carries far-reaching implications. It means that neither is to be elevated above the other, nor is either life choice to be deprecated as being of inferior worth. This theological outlook calls for a balanced emphasis on both expressions of human sexuality. It requires as well a sense of mutuality and mutual importance among both married and single persons.

The assertion that marriage and singleness are alternative and equally valid ways of life, however obvious it may appear, runs counter to what has actually been the practice in the church throughout much of its history.

The medieval church, for example, laid great emphasis on celibacy. The single, celibate life was elevated as the pathway to higher spirituality. In contrast, Protestants tend to endow marriage with normative status. Contemporary conservative churches often heighten this emphasis on the marital state further by centering attention on the nuclear family. Church growth programs, for example, focus on married persons, for the church is generally seen as being built on families. As a result, programming caters to the family, singleness is readily stigmatized, and single persons are relegated to the fringes of the church and its life. Singles' groups, even those which receive church support, are often viewed as Christian mate-finding services.

b. Biblical basis.   In contrast to the overemphasis on either marriage or singleness characteristic of church history, the New Testament documents display an emphasis on both. There is development in viewpoint concerning singleness from the Old to the New Testament, and this development forms the basis for the balance that ought to characterize our understanding of the role of marriage and singleness in the divine program.

(1) The Old Testament: marriage as the norm. On the whole, little place was given to singleness in ancient Hebrew society. In fact, the Old Testament suggests that singleness was actually deprecated.[5]

This was especially the case with single women. Although exceptions can be found, a woman's status was determined nearly always in terms of her presence in, or her being a part of a man's household. Her place began within the household of her father, where she generally remained until she moved to the house of her husband (or became a part of the larger household of her husband's father). In situations where neither of these was a viable option, a woman could become part of the household of her brother or her deceased husband's next of kin. The law made provisions, for example, for a childless widow to join the household of her brother-in-law, who was to produce offspring in the name of his deceased brother. An unattached woman, on the other hand, had little place in the ancient society. She was generally viewed as a threat to the social structure and is at times characterized in the Old Testament as a temptress to males.

Hebrew society afforded to men greater social status and thereby also greater marital flexibility. Nevertheless, no less than with women, singleness was not viewed positively as an option for men. Rather, marriage and the continuation of the genealogical line of one's fathers was simply expected as the natural course that all males would follow.

A possible exception to the general lack of status for the single state did develop in the Old Testament era. Singleness was an option in certain cases in which an individual was called by God to carry out a special divine or religious mission. In addition to isolated examples of specific persons, the call to special missions came to be institutionalized in two forms.

One of the institutionalized forms of special service was the order of the Nazirites. These special persons were dedicated to God from birth and as a result were to be characterized by a certain type of asceticism. Their hair was not to be cut, and they were not to drink wine. Yet, as the case of Samson indicates, the Nazirites were not required to follow either the single life nor celibacy.

Singleness was more prominent in a second structure, the prophetic community. There is indication that certain prophets, including Jeremiah, were single. But as in the case of the Nazirites, singleness was not required of the prophets. On the contrary, many prophets were married. One in particular, Hosea, was commanded by God to marry, in order to give additional symbolic value to his prophetic mission.

Religiously motivated singleness became more prevalent in the intertestamental era. During this time certain Jewish religious sects, such as the Essenes, developed within the broader structure of the religious community. These groups often placed emphasis on celibacy as a religious response to the call of God. This development, more than the Old Testament writings, therefore, provides the context for the place of celibacy and the single life found in the New Testament.

(2) The New Testament: a role for singleness. Beginning with Jesus, a major change in the role of the single person and the outlook toward celibacy within the program of God is visible. This change comes to the fore from time to time in the New Testament documents. They indicate that rather than being viewed as a deviation from the norm, singleness enjoyed a place within the church community. For the early Christians, the single life was one means through which a person might fulfill one's divine vocation.

Lying at the genesis of this important change were three powerful examples of single persons who fulfilled great roles in salvation history—John the Baptist, Paul, and Jesus. In none of these cases does the New Testament elevate the single status as being the fulfillment of the person's divine vocation, nor is singleness affirmed on the basis of an ascetic rejection of marriage.[6] What is significant is that each of these individuals as a single person carried out a God-given mission within the divine economy, indicating thereby that one need not be married to serve God.

There is no explicit declaration in the New Testament that John the Baptist was unmarried. Luke's recounting of the events surrounding his birth does indicate that John is to be viewed in the context of the background of the Old Testament Nazirite tradition, for the angel told Zacharias that John was to abstain from strong drink (Luke 1:15). His lifestyle as reported by Matthew (Matt. 3:4), however, lends credence to the conclusion that John abstained from sexual relations and marriage as well.

Paul's single status, at least during his postconversion life, is widely acknowledged. He indicated to the Corinthians, for example, that unlike Peter and others, he was not accompanied by a wife (1 Cor. 9:5). Later, when the movement to a celibate clergy was gaining momentum, the unmarried status of Paul came to be one New Testament example to which appeal was made.

More important than either John or Paul, however, is the case of Jesus. He has always been the most powerful exemplar of the single person in service to the divine program. That Jesus remained unmarried is nearly uncontested. The Gospels nowhere explicitly mention that he had a wife. The absence of any such reference is especially revealing in the descriptions of the circles of women present at the intimate scenes of his life, such as the crucifixion and the empty tomb. Jesus' unmarried status is indirectly indicated by Matthew's recounting of Jesus' response to the report that his mother and siblings were seeking him: "whoever does the will of my Father in heaven is my brother and sister and mother" (Matt. 12:50).

John the Baptist, Paul, and especially Jesus stand as examples that singleness is no barrier to service in God's program. In his discussion of marriage, Paul took this matter a step further. He declared that the single life may in certain circumstances be preferable to marriage, for it can be more advantageous for divine service:

> I would like you to be free from concern. An unmarried man is concerned about the Lord's affairs— how he can please the Lord. But a married man is concerned about the affairs of this world— how he can please his wife—and his interests are divided. . . . I am saying this for your own good, not to restrict you, but that you may live in a right way in undivided devotion to the Lord. (1 Cor. 7:32–35)

Paul clearly preferred the single life. He advised widows and unmarried persons to consider singleness as a valid alternative to marriage or remarriage (1 Cor. 7:8, 26, 40). Yet, in expressing his preference and this advice, Paul did not present singleness as a higher manner of spirituality. On the contrary, the teaching of a group of ascetics in Corinth, who sought to prohibit single persons from entering into marriage and married couples from engaging in sexual relations, probably occasioned his discussion of this topic.[7] Rather than declaring the single, celibate life a higher way, Paul set forth a pragmatic argument. Those who are unmarried should remain so "because of the present crisis" (v. 26).

The chief argument Paul put forth in defense of his preference for single-ness appeals to flexibility to do the Lord's work (1 Cor. 7:32–35). Marriage, he declared, adds additional concerns to one's life, namely, concerns for the world and for one's spouse. Singleness, in contrast, allows for undivided con-cern for the Lord's work. For this reason, remaining unmarried is a wise choice for the disciple, in his view. For the previously married, he offered the same advice, based, however, on his observation that "she is happier if she stays as she is . . ." (v. 40).

In spite of the new status afforded singleness in the New Testament, re-maining unmarried is never presented as a new law. Believers as a whole are never commanded to abstain from marrying. Even in his seemingly strong pref-erence for the single life, Paul was careful to declare that for others to marry is no sin and that for some, marriage might even be preferable (i.e., because of immorality—1 Cor. 7:2). Nor is singleness enjoined on Christian leaders in the New Testament. Paul indicated that most of the apostles, including Peter, were married and were even accompanied by their wives on their journeys. And the criteria for church officers (overseers and helpers) laid down in the Pastoral Epistles gives the impression that most office holders were married, for they were to be persons able to manage their households well (1 Tim. 3:4–5, 12).

In the New Testament, then, single persons are welcomed as full partici-pants in the work of the Lord. Their single status even offers pragmatic advan-tages for such service. But neither the single option nor a commitment to life-long celibacy are ever set forth as the higher road to spirituality for believers.

Singleness in a Theological Context

The New Testament brought an important change in outlook toward singleness and the potential role of the single person in the economy of God. Paul, John, and especially Jesus stand as models of fulfillment in singleness which have served as patterns for many Christians throughout church history. The New Testament, however, does not contain explicit theological reflection on this matter. Offered instead is a purely pragmatic approach. This is most obvious in 1 Corinthians 7, which constitutes the most explicit discussion of singleness found anywhere in the New Testament documents.

A theological treatment of human sexuality cannot end with the prag-matic consideration of the subject of singleness, however. It will, of course, in-corporate this perspective. But it must likewise move beyond the pragmatic to the theoretical and seek to understand the single alternative, like marriage, in a theological context. The question concerns not only whether there is a place for singleness in God's design (which has already been answered from the practical perspective), but also how singleness fits in the divine program. The answer to this question emerges from consideration of two related themes.

1. Singleness and Human Sexuality

En route to an answer to the question concerning how the single life fits in the divine will to community, consideration must be given to singleness within the context of human sexuality as a whole. A theological understanding of the single life, in other words, must place singleness within the context of this dimension of the human reality.

a. Single persons as sexual beings. Any attempt to understand singleness within the broader category of human sexuality raises a question which at first glance seems almost arrogant, but which on closer inspection turns out to be foundational: To what extent are single persons *sexual* beings? The answer to this question appears to be self-evident; single persons, like all persons, are always sexual beings.

Yet what appears obvious in thought is not always so self-evident in practice. We have little difficulty affirming in theory that all persons, regardless of marital status, are sexual beings. And we readily ascribe sexuality to single people who are in the prime marriage years or who are between marriages. But to ascribe sexuality to those who are voluntarily celibate or who remain single past the prime years of eligibility for marriage is often more problematic. To put it bluntly, our society finds it difficult to view priests and "old maids" as sexual creatures.

As was delineated in chapters 1 and 2, however, all persons are sexual creatures. To be human means to exist as male or female, to be an embodied being. And embodiment means sexuality. Singles, then, are sexual beings. And they remain so whether or not they engage in genital sexual acts, for affective sexuality is not dependent on genital expression. Even voluntary participation in a celibate lifestyle does not necessitate a denial of one's fundamental sexuality. On the contrary, it can actually comprise a concrete way of expressing it.

Singles remain sexual beings. They continue to see themselves as male or female. Their way of relating to the world, to other persons, and to themselves is affected in a fundamental way by their biological sex. And their fundamental sexuality—their existence as male or female—is readily noted by others.

b. Bonding: the specific sexual expression. In addition to the basic sexual dimension of relationship (seeing oneself and being seen by others as sexual), the deeper level of human sexuality—bonding—is operative in the single life as well as in marriage. Although singles do not engage in the primal human sexual bond (marriage), bonding nevertheless remains. As has been developed in previous discussions, sexuality is the dynamic behind the drive toward bonding in all its forms, even in the bonding that characterizes singleness.

The bonding indicative of the single life is, of course, quite different from marital bonding. It obviously does not take the form of the permanent, monogamous relationship between husband and wife entered by public covenant and nurtured by covenant renewal in the sex act. Single bonding is neither permanent nor one-person centered, and it is seldom entered through formal covenant.

Although the bonding indicative of singleness is of a different order than marital bonding, it is nevertheless true bonding. Bonding is foundational to the single life and is present on different levels and expressed in several ways. Two such expressions of single bonding are the most significant.

(1) The church. The New Testament indicates that the primary community for the Christian is to be the believing community, the church. And the primary bond is the covenant with God in Christ, and by extension with the covenant community. While this is to be true for all Christians regardless of marital status, the single Christian often experiences this primary bonding in a more vibrant way. For the single Christian the church can become not only ideally and theoretically but also quite practically the source of highest fellowship and the focal point for the development of one's closest relationships. Single believers readily look to their congregation to be "family" in the primary sense and discover within the church membership their deepest friends. Married Christians, in contrast, find community both in the church and in the home. Because of the deep family bonds they continually experience, they readily look primarily to the home as the primary source of fellowship.

According to its original intent, the church does indeed constitute a bonded fellowship, a community of persons. Like marriage, the church community is ultimately based on covenant, specifically, the covenant of believers to their common Lord and, by extension, of believers to each other. As an expression of this, the church is entered by a public declaration of covenant or a public convenantal act. For the early church the act of covenanting was that of water baptism (e.g., 1 Peter 3:21; 1 Cor. 12:13), which entailed not only an outward confession of faith, but membership in the covenanting community as well.

Not only is the community entered by a public act of covenanting, it is nurtured by public acts of covenant renewal. It is in this context that the Lord's Supper derives an important meaning. The continual observance of the memorial meal is to be understood as the occasion of the renewal of the covenant by the participants. Paul alluded to this idea in his warning to the Corinthian believers that a believer cannot drink both at the table of demons and at the Lord's table (1 Cor. 10:21). Participation in this rite is a declaration of loyalty to the Lord Jesus and thereby an act of solidarity with the community of his loyal followers.

Modern Western society with its individualistic emphasis has contributed to the loss of this understanding of the church. Unfortunately, singles' groups within churches often inadvertently foster or are caught in this same attitude. Such groups have a tendency to be individualistic in their approach to the nature of the church and express this individualism in a loose affiliation of the group to the host congregation. It is important therefore that single persons take seriously the church covenantal relationship.

In the midst of contemporary culture the people of God would do well to rediscover the covenantal, community nature of the church as a fellowship of people bonded together and bonded to Christ. Such a rediscovery would assist single Christians in viewing their bondedness as an important expression of their fundamental sexuality.

(2) Close friendships. The New Testament teaches that the primary binding fellowship for believers lies in the church. At the same time, individuals quite naturally form bonds with certain persons within the larger fellowship. For the married this "inner community" is most naturally that of their marriage and, by extension, the family formed thereby. Ideally such bonds develop within the context of the church, as a Christian seeks a believing spouse and as the resultant family is "Christ-centered," that is, takes its identity from the wider church community.

In a somewhat similar way, single Christians often develop close ties with a few others within the context of the church community. One example of such bonding is the sharing of living accommodations. Such bonds may even include a type of formalized covenant. Sharing an apartment, for example, can include some sort of public agreement, perhaps even a legal contract. Unlike marriage, however, most cases of single bonding lack public formalization. Nor do they include the genital sexual activities characteristic of marriage.

The reason is apparent as to why single bonding is informal in nature and cannot be expressed through genital sexual acts. These friendship bonds have purposes that differ from those of the marital bond. They are directed toward furthering the mission of each as a single person, which is, as will be seen subsequently, the task of each to express the inclusive love of God. This expression of the divine reality is not dependent on the bond itself. Rather, the bond arises as a way of fostering the higher goal. Its purpose is to assist in the fulfillment of the task by each individual who participates in the bonded relationship. In marriage, in contrast, the task of the covenant partners to express the intimacy and exclusivity of the divine love and of the divine will to community cannot be fulfilled by either person apart from the bond.

Further, the purpose of the bonds formed by single persons differs from marriage in two sexually related ways. In contrast to the marital bond, single bonding is not designed for procreation and child-rearing. Likewise, single bonding is not intended to include the celebration of the bond formed by the dialectic sameness/difference present in marriage.

(3) Single bonding and sexuality. As has been argued earlier, sexuality lies at the foundation of all human bonding. This relationship between sexuality and bonding is present in single existence as well, even though the sex act as the "sacrament" of the bond is absent. For the drive toward bonding is nevertheless

present, and this drive is always based on our existence as sexual beings—on our fundamental incompleteness, our inner restlessness, our desire for love and intimacy.

To understand this we must remind ourselves about the dynamics of sexuality and bonding. To exist as a human being is to exist as male or female, that is, as a sexual and a sexually determined being. It is this dimension of the human reality (being a sexual being, being male or female) that provides the impetus toward bonding, for the desire for bonded relationship arises out of our sexuality. To be sexual—to be male or female—means to be incomplete as an isolated individual. For as isolated individuals we are unable to reflect the fullness of humanity and thus the fullness of the divine image. We see the other who is sexually different from us, and as this occurs we are reminded of our own incompleteness.

The fullness of humanness, therefore, is reflected only in community. As a result, our existence as sexual beings gives rise to the desire to enter into community, and thereby to actualize our design as human individuals. Sexuality, then, is an expression of our nature as social beings. We are not isolated entities existing to ourselves; nor are we the source of our fulfillment. On the contrary, we derive fulfillment beyond ourselves. This need to find fulfillment beyond ourselves is the dynamic that leads to the desire to develop relationships with others and ultimately with God.

This dynamic is present in a person's life regardless of marital status. Married persons have entered into this intimate bond as a result of their sexuality. But the drive toward bonding as an expression of human sexuality is operative in the single life as well, albeit in a less formal way. Just as bonding is a dynamic of the single life, so also this drive to bond with others in community is an expression of our fundamental sexuality, a sexuality that goes deeper than body parts, potential roles in reproduction, and genital acts.

2. The Theological Significance of Singleness

The single life—even voluntary celibacy—does not constitute a setting aside of one's fundamental sexuality. This negative conclusion calls forth the search for its positive correlation. Can we also conclude that singleness has positive theological significance?

The search for the theological meaning of singleness looms more difficult than the discovery of the significance of marriage. As has been argued in previous chapters, as a central, divinely ordained expression of human sexuality, marriage is a reflection of God's nature and design for human community. The intimacy of bonding found within marriage and which motivates two persons to join together in the marital relationship reflects the intimacy of relationship within the Godhead. The general statement that marriage makes concerning

God links marriage both to the church as the central expression of God's work in salvation history and to the order of creation. As a result, marriage is both an institution of the church and of the state.

But what about the theological significance of singleness? In what sense does this way of life also reflect the divine nature and the divine will to community? To answer, we must notice that marriage is not the only divinely ordained expression of human sexuality. Nor does marriage constitute the sole reflection of the divine nature or of the divine will to community. On the contrary, the marital bond represents only one aspect, albeit an important aspect, of the nature of the God who designed human sexuality.

Singleness represents another dimension. The divine nature and the divine will as reflected in the single life must be viewed individually before a conclusion concerning the whole can be offered.

a. Singleness and the divine nature. Just as marriage speaks about one major aspect of the divine reality, so also singleness represents a complementary dimension. Both contexts can reflect the love of God. This occurs, however, in two different ways.

Marriage reflects the divine love as the dialectic of similarity and difference. The dynamic of the intertrinitarian life lies in the relationship between the Father and the Son as a relationship of divine trinitarian persons who are of the same essence but who nevertheless are differentiated from each other. This relationship is that of divine love, which is both the essence of the one Godhead and is made concrete in the third person of the Trinity, the Holy Spirit.

This divine relationship is reflected in the human marriage relationship, in that the bonding which brings man and woman together incorporates a similar dialectic of sameness and difference. Marriage is the joining of two persons who share a fundamental sameness as "flesh of one flesh" and yet differ from each other as male and female.

Marriage is likewise intended to form a reflection of God as the One who loves. Specifically, the exclusive nature of the divine love is presented in the marital bond. As it incorporates its divinely given design to be the intimate, permanent bond arising out of the dialectic of sameness and difference, marriage reflects the exclusive relationship of love found within the Trinity, for there is no other God but the Father, Son, and Spirit. Marriage is likewise an apt metaphor for the exclusive love of God for creation. It is a picture of the exclusive love relationship that God desires to share with the people of God, a theme developed by the prophetic movement and reiterated in Ephesians 5. Of course, the marriage partners are open to the expansion of their bond to include the new life that their love might produce. Yet, this expansive love is built on and always remains grounded in the exclusive love inherent in the husband-wife relationship.

Singleness, on the other hand, constitutes an equally powerful image of yet another dimension of the divine reality as the One who loves, namely, the universal, nonexclusive, and expanding nature of the divine love. This may be seen by means of a contrast to marriage. The marriage bond is fundamentally exclusive, broadened only in so far as the entrance of children as the fruit of the exclusive love of the spouses expands marriage into the family bond. In contrast, the bond formed by single persons is less defined and as a result is more open to the inclusion of others. The "family" formed by the love of single persons is not the product of the intimate sexual acts shared by two people, but arises more spontaneously out of a dynamic of love that is open beyond exclusive boundaries. As such, the less formal bonding of singles reflects the openness of the divine love to the continual expansion of the circle of love to include within its circle those yet outside its boundaries. In short, the single life can express the divine reality as characterized by a love that seeks relationship (community) nonexclusively.

b. Singleness and the divine will. Like marriage, singleness is related to the divine will to community. But it expresses a different aspect of that will. Marriage expresses the divine will to form a close community of fellowship on the basis of exclusive love and fidelity to covenant. The single life, in contrast, represents the expansive nature of the divine love that seeks to encompass all of humanity in the relationship of community.

Like the marriage relationship, the fellowship God desires with human beings is exclusive. The Bible presents God as a "jealous God." God demands holiness and hates idolatry. The community God's activity brings into existence is an intimate fellowship, one characterized by a close, intimate bond between God and human persons. These dimensions of the community God wills are represented by the marital bond. At the same time, the community willed by God, while a community of faithfulness and intimacy, is not limited to a few. It is open to "whosoever will." Throughout this age in which the gospel is universally proclaimed it remains incomplete and therefore cannot rest or become complacent. It is always seeking its own expansion, so that still more persons can enjoy the fellowship with God, which is the goal of this community.

For this reason, singleness is closely related to the order of the church. Because marriage is also part of the order of creation the marriage relationship derives theological meaning not only from salvation history and its relationship to the church, but also from creation itself. Not so with the theological significance of singleness. Because it is derived solely from the relationship of the single life to the will of God to form an expansive community, the theological significance of singleness is found solely in salvation history, most specifically in the church. For this reason, singleness finds its paradigm above all in Jesus and secondarily in celibate saints in the church from Paul to the present.

c. Conclusion. Marriage and singleness represent different but equally important aspects of the divine nature. For this reason both are significant. Both are legitimate options for Christians. Both have a gift to offer the one people of God as the body of Christ seeks to reflect the divine nature. Susan Annette Muto summarized this point well in declaring:

> In the Church today we need single men and women of profound spiritual depth who, out of the resources of their own interior life with the Lord, live as other Christs in the world and radiate that power to a population hungry for true Christian formation. Singles do have a mission in life to fulfill, a special yet foundational task fashioned for them by God. No matter how narrow or expansive their circumstances, no matter how limited or gifted their ability, they can and must radiate a meaning no other person can give to the world in present and future times.[8]

And this meaning, this task, is to reflect the expansive love of the Redeemer, who wills that all share in the eschatological community of male and female that even now may be found in proleptic fashion in the church. Single Christians, therefore, who because of their abstinence from genital sexual expression are often "in touch" with their affective sexuality,[9] have a unique ministry of love to offer in service to the Lord within the fellowship of the community of Christ.[10]

The Single Life and Celibacy

The discussion to this point has been oriented to the single life in general without taking into consideration the differing types of the single state of existence. The principles proposed have been simply viewed as applicable to the varieties of singleness. But one way of being single—chosen celibacy—is somewhat different from the others. For this reason, the celibate life must be viewed in itself.

1. Celibacy Versus Other Forms of Singleness

Although when viewed from the Christian perspective, celibacy shares with all expressions of singleness certain common characteristics, there are also important differences. These differences center on how the lifestyle is entered and the depth of commitment it demands.

a. Mode of entry. Celibacy differs from other expressions of singleness in the mode by which it is entered. A person may be single for various reasons. Some are single by virtue of the fact that they are young. Others are single because they are older; they have for various reasons not married and now have moved beyond the age in which marriage most generally occurs. Some persons move from the married state to singleness through the death of their spouses or through divorce.

Celibacy is entered in a manner that differs from all of these. A person is celibate by positive choice. An individual can never be celibate in a de facto manner, that is, simply because he or she is not yet married or was previously married. Rather, the celibate person has chosen the single life as the best option for the fulfillment of a personal calling.

b. Depth of commitment. The second difference between celibacy and other forms of singleness is related to the first. For many people, the single life is viewed as a temporary state of existence. They are not devoted to the life for itself, but rather see it as impermanent, the life to be lived or the option to be pursued until marriage or remarriage. For some, this stage cannot end too soon, for their real desire is to be married.

The celibate life, in contrast, is characterized by commitment to this way of living as an end in itself. The celibate person has made a decision to live in celibacy as a life choice. There is no intent to leave the single life for marriage.

c. Celibacy and personal motivation. An individual may enter celibacy for various reasons. For the believer, this choice is religiously motivated. The Christian understands celibacy in terms of being a divine call for the sake of service within the divine plan. The believer chooses this life because it is the way in which he or she can best fulfill a personal vocation in the kingdom of God.[11] Regardless of the exact motivation, the celibate life remains distinguished from other expressions of singleness by its chosen and (foreseeably) permanent nature.

2. The Significance of Celibacy

As a willful decision, based on theological and practical considerations, to live as a single Christian and in abstinence, celibacy is a significant way of life. It carries meaning in addition to that found in the single life in general. This significance lies in two directions, one pragmatic and the other theological.

a. The pragmatic significance. As the willful choice of singleness in response to a sense of divine call, celibacy carries a pragmatic function. The pragmatic importance of this life context was emphasized by Paul in 1 Corinthians 7:25–38. He explained, "I am saying this for your own good, . . . that you may live in a right way in undivided devotion to the Lord" (v. 35). Of course, Paul's point may conceivably be applied to the single life in general. Singleness in any form offers certain freedom from the cares of spouse and family, and thereby it allows for a more fully undivided devotion to service to the Lord.

In addition to the freedom afforded by singleness as a whole, however, celibacy entails deeper freedom. The celibate person has spoken a positive, willful "no," not only to the married life but also to the search for a spouse or the quest for genital sexual intimacy with another human. The psychological freedom this positive decision brings means that the celibate person can be even more devoted to the service of the Lord. His or her attention to the Lord's service is not diverted by the encumbrance of seeking or entering into sexual relationships with another person. The celibate person is most able to follow the advice of Paul.

It is not surprising, therefore, that a high number of celibate people have formed the core of the missionary force of the church. Such persons have offered effective service to the advancement of the gospel. Because of the freedom from not only the concern for spouse and family but also from the search for sexual relationships, celibacy indeed offers certain advantages in specialized areas of church service, such as pioneer missions, work among the destitute, or activity in especially dangerous or taxing circumstances.

b. The theological significance. In addition to the pragmatic meaning, celibacy carries significance as reflecting certain theological truths about the divine reality. This life context can be a vivid reflection of the self-sacrifice that characterizes the God of our salvation.

The sacrificial dimension of the meaning of celibacy arises out of the willful and permanent aspect of this life. In choosing celibacy a person must at the same time give up the other alternative. The celibate sacrifices the possibility of knowing the intimacy of the marriage bond and the joy of family life. Such personal sacrifice is made in view of what for this person is a higher good, namely, obedience to a personal divine calling. The celibate Christian sacrifices marriage and affirms singleness in order to fulfill a personal vocation in the kingdom of God.

Understood in this context, the choice of celibacy reflects an important dimension of the divine reality. It forms a picture of the self-sacrifice of the Son, who willingly laid aside all divine prerogatives in order to be an obedient servant in effecting salvation for lost humanity. It offers a picture of the depth of the divine love, which will go to great lengths in order to meet the needs of humans. Celibacy reflects the divine will to community that takes upon itself the cost of establishing community.

3. Candidates for Celibacy

We generally think in terms of persons in the prime marrying years as those eligible to make the choice to live the celibate life. This understanding carries

New Testament credence, for such persons come into view in Paul's discussion in 1 Corinthians 7. Those who choose celibacy in their youth can thereby offer entire lives of service to the kingdom of God as single persons.

The celibate life is not only for the not-yet married, however. The New Testament also knows of formerly married persons choosing to remain single following the loss of a spouse. In fact, Paul advised this alternative to the Corinthian widows as being the better and more fulfilling option (1 Cor. 7:39–40), although elsewhere he presented the opposite alternative for the case of younger widows (1 Tim. 5:11, 14). There is evidence that in the New Testament era widows who had chosen to remain single came to form a special group, which constituted a type of church office (1 Tim. 5:9). These women served in the education and care ministries of the church.

No explicit indication is found in the New Testament documents that divorced persons should chose celibacy as a life commitment. Yet, there is no reason to deny this possibility. The considerations offered here would be applicable to these persons as well. In addition to serving in ways available to others, they could offer helpful and needed service in certain specialized areas, specifically in ministering to the recently divorced.

4. Conclusion

Singleness and marriage are alternative life choices. The present discussion is not to be viewed as an elevation of the celibate life as a path to higher spirituality. The elevation of celibacy in this way was a mistake made by the medieval church.

Rather, each lifestyle has the potential to reflect an important dimension of the divine reality. And no one lifestyle represents every dimension of the nature of God. For this reason, the church as the community of the people of God must be open to each of these alternatives within its ranks. All people, whether single or married, have an important contribution to make to the work of the Lord and have an important role to play as the people of God seek to reflect the nature of God.

Lifestyle choice is an important matter which is not to be taken lightly. Each individual must choose whether to continue to live the single life or to enter into marriage. Ultimately this choice must be made according to one's sense of calling: To which way of life has God called me? Each believer must come to terms with one's own vocation in the kingdom of God and to the way of life that best allows for the fulfillment of that personal vocation.

Singleness and
10
Sexual Expression

As alternative contexts for the expression of human sexuality and thus alternative means of expressing the divine will to community, both marriage and singleness are related to the divine plan. In a way quite different, but not for that reason less important, singleness, like marriage, can be a means for the realization of the human destiny as the community of male and female. Like marriage, it can in this way be a reflection of the divine nature.

The previous chapter sought to describe the relationship between sexuality and singleness, focusing specifically on single adults. Likewise, it was argued that our basic sexuality as the dynamic that leads toward bonding is not limited to the bond that brings male and female together in marriage. It is present in the single life as well. In this way single persons, as well as married couples, give expression to the divine will to community and reflect an important dimension of the divine love.

Yet unanswered, however, is the question concerning the limits for the expression of sexuality within the single life. Are there boundaries to sexual expression inimical to singleness, just as there are limits on the expression of sexuality within the context of marriage? Related to this general consideration is the matter of sexuality among the not-yet-married. How ought persons in adolescence and young adulthood give expression to their emerging sexuality? To these questions we now turn.

Sexuality in Adolescence
and Young Adulthood

The previous chapter identified several varieties of singleness. One is a stage of life that all must pass through, regardless of one's lifestyle choice, the singleness of youth. It includes one's "growing-up" years, the period of life that precedes eligibility for marriage. The years that extend from puberty into young adulthood, including the teen-age years, are of great concern for the ethics of sexuality. In our society, this time of life is intended to offer opportunity to discover one's identity, develop one's potential, and prepare for one's future role in society.

The singleness characteristic of this stage does not generally entail a commitment to the single life itself, for in the minds of most young people, these years are a time of preparation for marriage. The de facto nature of the singleness at this stage means that most young people do not view being unmarried as an end in itself, but as the prelude to a possible future marriage. As a result, some do not conclude that this stage requires abstinence from genital sexuality activity. And even those who are not sexually active likely view such present inactivity, like the single state itself, not in terms of personal commitment to celibacy but as a temporary abstinence that will later give way to sexual activity. Its temporary nature and the attitudes attendant to it make this stage of life an ethically challenging one.

1. The Unique Situation of Modern Adolescence

Being young, of course, is not a recent phenomenon. All through history people have been confronted with the need to cope with the feelings of awakened sexuality that arise when a person reaches a certain stage of physical and emotional development. Despite the ancient and universal nature of this theme, however, there is a sense in which the contemporary situation poses a challenge unparalleled in history. Certain factors have placed the young person in the modern world in a unique situation.

a. The problem of adolescence. One factor that makes the situation faced by persons growing up in the modern world unique is the advent of adolescence. Adolescence is the stage in life between childhood and full adulthood, which is characterized by profound changes in one's total personal makeup. The individual not only experiences the quick growth to the full stature of adulthood, but also discovers a new force at work in the body, the sex drive that comes with the emergence of reproductive capacities. The goal of these physical changes is to endow the emerging adult with the physical characteristics necessary to function as an adult member of the species.[1]

Although growth to adulthood is not new, modern society has introduced a problem into this process which is of quite recent origin. In our world, a gap in time lies between the attainment of physical maturity and the recognition of adult status in society. This is often most evident in the matter of economic independence. Physical maturity precedes by several years financial self-sufficiency. Generally by the late teen-age years this physical development has been completed. Yet, the young person is not in a position to function as an adult in society. Not yet having completed the process of formal education which marks entrance into the work force as an independent person, he or she remains economically dependent on parents or other authority figures.

As a result of this gap, the years between physical maturity and social independence can be a period of frustration. This frustration extends to the sexual realm as well. Young persons are sexually vibrant and physically ready to engage in the sex act and in procreation. Yet, in the eyes of society, they are still juveniles and are not yet ready to assume the economic responsibility of spouse and offspring, let alone the psychological responsibilities. The difficulty of this situation is especially acute for young males, who reach the height of the sexual drive at age seventeen, an age deemed too young to engage in sexual activity.

One need not agree with his solution to see that Joseph Fletcher correctly pinpointed a problem in the current situation:

> Approximately forty percent of the sexually mature population are unmarried. . . . Social competition penalizes early marriage, and the postponement required by a lengthening period of training for career roles and functions pushes marriage farther and farther away from the biological pressure following puberty. Physical maturity far outstrips our mental, cultural, and emotional development. . . . No human culture in past history ever levied as much tension and strain on the human psychological structure as ours does.[2]

b. The pressures of secularized society. The difficult nature of adolescence is augmented by certain forces endemic to our culture. Among these, three interrelated pressures are most pronounced.

First, there is the impact of media. Modern media—from music to cinema—pervade all levels of society. Today youth are exposed to their influence to a degree unmatched in any previous time. But unfortunately the media have devoted disproportionate interest to the theme of sex. And their treatment of sex is often distorted and misguided, glorifying the sex act and sexual gratification to the detriment of the traditional sex ethic. Because of their natural interest in the subject due to the awakening of sexuality within them, young people are especially vulnerable to media portrayals concerning sex.[3]

A second force at work in the youth of today is the dating game.[4] Already in 1966, sociologist J. Richard Udry pointed out that "adolescent social life is increasingly oriented around heterosexual pairs," a phenomenon that adds importance to dating for young people.[5] This trend has continued into the present. However, in recent years youth have gained increasing access to automobiles. As a result, they are now more and more being entrusted with the responsibilities of dating without the benefit of adult guidance. And for many, dating has become the only activity that carries any real meaning at all. The pressure this situation poses to young people adds to the difficulty associated with this stage of life.

Peer influence is a third force that shapes the attitudes and actions of youth today.[6] In every generation friends have been influential in shaping attitudes among young people. But the role of peers has grown larger in recent years. This is so, in part, because "group consciousness" has increasingly filled the place of influence and leadership in the lives of youth which adults once held.[7] The impact of this phenomenon is felt in the area of sexual behavior as well. Recent research indicates that a young person's decision concerning involvement in premarital sexual activity is most heavily influenced by perceptions of whether or not one's best friends are engaging in various acts.[8] The influence of peers means that young persons are making decisions largely on the basis of input from those who are facing the same struggles as they are. As a result, they find themselves coping with the difficulties of forming a personal sexual identity without the benefit of assistance from those who have already passed through that stage of life.[9]

As in every generation, youth today are naturally interested in matters related to their sexuality. As never before, however, their attitudes toward sexuality are the product of forces—media, dating mores, and peers—that are not necessarily motivated by a genuine interest in what is best for the emerging generation. Lying at the foundation of the popular media's message is the profit motive. Because sex "sells," whereas programs, films, and music that offer a wholesome perspective on sexuality may not, sex receives a disproportional degree of media air time. The dating game as it is currently played encourages the coupling of young people into a series of semipermanent relationships, allows teens to spend time alone as couples, and fosters experimentation with sex. The glorification of sex that is proclaimed by the media and which forms the basis of the dating game is reinforced by the most crucial influence on young lives—"everybody"—their peers.

In this context, the Christian community seeks to offer guidance to the youth of society. Such guidance ought to be both *cautionary*—setting standards concerning the limits of healthy and helpful sexual activity—and *future* (goal-) *oriented*—counseling for the sexual expression that will be of most benefit to young people themselves in the long run. The purpose of Christian guidance is to assist the next generation as they enter into the task of creating communities of male and female that are able to reflect the divine love and the divine will to community.

2. Sexual Expression and the Young Adult

All recent surveys point to the same conclusion: young people are sexually active today in a way unprecedented in previous eras. Recent statistics, as cited by James Moore, indicate that as many as 85 percent of all university students in the U.S. have had at least one experience of sexual intercourse by the age of twenty-one.[10] And a recent newspaper report asserted that half of all teenagers may have had sex before graduating from high school, some as early as age twelve.[11] Other surveys concluded that religious convictions apparently have little impact on the sexual behavior and attitudes of youth who attend church.[12] In light of this situation the question gains new urgency: Are there parameters for sexual expression prior to marriage? If so, what are these, and why are they valid?

a. The question of sexual intercourse. Although the discussion of premarital sex ought not to be limited to debating the propriety of the sex act itself, the question of sexual intercourse is nevertheless foundational for the issue of premarital sexual expression. Is it morally acceptable for young adults to engage in the sex act prior to marriage? The traditional Christian sex ethic maintains that sexual intercourse is to be reserved for marriage. Unfortunately this assertion is often interpreted as the groundless prohibition by a religion that condemns the enjoyment of the body in the quest for the salvation of the soul. This caricature, while perhaps applicable to certain attitudes in the church's history, is wide of the mark. The traditional Christian sex ethic does proclaim a prohibition of sexual intercourse prior to marriage. But this stance is not the product of a body-denying attitude. On the contrary, the admonition to abstain from sex prior to marriage actually arises out of a positive intent, which is body-affirming. The prohibition against premarital sex is the outworking of the Christian concern for the protection of the meaning of the sex act and for the full establishment of the community of male and female.

(1) The sex act and meaning. The traditional prohibition of sex prior to marriage arises from the concern to preserve the meaning of the act. Sexual intercourse must be reserved for marriage, because single persons cannot express through this act the profound meanings intended by it.

As noted in chapter 4, the sex act is intended to be a beautiful means by which a couple gives expression to the deep dimension of their relationship. First, it is a recalling of their commitment to one another. Within marriage, sexual intercourse is a reenactment of the public vows which formed the outward seal of their inward commitment, designed both to represent and to effect the bond between them. An unwed couple simply cannot express this meaning. They may believe that in the sex act they are expressing love for each other. But the intended meaning of the act goes deeper than felt love. As Larry Richards correctly noted, "God didn't create sex to show affection. He invented it to seal commitment." For "sex is inherently a sign of total commitment."[13]

A second meaning of the sex act is mutual submission. Through sexual intercourse, a married couple express their desire to please each other in all areas of their relationship. Premarital intercourse, however, is rarely able to reflect this meaning. Generally, persons engaging in sex prior to marriage are not primarily motivated by the desire to express a willingness to give place to the other in all areas of their relationship. More often than not, their motives center on the gratification of self or the desire to manipulate the other.

Even when the couple is "in love," sexual intercourse can be manipulative, the young man encouraging his partner thereby to prove her love, and the young woman hoping that the act will serve to strengthen the commitment of her partner to the relationship.[14] In this way, one partner might agree to engage in an act, which is actually intended to be a celebration of the bond of commitment between male and female, with the hope that it will bring the other partner to the point of such commitment. This dynamic has been capsulized by Mary Calderone in a statement that has received wide echo:

> The girl plays at sex, for which she is not ready, because fundamentally what she wants is love; and the boy plays at love, for which he is not ready, because what he wants is sex.[15]

The basic point of this statement has been confirmed by Diamond and Karlen. Boys primarily want erotic satisfaction, and learn that to obtain it they must develop relationships, which they may come to value. Girls primarily want love, and through relationships learn to accept and perhaps value eroticism.[16]

The third meaning of the sex act is equally lacking in premarital sex. Sexual intercourse is intended as a vivid expression of the couple's openness beyond their relationship. Even though they may use contraceptives, married couples express in the sex act a willingness to welcome new life into the relationship, including the new life that might come as the fruit of the marital bond. However, unmarried couples generally approach the act with the opposite outlook. Their intent is rarely that of expressing an openness to the new life which could emerge as the product of their union. On the contrary, they are more likely to hope anxiously that no such new life is produced by the act.

The assertion that premarital sex cannot fully reflect the deep meaning intended by sexual intercourse does not suggest that the sex act is devoid of meaning when engaged in by the unmarried. For them the act can give expression to a love for each other which is deeply felt. In fact, one or both partners might truly view his or her love, and perhaps even their relationship itself, as permanent. Yet, until their commitment is given public expression and receives societal sanction, it remains rather tenuous. The future could reveal that neither their love nor their commitment was as deep or as permanent as they had hoped. Therefore, while the sex act may be a declaration of love, it cannot be the reenactment and reaffirmation of the publicly pledged permanent commitment of each to the other that makes intercourse such a beautiful act. Nor can the sex act serve as a sustaining reminder of that day when the couple publicly recited vows of fidelity.

(2) The sex act and a future choice of marriage. The traditional stance against sexual intercourse prior to marriage is motivated as well by the

concern for the ability of young persons to form healthy communities of male and female in the future. Thus, the prohibition looks to the future. The sex act must be reserved for marriage, because abstinence during youth allows the young person to choose with dignity and integrity from the two alternatives that will stand open to him or her in the near future—marriage and celibacy.

Most young people will eventually opt for the marriage alternative. The prohibition of premarital sex is motivated by a concern for the future fulfillment of this life choice, the possibility that the young person will eventually wish to enter marriage. Abstinence is intended to protect the possible future marriage, in that it presumes that lack of sexual experience on the part of both partners prior to marriage offers a better basis for a good and lasting marital bond.[17]

This thesis, of course, has come under heavy attack in recent years. Nevertheless, no one has yet been able to demonstrate that in the majority of cases sexual experience prior to marriage is healthier for the relationship than abstinence. As Richard Hettlinger concluded, "Contrary to widespread myth there is no scientific evidence to prove that premarital intercourse leads to successful marriage."[18] On the contrary, marriages in which both partners enter the relationship without prior experience of intercourse do have certain advantages.

A first important advantage arises out of the link between sexuality and bonding. In keeping with the imagery of the second creation story (Genesis 2), the apostle Paul speaks of this link in terms of becoming one flesh (1 Cor. 6:12–20), that is, the sex act is a *bonding* experience. Paul is surely correct, for through the act a type of bond is formed; the act significantly alters the relationship between the two people who engage in it.

Because of the bonding which occurs in sexual intercourse, the marriage whose partners have not engaged in sex has the advantage of being free from all extraneous bonds, which can be detrimental to the marital bonding process. Previous experiences may bring to the marriage additional bonds that pose psychological problems and thereby hinder the bonding process. For example, they can introduce into that process the ghosts of third parties who haunt the marriage relationship by being a constant reminder of a previously formed bond tucked away in the memory of one or both partners. As the thoughts of one or the other spouse wander back to previous partners, the formation of a solid marital bond is complicated by such factors as guilt, regret, jealousy, or the longing to relive the past.

Further, by virtue of the fact that they came to an end, previous experiences are never without negative effects which can greatly affect the present bonding process. As Tim Stafford rightly noted, "A nonvirgin has already made, and broken, at least one bond, which makes the second bond harder to form."[19] This problem is compounded by experiences with several lovers prior to marriage. From her research Audrey Beslow concluded that "each new lover decreases the potential for intimacy." Even "serial exclusiveness . . . develops a pattern of restraint, a protective covering" which hinders future relationships.[20]

The difficulties that premarital sex introduces into the marital bonding process extend beyond the psychological dimension; premarital experiences may adversely affect as well the forming of the sexual bond in marriage. This is especially evident in the case of young women. Given the context in which it often occurs and the feelings of uncertainty often associated with it, premarital sex runs the risk of being an unsatisfying, even painful experience, especially for the female partner.[21] The Kinsey report indicated that such experiences often lead to difficulties in marital sexual adjustment. As a result, Richard Hettlinger offered this word of counsel:

> If you are going to be able to develop happy and satisfying sexual relationships it is important that your early experiences of intimacy be positive, warm, and free of guilt or resentment. If your first experience of intercourse is colored by disappointment or disillusion rather than by love and understanding, your start with a real disadvantage.[22]

Young men who engage in sexual intercourse prior to marriage also face difficulties. They run the risk of developing exploitive, immature, and superficial sexual behavior patterns, rather than the sensitivity necessary to the future formation of a trusting sexual bond. Premarital relations can lead to a loss of the capacity to love and to feel intensely about someone.[23] This stunted development of maturity can lead to severe marital problems. In fact, the Kinsey report noted a correlation between premarital intercourse and subsequent adultery, among both male and female.[24]

A second, related advantage offered by premarital abstinence arises out of another potential psychological danger. This is one intrinsically introduced by the presence of prior sexual experiences—the danger of comparison and competition. Each partner brings into the marriage relationship all previous sexual experiences. The presence of such experiences makes comparison between one's marriage partner and all former lovers nearly unavoidable. Of course, the new partner might outshine the others. But even so, the presence of previous experiences can mean that the previous bed partners are always present in the psyche of both spouses, especially during the crucial early years of marriage when the bonding process is still fragile. For the nonvirgin spouse, this presence can take the form of disruptive memory, whereas for his or her spouse the ghost of the previous partners could form a continual threat to one's self-confidence.

This point can be viewed from another angle. One dimension of the contemporary romanticizing of sex has been the cult of the *first time*—"you always remember the first time," it is said. Despite the problems this view of sex poses, there is a truth involved in the dictum, one which relates to the Pauline assertion that intercourse is a unitive act. More so than the first time itself, the first partner comes to take on lasting psychological significance. Premarital sex introduces the risk of robbing four people—oneself, one's present partner, and both future spouses—of the privilege of sharing the first bonding experience with one's spouse.

Related to this risk is the psychological damage that can ensue if premarital sex does not eventually lead to the marriage of the two partners. By engaging in premarital sex, an individual is increasing the premarital experiences both of oneself and of another, thereby increasing the chance that neither partner will enter into what remains in the minds of most people today (especially males) as the ideal marriage—a relationship between two persons who have had no previous sexual encounters.[25]

Many young persons (especially young women) who engage in sex prior to marriage truly believe that they will eventually marry the partner with whom they are intimate, thereby avoiding the potential problems noted above. Two factors compound this romantic notion, however. First, many men and women who engage in sex do not marry each other, even though they may be "deeply in love" at the time of intercourse. Second, even in those cases in which marriage does eventually follow, sex prior to marriage carries the potential of future guilt feelings in one or both spouses as they later contemplate the possibility that their relationship might just as easily have not led to marriage or as they wonder why they did not save intercourse for marriage.

Premarital sex among those who do marry likewise carries the potential of disrupting the normal process of marital bonding through the addition of an unplanned child.[26] Rather than having sufficient time to cement the relationship prior to introducing offspring, couples who begin marriage pregnant have the added burden of adjusting to parenthood while they adjust to life together. This situation raises the potential for hostility and subsequent abuse.

A third advantage offered by premarital abstinence is the practical matter of freedom from sexually transmitted diseases. Simply stated, the best way to insure that one's future marriage, not to mention one's own future health, will not be complicated by certain health problems is through the practice of abstinence. Sexually transmitted diseases can indeed complicate the delicate process of marital bonding at its very beginning. In addition to the physical problems, contracting such a disease through one's spouse brings psychological difficulties that strain even the best of marriages. And the long-term effects of such illnesses may be equally devastating including the risk of sterility which could threaten the likelihood of the couple ever becoming parents.

Even though medical advances offer hope of cure for certain sexually transmitted diseases, the best course of action is to avoid all acts that open one to the possibility of contracting them in the first place.

More likely than being a positive assistance to the marital bonding process, then, previous relationships can be detrimental to the establishment of a good marriage. The coming together of husband and wife to form a community of male and female which can reflect the divine will to community is itself a difficult task. Previous sexual experiences so easily compound the process. Abstinence has positive value. In the words of J. Richard Udry, "Those who enter marriage with no premarital coital experience are most likely to have high marital adjustment and are least likely to be divorced."[27] Although the exact connection between premarital experience and marital maladjustment is subject to debate, abstinence prior to marriage performs a positive function, for it is one way of saying, "I value my future marital happiness, my future spouse, and my future family to the extent that I do not want to risk the future for the pleasure of the moment."[28] As Vance Packard aptly concluded from his discussion of the risks of premarital genital activity, "the case for sexual freedom as it is commonly understood—where every male and every female is free to behave sexually as he or she sees fit, as long as no one is hurt—seems to be a dubious goal."[29]

(3) Abstinence and a future choice of celibacy. Not only does abstinence protect the possible future marriage relationship. It also serves to protect a possible choice of the alternative vehicle for the building of the community of male and female—the single life within the context of the Christian community, and the possibility of embracing celibacy. A young person who willingly practices abstinence during this crucial stage of life keeps the door open to a future choice of foregoing the marital bond, in order to choose a life of celibate singleness, for the sake of service to God and others.

Abstinence protects this option, in that it allows the choice of the celibate life to be made apart from the bonds that would arise from a sexual relationship in early adulthood. Because the person is not entangled by the intimate sexual bonding that the sex act constitutes, he or she is free to choose unfettered the other alternative expression of human sexuality. This freedom includes being unencumbered by the pull toward marriage that is indicative of relationships in which sexual intercourse has occurred and being unencumbered by the psychological effects that the bond of sexual intercourse is designed to produce. As a result, abstinence protects the celibate option by allowing this choice to be made apart from any lingering feelings of personal guilt or responsibility to another. The person has no need to feel remorse for not marrying a previous sexual partner. Nor need he or she sense guilt for sinning against the Lord by entering into a sexual bond with another apart from marriage.

This is not to suggest that virginity constitutes a more sacred state of existence per se. Nor is it impossible for a sexually experienced person to choose to live the celibate life from that point on. Virginity and abstinence ought not to be elevated as a higher calling than sexual relations within marriage. Rather, celibacy is significant because of the deeper freedom it gives to the single life. Because the celibate person has spoken a definitive "no" not only to marriage, but also to the quest for sexual intimacy, he or she is able to devote this energy to service to the Lord and to others.

b. Sexual expression and young adulthood. The traditional Christian sex ethic rightfully counsels young people to reserve sexual intercourse for marriage. The admonition toward abstinence, however, ought not to be interpreted as suggesting that young adulthood is devoid of all sexual expression.

Were the sex act the only dimension of sexuality, as proponents of the so-called sexual revolution often assert, abstinence would be a denial of the sexuality of young adults. But as was noted in chapter 1, our sexuality encompasses aspects of our existence beyond genital activity, for it includes what is called *affective sexuality*. Sexuality, understood in its broader dimensions, forms the basis of our sensuousness, or enjoyment of sensory beauty. For this reason we express our sexuality in various ways. It is present insofar as we seek to look our best, not merely for the sake of attracting others to us in a physical-sexual manner, but in that we desire to allow our beauty to shine through. Our sexuality is present in our enjoyment of artistic beauty as well. As a result, involvement in a host of activities can be an expression of our sexuality. And the enjoyment of these activities is important in the lives of young persons as means toward the formation of their sexual identities.

In addition to these, sexuality is present among young people in its highest form as well, that is, as the dynamic toward bonding. Even though they do not as yet engage in forming the sexual bond of the marriage relationship, they nevertheless sense the tug toward bonding. In fact, in adolescence the drive toward bonding is especially strong.

Sexual expression in the nongenital ways noted above is properly present among those who are moving from childhood to adulthood. These years are to be a time of discovery of oneself as a sexual creation. Young people ought to be encouraged to engage in a positive quest to determine what it means to be a sexual being and what form their sexuality will eventually take—whether marriage or the single life. Youth, then, ought to be a highly sexual time of a person's life, albeit without genital sexual activity. The Christian sex ethic is not intended to deny the sexuality of young people, but rather to channel the process of sexual discovery in ways that will be the most beneficial to each individual in the long run. Its guidelines have as their goal the future day when each young person may be involved in forming a community of male and female within the community of Christ, whether as married or single.

3. The Christian Sex Ethic and Dating

The years between the onset of puberty and marriage are not a time of sexual indifference. On the contrary, during this stage of life young people are seeking to discover who they are as sexual creatures and to determine what lifestyle will form the context in which they will express their sexuality as adults. Western culture has elevated dating as the context for making many of these discoveries. The importance of this phenomenon in our society raises the question about the implications of the Christian sex ethic for dating: How does the experience of dating relate to the limits and the proper expressions of sexuality prior to marriage?

a. Dating behavior. The question of limits and proper expressions of sexuality quite naturally raises the matter of dating behavior. How ought a young person to conduct himself or herself while in the dating context?

(1) The purpose of dating. Foundational to a consideration of dating behavior is an understanding of the purpose of this social activity. Three are paramount. First, dating is intended to provide occasion for young people to enjoy the company of persons of their own age. In this manner such events include recreational times within the schedule of school, work, and home life. But not only does dating offer times of diversion from the routine, it also has educational value, as dating events provide opportunities for young persons to learn social skills.

Second, dating can assist a young person in the process of learning to relate to others as a sexual being. The social activities involving young men and women are to provide a sympathetic context in which they explore what it means to give proper respect to themselves and to members of the other sex as sexual beings. Such exploration ought to lead to a growing maturity in personal social confidence and in the ability to relate in positive ways to others. In this process young people often come to sense which option, marriage or singleness, looms as the best personal choice for their futures.

Dating carries a third purpose as well. It is designed to provide opportunity for young persons to determine the qualities that make for good marriage relationships. They also come to see what qualities they ought to be developing themselves as well as the characteristics they hope to find in their spouses. As these discoveries are made, through the dating experience a person sometimes finds the one with whom he or she desires to form the community of male and female within the context of marriage.

(2) Considerations for determining limits. Apart from the prohibition of sexual intercourse prior to marriage, there is a general hesitancy among Christian ethicists to set down explicit rules to govern conduct in all situations.[30] Nevertheless, several considerations are useful in assisting dating couples to form helpful and proper parameters for behavior, beyond the oversimplified approach that cautions them merely to maintain virginity.[31]

The purposes of dating outlined above indicate a foundational consideration about dating conduct. Basic in determining what constitutes proper dating behavior is the concern that one's conduct be conductive to building healthy relationships. The dating couple ought to give first consideration to utilizing social events as a context in which to assist each other in becoming mature persons who can relate to others in positive, beneficial ways. Dating, then, ought to be constructive for each person involved. For this reason, becoming preoccupied with physical sexual acts easily works to the detriment of a dating couple. Focusing on the physical dimension of their relationship directs them away from devoting themselves to assisting each other in exploring their gifts and potentials as persons. And it takes away from the joyous experience of growing as individuals through their relationship.

The foundational principle, *concern for dating behavior that will be conducive to building a relationship that will foster each person's growth*, provides a context in which to raise the question asked by many couples in serious dating relationships, "How far can we go?" To what extent can a dating couple engage in physical sexual expressions?

Here a second general consideration comes into view. Couples must keep in mind that once they get out on the path of sexual adventure, they can find it difficult to turn back. Further, it is rarely possible to return to a level of physical involvement lower than that to which a couple has already moved. A return to sexual expressions of a lesser magnitude than those currently practiced is rarely satisfying, but often frustrating. In fact, to sustain the same degree of pleasure and satisfaction often requires that a couple take the physical dimension of their relationship even deeper, that they engage in an increased level of physical activity. For this reason, a couple must exercise great caution from the beginning of their relationship and ought to be careful to move further along the way of increased involvement with deliberate slowness.

Third, a couple ought to respect several boundary lines in their physical behavior. For example, the line of respect for the other should never be crossed. A couple ought not to engage in any activity that would result in either one losing respect for the other, should the relationship come to an end. Rather, the attitude of each should include the desire to be able to continue to respect the other and be respected by the other, even after they are no longer dating.

Further, the line of future regret should never be crossed. A couple ought to avoid any activity that one or the other could possibly find to be a source of guilt in the future. Such regret may not only arise in situations in which the dating relationship ends. As has been indicated above, excessive premarital activity can also have detrimental effects on a man and woman who end up marrying each other. In addition, the line of uncontrollable passion dare not be crossed. Physical sexual activity is intended to lead to intercourse, if not willfully and deliberately arrested. For this reason, activities that raise the degree of passion can easily result in an unintended involvement in the sex act itself. Couples, therefore, must be careful to draw the line of activity well below the point at which the passion of the moment could blur their vision of their own ultimate good.

b. "Preceremonial" sex. But what about physical sexual expressions among engaged persons? Is an engaged couple a special case that leads to different conclusions about sexual behavior?

A biblical case could be made for greater laxity in sexual matters among engaged couples. The Old Testament, for example, stipulated that unmarried persons who engaged in sexual relations ought simply to be married, whereas persons who committed adultery were to be stoned. On that basis it could be argued that preceremonial sexual relations are not sinful, but merely serve to hasten the wedding day.

The seemingly straightforward outlook toward preceremonial sex in the Old Testament appears to have been related to an understanding of engagement as representing an irrevocable commitment to marriage. In ancient Hebrew culture, the permanency of the relationship began already with the engagement. In our society, engagement is viewed in a quite different way. It entails no binding promise of marriage, but is intended to allow time for each individual to move toward a firm commitment to the relationship and for the couple to prepare for their likely future marriage. As a result of this understanding of the nature of engagement, some engagements do not lead to marriage, but to an awareness on the part of one or both parties that the relationship is best terminated prior to the wedding day.

In our society, therefore, engagement is to be a time for final exploration of the relationship, in order that the couple might move into marriage.[32] This purpose may be thwarted if the two allow their energies and attention to be sidetracked by concern with the physical dimension of their relationship.

There is some validity to the suggestion that engagement be a time during which the future spouses develop an increasing comfort with each other physically, so that the transition to physical intimacy in marriage may not be too abrupt. Yet, the two will enjoy many years after the wedding ceremony in which to develop physical intimacy. For this reason, the goal of finding increased physical comfort ought not to be allowed to overshadow, but must take a subservient place to the greater goal of finding psychological and spiritual intimacy during engagement.

Recent studies have borne out the wisdom of refraining from sex prior to the marriage ceremony.[33] Premarital intercourse of any variety often brings a result opposite to what was intended. Whereas the female involved generally sought to strengthen the relationship by sex, involvement in the act usually weakened it. This phenomenon was evidenced even among engaged couples, for many found that new problems were introduced by participation in the sex act.[34] Sometimes these led to a broken engagement.

These various considerations indicate that the sex act is best reserved for marriage. Couples, regardless of the stage of their relationships, demonstrate great wisdom when they refuse to allow the pressures of the present to move them from a commitment to abstinence prior to marriage.

4. Masturbation

Masturbation, the act of "achieving sexual release by oneself through stimulating the erogenous zones of the body,"[35] has generated heated controversy both among Christian ethicists and psychologists, from the Vatican to Freud. It has been hailed by some as a way out of the dilemma of adolescence, as "God's provision" for "a temporary substitute for the full joys of sexual union."[36] Hettlinger, for example, lauds the practice as

> an escape valve, however inadequate in itself, which makes possible the survival of our society without the universal debasement of heterosexual intercourse to the level of purely animal satisfaction.[37]

With equal vigor, however, masturbation has been condemned by others in religious terms as a sinful, or in psychological terms a perverted, behavior pattern.[38]

Many Christian ethicists are moving away from either wholesale rejection or enthusiastic acceptance of the practice. They favor instead a position of qualified acceptance based on a differentiation of several types of masturbation.[39] The position of the Roman Catholic, John C. Dwyer, is somewhat typical. Masturbation, he wrote, "should not be stamped as 'perversion' but neither is it a particularly healthy use of our sexual powers."[40] Similarly, the evangelical Protestant Lewis Smedes concluded: "It is not morally wrong, but neither is it personally sufficient. It is not on the same casual level with other activities, but neither is it a terrible secret sin."[41]

Any acceptance of masturbation, regardless of how qualified, however, ought not to overlook the dangers that opponents of the practice point out. Three interrelated problems are especially difficult. First, masturbation is often practiced in connection with sexual fantasy, voyeurism, or even pornography. When unchecked, these associations can lead to mental pollution or to overt acts of aggression. Second, masturbation runs the risk of developing into a difficult habit or of becoming a compulsive behavior pattern. In this way it can lead to deep problems of guilt or self-abasement.[42] Finally, excessive involvement in this act can eventually result in maladjustment in future sexual roles. The masturbation habit might cause problems within the marriage relationship or become a type of fetish or obsession among single persons.

Despite dangers such as these, masturbation does offer certain benefits, as its proponents argue. Most importantly, when used within a context of restraint, it provides a way of coping with pent-up sexual energy without resorting to more dangerous or overtly aggressive practices. Hettlinger is surely correct in noting that "to make some responsible choice between, say, masturbation and using a prostitute is surely a mark of maturity."[43] In the same way, masturbation is a better alternative than premarital sex.

With these considerations in mind, two conclusions seem in order. First, the act of masturbation is in itself neither intrinsically moral nor immoral. Rather, the context and intent of the actor must always be considered. When the goal of the act is the occasional release of pent-up sexual energy which is a normal part of adolescent development (or is sometimes even present in adulthood), masturbation can be accepted as a phase of a person's growth. But when occasional release becomes compulsive escape, any positive value masturbation serves is destroyed. In such situations, it runs the risk of becoming a perversion and may also be a warning sign indicating the presence of deeper problems which require immediate attention.[44] The goal of such attention is concern to protect the well-being of the individual and his or her future ability to form a genuine, healthy bond of male and female.

Second, even when used within proper boundaries, masturbation is ultimately unfulfilling. Therefore, it can be accepted only as a phase en route to a higher level of sexuality and sexual expression. It may be a more mature way of coping with the tensions of adolescent sexual development than certain other alternatives, but it ought never to be afforded status as a positive expression of mature human sexuality.

Sexual Expression and the Single Life

A growing number of people pass through adolescence and young adulthood into a life of singleness of indefinite length. For some, this is but the de facto extension of the singleness of their youth, the continuation of the unmarried state beyond the "normal" marrying age. As a result, those who have remained single may continue to be characterized by attitudes toward marriage they held during their youth, still viewing singleness only as an interim state prior to marriage. They may not have given up the desire to be married, but only the hope of finding a spouse in the foreseeable future. Other unmarried persons come to affirm their singleness, which now becomes for them an end in itself, a chosen lifestyle. Whether they remain single de facto or by choice, some single men and women choose to be sexually active, whereas others are either involuntarily inactive or have chosen abstinence for personal reasons. A quite different approach to the single life is celibacy, the conscious choice of singleness without genital sexual activity, with the purpose accomplishing certain ends.

The previous chapter has addressed the ethical issues surrounding celibacy. Here we must mention only the question of the limits of sexual expression among single people who have moved beyond young adulthood and have not specifically dedicated themselves to the celibate life. The previous chapter put forth the thesis that singleness does not constitute having an asexual or nonsexual life. Single persons remain sexual beings. They too form bonds, the highest of which is to be the bond of the community of Christ. But what is the place of physical sexual expression in the lives of single persons?

1. The Single Life and the Sex Act: the Ethic of Abstinence

The central issue concerning the single life and sexual expression relates specifically to the sex act. Is it proper to engage in sexual intercourse? Previous discussion concluded that the marital bond requires sexual fidelity and that youth ought to be characterized by abstinence. But what about those who have passed the stage of young adulthood and are not married? Perhaps their situation is sufficiently different from either marriage or youth. Do older singles form a special case, so that they may express their sexuality through the sex act?

To this query, as to the question of premarital sex among young persons, the traditional Christian sex ethic responds with a prohibition. The single life in all its forms is to be characterized by abstinence. But this stance has often been interpreted as a groundless prohibition. Is there good reason for a single person to choose abstinence? The discussions in these chapters yield an affirmative answer to this query. From what has been said already, three considerations may be offered as a foundation for the choice of abstinence among all single persons.

a. Singleness as an improper context for the sex act. A first consideration approaches the question of sexual intercourse among singles from a negative direction. The principles outlined thus far in these pages lead to the conclusion that according to the understanding of the Christian sex ethic presented here, the sex act is to be reserved for marriage and practiced only within the context of the marital bond, because regardless of the age of the persons involved, singleness simply cannot provide the proper context for sexual intercourse. The limiting of the sex act to the marital bond and thus the corresponding assertion that the single life must be characterized by abstinence arises from a consideration of the importance of context for sexual intercourse. In chapter 4 the thesis was presented that acts do not carry their meaning wholly within themselves. Rather, meaning is a function of act and context (which includes the intention of the actors). This principle is applicable to the sex act. Within the context of marriage, sexual intercourse is able to carry deep and positive meaning. When practiced outside its proper context within marriage, however, the positive meanings it is designed to carry are diminished, or even lost completely.

This is not to say that apart from marriage the sex act is devoid of meaning. Were this so, a case could perhaps be made for engaging in the act outside of marriage merely for the sake of pleasure, a point that is sometimes argued. But to assert that the sex act is purely recreational and totally devoid of meaning is to deny our embodied existence, our fundamental sexuality. It is to suggest that sexual intercourse is an act which our bodies engage in apart from our real selves. But as was noted earlier, the sex act is not merely a function of the body. It is an act of our whole selves as sexual beings. As a result, it carries meaning whenever it is practiced.

When practiced beyond the boundaries of a loving relationship between two married persons, the positive meanings the sex act is designed to carry are replaced by other connotations, which are at best a poor substitute for the ideal meaning the act is intended to carry. Quite often such connotations constitute an actual denial of the intended meaning of the act. For outside of marriage sexual intercourse expresses the concept of bonding without permanency, that is, of a nonpermanent, nonbinding covenant, which is simply a contradiction.

Not only does it represent the permanent marital bond, the sex act is designed to seal that bond. It is a "life-uniting act," to cite the phrase of Lewis Smedes. Sex outside of marriage is a contradiction to reality, in that it entails involvement in a life-uniting act apart from a life-uniting intent.[45] To engage in sex as two single persons, in other words, is to bear false witness about the depth of the relationship shared by the two. It is to proclaim that a life-uniting commitment is present, where no such intent exists.

b. The relationship of abstinence to the advantages of singleness for ministry.

The second consideration approaches the question from the positive side. Not only is singleness an improper context for sexual intercourse because the meanings of the act cannot be expressed by an unmarried couple. The single life is properly characterized by abstinence, because only through the practice of abstinence can singleness maintain its pragmatic apologetic. Paul argues in favor of the single life on the basis of the advantages it offers for service to the program of God in the world. Single people are freed from concern for the affairs of a spouse and thereby are able to devote fuller attention to the Lord, he declares.

Singles who do not practice abstinence lose this advantage. Although he or she remain legally unmarried, the presence of a "significant other," a sexual partner, reintroduces the element of concern for the interests of the other person, which Paul declares to be the characteristic of the married life. The concern that arises in the life of a single person by the presence of a sexual partner can actually surpass that found in marriage. In contrast to stable marriage relationships, the relationship between a single person and a "significant other" is inherently instable. The impermanency of this situation leads to worries and anxiety over matters such as personal performance or the future of the relationship and to a sense of competition, which the permanent nature of marital commitment is intended to eliminate.

c. Abstinence and the single life as metaphor.   Finally, the single life is to be characterized by abstinence because of the theological metaphor which singleness is designed to be. The single life, it has been argued, is intended to serve as a picture of the expansive love of God and of the divine will to inclusive community. Abstinence is crucial for the fulfillment of this purpose. Within the context of the single lifestyle abstinence is an apt picture of the nonexclusive nature of the divine love. By abstaining from the act which celebrates exclusive bonding while remaining open to forming the bond of friendship with many people, the single person provides a picture of the God whose goal is the establishment of a human community, which although intimate in a nonsexual way, remains expansive.

Just as infidelity effaces the image of the love of God which marriage is designed to display, so where abstinence is not practiced, the intention of the single life as a picture of the divine love and of the divine will to community is effaced. To engage in sexual intercourse as a single person is to offer an ambiguous assertion concerning the divine reality. Among other meanings, the sex act, as the sacrament of the marital bond, is meant to represent the exclusive nature of the divine love and to reflect the divine will to establish an intimate community.

The single life, in contrast, is meant to express the inclusive, expansive nature of the divine love and the divine will to an inclusive community. As a result, engaging in the sex act within the context of the single life constitutes a denial of the theological significance of both the act and the single life. It gives a sense of nonexclusiveness to an act that is to represent exclusiveness, and it introduces a noninclusive dimension into a lifestyle that is to be open inclusively to others. As a result, the pictures of the dimensions of the divine reality the sex act and the single life are each intended to reflect are marred.

2. Abstinence and Contemporary Outlooks

The call for abstinence as integral to the single life is not a popular position in the wake of the sexual revolution. But before this position is dismissed, consideration should be given to the underlying world view of the current ethical climate, which forms a stark contrast to that of the Christian ethic of abstinence.

Foundational to the sexual revolution is an emphasis on personal rights. Proponents of the modern ethic generally present genital sexual expression as a "right" possessed by the individual. As a result any suggestion that certain lifestyles warrant abstinence from genital sex is rejected out of hand as constituting a violation of a fundamental right.

In actuality, however, genital sex is not to be viewed as one among several rights intrinsic to the human person.[46] Rather, it is an act designed to carry deep significance when practiced within its proper context. The essential context which bestows on the sex act its significance is the marriage bond. In this context the sex act carries the meanings outlined earlier. But even within marriage, the sex act does not become a "right" to be demanded. Rather, it is a gift instituted by the Creator in order to be offered freely by the partners to each other.

Viewed in this manner, we must conclude that the assertion that the single life is to be characterized by abstinence is not a violation of anyone's personal rights. On the contrary, the call to abstinence is an attempt to assist single persons in attaining fulfilled lives as participants in the program of God. In this context the call to abstinence functions in two directions. On the one hand, it has a negative purpose. It comes as a call to set certain boundaries to sexual expression, and thereby its intention is to help single people avoid the mistake of engaging in a practice which is inappropriate for their life context. But it also has an important positive purpose. The call to abstinence seeks to assist singles in allowing their life context to reflect the theological meaning it is intended to exhibit, namely, that of revealing a crucial aspect of the divine reality.

Further, any discussion of abstinence versus sexual involvement on the part of singles ought to avoid placing an undue emphasis on genital sexual expression as the path to the fulfillment of an innate human need. Lewis Smedes correctly observed that "sexual intercourse is not single people's most basic need. What takes top priority is the hunger for close personal relationships."[47] It is our culture, not biology, that places such great emphasis on genital involvement as the only means whereby we can find the closeness we all quite naturally desire.

3. Abstinence and Sexual Expression

At first glance, the call to abstinence as essential to singleness may appear to eliminate all sexual expression from the single life. Closer inspection, however, indicates that this is not necessarily the case. Singles remain sexual beings, and it would be quite natural to expect to find evidence that this foundational sexuality is being expressed even within the context of the single life. The crucial question, then, is not whether single persons express their sexuality. Instead, Christian sex ethics is concerned with the proper channeling of that expression.

a. Affective expressions of sexuality.   As has been repeatedly maintained throughout these pages, sexuality is more than physical body parts, and therefore there are significant dimensions of sexual expression besides the sex act. The various affective dimensions of sexual expression—including the appreciation of beauty and cultural, social, or aesthetic activity—are readily present in the single life regardless of age.

Some critics of the traditional Christian sex ethic find in any suggestion that sexuality can be expressed in nongenital ways merely a reintroduction of the concept of sublimation, which, they claim, has been discredited by recent research, such as the Kinsey report. Such criticisms, however, cannot boast universal acceptance even within the disciplines of the human sciences. Hettlinger, for example, noted that some psychologists view sublimation as offering "an effective, conscious therapeutic process," an assertion that "is an established fact in the experience of many people."[48] Regardless of the outcome of the debate in psychology concerning sublimation, a full understanding of human sexuality must include its relationship to dimensions of life beyond the genital (such as the aesthetic) and therefore be open to viewing activities related to such other realms as being important expressions of human sexuality.

Of the many affective sexual expressions, the most foundational and the most important in the present discussion is the crucial aspect called *bonding*. As noted in the previous chapter, this dynamic is not only present within marriage, but among single persons as well. For this reason, in this central dimension of the outworking of human sexuality abstinence does not constitute a denial of our sexuality. On the contrary, even the most fundamental expression of human sexuality, bonding, remains present among the nonmarried. And the highest focal point of bonding lies within the community of Christ, which is shared by single and married alike.

b. Sexual expression and personal relationships. But the question may nevertheless remain, where does that leave singles who have not chosen a life of celibacy. Are they totally to avoid entering into male-female relationships? In response, it is helpful to divide such potential situations into two broad categories.

The first potential situation is that of relationships that naturally develop within a community of friends. The single person ought not to limit his or her friendship circle to members of one's own sex. On the contrary, making friends of persons of both sexes, as well as with married couples, can be a mutually enriching, healthy experience for all single individuals. All such relationships are sexual, insofar as our fundamental sexuality lies at the basis of the quest for community, which leads to the process of making and enjoying friendships. At the same time, friendships with members of the other sex need not be overtly sexual. While they may include the more general experiences of touch or enjoyment of beauty, that are associated with our sexuality, they do not include the more specific sexual behaviors that relate to marital bonding.

The second type includes those relationships which could possibly lead to the process of marital bonding. It is not uncommon for dating relationships to emerge out of the wider circle of friendships. Should this occur, the desire to give physical expression to one's sexuality within the developing relationship will likely come into play.

This raises once again the question of the propriety of various sexual behaviors. We have already concluded that the sex act ought to be reserved for marriage. But short of sexual intercourse, what are the parameters of sexual expression for such relationships? The suggestions offered in the discussion of dating earlier in this chapter provide some assistance. Yet, singles who are no longer young adults often discover that their stage of life constitutes a situation much different from the teen-age or college-age years.

An appropriate beginning point for constructing a guideline for such couples can be found in a suggestion articulated by Karen Lebacqz, namely, the principle of vulnerability. According to Lebacqz sexuality involves becoming vulnerable, and therefore it needs protective structures: "The more sexual involvement there is to be, the more there needs to be a context that protects and safeguards that vulnerability."[49] But because it lacks the protections of marriage, singleness is "an unsafe environment for the expression of vulnerability."

Lebacqz's insights lead to the conclusion that adult singles must balance the depth of sexual expression they express within their relationship with the level of vulnerability that their relationship is able to protect. As in the case of dating in the earlier years, older singles must realize that their relationship might one day end; it might not necessarily lead to marriage. Therefore, they ought to give great care to the task of protecting the integrity and future well-being of both self and the other. As it matures their relationship may involve increased vulnerability on the sexual level, commensurate with the deepening vulnerability on all personal levels. Yet, regardless of age, full vulnerability is best avoided prior to the life-commitment of marriage.

c. Postmarriage singleness. Although this situation shares certain characteristics with the others, the experience of those living in postmarriage singleness is significantly different from that of other single persons. This state of single existence follows, rather than either precedes or sets aside, the experience of marriage. Postmarriage singles have a fundamentally different relationship to the sex act than those who have never been married. This different relationship means that the postmarriage state of singleness may be the most difficult context in which to practice abstinence. The desire for the experience of sex does not simply end with the loss of a spouse. Divorced and widowed persons, therefore, are especially vulnerable to exploitation or to mistaking sexual arousal with depth of relationship. As those who have experienced the joy of a bonded relationship that extended to all dimensions, including the physical, they likewise often discover that they are not content with the prospect of living without sex.

Despite these special problems and difficulties, the Christian call for abstinence apart from marriage extends to postmarriage single men and women as well. Again here, however, the ethic of abstinence is not intended to deny the fundamental sexuality of the individuals, but rather to provide parameters for sexual expression which are in their best interest. For this reason the considerations offered about the single life earlier in this chapter are appropriate in this context as well. But beyond its importance for singleness in general, abstinence offers an important vehicle for safeguarding the integrity of postmarriage single persons whose special vulnerability to exploitation and to self-deception potentially lead them into unhealthy or even damaging situations during a tender time of their lives.

By refusing to yield to the temptation to enter prematurely into sexual relationships, postmarital singles committed to abstinence outside of marriage are freed to concentrate on those relationships that will facilitate the healing of wounds and hurts with which they must now cope, because of their change of status. Only after healing has occurred are such persons able to sense whether or not they have gained the renewed strength and sense of personal identity necessary to give consideration again to the possibility of relationships that might lead to another marriage.[50]

Homosexuality

11

Sin or Alternative Lifestyle?

On June 28, 1969, New York police raided the Stonewall Inn, a bar frequented largely by persons of a homosexual orientation. While such actions were not uncommon, this raid ended differently than previous ones, for this time the customers retaliated. During the course of the incident the police barricaded themselves inside the bar for protection from the angry mob that had formed outside. The event at the Stonewall Inn is often viewed as marking the beginning of a new chapter in the ongoing struggle over the issue of homosexuality, the "gay activist era."

Homosexuality itself is not a new issue. Homosexual practices were known already in the ancient world. Several Greek philosophers, for example, reported their involvement in homosexual acts. Homosexual practices were also present in the ancient Semitic world, as is evidenced by injunctions against them found in the Hebrew Torah. So widespread were such acts in the Roman Empire that Paul listed them among the sins of the pagans that Christians were to avoid. Nor did the Christianization of the Western world mark the eradication of homosexual activity. On the contrary, church theologians and ethicists have grappled with this issue from the patristic era into the present.

Despite the apparent presence of homosexuality since ancient times, the contemporary discussion is in several respects quite unlike that of previous eras. Prior to modern times homosexuality was understood in terms of activities, and such practices were generally viewed as deviant, a perversion of normal sexual relations, if not blatantly sinful. As a result, engaging in homosexual acts generally carried social condemnation. Two recent developments, however, have brought sweeping changes in the outlook toward homosexuality. The modern outlook defines homosexuality more in terms of a personal orientation, a sexual inversion, seen as a lifelong pattern.

First, the rise of the modern discipline of psychology beginning in the nineteenth century has brought a shift in the understanding of the phenomenon. In fact, the first use of the term *homosexuality* is attributed to K. M. Benkert, a Swiss doctor, in 1869.[1] The definition of the phenomenon that views it as an orientation which may be normal for some people has gained wide acceptance in professional and academic circles, especially since the events of 1969. This is evidenced by the 1974 decision of the American Psychological Association, however motivated, to remove homosexuality from its list of pathological psychiatric conditions.

In addition to the definitional change, a second development has emerged since the Stonewall incident. A new social situation, gay activism, now forms the context for the ethical discussion of this newly defined sexual orientation. Since 1969 a movement has arisen which seeks to foster a revision not only of the terminology of professional psychologists, but also the attitudes of society as a whole. This new social context has witnessed an increasing number of persons who have not only "come out of the closet" and publicly affirmed their sexual preference but also actively assert that homosexuality as a sexual preference stands on equal footing with heterosexuality. Gay activists now demand that society not only tolerate homosexual acts, but accept the homosexual orientation as a legitimate, alternative lifestyle.

The voices calling for this profound change in societal attitude are not confined to radicals in the homosexual community, however. On the contrary, they include persons within the church and even certain Christian theologians and ethicists representing a broad range of traditions.[2]

The new social context in which homosexuality is put forth as a lifelong orientation and as an alternative way of sexual expression presents a formidable challenge to the development of a Christian sex ethic. Gay activism raises a crucial ethical question: Is the widely held rejection of the homosexual lifestyle valid, or is this outlook sorely in need of revision at this point? In other words, gay activism raises anew the question, is homosexuality sin or an alternative sexual expression?

Homosexuality as a Sexual Orientation

An appropriate point at which to begin the development of a response to this central issue is with the sexual orientation itself. Crucial to the larger discussion is a determination as to what homosexuality is. And related to an understanding of the nature of this phenomenon is an attempt to determine whether or not the orientation is to be viewed as intrinsically sinful.

1. The Nature of the Homosexual Orientation

What exactly does the term *homosexuality* refer to? And what is the genesis of this sexual preference?

a. Orientation or behavior. Most contemporary attempts to define homosexuality, whether by Christian ethicists or by researchers in the human sciences, focus on homosexuality as a sexual preference, and not as specific acts. The term, then, refers basically to the preference for sexual partners of the same sex or to the situation in which erotic feelings are nearly exclusively triggered by persons of one's own sex. An example of this modern approach with its emphasis on orientation rather than behavior is the definition offered by the Roman Catholic ethicist, John Dwyer. Preferring that "homosexuality" be used only to refer to the orientation, he defined the term as "*a preference,* on the part of *adults,* for *sexual behavior* with members of their own sex."[3]

The focus on orientation apart from behavior has led to two important results. First, the modern understanding has encouraged various researchers to attempt to determine the extent to which the homosexual preference is present in contemporary society. It is estimated that in the United States 3–5 percent of the adult male population, and a smaller percentage of females, are homosexual in orientation. Some researchers dispute these findings as being too high.[4] Recent findings also suggest that one fourth to one third of adult males have had some overt homosexual feelings or experience, generally between the onset of puberty and age sixteen.[5] This finding has led many researchers to differentiate between homosexual orientation as "a *phase* to be passed through and a *constant* to be lived with."[6] Second, the modern emphasis on orientation has led some ethicists to conclude that the biblical authors lacked an awareness of homosexuality as a sexual inversion, as a stable, lifelong sexual preference.[7]

The viewpoint that homosexuality is best understood as a lifelong sexual preference rather than in terms of activities has not attained universal adherence, however. Recently, the thesis has come under formidable attack. Sociologist David Greenberg, for example, rejects all such "essentialist" theories. He asserts that homosexuality is not an essence or condition that some people have and others do not. Rather than a static orientation, it is a behavior produced and interpreted in different ways by different societies at different times. Homosexual identity, then, is a social label, he maintains.[8] Although Greenberg's critique warrants further reflection, the more widely held differentiation between orientation and conduct will be employed for purposes of the discussion in this chapter.

b. The source of the homosexual orientation: heredity versus environment. Although recent discussions have led to broad agreement (despite critics such as Greenberg) that homosexuality is to be viewed primarily as a sexual orientation, the question concerning the source of the orientation has remained controversial. Two basic viewpoints have been defended in recent years. These two reflect to some extent the general discussion of heredity and environment carried out by biology and psychology.*

Since the early 1950s researchers have explored the thesis that certain

---

*For a helpful summary of the major positions, see Earl D. Wilson, *Counseling and Homosexuality* (Waco, Tex.: Word, 1988), 54–73.

inherited features are responsible for the homosexual orientation. Proposals have included genetic makeup, abnormal prenatal or postnatal hormonal levels, and distortions of the normal, unified development of various tissues related to sexuality and sexual behavior.[9] Despite their repeated use by persons sympathetic to the gay activist movement,[10] none of these proposals has been able to prove itself to be the sole cause of sexual preference.[11] Research into possible inherited causes has resulted in a general consensus that biological factors themselves are insufficient to produce the homosexual orientation.[12] To heredity must be added certain environmental stimuli. John Money's conclusion is representative of many researchers:

> . . . a prenatal disposition is probably in itself an insufficient cause, which needs to be augmented by postnatal social experience. In studying some, but by no means all, families, it is relatively easy to implicate familial interaction as a component factor in gender-identity maldifferentiation in one of the offspring. This same statement applies to obligative (as contrasted with facultative) homosexuality, and also to transvestism, transexualism and related psychosexual malfunctions.[13]

Others argue on the basis of the purported presence of homosexuality among animals. But this theory has likewise failed to generate widespread acceptance. Diamond and Karlen concluded that "homosexuality as we use the word of people, is uniquely human."[14] Building on the findings of the human sciences, Ruth Tiffany Barnhouse declared, "it seems clear that arguments in favor of the acceptance of homosexuality cannot be based on biological evidence, either animal or human. On the contrary, if such evidence is considered relevant at all, it points the other way."[15]

In the wake of the insufficiency of biological factors to explain sexual preference, the thesis that homosexuality as the product of psychological factors has gained importance. According to Masters and Johnson, it is a learned preference.[16]

Foundational for this view has been the work of Irwin Bieber, who suggested that disturbances in child development, especially in the area of parent-child relationships, are responsible.[17] Such disturbances result in confusion concerning the child's sexual identity. Possible situations that could lead to a same-sex preference in males include a possessive mother, a remote and unresponsive father, an early indoctrination with excessively negative ideas about sex, or enforced isolation from women. In addition to disturbed family relationships, some theorists point to other factors. They cite difficulties in establishing—or inability to establish—successful heterosexual relationships in adolescence as triggering a movement toward homosexuality. This sexual orientation frees the person from the perceived awesome responsibilities of heterosexuality.[18]

Hettlinger aptly capsulized the current understanding of the causes of male homosexuality:

> It is possible that some inherited characteristics may render a man susceptible to homosexual deviation; but without the contributing influences of inadequate family relationships and cultural pressures, these potentialities do not become decisive. Most authorities attribute the homosexual condition to a combination of psychological and sociological factors which prevent the individual from achieving full and free personal relationships with the other sex.[19]

And Lawrence J. Hatterer claimed as early as 1971 that because homosexuality arises from a confusion about sexual identity, homosexuals "are made, not born."[20]

2. Homosexuality and Sin

The debate concerning the nature of the homosexuality and the causes of same-sex preference forms a context for the theological question about the relationship of homosexuality, however understood, and sin. At this point the biblical documents enter into a discussion with the modern human sciences. Crucial in this dialogue are questions relating to homosexuality as it was known in the biblical era. What understanding of homosexuality is reflected in the several texts that are often cited as referring to this phenomenon? And do these texts declare that homosexuality is sinful?

a. Arguments against the sinfulness of homosexuality. According to some ethicists, the homosexual orientation is not sinful, for the Bible does not condemn it as such. Therefore acts that express this sexual preference are likewise not culpable. Two major arguments are offered in support of this conclusion.

(1) Homosexuality as "natural." Proponents of an acceptance of homosexuality argue that both the orientation itself and acts that express it are natural. Those who claim that this sexual preference is natural often appeal to the presence of the phenomenon in various societies and throughout history. Proponents, however, are not always unbiased in indicating how widespread the phenomenon is. In some societies it is virtually unknown.[21] And the homosexual behavior present in non-Western societies is rarely similar to the lifelong orientation that is claimed to be natural. Rather, such acts are often associated with adolescent sexual development, becoming ritualized rites of passage.[22] The same was true of homosexual practices in ancient cultures.[23]

Nor does the often-cited presence of homosexuality in ancient Greece offer a model for the contemporary phenomenon. The Greek philosophers routinely mentioned by proponents actually engaged in pederasty, that is, homosexual acts with boys between puberty and age twenty, and not in the same-sex be-havior between men advocated today. Although some philosophers hailed re-lations between men and youths as the highest form of love, their outlook was probably more reflective of a dualistic anthropology and a bias against women than an actual affirmation of homosexuality as a general practice. And even those who extolled the beauty of such liaisons were troubled by their inevitable instability and the fact that such acts could not be reciprocal. As a result such relationships came to be spiritualized and the sexual content increasingly di-minished.[24] In the wider Greek society, homosexuality was considered deviant and was generally illegal.[25]

For Christian ethicists the question of the naturalness of homosexuality has spilled over into the area of biblical exegesis. It is, of course, difficult to avoid the conclusion that certain biblical texts speak of some homosexual acts in a negative manner. The passages at issue include the story of Lot and Sodom (Gen. 19:4–11 plus other references to the sin of Sodom), the incident in Gibeah (Judg. 19), the prohibitions of the Holiness Code (Lev. 18:22 and 20:13), and the Pauline condemnation of sinful practices (Rom. 1:26–27; 1 Cor. 6:9; and 1 Tim. 1:10). Advocates of an openness to homosexuality, however, do not find in these texts a definitive rejection of homosexuality as such. Rather, they claim that homosexuality as a natural, lifelong orientation was not what the biblical prohibitions have in view.

Scholars who come to a sympathetic view with regard to homosexuality generally follow one basic line of argument. The sin of Sodom and of the in-habitants of Gibeah was not homosexuality per se, but inhospitality, attempted rape, or even the desire to cohabit with angels.[26] The prohibitions found in the Holiness Code refer to idolatrous sexual relations. The Pauline injunctions ei-ther continue the Leviticus condemnation of such acts associated with idola-try, or refer to practices known in ancient Greece, such as pederasty or ho-mosexual prostitution (1 Cor. 6:9; 1 Tim. 1:10).[27] The current phenomenon of homosexually oriented persons, the argument concludes, was unknown to the biblical authors, and therefore neither the natural homosexual preference nor its behavioral expression is what is prohibited by the Bible.

The biblical texts cited above demand a cautious approach. Regardless of the conclusion reached, the exegesis offered by persons sympathetic to ho-mosexuality has at certain points provided helpful insights into the biblical texts that deal with this matter. For example, although the sexual context of the episodes of both Sodom and Gibeah are undeniable (cf. Gen. 19:8), it is indeed unlikely that homosexual activities per se are in view here. Rather, the practice, found in various cultures, to utilize homosexual anal violation as a reminder of subordinate status,[28] might provide a clue to the intent of wicked residents of these two cities. It is possible that their purpose was not to engage in homosexual acts as such, but to employ this heinous cultural practice as a way of showing inhospitality to the strangers Lot was harboring.

This interpretation would fit with Ezekiel's characterization of the sins of Sodom (Ezek. 16:49–50). And the Jude commentary on Sodom, that the men went after "strange flesh" (verse 7, KJV), might not focus on homosexuality either. This reference follows immediately the mention of sinful angels (verse 6), which some scholars interpret as a reference to the cohabitation of angels and humans, presumably found in Genesis 6:1–4. Jude, therefore, might have in view the desire of the Sodomites to have sexual relations with angelic beings.

Despite the positive assistance it offers at some points, the case presented by contemporary exegetes is not without difficulties. The references found in the Holiness Code form an example. H. Darrell Lance, who made the point above regarding the practice of anal violation and who himself favors a more open stance toward homosexuality, nevertheless concluded, "Both Leviticus 18:22 and 20:13 are unambiguous in their practical effect: homosexual relations between Israelite men are forbidden and are punishable by death." This prohibition is grounded not only in the connection to idolatry—which is likely not to be understood in terms of male cult prostitutes, as some would maintain.[29] It is grounded also in creation: "Such acts violated the created order of male and female and are *tô'ēbāh*: they are an idolatrous affront to the integrity of the deity."[30] One need not advocate a continuation of the Old Testament punishment by death (as some would erroneously claim necessarily follows) to assert that the prohibition continues to carry its import into the present.[31]

The question at issue in 1 Corinthians 6:9 is the meaning of the Greek words, *malakoi* and *arsenokoitai,* the latter of which is repeated in 1 Timothy 1:10. Many exegetes have been quick to accept the conclusion of John Boswell that neither of these terms "connoted homosexuality in the time of Paul or for centuries thereafter."[32] Some do offer interpretations of the words that relate them to specific homosexual behaviors, however, whether to the "callboy" and his patron[33] or to the Greek practice of pederasty (homosexual acts between men and youths).

Boswell's conclusion, however, is not without its critics. From his survey of the pertinent literature, David F. Wright, for example, concluded, "It is difficult to believe that *arsenokoitai* was intended to indict only the commonest Greek relationship involving an adult and a teenager."[34] Rather, as its uses by Philo and Josephus indicate, it was a more generic term for male activity with males.

Of the various texts, the exegesis of Romans 1 is most problematic. Those who claim that Paul's condemnation of homosexual activity is not applicable to the contemporary phenomenon generally follow one basic tactic. Paul, they claim, was referring to individuals who pervert their own heterosexual orientation and engage in homosexual practices (e.g., pederasty), and not to persons who find in themselves a "natural" homosexual preference (inversion), concerning which Paul supposedly knew nothing.

This approach, however, fails to understand the development of Paul's indictment of the pagan world of his day. As Richard Hayes noted in his response to Boswell's book,[35] it is highly improbable that the apostle had in mind the life histories of a certain group of his contemporaries who had moved from heterosexuality to homosexuality. Rather, his purpose was to offer a corporate indictment of pagan society. The story he narrated is that of humankind; he offered a general sweep of the corporate downward spiral into an ever deeper pit of sin. Humankind had distorted even the basic sexual identity which had been given in God's created order as indicated by the Genesis story.

But on what basis did Paul assert that heterosexuality is "natural" and homosexuality "unnatural?" Some exegetes, such as H. Darrell Lance,[36] have argued that by "nature" Paul was not appealing to the created order, but to what is "characteristic of a certain group or species." Although Lance's characterization could possibly apply to 1 Corinthians 11:14–15, as he asserted, it simply cannot be the case in Romans 1. The inclusion of same-sex relations between women in Paul's indictment indicates that he had more than the contemporary practice of pederasty in view. And the mood of the text with its repeated emphasis of God's acting in judgment suggests that the perversion Paul had in mind is far more serious than the violation of species characteristics; it is rather the violation of God's intent in creation.

For Paul, then, the only proper model of sexual relations is that patterned after the creation story in Genesis 1–2. In keeping with the injunctions of the Holiness Code, Paul concludes that this model is natural,[37] for it alone was instituted by the Creator. Homosexual relations, whether between men or women, are against nature, because they are contrary to the pattern placed within creation itself.

One final problem with the appeal to the naturalness of homosexuality remains. Even if the homosexual orientation could be shown to be the "natural" inclination for a certain percentage of the population in any given society, that fact alone would not necessitate an acceptance of homosexual activity. Ethics is not merely a condoning of what comes naturally. On the contrary, Christian theology warns us that we dare not always entrust ourselves to what we sense to be "natural." Our natural inclinations are not a sure guide to proper human conduct, but share in our fallenness. Jesus himself warned his followers that evil can proceed from the human heart (Mark 7:21). For this reason, disciples of the Lord are often called to deny what they may perceive to be their natural desires and inclinations, in order to follow the radical ethic of the Master.

Caution is warranted as much in the area of sexual conduct as in any other. Even though some researchers conclude that males are naturally promiscuous, this supposedly natural inclination does not set aside the biblical ethic of fidelity. So also, the felt "naturalness" of same-sex preference among a certain percentage of persons does not set aside the biblical ethic which limits genital sexual expression to the context of monogamous heterosexual marriage.

(2) Homosexuality as not the product of conscious choice. Closely related to the argument that homosexuality is "natural" and therefore acceptable is the assertion that it is an orientation that the person does not choose, but discov-

ers as a given. The individual does not actively seek to develop a same-sex preference, the argument asserts. She or he simply discovers this to be one dimension of her or his personal reality.

Further, the basic givenness of sexual orientation is not altered by the outcome of the question of heredity verses environment. Whether a person's homosexuality is due to genetic makeup or to postnatal pyschological factors and parental relationships does not alter the fact, it is argued, that an individual discovers this orientation, rather than consciously chooses it.

The argument from the unchosen nature of sexual preference does remind us of an important point. It is surely correct that most persons do not consciously set out to develop a same-sex orientation. Further, insofar as the attitudes and actions of others, especially parental influences, contribute to the development of sexual preference, there is a sense in which many persons who discover in themselves a same-sex preference are to be viewed in part as the "sinned against." Other persons have contributed to their present situation.

But the argument that homosexuality is unchosen and therefore acceptable is not without problems. It must be faulted as presenting an overly simplistic picture of the development of sexual orientation in at least two ways. First, even though genetic makeup and external factors dispose a person to one sexual orientation, the element of personal choice is generally not fully lacking. Most individuals are to some extent actively involved in the development of personal sexual orientation.

This viewpoint is gaining adherence among psychologists. Many now argue that although experiences in early childhood are crucial, final sexual preference does not solidify until after puberty,[38] perhaps not until early adulthood. Some researchers refuse to speak of the presence of a permanent homosexual orientation in persons younger than about twenty-five years.[39] Homosexuality, then, is a pattern that develops over time and one in which the individual involved might actually have some active role.

Second, Christian ethics maintains that personal responsibility is not limited to matters in which we exercise full choice. This is true both of our involvement in particular acts and in sin in general. We are enslaved to sin, the Bible indicates. Although this situation might not be the result of a conscious, personal choice, we remain responsible. The Bible, then, never seeks to excuse persons on the basis of the suggestion that they are not responsible, because they did not consciously choose to be the way they are. Rather, the answer the Bible offers is the grace of God becoming active in the midst of our fallenness, failure, and sin.

b. The dimension of sin in homosexuality.   Neither its supposed naturalness nor its supposed inevitableness requires that homosexuality simply be accepted. But the question remains as to whether or not this phenomenon ought to be termed "sin," and if so in what sense it is sinful.

(1) Fallenness, sin and condemnation. En route to an answer to the question

of the sinfulness of homosexuality, it is important to delineate an understanding of sin itself and the relationship between sin and both fallenness and condemnation. Christian theology maintains that the present world is fallen; it does not measure up to the fullness of the intent of God. Even creation, Paul indicated, longs for liberation from the fallen state, a liberation that it will experience at the consummation of God's activity in history. We too are fallen, for each of us does not measure up to God's design for our lives. This fallenness extends beyond our actions to our existence in its various dimensions—including body (which will be transformed at the resurrection) and disposition (which one day will be conformed to the character of Christ).

Because our fundamental fallenness is not in accordance with God's intent, it is related to the concept of sin. The latter term refers basically to the failure to measure up to God's standards. For this reason, "sin" could aptly be used with reference to every dimension of human life, including the physical and the dispositional, that fails to reflect the design of God. For this design will only be fully present in the future. Generally, however, we use the term *sin* only to speak about human actions that fail to conform to the divine standard of morality, that is, to human failure to do what God commands or to human transgression of divine prohibitions.

"Fallenness" and "sin" introduce a third term, "condemnation." The Bible speaks of divine judgment and condemnation in a twofold sense. On the one hand, every dimension of the fallenness of creation will be transformed at the consummation of the age; in this sense our fallenness comes under divine judgment. But on the other hand, "condemnation," while not unrelated to fallenness, is generally used of sinful actions. In fact, the texts that deal with the subject consistently speak of divine judgment and condemnation in terms of testing what we do (e.g., Romans 2:3; 2 Cor. 5:10; Rev. 20:12). Putting the two dimensions together, we may conclude that our fallenness will be made whole at the final judgment, whereas our sinful actions will be condemned.

(2) Condemnation and homosexuality. The connection among the terms "fallenness," "sin," and "condemnation" provides a clue to an understanding of the sinful dimension of homosexuality. It suggests that a differentiation must be made between disposition and action in the area of sexual preference, as in every other area.

When compared to the biblical understanding of the creative intent of God, the homosexual orientation falls short of God's ideal. The Genesis creation stories indicate quite clearly that heterosexuality forms the basis of the dynamic of human sexual bonding from the beginning, an outlook confirmed by Jesus himself. Although the homosexual orientation is not God's ideal, this conclusion does not mean that the disposition itself is condemnable. Short of the eschatological renewal of human fallenness in its entirety, the condemnation of God rests not on human dispositions themselves, even though they participate in human fallenness, but on actions that flow from them. In the case of homosexuality, the tendency to be erotically aroused by members of the same sex, while potentially dangerous and placing the person at certain disadvantages, does not itself invoke the condemnation of God. Rather, sin as the transgression of divine prohibition occurs only when this disposition is allowed to express itself in actions contrary to God's intention that genital sexual activity occur within the context of monogamous heterosexual marriage.

Actually, the same principle is operative in the heterosexual orientation as well. The Genesis narratives indicate that the male-female difference lies at the basis of the forming of human sexual bonding. But even though heterosexuality is in keeping with the intent of the Creator, not all expressions of this disposition are ethically acceptable. On the contrary, the opposite-sex preference, like the same-sex orientation, can lead to sinful acts. Lust, premarital sex, incest, rape, and adultery are all condemnable, whether perpetrated by persons of a heterosexual or a homosexual orientation. In short, there are proper parameters for sexual expression. Sexual acts outside their proper context must be judged inappropriate. This principle is applicable regardless of the degree to which an individual was consciously involved in the choice of sexual preference. We may have only limited control over our orientation. We are nevertheless responsible for the choices we make about its expression.

Although the homosexual preference need not be judged as condemnable in itself, at the same time this orientation ought not to be put forth as normal nor be accepted as an alternative on an equal level with heterosexuality. The fact remains that the Bible sets forth heterosexuality as God's design for creation.

Recent findings among the human sciences indicate that adolescents move through a stage of development in which certain same-sex activities are often present. But the ideal is for individuals to move beyond that stage, rather than to develop permanent homosexual behavior patterns.[40] Ruth Tiffany Barnhouse, therefore, is surely correct in speaking of homosexuality as "immature," as constituting a less developed sexuality. In a similar way Elizabeth Moberly classified homosexuality as a state of incomplete development or of unmet needs.[41] Theologically seen, this orientation constitutes an unfortunate truncation of development into God's ideal as found in creation.

Not only is homosexuality less than the divine ideal, an arresting of normal sexual development at an immature stage, there is growing opinion that it is "positively harmful" because of its effect on the young. Barnhouse is again instructive at this point:

> Adolescence is a period which requires the utmost of young people in working their way through the enormously difficult transition from childhood to adulthood. . . . the anxieties surrounding the psychosexual maturation process are severe, and the temptation to opt for less than one is capable of is very great. While it is probably true that one cannot proselytize the invulnerable, there are a great many

youngsters whose childhoods have been sufficiently problematic so that homosexuality presented to them as an acceptable alternative would be convincingly attractive.[42]

Homosexuality, then, is not in itself condemnable as an orientation. Yet, it falls short of God's best for human beings and poses certain dangers. Persons caught in this arrested stage of sexual development are not to be condemned, but like all fallen human beings they are to be viewed as objects of God's concern and in need of experiencing God's grace.

3. Can the Orientation be Altered?

The homosexual orientation apart from its expression in actions and behaviors is not itself condemnable. Nevertheless, it falls short of God's intent in creation. This conclusion raises the ticklish question of the possibility of an alteration of the orientation. Can a homosexual person become heterosexual?

Researchers offer a mixed opinion as to the possibility of change in sexual orientation. Recent statistics indicate anywhere from a one-third to two-thirds success rate,[43] apparently depending in part on the degree of motivation for change.

Even evangelicals are divided on the issue of the possibility of a change in sexual orientation. Groups such as Homosexuals Anonymous or Exodus International, an umbrella organization for about fifty ministries, are part of a fledgling ex-gay movement. The assertion that homosexuals can and ought to change, as well as the ex-gay movement itself, is attacked by Evangelicals Concerned, an organization that promotes monogamous relationships between Christian homosexuals. Writing in *Christianity Today,* Tim Stafford concluded his study of the various groups with "cautious optimism": He said, "The degrees of healing vary. But the possibility of living an adjusted, hopeful, and fruitful life in a sin-distorted world—and the possibility of growing more joyful and consistent in life—remain."[44]

All researchers, however, are in agreement on one point. If change is to come, it is difficult. According to Jones and Workman,

> No study suggests that change comes from willingness to change or some simple set of procedures. There seems to be a consensus of opinion that change is most likely when motivation is strong, when there is a history of successful heterosexual functioning, when gender identity issues are not present, and when involvement in actual homosexual practice has been minimal. Change of homosexual orientation may well be impossible for some by any natural means.[45]

Despite the difficult nature of the process, many hold out the possibility for change. Psychotherapist Martin Hoffman, for example, counsels his colleagues who work with homosexual persons to begin by helping their clients assess their motivation for change.[46] Hoffman's next step is to aid patients in accepting themselves as they are, while reminding them that acceptance does not preclude, but may in fact enhance, change. The goal of such efforts is to help them achieve a sense of their own value as persons.

Other researchers and counselors are even more optimistic. Elizabeth Moberly has articulated a position that is widely held among evangelicals. She focuses on the need to address the parental relationship that in her estimation originally gave rise to a person's homosexual orientation. The homosexual situation, she theorizes, arises from a deficit in same-sex, not opposite-sex relationships. As a result, she advocates loving, nonsexual same-sex relations as crucial for the process of changing a homosexual orientation.[47]

Douglas A. Houck of Outpost, a ministry based in St. Paul, Minnesota, built from Moberly's thesis a four-stage program. In the first, the homosexually oriented person responds to God's call to obedience by changing one's behavior. The second stage focuses on the establishment of self-esteem founded on God's grace and including self-acceptance. Third, the individual seeks to establish healthy same-sex relations in order to meet the needs of same-sex love lacking in one's past. Only then can the fourth stage emerge, namely, the acceptance of heterosexuality.

The basic position of Moberly finds echo in the approach of Paul D. Meier, psychiatrist at the Minirth-Meier Clinic in Richardson, Texas. He too focuses on the needs that remained unmet in childhood. In the case of males, "primary emphasis should be on developing friendships with males their own age and older, with whom they can begin to identify and from whom they can receive emotional and spiritual affection to help fill the father vacuum,"[48] says Meier.

Homosexuality and Sexual Expression

The discussion thus far has yielded several conclusions. Understood as a stable sexual orientation, homosexuality falls short of God's ideal in creation and constitutes a truncated sexual development. It does not for this reason, however, fall under divine condemnation.

With this in view, attention must now shift from orientation to behavior. It has already been suggested that certain expressions of a same-sex orientation are ethically problematic. This thesis requires further elaboration, as we look at expressions of a same-sex preference.

1. The Outward Expression of the Homosexual Orientation

The question the previous discussion raises is whether or not the homosexual orientation can find proper expression. This question must be raised in connection with the central sexual act, before turning to other dimensions of the expression of human sexuality.

a. Homosexuality and the sex act. The first act that comes into view is that of genital sex. What is the relationship of the expression of homosexuality and sexual intercourse? Two major considerations lead to the conclusion that the sex act cannot be viewed as a proper vehicle of expression in the case of homosexual persons.

(1) Marriage as the proper context of the sex act. In previous chapters the point was repeatedly made that the only proper context for the sex act is marriage as the community of male and female characterized by an exclusive bond. If this is the case, it follows that a homosexual relationship cannot form the context for the sex act. Sexual intercourse simply cannot express in the context of such a relationship what this act is intended to convey.

The insufficiency of homosexual relationships to form the proper context for the sex act is actually twofold. It is due to the fact that the marriage bond is not thereby being celebrated, and it is likewise due to the nature of the relationship involved. Often the persons who engage in homosexual relations are single, and as was argued in earlier chapters, the single life cannot include involvement in sexual intercourse. At other times same-sex relations include one partner who is married to someone else. But such acts are problematic, if for no other reason than because they are extramarital, making the sexual activity involved illicit and adulterous.

(2) Same-sex acts and the sex act. Genital sexual activity between members of the same sex is technically not the sex act. This assertion raises, of course, the question of the nature of that act. Earlier we argued that the significance of any act, including sexual intercourse, is determined not only by the physical act itself, but by its context, so that the context of marriage is crucial for the appropriate meaning of the sex act. Whereas this argument focused on the importance of context, now the significance of the other dimension, the physical act itself, comes into view. Not only is a proper context crucial, but the physical act must at the same time be appropriate for the meaning it is intended to convey.

The application to the sex act is obvious. Sexual intercourse is intended to convey the union of two persons in their entirety as two sexual beings: the two becoming one. For this meaning to be fully expressed, the physical act itself must be one whereby the dialectic of sameness and difference is taken up into a union. This occurs when each of the partners contributes himself or herself in entirety, so that this contribution results in a uniting of the two into a supplementary union.

The sex act, then, is more than the experience of sexual "climax." Climax, therefore, ought not to be equated with the sex act. That this is the case becomes obvious when we remember that sexual climax can actually occur apart from intercourse (apart from penis in vagina), such as through self-manipulation (masturbation) or by the manipulation of the genitals by another. More crucial than the ability to attain climax, therefore, is the capability of the sex act to symbolize the uniting of supplementary sexual persons into a whole. This significance is readily evident in the heterosexual act of intercourse. In this act, male and female as whole sexual beings that supplement one another are symbolized by the most obvious unique physical features that both separate male from female and allow male and female to supplement the other (namely, penis and vagina). Thereby the act itself serves as an apt symbol of the union of supplements.

Same-sex genital activity simply lacks this symbolic dimension. No act engaged in by two members of the same sex can be the physical uniting of supplements. Same-sex genital activity can at best only imitate this symbolized unity. In the words of Hanigan, such actions are ultimately "only pretense or imaginative simulations of the real thing."[49]

The deficiency of all same-sex physical acts is readily evident. In a lesbian relationship, sex acts are limited to mutual masturbation to climax, sometimes with the use of some artificial substitute for a penis. Through the use of oral or anal intercourse, male homosexual acts might appear to approximate more closely heterosexual intercourse. But both methods involve the use of an inappropriate receptacle. Neither of these two body parts (anus and mouth) is intended for the sex act. They are totally unrelated to the procreative process. (No one ever begets children in this way). Further, neither was designed for the purpose of intercourse, which is readily evident from the physical injuries that often arise from such practices. And finally, neither body part is able to provide an apt symbol of the supplementary nature which is to characterize one's sexual partner.

In the final analysis, the conclusion of John Harvey is correct: the homosexual act "does not lead to a true union of human persons on the physical genital level. . . . this maladaptation of parts is symbolic of the pseudo-complementarity on the psychological and spiritual levels."[50] Same-sex activity, therefore, is simply not the sex act in its full sense.

b. Homosexuality and genital sexual activity.   If same-sex behavior is deficient sexual activity, then how are such acts to be evaluated? Four major viewpoints are currently defended. Either the acts are intrinsically evil, are essentially imperfect, are to be evaluated in terms of their relational significance, or are essentially good and natural.[51] The considerations outlined in this chapter and the understanding of the sex act articulated earlier lead to a conclusion somewhat different from all four. All such acts are to be evaluated in terms of the meaning they derive from their contexts, in this case, within the homosexual relationship. When so evaluated, same-sex genital behavior comes up short, because it fails to carry the intended meaning of the sex act.

(1) Same-sex activity and the meaning of the sex act. A consideration of the nature of the meaning of the sex act leads to the conclusion that same-sex activity is deficient. *All acts carry meaning,* it has been argued, *and this meaning is derived from the act and its context, including the intent of the actors.* In same-sex genital activity, the intent of the actors is generally that of engaging in a substitute for the sex act. But such activity cannot carry the meaning the sex act is intended to convey, as presented in chapter 4.

It is obvious that same-sex genital acts cannot depict the third meaning of the sex act, openness of the couple to new life as arising from their bond, for children are simply not procreated in this manner. Their ability to serve as the sacrament of marriage (the first meaning of the sex act) is likewise problematic. Even if other considerations were favorable to same-sex acts, the bond of same-sex relationships is simply too fragile to warrant the sex act as its symbol. Same-sex acts are perhaps more capable of expressing the second meaning of the sex act, mutual submission. But here again, the bond which forms the context of the act is generally too fragile to sustain this meaning over a greater length of time.

The fragile nature of the homosexual bond is borne out by findings which indicate that such relationships are generally unstable. This is especially the case with male relationships, which appear to be inherently promiscuous. The research of Bell and Weinberg (1978), for example, indicated that only 17 percent of white homosexual males had had fewer than 50 partners, while 28 percent reported having had 1000 or more partners.[52] A 1982 study indicated that the median number of lifetime sexual partners for a group who had contracted AIDS was 110 with a few men reporting as many as 20,000. This compared with a median of 550 for a homosexual control group without AIDS.[53] The propensity to promiscuity among homosexual males has led some researchers to view the practices of the gay community as the distillate of male sexuality "uncontaminated" by the female ethos.[54]

(2) The meaning of same-sex behavior. Although deficient in its ability to express the meaning intended by the sex act, same-sex activity, like all acts, is not devoid of meaning. However, the meaning it conveys is generally inappropriate for its context. This may be seen in two ways.

First, its connection with the sex act as a substitute for that act means that same-sex acts are intended to declare, "I desire to form an exclusive bond with you." Despite this connection, however, this is seldom the actual intent of the actor. Even if it were, as has been argued previously, exclusive bonding with a person of the same sex is inappropriate. And as recent findings indicate, same-sex bonding is rarely permanent.

Second, more often same-sex acts are intended to say, "I find you attractive," or even, "I love you." But mutual attraction is never a sufficient basis for sexual intimacy, regardless of the sexual orientation of the persons involved. As Edward Batchelor pointed out, "love does not always justify sexual union."

Rather, it is every bit as likely that the love of man for man or woman for woman bids them refrain from sexual intercourse as that it urges them to it."[55] And as the creation story indicates, the kind of sexual attraction that leads to the sex act is meant to be between male and female.

(3) Same-sex behavior and the sex drive. The appeal to the creation story introduces a third consideration. Not only do same-sex sexual relations express an inadequate, even incorrect meaning, they constitute a misuse of the sex drive.

As was developed in previous chapters, human sexuality is intended to form the basis for the drive toward bonding. This bonding is to lead ultimately to the bond of the people of God with their Creator, the foretaste of which is now to be found in the community of Christ. Within that overarching purpose, heterosexual marriage and singleness form alternative contexts for the expression of human sexuality, only the former of which is to include exclusive bonding and genital sexual expression. Homosexual relationships, however, constitute a confusion of the single and marital alternatives. The sex drive, which was intended to bring male and female together in marriage, now is used to bring male and male or female and female together in a sexual relationship.

Not only do such relationships move against the purpose of human sexuality in general, in same-sex relationships the sex drive itself is misused, for it often is reduced to sexual self-gratification. This difficulty is in part an outworking of the inherent lack of the dimension of supplementary completeness in all such relationships. As a result, the relationships are prone to the erroneous dualist anthropology in which the body is used as an instrument in the service of a self-centered goal.[56] In this context Hettlinger's critique of male relations is insightful: "Because for most of them sexual gratification is purely a physical relief and the other man holds no prospect of being a true partner, far more of their encounters approximate to the level of prostitution in the heterosexual's experience."[57]

In summary, homosexuality is at best an inferior or distorted expression of human sexuality. It is perhaps this distortion that leads to the instability of the homosexual relationship. The distortion of the relationship and of the sex act inherent in same-sex behaviors go hand in hand. Hettlinger aptly summarized this point with respect to male homosexuality:

> Because the natural complementariness of womanhood is divorced from one of the basic natural expressions of sex—vaginal coitus—it is always incomplete and always to some extent distorted. Because the natural complementariness of womanhood is rejected, and the fulfilling bond of parenthood impossible, the homosexual's appetite can never be satisfied; he is always searching for "an ideal lover who exists nowhere on the face of this planet."

As a result, "the average man with sexual drives of normal strength, who chooses to accept the homosexual role, will probably seek physical satisfaction through contacts with other men and is destined to increasing frustration and ultimate loneliness."[58]

2. The Question of Homosexual Marriage

Some who acknowledge the instability and promiscuity of same-sex relations suggest that homosexual "marriages" form a solution to the problem. Rather than affirming heterosexuality as the norm, they argue, we ought to find ways to encourage persons of the same-sex preference to form permanent bonds. In response several considerations are in order.

a. The propriety of homosexuality. The case for homosexual marriages presupposes that homosexuality is to be acknowledged as right and proper for at least those persons who sense that this orientation is "natural." We evaluated and rejected this position in the preceding discussion.

b. The promiscuity of homosexuality. A second important point in considering the possibility of homosexual marriages is that of the apparent promiscuity of homosexual relations. Even if homosexuality could be acknowledged as in some sense natural, recent studies hold out little hope that encouraging the formation of permanent same-sex bonds would be successful, especially among males. As noted above, homosexuality appears to be inherently promiscuous. For this reason, the formation of stable, permanent bonds among homosexuals is difficult. A study by psychiatrist Charles Socarides indicated that only about 2 percent of homosexual males are able to live in a committed relationship like marriage.[59]

Some proponents of homosexual marriage respond to such pessimistic statistics by suggesting that homosexual promiscuity is the product of social repression on the part of the wider society. The implication is that a change in societal attitude would result in a decrease in homosexual instability.[60] But even Martin Hoffman, who offers this thesis, admits that the problem of promiscuity is deeper than the attitude of the dominant heterosexual society. He himself admits that the homosexual community itself is partially responsible: "Since large sections of the gay world view the homosexual as a commodity and judge him by his cosmetic qualities, he soon begins to develop that same view of himself."[61]

c. The impermanence of homosexual relationships. A further consideration looks at the prospects for permanency within homosexual bonds. It seems that same-sex marriages generally cannot offer hope of being permanent and stable. This, too, is indicated by recent findings. Bell and Weinberg concluded from their research that only 10 percent of male homosexual respondents could be classified as existing in "close couple" relationships. And even these relationships could only be characterized as "relatively monogamous" or "relatively less promiscuous."[62]

Many relationships that appear stable from the outside are actually filled with tension and uncertainty. In fact, Hettlinger went so far as to theorize that such "marriages" are intrinsically unstable:

> Even when two male homosexuals establish a "marriage," the permanence of their never-consummated sexual union is always threatened by disruptive factors additional even to those experienced by normally married people. Both parties to the contract immediately become the object of jealous younger suitors to whom they are easily attracted; and lacking any binding obligation, the relationship has no protection from dissolution.[63]

d. The deficiency of same-sex marriage. Finally, even under the best of conditions, same-sex marriages suffer from a deficiency. This deficiency is apparent in four dimensions.

First, because they do not encompass male and female, they cannot represent or serve as models of the community of humankind. Such a marriage may be, of course, a unity of friends, and thereby it may reflect to a certain degree the dialectic of sameness and difference intrinsic in human bonding. But the marriage remains deficient even on this level, for the dialectic of sameness and difference present in it does not extend to the sexual realm, which, however, is an integral dimension of our essential personhood. Therefore, same-sex "marriages" can never be viewed as marriage in its full sense, and for this reason can never be an appropriate symbol of what marriage is intended to convey.

Barnhouse aptly appealed to the author of the Song of Songs as one who has understood that "sexuality itself is a symbol of wholeness, of the reconciliation of opposites, of the loving at-one-ment between God and Creation."[64] Because it is not built from the union of male and female—the two foundational ways of being human—the homosexual relationship cannot serve as an appropriate symbol of reconciliation.

Second, same-sex marriages are deficient, because even on the theoretical sphere they simply cannot be procreative. Such relationships include genital sexual activities within the context of a deliberate choice to forego procreation. As has been argued earlier, procreation is not definitive for sexual union. But at the same time it is not for this reason inconsequential.

James Hanigan stated this succinctly: "for the sexual union of human beings finds part of its Christian, human meaning in the procreative power of a freely shared, embodied love to produce a new reality, one that participated in and is yet different from the reality of the two partners."[65]

Third, such marriages are deficient, because they are inherently nonbinding. Even if same-sex marriages came to carry legal sanction and received ecclesiastical blessing, they would never require the same seriousness inherent in heterosexual marriage. The breakup of a homosexual relationship does not, and cannot, carry the sense of moral failure found in heterosexual marriage. It could mark at most the transgression of a legal contract. The breakup of a heterosexual union, in contrast, always entails the effacing of the community of male and female and the destruction of the divinely intended metaphor of God and God's people.

For this reason, to sanction same-sex relationships would do more than acknowledge a deficient relationship. Such sanction would also cause injury to the concept of marriage itself. It would reduce the significance of marriage as a moral commitment.

Finally, same-sex marriages are deficient because they cannot be sealed with the sex act. As has been noted earlier, some type of genital sexual activity can occur between members of the same sex, but the sex act itself cannot. Of course, the sex act is not necessary for the presence of marriage; persons who for various reasons cannot engage in sex remain married. However, same-sex "marriages" form a case apart from those exceptional situations involving marriages of male and female. In the latter, sexual relations are precluded by some mitigating circumstance. In the former, in contrast, such relations are intrinsically impossible.

3. Options for Homosexuality

The conclusions reached above, namely, that same-sex relations are to be avoided and that homosexual unions are deficient, raises the question as to what the viable options are for persons of a same-sex preference. What lifestyle alternatives are available to them? And what does a reduction of such alternatives mean for the expression of sexuality among homosexual persons?

a. Marriage or abstinence.   On the basis of previous conclusions, only two alternatives present themselves: a change of orientation leading to monogamous, heterosexual marriage; or abstinence. Proponents of openness to homosexuality generally respond to any such limitation by claiming that this position is unusually harsh on persons with a same-sex orientation. In response, several considerations are worthy of note.

First, this limitation is simply in keeping with the position developed throughout this work that heterosexual marriage or the single life characterized by abstinence are the only two alternative contexts for the expression of human sexuality. Such a limitation, then, is not directed specifically to homosexual persons, but encompasses all persons regardless of sexual orientation. The fact that heterosexuals find it easier to actualize the option of marriage than homosexuals does not mitigate against the fairness of the position as extending to all persons.

Second, this limitation, while not unfair, does work against the widespread contemporary emphasis on rights and self-expression. John J. McNeill stands as an example of those who have defended homosexuality on the basis that "every human being has a God-given right to sexual love and intimacy."[66] However, the ethic of the New Testament does not appeal to the actualization of perceived rights, but to the willingness of the disciple to follow the example of Jesus in freely laying aside rights for the sake of a higher good. Jesus himself noted that certain persons would willingly set aside the sex act for the sake of the kingdom of God (Matt. 19:12).

The possibility of practicing abstinence for the sake of a higher good is confirmed by the modern human sciences, which conclude that sexual activity is not a human necessity. In the words of Jones and Workman, "There is no basis in behavioral science or Christian theology to suggest that abstinence is detrimental to human welfare, or that expression of genital eroticism is necessary for wholeness."[67]

Rather than possessing "a God-given right to sexual love," as McNeill asserted, all human beings are called to give expression to their fundamental human sexuality in ways that bring glory to God. This call requires chastity of all persons, whether homosexual or heterosexual in orientation, a chastity that is to be understood as being responsible creatures who know the boundaries of sexual expression.[68]

b. Sexual expression among homosexuals.   To offer marriage and abstinence as the only two proper alternatives for persons of a same-sex orientation does not mean that their life is destined to be devoid of all sexual expression. On the contrary, those who remain single, whether because they are unable to undergo a change of orientation or who simply choose that alternative, may experience the same dimensions of affective sexual expression as other single persons.

At this point, however, it is important to reiterate the differentiation between sexual desire and the desire for sex. Sexuality is the basis for the drive toward bonding, and it is operative in the lives of all humans. Sexual desire, then, refers to the need to form bonds with other humans, to live in community with others and with God. This is natural and wholesome. Sexual desire, however, need not lead to actual genital sexual activity, as most of our day-to-day relationships with others indicate. Only the bonding of marriage, which is but one form that results from sexual desire, provides the proper context for the expression of the sex urge in terms of genital sexual activity between persons.

Persons regardless of sexual preference may experience other types of bonding besides marriage, the highest form being the bond of the community of Christ. Within this primary bond of the community of Christ, bonding between persons of same sex can occur, as they develop close, even intimate friendships, albeit excluding sexual intimacy in the form of genital relations.

4. The Church and Homosexuality

Mention of the community of Christ as the context for the building of caring, intimate friendships among persons introduces the topic of the church and homosexuality. How ought the church to respond to the issue of homosexuality? And more importantly, how ought the church to respond to persons of a same-sex orientation?

a. The church and homosexuality in an age of AIDS. Unfortunately, the relationship between the church in general and the homosexual community, which has never been characterized by mutual openness to dialogue, has become even more uneasy in the era of Acquired Immunodeficiency Syndrome (AIDS). When AIDS first became a public concern, some Christians were quick to term it "the gay disease" or even to claim that it is caused by homosexual acts themselves. Medical science, however, has assisted in clearing the air about how the disease is and is not contracted. And writings of several ethicists have attempted to assist Christians in overcoming many widespread but incorrect assumptions and unwholesome attitudes.[69]

Through the help of medical research, Christians are beginning to see that although certain types of homosexual activity place one at greater risk, AIDS itself is not a gay disease. And various Christian writers have called on the church to see the AIDS epidemic as an opportunity for compassionate service in the name of Christ. We can only hope that this horrible epidemic will be a catalyst not for a wholesale rejection of homosexual persons on the part of Christians, but rather for a new openness to look beyond sexual orientation and see persons in need of God's grace.

b. The church's ministry in the face of homosexuality. The gay movement, AIDS, and the rise in awareness of homosexuality provide a grave challenge to the church for ministry. To be effective, this ministry must move in at least two directions.

(1) A ministry of prevention. To meet the contemporary challenge, the church must engage in a ministry of prevention. Recent findings indicate that the same-sex orientation is not simply inborn, but is in part the product of socialization, especially, parental relations. If this is the case, Christians would do well to seek to strengthen parents in the task of training their children properly. This point is not the sole property of conservative Christians. It was raised even by Derrick Sherwin Bailey, who concluded his epoch-making study of homosexuality with a plea for both an even-handed treatment of all sexual sins and the fostering of home life:

> the only solution is to attack the problem at its root—to deal with
> the social and sexual evils in which the condition of inversion frequently originates. Promotion of good marriages and happy homes

will achieve a result immeasurably greater and more valuable than punitive legislation aimed at the private practices of adult homosexuals, while the adulterer and adulteress are allowed to pursue their anti-social designs unchecked.[70]

(2) A ministry of support. It has been argued here that the homosexual orientation does not carry the condemnation of God, but nevertheless must be candidly viewed as in various ways a deficient mode of human sexuality. Likewise, we concluded that the expressions of sexuality that take the form of same-sex genital activity are improper. But such conclusions do not mean that the church has no ministry to persons of a same-sex orientation. On the contrary, the mandate given to the church includes reaching out to all persons, regardless of orientation and lifestyle. This mandate extends to ministry to homosexuals as well.

Christians, in fact, can offer to persons struggling with sexual problems a climate which can be found nowhere else, and this without compromising what they believe to be the biblical sex ethic. The climate which the church ought to seek to create for persons of a same-sex orientation is twofold.

First, the church can create a climate of acceptance. Such acceptance cannot extend to actions which the Bible views as sinful, of course. But that acceptance can move to a far deeper level, acceptance of all individuals as persons whom God loves. By seeking to mediate to others the love and compassion of God that extends to all regardless of the type of personal sins, Christians can provide a healthy, healing alternative to the gay community, which often tends to view persons as commodities and to accept others insofar as they have something to offer in return.

Second, the church can create a climate of assistance. Although some might genuinely prefer the homosexual orientation, many others feel trapped and long for release. Christians can lend a sympathetic hand to help and support such persons through the struggles associated with coping with their sexual orientation. By standing with them during the difficult periods of the coping process, Christians who extend unqualified support, coupled with the assurance of divine assistance, can provide such persons the boost needed to gain full liberation from their past and from their sexual orientation.

(3) A ministry within the church. The community that the church seeks to be for persons struggling with a same-sex orientation must not become only a one-way enterprise. The church must also be open to accept the ministry that these persons offer to the community of Christ. This will include welcoming them into the fellowship of the church on the same basis as all other sinners (which includes all Christians, for all are only "sinners saved by grace").

Offering a place for ministry in the Christian community means as well that leadership positions and even ordained roles are to be open to persons regardless of sexual orientation. Sexual orientation itself does not preclude ministry in

Christ's vineyard. Rather, it is the continuation of sinful practices that forms a barrier to service and leadership. In all situations, the sexual sins of homosexuals in the community of Christ are to be treated like those of heterosexuals.

No believer, therefore, must complete a transition to heterosexuality in order to serve in any capacity in the church. What is required of all persons who are selected to lead is that they be living exemplary lives. In the case of persons of a same-sex orientation, leading an exemplary life means that they have forsaken all sinful sexual practices associated with their orientation, just as heterosexual Christians must forsake the sins that arise out of the improper expression of their sexuality.

Homosexuality forms a challenge to the Christian sexual ethic. Christians are compelled to accept and acknowledge persons, regardless of lifestyle, as the objects of God's compassion, concern, and love. From the vantage point of the divine design and intention in creation, a same-sex orientation must be seen as an unfortunate and deficient situation. It becomes ethically problematic whenever it is given expression in the form of genital behavior. Although homosexual relationships cannot be condoned as alternatives to monogamous heterosexual marriage, the good news of the gospel is that persons of a same-sex orientation, like heterosexuals, can live full lives. They can find fulfillment as singles who practice abstinence while finding their primary bonded community within the fellowship of Christ. Those who are not called to the single life can claim the grace of God to work a change in orientation leading to a wholesome life within monogamous, heterosexual marriage.

For Christians of either sexual orientation, the call to live out one's sexuality in ways that bring honor to God is a difficult challenge, especially in the midst of our permissive society. Yet, the resources of the Holy Spirit are greater than the difficulty of the calling, and obedience to the divine design is the path to greatest joy.

Epilogue:
The Church and Human Sexuality

The Christian sex ethic finds its beginning point in the premise that humans are sexual beings. Our sexuality is a dimension of our existence as created beings. As a dimension of our creaturely existence our sexuality is given by the will of God, and therefore it participates in the divine design for humanity. This book has presented the thesis that the design of God for us as arising out of our sexuality is related to the drive toward bonding, the highest expression of which is the bond of the community of Christ. Because we are created as sexual beings, we are called to become the community of male and female. And the highest earthly expression of that design is the community shared among the Master's disciples.

Despite the importance of sexuality for the dynamic of bonding that forms that basis of the development of community, the contemporary church has not always been cognizant of this dimension of the human reality. The church has at times shown meager interest in reflecting within itself the importance of sexuality to human existence. Nevertheless, an understanding of human sexuality could provide an important dimension in the life of the church.

Sexuality and the Community of God

Because of its importance for the process of bonding that gives rise to the community of male and female, human sexuality ought to play an important role in the life of the church community. This role arises naturally out of an understanding of the relationship between sexuality and the community of God. Various themes outlined earlier in this volume contribute to such an understanding.

1. Bonding and Community with God

One applicable thesis presented earlier is that community with God is the result of the sexually related drive toward bonding. This thesis requires further elaboration.

***a. Community with God as the highest expression of the drive to-
ward bonding.*** God created us as sexual creatures with a purpose in view.
The divine purpose relates to the fundamental human drive toward bonding
that finds its fulfillment only in community with God. But how does sexuality
lead to community with God?

The first step in understanding the path to community with God charted
by human sexuality lies in the close relationship between our sexuality and incompleteness. It is as sexual beings that we are incomplete. And because we
are incomplete as sexual beings we become aware of our need to be supple-
mented by the other, an awareness that leads us to enter into community.

This twofold relationship between sexuality and incompleteness is evidenced in the second creation narrative. Adam's solitude was a result of the
lack of an appropriate bonding partner for him: "But for Adam no suitable
helper was found" (Gen. 2:20). There was in him a void that none of the animals could fill. Nor could his relationship with God eliminate the need for him
to exist in human community. A suitable other was needed as the remedy for
his fundamental incompleteness. Further, Adam's sense of solitude was heightened with the creation of the female. Only at this point does he realize that his
solitude is due to the fact that he is a sexual being (in his case, a man), for
only as he gazes on the female, on *'ishshāh,* is he referred to as *'îsh,* "male,"
and not *'ādām,* the earth-creature. Only in relationship to, or in community
with his counterpart, therefore, is Adam fully aware of his own sexuality, of
the sexually based nature of his solitude, and of the liberation from solitude
offered to him by the presence of the other human being.

The primal experience of solitude presented in Genesis 2 forms the basis
for the drive toward bonding which is characteristic of human life. As noted
earlier, this drive constitutes the foundation for various expressions of human
community, beginning with marriage and including society, for human beings
were designed to live in community. And the drive toward community constitutes the basis even for the quest for the highest fellowship, life together as a
people in relation with God.

This, too, finds expression in the creation narrative. As sexual beings exist in community, human community with God emerges. In the first narrative,
the divine desire to form a creature in the image of God results in the creation
of humankind as male and female. In the second narrative the point is less
striking, but nevertheless not absent. Prior to the forming of the female, God
gave Adam both a task—to care for the garden (Gen. 2:15)—and a prohibition—not to eat of the one tree (2:17).

The task and the prohibition mark out a relationship of responsibility before the Creator. But at this point there is no mention yet of a relationship of fellowship with God. Despite the presence of some type of relationship between
God and Adam, Adam experiences solitude, a situation that is remedied only
with the creation of the female. The text gives no indication that in his solitude

Adam was able to hear "the sound of the Lord God as he was walking in the garden in the cool of the day." This language is employed only of "the man and his wife" (3:8).

More important than the creation stories, however, the story of salvation points toward community with God as the highest expression of the drive toward bonding. The central theme of the Bible is God's action in reconciling alienated humankind in Christ and thereby bringing reconciled humanity into relationship with God. The book of Ephesians presents this theme in terms of the overcoming of the barrier between Gentile and Jew. The purpose of Christ was "to create in himself one new man out of the two, thus making peace, and in this one body to reconcile both of them to God through the cross, by which he put to death their hostility" (2:15–16).

The sexually based drive toward bonding, therefore, finds its final completion only when a reconciled people enjoy fellowship with the Creator. For this reason, community with God—the community shared by reconciled humanity—is the highest expression of the drive toward bonding. The ultimate goal of human sexuality, therefore, is corporate fellowship with the Designer of our existence as sexual beings.

b. Community with God as the eschatological expression of the drive toward bonding. The sexually motivated drive toward bonding is ultimately fulfilled only in community with God. This community, however, is eschatological. The eschatological nature of community with God may be viewed from two angles.

First, community with God is eschatological in a teleological sense. It is the culmination of the divine purpose. God's intent is to enter into fellowship with creation, specifically by forming a bond with humankind as the divine image bearer. Community with God, therefore, is the "last thing," the *telos* or goal of God's salvific activity and the goal of creation and history. As humans enter into fellowship with God, the design of the Creator in making sexual beings, beings who seek to form bonds, comes to completion.

Second, community with God is eschatological in a temporal sense. The vision of the Bible speaks of fellowship with God as a community formed by the presence of God with us. But according to the prophets and apocalypticists, this goal is not fully realized in the present. Rather, the time when God is fully "with us," when we experience the complete presence of God, is yet future, coming only at the climax of the age. For the New Testament, the consummation of history occurs at the return of the ascended Lord, when all history is brought to completion.

The seer in Revelation provides a grand articulation of this vision. Concerning the time following the capture of Satan and the judgment, he declares:

> Then I saw a new heaven and a new earth, for the first heaven and
> the first earth had passed away, and there was no longer any sea.

I saw the Holy City, the new Jerusalem, coming down out of heaven from God, prepared as a bride beautifully dressed for her husband. And I heard a loud voice from the throne saying, "Now the dwelling of God is with men, and he will live with them. They will be his people, and God himself will be with them and be their God. He will wipe every tear from their eyes. There will be no more death or mourning or crying or pain, for the old order of things has passed away." (Rev. 21:1–4)

He describes the perfection of that coming time as due to the presence of God within the human community:

Then the angel showed me the river of the water of life, as clear as crystal, flowing from the throne of God and of the Lamb down the middle of the great street of the city. On each side of the river stood the tree of life, bearing twelve crops of fruit, yielding its fruit every month. And the leaves of the tree are for the healing of the nations. No longer will there be any curse. The throne of God and of the Lamb will be in the city, and his servants will serve him. They will see his face, and his name will be on their foreheads. There will be no more night. They will not need the light of a lamp or the light of the sun, for the Lord God will give them light. And they will reign for ever and ever. (Rev. 22:1–5)

c. Community with God as the community of male and female.

Often the vision of the final reign of God pictures a nonmaterial, sexless world. Proponents of such a vision appeal to Jesus' response to the Sadducees, in which the Lord declares that in the kingdom era people will not marry, but will be like the angels (Matt. 22:30). Yet it is instructive to note that Jesus' statement does not declare that in the reign of God people will no longer be sexual creatures. On the contrary, as has been argued previously, both Jesus' own resurrection and the doctrine of the resurrection in general indicate that human sexual distinctions (albeit in a transformed manner) are taken into existence in the community of God.

In that community, we remain embodied persons, albeit people whose embodied existence has been transformed through the resurrection. Because sexuality is a crucial dimension of our existence as embodied creatures, we remain sexual beings in the community of God. At the same time, our sexuality, like our embodiment as a whole, is transformed. One important result of this transformation, as Jesus indicates in his statement to the Sadducees, is that we no longer will express our sexuality in genital intercourse, for this act is related solely to the marriage bond, which will no longer be present in the community of God.

Although genital sexual activity has no place in the eschatological reign of God, sexuality will be present in various forms.

Sensuality, for example, will remain; in fact, we will experience even a heightened appreciation of sensual joy, as is indicated by the use of sensuous imagery in the biblical vision of the reign of God. Sexuality is present in the form of the aesthetic sense, as is evidenced by the biblical vision of the beauty of the place of God's eschatological reign. But of highest importance, sexuality remains present in the form of mutuality. According to the biblical vision, the eschatological community is a bonded society, a city or a kingdom. It is the society of transformed yet embodied human beings, the perfect community of male and female, in which all experience the fullness of interpersonal relationships.

2. Bonding and Community with Christ

The vision of the community of God, which will one day be present in its fullness, has an important implication for our understanding of the church. Although the fullness of community with God is future, a partial, yet real fellowship may be enjoyed in the present. According to the New Testament, the focus of the present experience of the eschatological reality is the community of Christ, that is, the present experience of fellowship with Christ and Christ's disciples. Community with Christ, i.e., the relationship of believers with their Lord and therefore with each other, is designed to be a foretaste of the full eschatological community, the society of humankind in fellowship with God. For this reason, in the present time the community of Christ is to form the context for both contexts for expressing human sexuality—marriage and singleness.

The significance of the church of Jesus Christ arises in this context. The church is related to the community of Christ as its visible expression. The task of each local congregation is that of being the church of Jesus Christ in miniature and thereby living out the mandate given to the church by its Lord. This mandate includes seeking to be the community of Christ and in this way being a concrete foretaste of the eschatological community of God in this age. Each congregation is to be the church—a visible expression of the community of Christ. Each is to be a place where believers experience community and become community to one another.

The Role of Human Sexuality
in the Church

As the visible expression of the community of Christ, the church is to be the place where community may be experienced. This requires that the church incorporate the sexual nature of humankind into its life, affirming our basic sexuality and utilizing the gift of sexuality for the purposes of advancing its divinely given mandate. Human sexuality can become an integral part of the life of the church in many ways. Three general considerations are sketched here.

1. As the Church Welcomes
the Gifts of Both Marriage and Singleness

One important means by which the church can incorporate the sexual nature of humankind into its life is by welcoming the gifts of both marriage and singleness into its fellowship. Our sexuality and the different contexts in which it is to be lived out are crucial to the task of the church to become the expression of community God intends it to be. Both the gift of marriage and the gift of singleness play a role in the completion of this task.

The presence of both married and single persons is theologically important to the task of the church. In anticipation of the community of God, the church has a task that is related to the concept of the image of God. Because it is to be a foretaste of the eschatological community of God, the church is to reflect the nature of the divine character, namely, love.

But the divine love has two dimensions, necessitating the presence in the church of the two basic sexual lifestyles. The presence of married persons within the fellowship serves to remind the community of the holy and exclusive nature of the divine love, whereas single persons are needed as a reminder of its universal and inclusive nature. Without the contribution of the symbol of marriage, the community runs the risk of becoming simply another human institution without an awareness of its holy and exclusive calling. But without the presence of the symbol of singleness, it could degenerate into an introverted "holy club" with no understanding of its inherent drive toward inclusiveness.

The theological importance of the presence of both lifestyles in the church forms the context for the practical importance of each. As noted earlier, in the New Testament era marriage served as an important vehicle for the ongoing mission of the church in various ways. Marriage facilitated the movement of the gospel from spouse to spouse, from parents to children, and from home into the community. This role of marriage remains crucial for the ministry of the church today. Singleness serves the mission of the church as well. As in the first century, single persons today are in a position to be undivided in devotion to the Lord's service and thereby are free to serve in certain capacities within the church that would be complicated by responsibilities to spouse and children.

Many churches today have little difficulty facilitating the incorporation of married couples and families into their programs. A greater challenge is that of helping single persons find places of service. In part this may be a vestige of the Protestant reaction to the Roman Catholic emphasis on celibacy for priests and nuns. But it may also reflect a type of captivity to present culture. In either case, the challenge that singleness poses to the church must be met for the sake of the mission of the people of God. Single persons must be encouraged to minister within the congregation, in order thereby to fulfill their calling to employ their lifestyle choice to serve the Lord. As both married and single persons find places of service, the congregation is able to carry out its corporate mandate to be the foretaste of the eschatological community of male and female.

2. As the Church Welcomes the Gifts of Both Sexes

The church can incorporate into its life the sexual dimension of human nature as it welcomes and utilizes the gifts of both male and female. In the past, the church has often been a male-centered and male-dominated institution. Even today, many congregations relegate women to a lesser status in the fellowship by limiting them to certain roles in church life. The congregation that would truly be a foretaste of the eschatological community of male and female, however, discovers the importance of welcoming the contribution of both sexes in its life and mission. It is beyond the scope of this volume to deal with the controversial contemporary issues of ordination and office structure. Nevertheless, the conclusions presented in this study yield a general principle regarding the role of men and women in the church.

As has been argued previously, men and women are different in ways that are more fundamental than simply their roles in the reproductive process. The differences lie even in the basic ways in which we view ourselves and the world. Men and women think differently; they approach the world differently. The fundamentally different outlooks toward others, life, and the world that characterize males and females mean that the two sexes are supplementary. Each sex needs the supplemental approach to reality offered by the other in all the various dimensions of human life together.

This observation is readily applicable to the church. If it is to be the foretaste of the community of God, the church must welcome the unique contribution of both male and female in its midst. This is both a theological and a practical necessity. Theologically, the presence and activity of both sexes is vital, if the church is to point toward the perfect community of God, the fellowship of God with humankind that will characterize the eschatological reign of God. Because this future reality will be the society of human beings existing in supplementary community with each other (the community of male and female), the church must strive to reflect that eschatological vision in its present life.

The mutual contribution of both sexes is vital on the practical level of church life as well. If the church is to develop a well-rounded ministry that can serve all humankind, it must value the gifts and contributions of both sexes. No congregation can genuinely expect to complete the mandate given by the Lord, if its structures allow only the male voice to be heard during the planning and decision-making process. Important to the ongoing ministry of the people of God are the wisdom and insights of male and female, which are born out of experiences filtered through quite different approaches to life. The congregation that is intent on being the reflection of the community of God and on fulfilling its mandate to worship God, edify its membership, and reach into the world, therefore, would do well to welcome the contribution of both male and female in all areas of its corporate life.

3. As the Church Includes the Sexual Dimension of Life

Finally, the church can incorporate our basic sexuality in its life as it consciously takes this dimension of human existence into the heart of its ministry. The worship aspect of the church's mandate offers an appropriate example of this principle.

Because of its foundation in the Reformation, Protestant worship is generally word-oriented, focusing attention on the hearing of the proclaimed message. This orientation is basically correct, for the spoken word is rightly foundational to the fulfillment of the church's mandate as a whole. And the proclamation of the word must form the context for all the various ingredients of Christian worship, if these are to remain understandable to the worshiping community. At the same time, however, the emphasis on "the Word" must be tempered with two additional considerations.

First, the proclamation and hearing of the word, while focusing on logical discourse, need not be restricted to it. Within preaching and teaching there is also a place for using sound to create sensation and imagery or to spark the imagination. This could include simply the use of narratives about life in order to assist the hearer in comprehending spiritual truth or to elicit an emotive response, just as Jesus used parables in his teaching to this end. Hearing can also move beyond the spoken word, however. Music is one powerful means of evoking sensation or creating desired mood. To cite one example, for many Christians the hymn, "How Great Thou Art," carries great emotive and mood-producing power.

The second consideration takes us beyond the confines of the sense of hearing. Hearing is not the only human sense that can be harnessed in the service of the worship life of the church. The other senses are also worthy of being utilized. The sense of sight can be employed through the use of banners, pictures, and art. Modern psychology has confirmed the importance of the sense of touch to human well-being. The propriety of touch in Christian worship is indicated by the widely-used hand clasp as a symbol of Christian unity. Our sense of smell allows various fragrances to become symbols of aspects of God's being and activity, such as the divine holiness, creativity, and salvific love. And through the ability to taste we are able to understand more fully certain spiritual truths, especially as we savor the elements at the celebration of the Lord's Supper.

Because our sensuality is connected with our sexuality, the use of the various senses within the worship life of the church is a way of celebrating this central dimension of our being. The senses can be used to celebrate the creative activity of God, for God is the creator of nature and of our ability to enjoy nature as God's handiwork. Beyond the celebration of God as Creator, however, sensuality is an appropriate vehicle to celebrate God's action in salvation history. For our God is the Savior or Redeemer of humankind in all the dimensions of human life.

The central events of the church year offer appropriate occasions for the use of human sensuality as an aid to understanding spiritual truth. At Christmas the manger scene could be constructed in a barn, as a means of sensing the lowly birth of our Lord. Christmas gift-giving, as a continuation of a tradition begun by the magi, can become an apt way of celebrating God's gift of Immanuel to us and of our giving of ourselves to God and to one another in return. During Holy Week the cross draped in black can serve as a means of feeling the pain of Christ's passion and of sharing the disciples' sense of loss. Then the grand victory of the resurrection can be experienced through the use of light, colors, and even joyful dance to the Lord.

The ongoing use of sensuality in the church can be evidenced through the inherent sensual nature of the ordinances or sacraments. By its very nature, baptism is a vivid picture of a spiritual truth. The wetness of the baptismal water is a reminder of our spiritual washing. For the one who is immersed, the sensation of being under the water facilitates a sensually-based understanding of the truth of dying with Christ, followed by the bursting forth from the water as a preview of newness of life. Those who watch this event are led thereby to remember their own baptism and to be reminded of their own death and life in Christ. In the same way, the Lord's Supper is filled with sensual imagery. Seeing the one loaf assists us in imagining our fundamental oneness as the community of Christ, which it symbolizes. And by savoring the taste of the bread and the wine we are reminded that spiritual vitality is our through "feeding" on Christ. In these and other ways the sensual dimension of our existence is incorporated into the worship life of the church.

The Penultimate Nature of Sex Ethics

We are sexual beings. Our sexuality is a central and pervasive dimension of our humanness. For this reason, sexual expression and its proper contexts are worthy topics for deliberation, and ethical standards relating to them ought to be taken seriously. However, this process must be tempered with three additional considerations that indicate the nonfinal nature of the discussion of marriage and singleness as alternative contexts for the expression of human sexuality. As the church boldly proclaims and practices the sex ethic it derives from the Bible, it is crucial that it not lose sight of the fact that issues surrounding marriage and singleness are for this age only. They will pass away in the eschatological community of male and female in the reign of God.

1. The Relationship between Ethical Guidelines and God's Ideal

The first consideration that reflects the nonfinal status of sex ethics relates to the penultimate nature of ethics in general. This can be illustrated through the relationship between laws and true fellowship. Rules are essential for human community in all its forms. Nevertheless, rules of social interaction ought never to be confused with the human fellowship they are intended to serve. The moral law does not produce the life of the community, but only provides the boundaries within which community life can happen.

This relationship is expressed in the Bible in terms of the Pauline distinction between law and spirit. The law, Paul declares, does not give life; only God's Spirit is the source of life (e.g. Rom. 8:1–4). At the same time, however, the law is important. For Paul, it gives insight into God's standards (Rom. 7:7) and is a schoolmaster leading us to Christ (Gal. 3:24).

The Reformation sought to clarify this Pauline declaration. According to Luther the law has two functions. It shows human sin, and it functions as a brace against uncontrolled sinfulness in society. To these two, Calvin added the so called third use of the law, the law as forming the guide for Christian conduct. This third function can be viewed as carrying an additional interpretation. The law, it may be argued, offers the parameters within which the Christian in community can hope to find community life. It provides the boundaries within which the truly Christian "law"—love—may freely operate and be found. Love goes beyond the law, according to the New Testament writers. In so doing, however, love does not transgress the law, but rather is its fulfillment (e.g. Matt. 22:37–40). It moves within the boundaries the law provides and thereby brings into being what the law intends, but is powerless to effect.

This understanding is directly applicable to sexual expression and community. The biblical sex ethic, presented as it is in terms of "law," provides the parameters in which true community, the community of love, can emerge. Adultery provides one example. The prohibition of adultery—or the emphasis on marital sexual faithfulness, to offer the positive dimension of the negative injunction—does not guarantee a living, vital marital relationship. Rather, it indicates the parameters within which a loving relationship can be experienced. The ultimate goal for marriage is love, not merely sexual fidelity. Christians maintain that in the final analysis love can be learned only from God, only in relationship to God, and not through the study of law. Ultimately, therefore, personal commitment to God, and not the prohibition of adultery, provides the best basis for a fulfilling marital relationship. Nevertheless, the prohibition assists us in understanding the context in which that loving relationship can emerge, for it declares that any act of adultery lies beyond what can be considered loving, God-honoring behavior.

In the same way the biblical call to abstinence apart from marriage does not guarantee that loving relationships among single males and females will emerge. But it does indicate the parameters of proper conduct. Outside of these parameters actions cannot be termed truly loving. And by being careful to act within them, single people may hope to discover truly loving relationships.

2. The Noneternal Nature of Human Genital Expression

Our sexuality, all pervasive as it is, is only one aspect of our humanness. For this reason, issues of human sexuality must be kept in a proper perspective. They are crucial. But they must not be presented as the only issues worthy of being addressed. More specifically, marriage is of vital concern to the Christian. Yet, as an expression of human sexuality, marriage belongs to the present order. It will be laid aside, when the eschatological reign of God comes in its fullness. Marriage and issues related to it, therefore, must never be treated as having ultimate status in themselves. In the same way, concern over the proper expression of sexuality within the single life is also of penultimate importance, for in the reign of God genital sexual activity will be a thing of the past.

3. The Divine Grace as the Ultimate Principle

A final principle—divine grace—must be emphasized in any treatment of issues surrounding human sexuality and its expression. According to the Christian gospel, God forgives, redeems and transforms all dimensions of human existence. This gracious activity of God encompasses the sexual aspect of our being as well. As the people of God, the church in turn is to be a community of forgiveness and hope, not a court of judgment and condemnation. Sin must be treated seriously, but the final goal of such treatment must always be redemption and reconciliation, not ostracism.

The people of God are called to espouse and live truly biblical sex ethic in the midst of the contemporary world. To this end we must take sexual conduct seriously and treat sexual transgressions as being the significant acts that they are. At the same time, the mandate of the church includes that of being the reconciling community, proclaiming the good news of the grace and power of God that is available to sinful and fallen creatures, among whom all believers are to be numbered (1 Cor. 6:9–11). Only in this way can the community of Christ become what it is intended to be—the foretaste of the eschatological community of male and female that God wills as our human destiny.

Notes

Introduction

1. The use of sex in advertising and in the media was documented in the 1960s by Vance Packard, *The Sexual Wilderness* (New York: David McKay Co., 1968), 54–63. For the situation in the 1980s, see Randy C. Alcorn, *Christians in the Wake of the Sexual Revolution* (Portland, Ore.: Multnomah, 1985), 81–102.
2. Congregation for the Doctrine of the Faith, "Instruction on Respect for Human Life in its Origin and on the Dignity of Procreation: Replies to Certain Questions of the Day" (Vatican City, Feb. 22, 1987).
3. Summaries of the history of Christian attitudes toward sexuality abound. See, for example, Geoffrey Parrinder, *Sex in the World's Religions* (New York: Oxford, 1980), chapter 10. The recent literature concerning the history of general outlooks toward sexuality forms the basis for a summary by historian Lawrence Stone, "Sex in the West," *The New Republic* (July 8, 1985): 25–37.
4. Clement of Alexandria, *The Stromata, or Miscellanies* in Alexander Roberts and James Donaldson, eds. *The Ante-Nicene Fathers: Translation of the Writings of the Fathers Down to A.D. 325,* (Grand Rapids: Eerdmans, 1962), 2:377–78.
5. Although flawed at points, a helpful recounting of the rise of sexual renunciation in the church is offered in Peter Brown, *The Body and Society: Men, Women and Sexual Renunciation in Early Christianity* (New York: Columbia University Press, 1988). See also the review of this book by Raymond J. Lawrence in *St. Luke's Journal of Theology* 32/4 (1989): 283–87.
6. Donald Goergen, *The Sexual Celibate* (New York: Seabury, 1974), 7.
7. For a recent discussion of Augustine's understanding of marriage written from a Roman Catholic perspective, see Theodore Mackin, *The Marital Sacrament* (New York: Paulist, 1989), 197–227.
8. For a sampling of medieval sexual repression, see Dwight Hervey Small, *Christian: Celebrate Your Sexuality* (Old Tappan, N.J.: Revell, 1974), 79.
9. For a helpful discussion of Reformation sexual ethics, see Eric Fuchs, *Sexual Desire and Love* (New York: Seabury, 1983), 135–48.
10. See, for example, Luther's comments on marriage, Jaroslav Pelikan, ed. *Luther's Works,* Vol. 2, Lectures on Genesis Chaps. 6–14 (St. Louis: Concordia Publishing House, 1960), 356–57.
11. The Puritan sexual ethic has been reevaluated recently by Leland Ryken, "Were the Puritans Right about Sex?" *Christianity Today* (April 7, 1978): 13–18. Ryken finds several Puritan themes concerning sex in the literature of the period: "the

biblical basis . . . for affirming sex, the differentiation between animal lust and human love, the domestic context into which sexual fulfillment is put, and the privacy of the sexual relationship between two persons."

12. Milton Diamond and Arno Karlen, *Sexual Decisions* (Boston: Little, Brown and Co., 1980), 262. See also Small, 90, 93.

13. An interesting narrative of the story of the move from sin to innocence in the view of sex which is characteristic of the last three centuries is given in Peter Gardella, *Innocent Ecstasy* (New York: Oxford, 1985).

14. John Leo, "The Revolution Is Over," *Time* 123/15 (April 9, 1984): 74–83.

15. For a description and critique of the contemporary emphasis on intimacy, see Tim Stafford, "Intimacy: Our Latest Sexual Fantasy," *Christianity Today* (Jan. 16, 1987): 21–27. An attempt to mine the term for a Christian ethic is found in Robert M. Cooper, "Intimacy," *St. Luke's Journal of Theology* 30/2 (1987): 113–24.

Chapter 1: The Nature of Human Sexuality

1. Besides the primary sexual differences, biologists point to certain secondary differences between the physiology of males and females. For a discussion of these, see J. Richard Udry, *The Social Context of Marriage* (Philadelphia: J. B. Lippincott, 1966), 62–64.

2. George H. Tavard, "Theology and Sexuality," in *Women in the World's Religions, Past and Present,* ed., Ursula King, (New York: Paragon, 1987), 74.

3. Milton Diamond, "Biological Foundations for Social Development," in ed., Frank A. Beach, *Human Sexuality in Four Perspectives* (Baltimore: Johns Hopkins University Press, 1967), 25–27.

4. For a discussion of these differences, see Jerome Kagan, "Psychology of Sex Differences," in Beach, ed., *Human Sexuality in Four Perspectives,* 103–10.

5. A helpful study of this topic is found in Robert L. Solnick, ed., *Sexuality and Aging,* rev. ed. (Los Angeles: University of Southern California Press, 1987).

6. Milton Diamond and Arno Karlen, *Sexual Decisions* (Boston: Little, Brown and Co., 1980), 91.

7. For a discussion of this distinction in Freud and the neo-Freudians, see Donald Goergen, *The Sexual Celibate* (New York: Seabury, 1974), 51–57.

8. Martha Smith Good, "Singleness and Sexuality: A Gift from God," in ed., Bruce Yoder and Imo Jeanne Yoder, *Single Voices* (Scottdale, Penn.: Herald, 1982), 66–67.

9. Goergan, 53.

10. The etymological relationship between the two terms is in doubt. The root of the feminine term, *'ishshāh,* is presumed to be *'nsh,* from which is derived the general masculine term *'enosh.* The more individual masculine term *'ish* is derived either from *'ysh* (*'wsh*) or possibly from the same root as *'ishshāh.* Despite these uncertainties in rootage, N. P. Bratsiotis, writing in the *Theological Dictionary of the Old Testament,* maintains that the connection between *'ishshāh* and *'ish* made in Genesis 2:23 "is probably to be interpreted as a popular etymology" (*"ish," TDOT,* revised edition, I:222). This indicates that

whatever the actual historical connection between the two terms, the Genesis writer is employing a connection that was assumed by his readers.

Bratsiotis also draws out the significance of the fact that *'iysh* is noted here for the first time in the narrative: "for the first time he (i.e., the *'ādām*) becomes aware of standing in the presence of a fellow creature merely with the same nature but also of a different sex . . . now he also realizes that he is of a different sex from the *'ishshāh,* 'woman,' and thus recognizes the peculiarity of his being a 'man' (*me'ish*). Therefore, he is *'ish* and she is *'ishshāh*" (226). What is significant in the author's choice of this pair of words, is their striking similarity.

11. Gary Anderson, "Celibacy Consummation in the Garden? Reflections on Early Jewish and Christian Interpretations of the Garden of Eden," *Harvard Theological Review* 82/2 (1989): 148.

12. V. A. Demant, *Christian Sex Ethics* (New York: Harper and Row, 1963).

13. In his classic work, *The Four Loves,* C. S. Lewis draws a similar distinction between *venus* and *eros.* (London: Collins, 1960), 86–87.

14. Tavard incorrectly limits the procreative dimension as the expression of continuity of humankind with the animal world. "Theology and Sexuality," 77.

15. At this point certain religious groups (such as the Mormons) are in error—they rightly see sexuality as present in the kingdom, but mistakenly see it as expressed in marriage and procreation.

16. J. Richard Udry, *The Social Context of Marriage* (Philadelphia: J. B. Lippincott, 1966), 37. A 1963 study suggested that these differing modes of orientation are present among children as well. Girls are more likely to order objects according to "functional" groupings, whereas boys tend toward "analytic" groupings. Eleanor E. Maccoby, "Women's Intellect," in, ed., Seymour M. Farber and Robert H. L. Wilson, *The Potential of Woman* (New York: McGraw-Hill, 1963), 30–31.

17. A discussion of this differentiation is presented in James P. Hanigan, *Homosexuality: The Test Case for Christian Sexual Ethics* (Mahweh, N.J.: Paulist, 1988), 143–44.

18. Anthony Kosnik, et al., *Human Sexuality: New Directions in American Catholic Thought* (New York: Paulist, 1977), 81.

19. "Human Sexuality and Sexual Behavior," a statement adopted by the Tenth General Convention of the American Lutheran Church.

20. Letha Dawson Scanzoni, *Sexuality* (Philadelphia: Westminster, 1984), 14.

21. The tendency to distinguish in relationships between members of the same sex and members of the opposite sex is present regardless of a person's sexual orientation. The way of relating will differ between heterosexuals and homosexuals, but the phenomenon of relating differently according to the sex of the other remains.

22. V. A. Demant cites Nicholas Berdyaev as a twentieth-century theologian who expounds a view similar to the Greek androgyny myth (*Christian Sex Ethics,* 15). See also James B. Nelson, *The Intimate Connection* (Philadelphia: Westminster, 1988), 97. This approach to Genesis 2 is reflected in the exegesis of Phyllis Trible, *God and the Rhetoric of Sexuality* (Philadelphia: Fortress Press, 1978), 79–105.

23. For an example of the application of the Jungian perspective to human sexuality within a Catholic theological context, see John A. Sanford, *The Invisible Partners* (New York: Paulist, 1980).

24. Tavard, "Theology and Sexuality," 78–79. He develops this thesis more fully in *Woman in Christian Tradition* (South Bend: University of Notre Dame Press, 1973).

25. For a synopsis of Money's findings and their implications for current debates, see John Money, "Human Hermaphroditism," in ed., Frank A. Beach, *Human Sexuality in Four Perspectives* (Baltimore: Johns Hopkins Press, 1976). His findings are likewise summarized in Peter DeJong and Donald R. Wilson, *Husband and Wife* (Grand Rapids: Zondervan, 1979), 38–44.

26. For a description of psychosexual development in humans, see Herant A. Katchadourian and Donald T. Lunde, *Fundamentals of Human Sexuality,* 2d ed. (New York: Holt, Rinehart and Winston, 1975), 213–58.

27. Karl Barth's exegesis of Genesis 2 stands as a classic theological assertion of the essential nature of human sexuality. Concerning the primal pair, he wrote: "Humanity was not for them an ideal beyond masculinity and femininity. But masculinity and femininity themselves, in their differentiation and unity, constituted humanity." *Church Dogmatics* III/1, trans. by J. W. Edwards, O. Bussey, and Harold Knight (Edinburgh: T. & T. Clark, 1958), 309.

28. In the Old Testament, "soul" (Heb. *nephesh*) emphasizes the living nature of a being, not its rational nature. Thus, even certain animals are characterized by the term (e.g., Gen. 1:20, 21, 24, 30; 2:19; 9:10, 12, 15–16).

29. The understanding of the resurrection state that views it as nonsexual is widely held among evangelicals. This is indicated by the matter-of-fact way in which Gene A. Getz builds from the thesis in the popularly written book *The Measure of a Family* (Glendale, Calif.: Gospel Light/Regal Books, 1976), 47. Getz's conclusion is valid (i.e., the spiritual equality of the sexes), even though his premise may be faulty.

30. Vance Packard, *The Sexual Wilderness* (New York: David McKay, 1968), 434.

Chapter 2: Male and Female:
Humankind as a Sexual Creation

1. The broader interpretation of helper is offered by many exegetes of Genesis 2:20. See for example, Samuel L. Terrien, *Till the Heart Sings* (Philadelphia: Fortress, 1985), 10–11.

2. The ancient Hebrews were not unique in this respect. According to sociologist Talcott Parsons, "the family is the 'primordial' solidarity unit of all human societies." From "The Normal American Family," reprinted in *Sourcebook in Marriage and the Family,* ed., Marvin B. Sussman, 3d ed. (Boston: Houghton Mifflin Co., 1968), 40.

3. A corresponding relationship between loneliness and community is presented by Dwight Hervey Small, *Design for Christian Marriage,* (Westwood, N.J.: Revell, 1959), 30.

4. Augustine's famous statement is found on the opening page of his *Confessions.*

5. This theory is based in part on the studies of the anthropologist George Murdock. For a helpful presentation of the theory, see Peter DeJong and Donald R. Wilson, *Husband and Wife* (Grand Rapids: Zondervan, 1979), 68–75.

6. Marianne H. Micks notes that one feminist's writings took this point so far so as to earn the accusation "of thinking that if we ignored our different reproductive organs we would all be the same." *Our Search for Identity* (Philadelphia, Fortress, 1982), 18.

7. This difficulty has been noted even by proponents of the concept of androgyny. Some have moved beyond the older goal of establishing a single ideal for everyone (termed "monoandrogynism") to advocating a variety of options ("polyandrogynism"). See Joyce Trebilcot, "Two Forms of Androgynism," in *"Femininity," "Masculinity," and "Androgyny,"* ed., Mary Vetterling-Braggin (Totowa, N.J.: Rowman and Allanheld, 1982), 161–69. Others, such as Mary Ann Warren, look to the day when the concept of androgyny will "become obsolete" and "we will be comfortable with our natural human differences" ("Is Androgyny the Answer to Sexual Stereotyping?" in Vetterling-Braggin, 184–85). A critique of the two types of androgyny is presented in James B. Nelson, *The Intimate Connection* (Philadelphia: Westminster, 1988), 98–99.

8. Psychologists Janet T. Spence and Robert L. Helmreich note that gender roles are present in some form in all societies, even though their exact forms vary. *Masculinity and Femininity* (Austin: University of Texas Press, 1978), 4–5.

9. Paul K. Jewett, *Man as Male and Female* (Grand Rapids: Eerdmans, 1975), 27.

10. Nelson, 75.

11. The importance of this difference for women's development is explored in Carol Gilligan, *In a Different Voice* (Cambridge, Mass.: Harvard University Press, 1982).

12. Spence and Helmreich, 18.

13. Milton Diamond and Arno Karlen, *Sexual Decisions* (Boston: Little, Brown and Company, 1980), 447–48. A lengthier list of gender differences and their application to psychological therapy is found in Ron Johnson and Deb Brock, "Gender-Specific Therapy," *Journal of Psychology and Christianity* 7/4 (winter, 1988): 56–57. See also, Vance Packard, *The Sexual Wilderness* (New York: David McKay Co., 1968), 338–60.

14. Jerome Kagan, "Psychology of Sex Differences," in ed., Frank A. Beach, *Human Sexuality in Four Perspectives* (Baltimore: Johns Hopkins University Press, 1976).

15. For a summary of the differences in brain development, see Milton Diamond, "Human Sexual Development: Biological Foundations for Social Development," in Beach, ed., *Human Sexuality in Four Perspectives,* 51–52.

16. Ron Johnson and Deb Brock, "Gender-Specific Therapy," 56.

17. The work of neuropsychologists Jerre Levy and Roger Sperry is summarized by John C. Dwyer, *Human Sexuality: A Christian View* (Kansas City, Mo.: Sheed and Ward, 1987), 142–44. The implications for theology of such research is sketched in James B. Ashbrook, "Ways of Knowing God: Gender and the Brain," *Christian Century* 106 (1989): 14–15.

18. For an intriguing discussion of "womanly" versus "manly" existence based on recent findings in neuropsychology, see Dwyer, 145–48.

19. Lisa Sowle Cahill, *Between the Sexes* (Philadelphia: Fortress, 1985), 91.

20. Behavioral scientists have been keenly interested in the relationship between heredity and environment in shaping individual human life. For a good summary of the implications of such research for gender roles, see Micks, 19.

21. A call to move in this direction was issued already in 1968. See Vance Packard, *The Sexual Wilderness*, 360–79, 392.

22. Milton Diamond, "Human Sexual Development: Biological Foundations for Social Development," in ed., Beach, *Human Sexuality in Four Perspectives*, 58. His understanding is developed further in Diamond and Karlen, *Sexual Decisions*, 441–61.

23. Emil Brunner, *The Divine Imperative* (Philadelphia, Westminster, 1947), 376.

24. Advertisement in *Christianity Today*, 33/1 (Jan. 13, 1989). See also Gene A. Getz, *The Measure of a Family*, (Glendale, Calif.: Gospel Light/Regal, 1976), 41–43. Getz attempts to chart a middle position by concluding, "woman's submissive role to man, then, antedates the Fall, but was complicated by the Fall" (43).

25. Many conservative authors interact with the biblical materials dealing with gender roles. For a helpful presentation from an egalitarian perspective, see DeJong and Wilson, 121–76.

26. This point is argued successfully in the classic evangelical work by Paul K. Jewett, *Man as Male and Female*, 120–28.

27. See for example Rosemary Nixon, "The Priority of Perfection," *The Modern Churchman*, 27/1 (1984): 36. Even Barth hints in this direction in his discussion of this text in *Church Dogmatics* III/1, trans. by J. W. Edwards, O. Bussey, and Harold Knight (Edinburgh: T. & T. Clark, 1958), 294. For a discussion and critique of Barth's position, see Jewett, 33–40, 82–86.

28. For an interesting example of an egalitarian exegesis of Genesis 2, see Samuel Terrien, *Till the Heart Sings*, 7–17.

29. Peggy Reeves Sanday, *Female Power and Male Dominance* (New York: Cambridge University Press, 1981), 172. Sanday's study is noted by Lisa Cowle Cahill, *Between the Sexes*, 95.

30. Cahill, 55.

31. The significance of the Hebrew assertion of the celibacy of God in contrast to the outlook of the surrounding religions is put forth by Joseph Blenkinsopp, *Sexuality and the Christian Tradition* (Dayton, Ohio: Pflaum Press, 1969), 24–27. See also Tikva Frymer-Kensky, "Law and Philosophy: The Case of Sex in the Bible," *Semeia* 45 (1989): 90–91. Nevertheless, the situation may not have been so simple, as is argued by Mark S. Smith, "God Male and Female in the Old Testament: Yahweh and His 'Asherah,'" *Theological Studies* 48 (1987): 333–40.

32. For a helpful discussion of the significance of the dominance of paternal rather than maternal metaphors to speak of the nature of God, see Terrien, 59–70.

33. The basically masculine orientation of the trinitarian actions is noted by Urban T. Holmes, "The Sexuality of God," in ed., Ruth Tiffany Barnhouse and Urban T. Holmes III, *Male and Female: Christian Approaches to Sexuality* (New York: Seabury, 1976), 264–65.

34. Terrien, 57.

35. Derrick Sherwin Bailey, *Sexual Relation in Christian Thought* (New York: Harper and Brothers, 1959), 267.

36. This is an apparent weakness of Dwight Hervey Small's otherwise helpful treatment of this theme in *Christian: Celebrate Your Sexuality,* (Old Tappan, N.J.: Revell, 1974), 130–40.

37. Paul T. Jersild and Dale A. Johnson, eds. *Moral Issues and Christian Response,* 4th ed., (New York: Holt, Rinehart and Winston, 1988), 50.

Chapter 3: Marriage in a Christian Perspective

1. Frank A. Beach, ed., *Human Sexuality in Four Perspectives* (Baltimore: Johns Hopkins University Press, 1977), 116.

2. For a discussion of the development of the Roman Catholic view of marriage, see Theodore Mackin, *What Is Marriage?* (New York: Paulist, 1982).

3. For a statement of this view, see Charles Erdman, *The First Epistle of Paul to the Corinthians* (Philadelphia: Westminster, 1928), 65–70.

4. The relation of marriage to the order of creation and salvation is outlined by Kari Jenson, "On Marrying," reprinted in ed., Paul T. Jersild and Dale A. Johnson, *Moral Issues and Christian Response,* 4th ed. (New York: Holt, Rinehart and Winston, 1988), 79.

5. Vance Packard, *The Sexual Wilderness* (New York: David McKay Co., 1968), 230–31.

6. This phrase is developed in Lester A. Kirkendall, "Understanding the Male Sex Drive," in Isadore Rubin and Lester A. Kirkendall, eds., *Sex in the Adolescent Years* (New York: Association Press, 1968), 52.

7. The universality of some form of marriage is widely documented. Nena and George O'Neill go even further, claiming universality for monogamy. *Open Marriage: A New Life Style for Couples* (New York: Avon, 1972), 21.

8. Perhaps Small overstates his point in saying, "marriage needs sex to give it an exclusive and profoundly intimate bond." Dwight Hervey Small, *Christian: Celebrate Your Sexuality* (Old Tappan, N.J.: Revell, 1974), 176.

9. See Theodore Mackin, *What Is Marriage?* (New York: Paulist, 1982), 26.

10. Congregation for the Doctrine of the Faith, "Instruction on Respect for Human Life in its Origin and on the Dignity of Procreation: Replies to Certain Questions of the Day" (Vatican City, Feb. 22, 1987).

11. For a summary and discussion of these changes, see Mackin, *What Is Marriage?* 5–37.

12. The importance of the presence of both male and female role models for child development has been confirmed by many studies. For an example, see John Money, "Human Hermaphroditism," in Beach, ed., *Human Sexuality in Four Perspectives,* 78–79. The importance of the father is described in Vance Packard, *The Sexual Wilderness,* 390–91.

13. Dwight Hervey Small argues that marriage has been affected by industrialization, urbanization, and mobility, with the result that marriage and family are viewed as a haven of intimacy in a world of anonymity. *Design for Christian Marriage,* (Old Tappan, N.J.: Revell, 1959), 40–44.

14. Diana S. Richmond Garland and David E. Garland, *Beyond Companionship*

(Philadelphia: Westminster, 1986), 97. For a quite different critique of the traditional companionship model, see Nena and George O'Neill, *Open Marriage.*

15. Garland and Garland, 97.

16. Lewis B. Smedes, *Caring and Commitment* (San Francisco: Harper and Row, 1988), 80.

17. For summaries of Hebrew marriage customs, see Erhard Gerstenberger, *Woman and Man, Biblical Encounters Series* (Nashville: Abingdon, 1980), 40–48; Tom Horner, *Sex in the Bible* (Rutland, Vt.: Charles E. Tuttle, 1974), 18–23.

18. This has become an important issue even in the Roman Catholic Church as is evidenced in the three-volume work by Theodore Mackin, *Marriage in the Catholic Church* (New York: Paulist, 1982, 1984, 1989).

19. For an interesting critique of the contemporary emphasis on romantic love, see William J. Lederer and Don D. Jackson, "False Assumption 3: That Love Is Necessary for a Satisfactory Marriage," reprinted in, ed., Eleanor S. Morrison and Vera Borosage, *Human Sexuality: Contemporary Perspectives* (Palo Alto: Mayfield Publishing Company, 1977), 438–45.

20. A helpful discussion of *agape* as central to marriage and of its relationship to *eros* is found in Lewis B. Smedes, *Sex for Christians* (Grand Rapids: Eerdmans, 1976), 96–99.

21. Kari Jenson, "On Marrying," reprinted in Jersild and Johnson, eds., 76.

22. A summary of the recent European discussion of the civil and ecclesiastical dimensions of the wedding is given in Urs Baumann, *Die Ehe—Ein Sakrament?* (Zurich: Benzinger, 1988).

Chapter 4. The Sex Act within the Context of Marriage

1. Raymond J. Lawrence, "Bench Marks for a New Sexual Ethics," reprinted in, ed. Paul T. Jersild and Dale A. Johnson, *Moral Issues and Christian Response,* 4th ed. (New York: Holt, Rinehart and Winston, 1988), 60.

2. For examples of this argument found in contemporary culture, see Richard Hettlinger, *Sex Isn't That Simple* (New York: Seabury, 1974), 74–75.

3. The traditional exegesis understood this statement as Paul's own assertion. However, many contemporary scholars now conclude that this actually formed a slogan of the ascetics in the church, whose teaching Paul combats in the chapter. For a presentation of this view, see O. Larry Yarbrough, *Not Like the Gentiles,* SBL Dissertation Series 80 (Atlanta: Scholars Press, 1985), 93–96. This view is likewise put forth in Gordon Fee, *The First Epistle to the Corinthians,* (Grand Rapids: Eerdmans), 198.

4. Hettlinger, *Sex Isn't That Simple,* 80.

5. Abraham Maslow, "Self-Esteem (Dominance-Feeling) and Sexuality in Women," in, ed., M. F. DeMartino, *Sexual Behavior and Personality Characteristics* (New York: Grove, 1966), 103.

6. Christian writers have offered many suggestions as to how the meanings of the sex act can be summarized. Dwight Hervey Small, for example, argues that marital sex is creative, recreative, and procreative. *Christian: Celebrate Your Sexuality* (Old Tappan, N.J.: Revell, 1974), 186–87.

7. The application of the term "sacrament" to the sex act was made as early as 1959 in Dwight Hervey Small, *Design for Christian Marriage* (Old Tappan, N.J.: Revell, 1959), 80–89.

8. J. Richard Udry. *The Social Context of Marriage* (Philadelphia: J.B. Lippincott, 1966), 439–40.

9. An intriguing, albeit overdrawn, development of a sacramental understanding of marriage by means of a comparison of marital sexuality with baptism and the Lord's Supper is given in William E. Phipps, *Recovering Biblical Sensuousness* (Philadelphia: Westminster, 1978), 86–97.

10. For a recent description of the development of the sacramental state of marriage and its implications for today, see Urs Baumann, *Die Ehe—Ein Sakrament?* The historical development of the Roman Catholic view is described in Theodore Mackin, *The Marital Sacrament* (New York: Paulist, 1989).

11. The nonreligious understanding of sexuality in the Old Testament is the topic of Tikva Frymer-Kensky, "Law and Philosophy: The Case of Sex in the Bible," *Semeia* 45 (1989): 89–102. While Frymer-Kensky's discussion is helpful, his case appears to be overstated.

12. This point is made even by secular psychology. See, for example, Udry, 440.

13. For a succinct discussion of the pleasure dimension of the sex act, see Diana and David Garland, *Beyond Companionship* (Philadelphia: Westminster, 1986), 139–40.

14. Letha Dawson Scanzoni, *Sexuality* (Philadelphia: Westminster, 1984), 35. She develops this point as well in *Sex Is a Parent Affair* (Glendale, Calif.: Regal, 1973), 23–24.

15. For a recent discussion of the celebrative understanding of the Song of Songs, see Richard M. Davidson, "Theology of Sexuality in the Song of Songs," *Andrews University Seminary Studies* 27/1 (Spring, 1989): 1–19.

16. The link between *eros* and *agape* is eloquently developed by Helmut Thielicke, *Theological Ethics,* trans. John W. Doberstein (Grand Rapids: Eerdmans, 1979), 3:17–98.

17. In this sense, the sex act opens especially to the husband a means of overcoming the male tendency toward aggressiveness. Through sexual intercourse the man can offer himself to his wife, rather than demand from her, allowing her then to respond to his offering. See Dwight Hervey Small, *Christian: Celebrate Your Sexuality,* 202.

18. For a thought-provoking statement concerning the integral relationship between marriage and procreation, see Ellen Wilson Fielding, "Love and Marriage," *Human Life Review* 14/4 (Fall, 1988): 70–76. Fielding overstates the matter, however, in claiming, "marriage holds its special position only because of children" (75).

19. Congregation for the Doctrine of the Faith, "Instruction on Respect for Human Life in its Origin and on the Dignity of Procreation: Replies to Certain Questions of the Day," (Vatican City, Feb. 22, 1987). For a discussion by this author, see Stanley J. Grenz, "What Is Sex For?" *Christianity Today* (June 12, 1987): 22–23.

20. For a discussion of the problems in this text, see Gordon D. Fee, *The First Epistle to the Corinthians* (Grand Rapids: Eerdmans, 1987), 270–84.

21. See Eric Pfeiffer, "Sexuality in the Aging Individual" in, ed., Robert L. Solnick, *Sexuality and Aging,* rev. ed. (Los Angeles: University of Southern California Press, 1987), 28.
22. For a discussion of sexual expression in older adults, see Margaret Neiswender Reedy, "What Happens to Love? Love, Sexuality and Aging" in Solnick, ed., 184–95.
23. Robert N. Butler and Myrna I. Lewis, "The Second Language of Sex," in Solnick, ed., 176–78.
24. Raymond J. Lawrence, "Bench Marks for a New Sexual Ethics," reprinted in *Moral Issues and Christian Response,* 62.
25. Frank A. Beach, ed. *Human Sexuality in Four Perspectives* (Baltimore: Johns Hopkins University Press, 1977), 116.
26. Emil Brunner, *The Divine Imperative,* 382–83.

Chapter 5: The Marital Bond:
Fidelity versus Adultery

1. The exact meaning of 1 Thess. 4:3–6 is in doubt. That Paul is referring to marriage in the text is strongly argued by O. Larry Yarbrough, *Not Like the Gentiles,* SBL Dissertation Series 80, (Atlanta: Scholars Press, 1985), 65–87.
2. For a summary of the place of women in Hebrew society as being out of line with Hebrew and Greek creation stories, see Helmut Thielicke, *Theological Ethics* translated by John W. Doberstein (Grand Rapids: Eerdmans, 1979), 3:104–106.
3. See Paul K. Jewett, *Man as Male and Female* (Grand Rapids: Eerdmans, 1975), 86–94.
4. Margaret Mead, *Male and Female* (New York: William Morrow and Co., 1967), 195.
5. Vance Packard, *The Sexual Wilderness* (New York: David McKay Co., 1968), 282.
6. Eric Fuchs, *Sexual Desire and Love* (New York: Seabury, 1983), 182.
7. Sidney Callahan, "Human Sexuality in a Time of Change," reprinted in, ed., Paul T. Jersild and Dale A. Johnson, *Moral Issues and Christian Response,* 3d ed. (New York: Holt, Rinehart and Winston, 1983), 72.
8. Emil Brunner, *The Divine Imperative* (Philadelphia: Westminster, 1947), 347.
9. For a positive treatment of the advantages of fidelity, see Donald M. Joy, *Rebonding: Preventing and Restoring Damaged Relationships* (Waco, Tex.: Word, 1986).
10. Raymond J. Lawrence, "Bench Marks for a New Sexual Ethics," reprinted in, ed. Paul T. Jersild and Dale A. Johnson, *Moral Issues and Christian Response,* 4th ed. (New York: Holt, Rinehart and Winston, 1988), 63.
11. Raymond J. Lawrence, "Toward a More Flexible Monogamy," reprinted in Jersild and Johnson, eds. *Moral Issues and Christian Response,* 3d ed., 107. See also Nena and George O'Neill, *Open Marriage* (New York: Avon, 1972), 236–56.
12. The concern for monogamy is evidenced by the definition of "open marriage"

as "an honest and open relationship between two people" offered by the O'Neills in *Open Marriage,* 38. See also the guidelines they offer, 72–73.

13. Criticism of the "open marriage" idea is not limited to Christian writers. Clinical psychologist Diane Medved, for example, argues against the suggestion that an affair may be good for a marriage. For support she cites the reversal in the position of Joyce Brothers between 1975 and 1984. *The Case Against Divorce* (New York: Donald I. Fine, 1989), 130.

14. O'Neill and O'Neill, 224.

15. Joseph L. Allen, *Love and Conflict* (Nashville: Abingdon, 1984), 242.

16. Joseph Fletcher, *Situation Ethics: The New Morality* (Philadelphia: Westminster, 1966).

17. According to Fletcher, "for the situationist there are no rules—none at all." Ibid., 55.

18. Ibid., 68.

19. Ibid., 140.

20. Aaron H. Gerber, however, rejects the suggestions that Old Testament adultery laws were motivated by concern for male property rights. Rather, "adultery is not merely a private sin but a violation of God's commandment; moreover it is an evil which undermines a nation by disrupting the family." *Biblical Attitudes on Human Sexuality* (Great Neck, N.Y.: Todd and Honeywell, 1982), 158.

21. Rollo May, "What Is Our Problem?" reprinted in *Human Sexuality: Contemporary Perspectives,* Eleanor S. Morrison and Vera Borosage, eds., 2d ed. (Palo Alto, Calif.: Mayfield, 1977), 395.

22. Although not using the term *dualism,* Rollo May offers a similar critique, viewing the modern sexual attitudes as "alienation from the body and feeling, and exploitation of the body as though it were a new machine," "What Is Our Problem?" in *Human Sexuality,* 395.

23. James B. Nelson, *Embodiment* (Minneapolis: Augsburg, 1978), 66.

24. This point with respect to fathers is argued by Packard, 390–91.

25. Packard, 472.

26. Allen, 243.

Chapter 6: Divorce:
The Ultimate Severing of the Marital Bond

1. For a succinct summary of the sexual morality of Greco-Roman society, see O. Larry Yarbrough, *Not Like the Gentiles,* SBL Dissertation Series 80 (Atlanta: Scholars Press, 1985), 63.

2. For a detailed description of the outlook of the church throughout its history, see Theodore Mackin, *Divorce and Remarriage* (New York: Paulist, 1984).

3. Donna Schaper, "Marriage: The Impossible Commitment?" reprinted in, ed. Paul T. Jersild and Dale A. Johnson, *Moral Issues and Christian Response,* 4th ed. (New York: Holt, Rinehart and Winston, 1988), 77–79. An interesting discussion of the phenomenon of divorce among "good marriages" is offered by Diana S. Richmond Garland and David E. Garland, *Beyond Companionship*

(Philadelphia: Westminster, 1986), 151–55. The factors in modern society that contribute to marital demise are likewise discussed in Vance Packard, *The Sexual Wilderness* (New York: David McKay Co., 1968), 283–96.

4. This information is based on charts found in *The 1989 Information Please Almanac,* Otto Johnson, ed. (Boston: Houghton Mifflin Co., 1989), 140, 794–95, and *The World Almanac and Book of Facts 1990,* Mark S. Hoffman, ed. (New York: Pharos Books, A. Scripps Howard Company, 1989), 852.

5. Talcott Parsons, "The Normal American Family," reprinted in, ed. Marvin B. Sussman, *Sourcebook in Marriage and the Family,* 3d ed. (Boston: Houghton Mifflin Co., 1968), 44.

6. The significance of society's lack of community for the breakup of marriage is noted by Packard, 286.

7. The role of sexual dissatisfaction as a factor in the rise of infidelity is noted by Packard, 290.

8. Garland and Garland, *Beyond Companionship,* 155.

9. Craig A. Everett, "Introduction," *Journal of Divorce* 12/2-3 (1989): 1.

10. Case studies concerning the effects of divorce on children are offered in Judith S. Wallerstein and Sandra Blakeslee, *Second Chances: Men, Women, and Children a Decade After Divorce* (New York: Ticknor and Fields, 1989). Summaries of their findings are supplied on pp. 10–15, 296–300.

11. This point is argued at length in William F. Luck, *Divorce and Remarriage* (San Francisco: Harper and Row, 1987), 47–67.

12. The school of the Rabbi Shammai offered a strict interpretation of Deuteronomy 24:1 as allowing divorce only in cases of sexual infidelity, whereas the school of Hillel advocated a broader view which allowed a man to divorce his wife for nearly any reason.

13. Ellen Wilson Fielding, "Love and Marriage," *Human Life Review* 14/4 (Fall, 1988), 74.

14. William F. Luck finds Old Testament legal precedence for divorce in the case of abuse in Exodus 21:10f, 26f. *Divorce and Remarriage,* 50–51.

15. The evangelical tendency toward a new legalism is reflected in various recent treatments of divorce. For example, see Gene A. Getz, *The Measure of a Family* (Glendale, Calif.: Regal, 1976), 169. The evangelical tendency toward legalism is bemoaned by Bernard L. Ramm, *The Right, the Good and the Happy* (Waco, Tex.: Word, 1971), 87.

16. The nonlegalistic orientation of these texts is argued in Helmut Thielicke, *Theological Ethics,* translated by John W. Doberstein (Grand Rapids: Eerdmans, 1979), 3:108–24.

17. For an example of an exegesis of Matthew 19 that presents a similar viewpoint, see Phillip H. Wiebe, "Jesus' Divorce Exception," *Journal of the Evangelical Theological Society* 32/3 (September, 1989): 327–33.

18. For a similar interpretation, see Thielicke, 3:166.

19. In *The Case Against Divorce* (New York: Donald I. Fine, 1989), clinical psychologist Diane Medved argues against the tendency in society today to downplay the trauma of divorce. She maintains that divorce ought to be sought only in exceptional situations. (For a discussion of such situations, see pp. 104–22.)

20. In his helpful discussion of the marital covenant, Joseph L. Allen extrapolates from Christian just-war theory three factors which together could result in divorce becoming an expression of covenant love: (1) a grave wrong to be prevented or a crucial right to be protected, (2) divorce as a last resort, and (3) a right intention. *Love and Conflict* (Nashville: Abingdon, 1984), 249–52. These three criteria, it would seem, could all be subsumed under the concern to follow the principle of peace outlined here. Under adverse conditions, fidelity to this principle overrides but never sets aside the evil of divorce as the violation of the marriage covenant.
21. For a discussion of this issue in the Roman Catholic tradition, see Mackin, *Divorce and Remarriage.*
22. For an example of this position, see Getz, 167–75.
23. William F. Luck describes the position on divorce and remarriage with which he was raised, but which he later forsook, in terms similar to these. *Divorce and Remarriage,* ix.
24. For a discussion of the difficulties encountered by widowed persons to remarriage, see Robert R. Bell, *Marriage and Family Interaction,* revised ed. (Homewood, Ill.: Dorsey, 1967), 501–502.
25. Several "scars" typical of the divorced person are outlined by Medved, 217–20.
26. The complications of remarriage after divorce are so great that, as statistics indicate, the chances of divorce increase after each failed marriage. As a result some psychologists now speak of "divorce-proneness" and divorce-prone persons. See Bell, 511–12.
27. As early as 1971, Bernard Ramm called for the church to follow the rule of redemption. *The Right, the Good and the Happy,* 88.
28. This redemptive approach advocated here is somewhat similar to that outlined, after a brief summary of the eight major options for a congregation in dealing with divorce, in G. Edwin Bontrager, *Divorce and the Faithful Church* (Scottdale, Penn.: Herald, 1978), 156–60.
29. This viewpoint is gaining adherents among evangelicals. Even a person as conservative as Gene Getz argues that a divorced person can serve as a spiritual leader. *The Measure of a Family,* 173. Helmut Thielicke, in contrast, states that a divorced member of the clergy "must give up his office." *Theological Ethics,* 3:177.

Chapter 7: Technology and the Prevention of Pregnancy

1. Augustine, *The Good of Marriage,* chapter x, paragraph 11, translated by Charles T. Wilcox, *The Fathers of the Church* (Westminster, Md.: Christian Classics, 1948), 27:24.
2. Ibid, chapter vi, paragraph 6, (p. 17).
3. Thomas Aquinas, *Summa Theologica,* part II, question 153, article 2, trans. by Father of the English Dominican Province (Westminster, Md.: Christian Classics, 1948), 4: 1805.
4. *Summa Theologica,* II, question 154, article 1 (p. 1809).
5. Pope Pius XI, "Casti Connubi," iv, 55. Printed in *Social Wellsprings volume II:*

Eighteen Evangelicals of Social Reconstruction, Joseph Husslein, ed, (Milwaukee: The Bruce Publishing Company, 1942), 122–73.

6. For a discussion of the changing Roman Catholic view of the purposes of marriage and the sex act, see Theodore Mackin, *What Is Marriage?* (New York: Paulist, 1982), 5–37.

7. The Congregation for the Doctrine of the Faith, "Instruction on Respect for Human Life in its Origin and on the Dignity of Procreation: Replies to Certain Questions of the Day" (Vatican City, Feb. 22, 1987). Birth control is discussed in Part II, B4a.

8. Martin Luther, *Lectures on Genesis* in *Luther's Works,* Jaroslav Pelikan, ed. (St. Louis: Concordia Publishing House, 1958), 1:217.

9. Martin Luther, *Lectures on Genesis* 4:304–05.

10. Lloyd A. Kalland, "View and Position of the Christian Church—An Historical Review," in ed., Walter O. Spitzer and Carlyle L. Saylor, *Birth Control and the Christian* (Wheaton, Ill.: Tyndale House, 1969), 452–53. See also Alvah W. Sulloway, *Birth Control and Catholic Doctrine* (Boston: Beacon Press, 1959), 29–30.

11. For a discussion of factors that a couple should consider before accepting the challenge of parenting, see Diane Payette-Bucci, "Voluntary Childlessness," *Direction* 17/2 (1988): 26–41.

12. Origen, *On First Principles,* book IV, translated by Rowan A. Greer in *Origen, The Classics of Western Spirituality* (New York: Paulist Press, 1979), 186, 198.

13. This is standard Mormon teaching, which generally draws from *The Pearl of Great Price,* Moses 3:5, and Joseph Smith's *History of the Church of Jesus Christ of Latter-day Saints, Period I,* ed. B. H. Roberts, 2d ed., (Salt Lake City: Deseret News Press, 1950), 6:308–12. For an example of the development of this doctrine, see Sterling M. McMurrin, *The Theological Foundations of the Mormon Religion* (Salt Lake City: University of Utah Press, 1965), 25–26, 50.

14. For the medical dimensions of various birth control methods, see Milton Diamond and Arno Karlen, *Sexual Decisions* (Boston: Little, Brown and Co., 1980), 402–19, and Herant A. Katchadourian and Donald T. Lunde, *Fundamentals of Human Sexuality,* 2d ed. (New York: Holt, Rinehart and Winston, 1975), 151–71.

15. For preliminary assessments of the impact of Webster, see Kim A. Lawton, "Confrontation's Stage Is Set," *Christianity Today* 33/11 (Aug. 18, 1989): 36–38; and Rob Boston, "Different Doctrine," *Church and State* 42/8 (September, 1989): 7–8.

16. The history of the abortion issue is summarized in Mary Anne Warren, "The Abortion Struggle in America," *Bioethics* 3/4 (1989): 320–32. For an evangelical interpretation of this history, see Tim Stafford, "The Abortion Wars," *Christianity Today,* 33/14 (Oct. 6, 1989): 16–20.

17. This issue is treated in Norman M. Ford, *When Did I Begin? Conception of the Human Individual in History, Philosophy and Science* (Cambridge: Cambridge University Press, 1988).

18. Implantation is set forth as the beginning of life in Elizabeth Hall, "When Does Life Begin? A Conversation with Clifford Grobstein," *Psychology Today* 23/9 (September, 1989): 42–46.

19. Plato, *Republic* 5:457D–60D, translated by Paul Shorey, in *The Collected Dialogues of Plato,* Edith Hamilton and Huntington Cairns, eds. (Princeton: Princeton University Press, 1961), 696–99.
20. A. H. Sturtevant, *A History of Genetics* (New York: Harper & Row, 1965), 131.
21. H. J. Muller, "Means and Aims in Human Genetic Betterment," in *The Control of Human Heredity and Evolution,* T. M. Sonneborn, ed. (New York: Macmillan, 1965), 100.

Chapter 8: Technology and Pregnancy Enhancement

1. John and Sylvia Van Regenmorter and Joe S. McIlhaney, Jr., M.D. *Dear God, Why Can't We Have a Baby?* (Grand Rapids: Baker Book House, 1986), 9. See also Claudia Wallis, "The New Origins of Life," *Time* 124:11 (Sept. 10, 1984): 46–50.
2. Claudia Wallis, "The Saddest Epidemic," *Time* 124, no. 11 (Sept. 10, 1984): 50.
3. Ibid.
4. Robert R. Bell, *Marriage and Family Interaction,* revised ed., (Homewood, Ill.: Dorsey, 1967), 387.
5. The Congregation for the Doctrine of the Faith, "Instruction on Respect for Human Life in its Origin and on the Dignity of Procreation: Replies to Certain Questions of the Day" (Vatican City, Feb. 22, 1987), Part II, B4a.
6. The term "childfree" is offered as preferable to "childless" by Diane Payette-Bucci, "Voluntary Childlessness," 39.
7. Van Regenmorter and McIlhaney, Jr., *Why Can't We Have a Baby?,* 141.
8. For a helpful, succinct discussion of the joys and difficulties surrounding adoption, see ibid., 139–48. The difficulties involved in the adoption process are the subject of a recent *Time* cover story. Nancy Gibbs, "The Baby Chase," *Time* (Oct. 9, 1989): 86–89.
9. The situation of "special-needs" children is described in Richard Lacayo, "Nobody's Children," *Time* 134, no. 15 (Oct. 9, 1989): 91–95.
10. Cases of adopted children and genetic parents finding each other are widely publicized. For a recent report, see Elizabeth Taylor, "Are You My Mother?" *Time* (Oct. 9, 1989): 90.
11. For a fuller development of the motivations for childlessness, see Diane Payette-Bucci, "Voluntary Childlessness."
12. For a discussion of methods of technological assistance in procreation see William Walters and Peter Singer, eds. *Test Tube Babies: A Guide to Moral Questions, Present Techniques and Future Possibilities* (Melbourne: Oxford University Press, 1982), and Mary Warnack, ed. *A Question of Life: The Warnack Report on Human Fertilization and Embryology* (New York: Basil Blackwell Ltd., 1984).
13. Acceptance of AIH is not universal, however. Another argument voiced against AIH is the cleavage it produces between sexual love and procreation. See Leon Kass, "New Beginnings in Life," in *The New Genetics and the Future of Man* ed., M. Hamilton (Grand Rapids: Eerdmans, 1972), 53–54.
14. See Lori B. Andrews, "Yours, Mine and Theirs," *Psychology Today* 18/12 (December, 1984): 24.

15. Some donors have sought court action in order to gain the right to visit children produced by their sperm. Lori B. Andrews, "Yours, Mine and Theirs," 29.

16. For a discussion of a variety of purported ethical issues surrounding IVF, see William B. and Priscilla W. Neaves, "Moral Dimensions in In Vitro Fertilization," *Perkins Journal* 39/1 (1986): 10–23.

17. Neaves and Neaves, 20. A recent report suggests that the success rates of infertility clinics may not be as high as they would have their patients believe. See "What Do Infertility Clinics Really Deliver?" *U.S. News and World Report* (April 3, 1989): 74–75.

18. Otto Friedrich "A Legal, Moral Social Nightmare," *Time* 124/11 (Sept. 10, 1984). 54–56.

19. David T. Ozar argues that regardless of the answers to these questions, frozen embryos ought to be kept in their frozen state until implanted in a womb or are no longer capable of surviving implantation. "The Case Against Thawing Unused Frozen Embryos," *Hastings Center Report* 15/4 (1985): 7–12.

20. Neaves and Neaves, 22.

21. The guidelines for freezing embryos offered by Grobstein, Flower, and Mendeloff serve as an example: "The clinical community involved with in vitro fertilization should voluntarily limit use of embryo freezing to the initial purpose—i.e., to circumvent infertility in patients. Freezing should be carried out only with surplus embryos obtained from a clinically justifiable laparoscopy, and on thawing, embryos should be returned to the uterus of the donor, usually after an unsuccessful first attempt to transfer unfrozen embryos. Thawed embryos should be transferred to a nondonor only with the consent of the donor and an institutional review board or hospital ethics committee. Frozen embryos should be kept in storage for not more than five years or until the establishment of relevant public policy. Under such a voluntary arrangement, experience could be gained with freezing through clinical trials as an adjunct to in vitro fertilization but without public anxiety that other purposes might be served that had not been carefully considered. The purpose of the arrangement would be to avoid precipitate limitation of freezing for purposes that appear to be publicly acceptable, out of suspicion and fear of unsanctioned purposes, such as uncontrolled experimentation." Clifford Grobstein, et al., "Special Report: Freezing Embryos: Policy Issues," *The New England Journal of Medicine* 312/24 (1985): 1588.

22. Florence Isaacs, "High-Tech Pregnancies," *Good Housekeeping* 202 (February, 1986): 82.

23. Lori B. Andrews, "Yours, Mine and Their," 22.

24. For a discussion of the question of fetal tissue transplants from a philosophical point of view, see Barbara Miller, "Baby Harvest: Year Two-thousand Twenty," *Contemporary Philosophy* 12/7 (January, 1989): 29–30.

25. For a discussion of this possibility, see Neaves and Neaves, 17–19.

26. William D. Hamilton, "Sex and Disease," in, ed., George Stevens and Robert Bellig, *The Evolution of Sex* (San Francisco: Harper and Row, 1988), 90.

27. Janet Dickey McDowell, "Ethical Implications of In Vitro Fertilization," *Christian Century* (Oct. 19, 1983): 938.

Chapter 9: The Single Life

1. Unfortunately, some evangelical writers, in their attempts to articulate the goodness of sexuality and marriage, have inadvertently left no place for single Christians. Reflecting a view held in the late fifties, Dwight Hervey Small, for example, declared that "the loneliness of an unmarried person . . . is the condition of being less than a complete person." The solution he set forth is "real completeness between a husband and wife." *Design for Christian Marriage,* (Westwood, N.J.: Revell, 1959), 31. For an alternative understanding of loneliness, see Bruce Yoder, "Singleness and Spirituality: Holy Loneliness," in *Single Voices,* Bruce Yoder and Imo Jeanne Yoder, eds. (Scottdale, Penn.: Herald, 1982), 82–89.

2. For a citation of census statistics and their implications, see Susan Annette Muto, *Celebrating the Single Life* (Image Books, Garden City, N.Y.: Doubleday, 1985), 9–10.

3. For a Christian perspective on the motivation for celibacy, see Donald Goergen, *The Sexual Celibate* (New York: Seabury, 1974), 108–14.

4. The road to a celibate clergy is summarized in Goergen, 7.

5. See, for example, Herant A. Katchadourian and Donald T. Lunde, *Fundamentals of Human Sexuality,* 2d ed. (New York: Holt, Rinehart and Winston, 1975), 528–29.

6. This point is made by Erhard S. Gerstenberger and Wolfgang Schrage, *Woman and Man,* trans. by Douglas W. Stott, Biblical Encounters Series (Nashville: Abingdon, 1981), 174–79.

7. For a discussion of the nature of the opposition to Paul at Corinth, see Gordon D. Fee, *The First Epistle to the Corinthians* (Grand Rapids: Eerdmans, 1987), 267–70, 322–24.

8. Muto, 188.

9. The affective nature of the single experience is developed by Martha Smith Good, "Singleness and Sexuality: A Gift from God," in *Single Voices,* Bruce Yoder and Imo Jeanne Yoder, eds., (Scottdale, Penn.: Herald, 1982), 66–69.

10. This special ministry of single persons is articulated by Rhena Taylor, *Single and Whole* (Downers Grove, Ill.: InterVarsity, 1984), 35–36.

11. William A. Heth argues correctly that vocation within the kingdom and not asceticism lies behind the statement of Jesus in Matthew 19:12. "Unmarried 'for the Sake of the Kingdom' (Matthew 19:12) in the Early Church," *Grace Theological Journal* 8/1 (1987): 55–88.

Chapter 10: Singleness and Sexual Expression

1. Herant A. Katchadourian and Donald T. Lunde use three terms to describe this stage of life: adolescence ("the phase of psychological development that culminates in full genital and reproductive maturity"), puberty ("which begins with the appearance of secondary sexual characteristics and extends to the inception of reproductive capacity"), and nubility ("during which full reproductive fertility is reached"). *Fundamentals of Human Sexuality,* 2d ed. (New York: Holt, Rinehart and Winston, 1975), 214.

2. Joseph Fletcher, "Ethics and Unmarried Sex," in, ed., Paul T. Jersild and Dale A. Johnson, *Moral Issues and Christian Response,* 3d ed. (New York: Holt, Rinehart and Winston, 1982), 82.

3. The influence of cinema and television was decried already in the 1960s. See, for example, Vance Packard, *The Sexual Wilderness* (New York: David McKay, 1968), 55–58. The sexual confusion that results from media portrayals is outlined in Robert R. Bell, *Marriage and Family Interaction,* revised ed., (Homewood, Ill.: Dorsey, 1967), 179. The influence of media has not abated since the 1960s.

4. The modern phenomenon of dating is described in J. Richard Udry, *The Social Context of Marriage* (Philadelphia: Lippincott, 1966), 108–24.

5. Udry, 111.

6. The youth subculture has been a significant dimension of Western society throughout the second half of the twentieth century. For a description of this phenomenon and its impact on young people, see Bell, 438–42.

7. John DeLamater and Patricia MacCorquodale, *Premarital Sexuality: Attitudes, Relationships, Behavior* (Madison: University of Wisconsin Press, 1979), 230.

8. DeLamater and MacCorquodale, 222.

9. The decline of parental guidance over the "awakening process" is noted by Packard, who sees the media as "encouraging the generational gulf." *The Sexual Wilderness,* 35–36.

10. Cited by James F. Moore, *Sexuality and Marriage* (Minneapolis: Augsburg, 1987), 30.

11. Janet Lively, "An 'F' in Family Planning," *Sioux Falls (S.Dak.) Argus Leader,* Jan. 22, 1989, sec. A, p. 1.

12. Jill Lawrence, "Poll: Students Discount Religion in Sex Life," *Sioux Falls (S. Dak.) Argus Leader,* Jan. 22, 1989, sec. A, p. 5. A recent poll among youth within the theologically conservative Baptist General Conference confirmed these results: "the sexual attitudes and behavior of BGC teens closely match those of adolescents from ten other evangelical denominations and are, unfortunately, not significantly different from those of unchurched teens." Sharon Sheppard, "Sexual Attitudes and Practices of BGC Teens," *The Standard* 79:10. (November 1989), 38.

13. Larry Richards, *How Far Can I Go?* (Chicago: Moody, 1969), 92–93.

14. For a discussion of gender-based psychological differences in motivation in premarital sex, see Richard Hettlinger, *Sex Isn't That Simple* (New York: Seabury, 1974), 165–67.

15. Mary Calderone, "How Young Men Influence the Girls Who Love Them," *Redbook* (July, 1965), quoted in Richard Hettlinger, *Living with Sex* (New York: Seabury, 1966), 119. See also Packard, 398.

16. Milton Diamond and Arno Karlen, *Sexual Decisions* (Boston: Little, Brown and Co., 1980), 119. For the basis in adolescence of these differing outlooks between young men and young women, see Ruth Tiffany Barnhouse, *Homosexuality: A Symbolic Confusion* (New York: Seabury, 1977), 71–72.

17. Studies have indicated that premarital relations with spouse and others lower the probability of general marital success. See Lester Allen Kirkendall, *Premarital Intercourse and Interpersonal Relations* (New York: Julian Press,

1961), 204. Such findings do not suggest that virginity per se offers a better start for marriage, for when intercourse is limited to one's future spouse marital success may not suffer. Yet, the lack of permanent commitment of all premarital relations means that such relationships offer little guarantee that intercourse will indeed be limited to one's future spouse. Should the couple break up and both marry others, the chance of their enjoying successful marriages is reduced. From this perspective the introduction of intercourse into their relationship did indeed increase the risk to the future marriages of each.

18. Richard Hettlinger, *Growing Up with Sex* (New York: Seabury, 1971), 80.
19. Tim Stafford, *The Sexual Christian* (Wheaton, Ill.: Victor, 1988), 119.
20. Audrey Beslow, *Sex and the Single Christian* (Nashville: Abingdon, 1987), 74.
21. Packard, 398.
22. See Hettlinger, *Growing Up with Sex,* 82. Bernard L. Ramm is more specific. He claims that premarital promiscuity can be a cause of frigidity in marriage. *The Right, the Good and the Happy* (Waco, Tex.: Word, 1971), 119.
23. Packard, 429–30.
24. Hettlinger, *Living with Sex,* 133. See also Packard, 432. The Kinsey data with respect to females is presented in Udry, 432.
25. Packard, 431.
26. It may be argued that the availability of contraceptives greatly reduces the chances of premarital sex leading to an unwanted child. Research reveals, however, a lack of widespread use of such measures. Respondents to a survey conducted in Canada, for example, indicated an aversion to condoms for reasons such as embarrassment in purchasing them or the belief that their use diminishes sexual pleasure. See Jack Hanna, "Sexual Abandon," *Maclean's* 102/39 (Sept. 25, 1989): 48. Couples may avoid using contraceptives, because their use indicates that engaging in sex is premeditated; many seek to maintain the appearance that their involvement in premarital sex is unplanned and spontaneous.
27. Udry, 157.
28. Proponents of the traditional Christian ethic with its emphasis on abstinence prior to marriage may find heartening reports that a small but growing number of states now mandate sex education programs in the public schools that promote premarital abstinence. See Ken Sidey, "Kids Get the Message: It's Okay to Say No," *Christianity Today* 33/14 (Oct. 6, 1989): 40.
29. Packard, 434.
30. A strong stance against petting is offered, however, in Dwight Hervey Small, *Design for Christian Marriage.* (Westwood, N.J.: Revell, 1959), 153–75.
31. Several Christian ethicists have noted that persons who maintain "technical virginity" while being involved in a variety of sexual activities are not necessarily following an ethic of abstinence. See, for example, Donald Goergen, *The Sexual Celibate,* (New York: Seabury, 1974), 132–35.
32. The purposes of engagement in the modern setting are outlined in Small, 198–221.
33. A shocking recent discovery is that couples who live together before marriage are surprisingly violent. See Andrea Sachs, "Swinging-and-Ducking-Singles," *Time* 132/10 (Sept. 5, 1988): 51.

34. Lester A. Kirkendall, *Premarital Intercourse and Interpersonal Relationships,* cited in Hettlinger, *Growing Up with Sex,* 80, *Living with Sex,* 134.
35. Masturbation as defined by John C. Dwyer, *Human Sexuality: A Christian View* (Kansas City, Mo.: Sheed and Ward, 1987), 56.
36. Hettlinger, *Living with Sex,* 92.
37. Ibid.
38. For a summary of the various positions on masturbation, see Michael S. Patton, "Twentieth-Century Attitudes toward Masturbation," *Journal of Religion and Health* 25/4 (1986): 291–302. See also Hettlinger, *Living with Sex,* 82–83.
39. See, for example, the discussion in Goergen, 196–201.
40. Dwyer, 57.
41. Smedes, *Sex for Christians* (Grand Rapids: Eerdmans, 1976), 162.
42. Lewis Smedes, for example, argues that compulsive masturbation is a form of self-punishment that arises from a heavy load of unattached guilt. Ibid., 163.
43. Hettlinger, *Living with Sex,* 78.
44. See the helpful discussion of masturbation in Letha Scanzoni, *Sex Is a Parent Affair* (Glendale, Calif.: Regal, 1973), 188–93.
45. Smedes, 128, 130.
46. This point is aptly made by James P. Hanigan, *Homosexuality: The Test Case for Christian Sexual Ethics* (Mahwah, N.J.: Paulist, 1988), 72.
47. Smedes, 112.
48. Hettlinger cites the Italian psychotherapist Roberto Assagioli and Havelock Ellis, *Living with Sex,* 77. For a recent statement concerning proper sexual expression within the single life, see Julia Duin, *Purity Makes the Heart Grow Stronger* (Ann Arbor, Mich.: Vine Books, 1988).
49. Karen Lebacqz, "Appropriate Vulnerability: A Sexual Ethic for Singles," *Christian Century* 104/15 (1987): 437.
50. For a firsthand discussion of the difficulties of following the rule of abstinence as a divorced single, see Keith Miller and Andrea Wells Miller, *The Single Experience* (Waco, Tex.: Word, 1981), 216–43.

Chapter 11`: Homosexuality:
Sin or Alternative Lifestyle?

1. Peter Coleman, *Christian Attitudes to Homosexuality* (London: SPCK, 1980), 2, 4.
2. One of the first voices calling for a reappraisal of the biblical documents was a British Anglican, Derrick Sherwin Bailey, *Homosexuality and the Western Christian Tradition* (London: Longman, Green and Co., Ltd., 1955). The major outlooks were classified into four categories in James B. Nelson, *Embodiment* (Minneapolis: Augsburg, 1978), 180–210. A call for openness to homosexuality was issued by the Roman Catholic, John J. McNeill, *The Church and the Homosexual* (Kansas City, Mo.: Sheed, Andrews, and McMeel, 1976). A similar position has been articulated by Letha Scanzoni and Virginia Mollenkott, *Is the Homosexual My Neighbor?* (San Francisco: Harper and Row, 1978).
3. John C. Dwyer, *Human Sexuality: A Christian View* (Kansas City, Mo.: Sheed

and Ward, 1987), 64. The distinction between orientation and activity is spelled out more clearly in the definition offered by Jones and Workman. Behaviorally, the term refers to "acts between two persons of the same sex that engender sexual arousal (usually to the point of orgasm)"; as an orientation, homosexuality is "a stable erotic and-or affectional preference for persons of the same sex." Stanton L. Jones and Don E. Workman, "Homosexuality: The Behavioral Sciences and the Church," *Journal of Psychology and Theology* 17/3 (1989): 214.

4. Estimates are generally based on the Kinsey findings. For a critical evaluation of that report, see Milton Diamond and Arno Karlen, *Sexual Decisions* (Boston: Little, Brown and Co., 1980), 219–22.

5. John M. Livingood, M.D., ed., National Institute of Mental Health Task Force on Homosexuality: Final Report and Background Papers (Rockville, Md.: National Institute of Mental Health, 1972), 27.

6. Edward Batchelor, Jr., *Homosexuality and Ethics* (New York: Pilgrim, 1980), 24.

7. The implication of this approach to the Bible is far-reaching. It suggests that the biblical restrictions on homosexuality are to be read as condemning only those homosexual acts that are a perversion of the natural sexual inclination of the perpetrator, and not the sexual expressions of those who are naturally inclined toward homosexuality. Thus, only naturally heterosexual persons who engage in homosexual acts are guilty of sin. This matter will be discussed subsequently.

8. David Greenberg, *The Construction of Homosexuality* (Chicago: University of Chicago Press, 1988), 3.

9. Milton Diamond, "Biological Foundations for Social Development," in *Human Sexuality in Four Perspectives,* Frank A. Beach, ed. (Baltimore: Johns Hopkins University Press, 1976), 40–42.

10. The biological theory is articulated in John Shelby Spong, *Living in Sin?* (San Francisco: Harper and Row, 1988), 71–74. Spong cites recent studies in East Berlin that point to prenatal hormonal processes as the source of homosexuality. For a summary of the prenatal versus developmental discussion, see Diamond and Karlen, 228–30.

11. For a discussion of the shortcomings of the various theories of hereditary causes, see Jones and Workman, 218–19.

12. Herant A. Katchadourian and Donald T. Lunde, *Fundamentals of Human Sexuality,* 2d ed., (New York: Holt, Rinehart and Winston, 1975), 336.

13. John Money, "Human Hermaphroditism," in Beach, 80.

14. Diamond and Karlen, 219.

15. Ruth Tiffany Barnhouse, *Homosexuality: A Symbolic Confusion* (New York: Seabury, 1977), 40. Richard Hettlinger confirms this viewpoint: "The theory, strongly argued a few decades ago, and still attractive to many confirmed homosexuals who want to avoid any sense of responsibility for continuing their practices, that hereditary, biological, or glandular factors determine the individual's sexual constitution, is now generally abandoned." *Living with Sex* (New York: Seabury, 1966), 111.

16. William H. Masters and Virginia E. Johnson, *Homosexuality in Perspective* (New York: Bantam Books, 1982), 271.

17. For a summary of Bieber's findings and their significance, see Jones and Workman, 219. See also Vance Packard, *The Sexual Wilderness* (New York: David McKay Co., 1968), 129–30.

18. Jerome Kagan, "Psychology of Sex Differences," in Beach, 103.

19. Hettlinger, *Living with Sex,* 111. In *Human Sexuality: A Christian View,* Roman Catholic ethicist John Dwyer echoes this conclusion. He declares that homosexuality is "the result of an early fixation on one parent" (68). And again, "male homosexuality seems to be the result of a definite pattern of child-rearing and acculturation . . ."(69).

20. Lawrence J. Hatterer, "What Makes a Homosexual?" condensed from *McCall's* (July, 1971) in *The Reader's Digest* (September, 1971): 60–63.

21. Diamond and Karlen, 227.

22. See William H. Davenport, "Sex in Cross-Cultural Perspective," in Beach, 156. See also Diamond and Karlen, 228.

23. Diamond and Karlen, 228.

24. Michael Foucault, *The History of Sexuality, Vol. 2: The Use of Pleasure* (New York: Pantheon Books, 1985), 245.

25. For a response to the sympathetic retelling of the historical development of homosexuality, see Barnhouse, 24–31. See also Diamond and Karlen, 228. This point has recently been questioned by Greenberg, 142.

26. See, for example, Spong, 139–40.

27. A succinct summary of the newer exegesis of the New Testament texts and the relevant literature is provided in Joseph J. Kotva, Jr., "Scripture, Ethics, and the Local Church: Homosexuality as a Case Study," *Conrad Grebel Review* 7/1 (Winter, 1989): 56–57.

28. H. Darrell Lance, "The Bible and Homosexuality," *American Baptist Quarterly* 8/2 (1989): 143.

29. That male cult prostitutes were found in the fertility rites of surrounding religions and therefore formed the context for the prohibitions of the Holiness Code is argued by Scanzoni and Mollenkott, 59–60. However, this theory is rejected even by Bailey, 30. See also Joseph Jenson, "Human Sexuality in the Scriptures," in *Human Sexuality and Personhood* (Chicago: Franciscan Herald Press, 1981), 23.

30. Lance, 145.

31. A helpful development of this argument is offered by P. Michael Ukleja, "Homosexuality and the Old Testament," *Bibliotheca Sacra* 140/559 (1983): 264–65.

32. John Boswell, *Christianity, Social Tolerance and Homosexuality* (Chicago: University of Chicago Press, 1980), 353.

33. E.g., Kotva, 57.

34. David F. Wright, "Homosexuals or Prostitutes?" *Vigiliae Christianae* 38/2 (1984): 146.

35. See Richard Hays, "Relations Natural and Unnatural: A Response to John Boswell's Exegesis of Romans 1," *Journal of Religious Ethics* (Spring, 1986), 200.

36. Lance, 148.

37. For a discussion of Paul's use of the term "natural" see James B. DeYoung,

"The Meaning of 'Nature' in Romans 1 and Its Implications for Biblical Proscriptions of Homosexual Behavior," *Journal of the Evangelical Theological Society* 31/4 (1988): 429–41.

38. Robert Friedman "The Psychoanalytic Model of the Male Homosexuality: A Historical and Theoretical Critique," *The Psychoanalytic Review* 73/4 (Winter 1986): 85. Elizabeth Moberly, *Homosexuality: A New Christian Ethic* (Greenwood, S.C.: Attic Press, Inc., 1983), 2–8.

39. Barnhouse, 61.

40. For a discussion of certain adolescent activities, see Dwyer, 65.

41. Elizabeth Moberly, *Homosexuality: A New Christian Ethic* (Greenwood, S.C.: Attic, 1983), 2–8.

42. Barnhouse, 152–53.

43. For a short summary, see Jones and Workman, 221. See also Barnhouse, 109. Diamond and Karlen report a one-third success rate with an additional one-third changing to "a partly heterosexual pattern," 231.

44. Tim Stafford, "Coming Out," *Christianity Today* 33/11 (Aug. 18, 1989): 21.

45. Jones and Workman, 221.

46. Martin Hoffman, "Homosexuality," in Beach, 186–88.

47. Moberly, 18–19. See also the conclusion of Wilson, 72–73.

48. Paul D. Meier, "Counseling Homosexuals," *Fundamentalist Journal* 4/3 (March, 1985): 21.

49. James P. Hanigan, *Homosexuality: The Test Case for Christian Sexual Ethics* (Mahwah, N.J.: Paulist, 1988), 102.

50. John Harvey, "The Traditional View of Homosexuality as Related to the Pastoral Situation of Homosexual Persons," as quoted by Eileen Flynn, *AIDS: A Catholic Call for Compassion* (Kansas City, Mo.: Sheed and Ward, 1985), 71.

51. These are the four main positions as presented in Anthony Kosnik, et. al., *Human Sexuality: New Directions in American Catholic Thought* (New York: Paulist, 1977), 200–209. A similar fourfold delineation is found in James B. Nelson, *Embodiment,* 188–89. For a helpful discussion of the four major positions, see Hanigan 59–88.

52. A. P. Bell and M. S. Weinberg, *Homosexualities: A Study of Diversity among Men and Women* (New York: Simon and Schuster, 1978), 308.

53. Nikki Meredith, "The Gay Dilemma," *Psychology Today* 18/1 (January, 1984), 56.

54. Ibid., 58–59. Meredith cites a 1978 survey conducted by Alan P. Bell and Martin S. Weinberg. Meredith also cites anthropologist Donald Symons, who in his book *The Evolution of Human Sexuality* (New York: Oxford University Press, 1979) declares that in homosexuality one finds male and female sexualities in their pure, uncompromised form.

55. Edward Batchelor, Jr., *Homosexuality and Ethics* (New York: Pilgrim, 1980), 76.

56. Barnhouse offers a similar critique on the basis of the assertion that "the true religious goal of human sexuality can thus be seen not as satisfaction, but as completion" (172).

57. Hettlinger, *Living with Sex,* 105.

58. Ibid., 104, 106–107.

59. Charles Socarides, quoted by Michael McManus, "Homosexuals Anonymous Gives Gay Christians a Way Out," *Sioux Falls (So. Dak.) Argus Leader* March 7, 1987, sec. A, p. 9.
60. For example, see Hoffman, 182–85.
61. Ibid. 182.
62. Bell and Weinberg, 346. For an analysis of Bell and Weinberg's research, see Jones and Workman, 216.
63. Hettlinger, *Living with Sex,* 105.
64. Barnhouse, 172.
65. Hanigan, 99.
66. This position, articulated in John J. McNeill's important work, *The Church and the Homosexual* (Kansas City, Mo.: Sheed, Andrews and McMeel, 1976), was presented in the recent article, "Homosexuality: Challenging the Church to Grow," *Christian Century* 104/8 (March 11, 1987): 243.
67. Jones and Workman, 224.
68. A similar understanding of chastity is developed in Donald Goergen, *The Sexual Celibate* (New York: Seabury, 1974), 101–103.
69. Many excellent treatments of the subject of AIDS have appeared in recent years. See also Wendell W. Hoffman and Stanley J. Grenz, *AIDS: Ministry in the Midst of an Epidemic* (Grand Rapids: Baker, 1990).
70. Bailey, 168.

Bibliography

Alcorn, Randy C. *Christians in the Wake of the Sexual Revolution*. Portland: Multnomah, 1985.

Allen, Joseph L. *Love and Conflict*. Nashville: Abingdon, 1984.

American Lutheran Church. "Human Sexuality and Sexual Behavior." Statement adopted by the Tenth General Convention.

Anderson, Gary. "Celibacy or Consummation in the Garden? Reflections on Early Jewish and Christian Interpretations of the Garden of Eden." *Harvard Theological Review* 82, no. 2 (1989): 121–48.

Andrews, Lori B. "Yours, Mine and Theirs." *Psychology Today* 18, no. 12 (December 1984): 20–29.

Aquinas, Thomas. *Summa Theologica*. Translated by Fathers of the English Dominican Province. Westminster, Md.: Christian Classics, 1948.

Ashbrook, James B. "Ways of Knowing God: Gender and the Brain." *Christian Century* 106 (1989): 14–15.

Augustine. *Confessions*.

———. *The Good of Marriage*. Vol. 27 of *The Fathers of the Church*. Translated by Charles T. Wilcox. Westminster, Md.: Christian Classics, 1948.

Bailey, Derrick Sherwin. *Homosexuality and the Western Christian Tradition*. London: Longmans, Green and Co., Ltd., 1955.

———. *Sexual Relation in Christian Thought*. New York: Harper and Brothers, Publishers, 1959.

Barnhouse, Ruth Tiffany. *Homosexuality: A Symbolic Confusion*. New York: Seabury, 1977.

Barnhouse, Ruth Tiffany, and Urban T. Holmes, III., eds. *Male and Female*. New York: Seabury, 1976.

Barth, Karl. *Church Dogmatics*. Vol. 3:1, Translated by J. W. Edwards, O. Bussey, and Harold Knight. Edinburgh: T. and T. Clark, 1958: 176–329.

Batchelor, Edward, Jr. *Homosexuality and Ethics*. New York: Pilgrim, 1980.

Baumann, Urs. *Die Ehe—Ein Sakrament?* Zurich: Benzinger, 1988.

Beach, Frank A., ed. *Human Sexuality in Four Perspectives*. Baltimore: Johns Hopkins University Press, 1977.

Bell, A. P., and M. S. Weinberg. *Homosexualities: A Study of Diversity among Men and Women*. New York: Simon and Schuster, 1978.

Bell, Robert R. *Marriage and Family Interaction.* Rev. ed. Homewood, Ill.: Dorsey, 1967.

Beslow, Audrey. *Sex and the Single Christian.* Nashville: Abingdon, 1987.

Blenkinsopp, Joseph. *Sexuality and the Christian Tradition.* Dayton, Ohio: Pflaum Press, 1969.

Bonhoeffer, Dietrich. *Creation and Fall.* New York: Macmillan, 1959.

Bontrager, G. Edwin. *Divorce and the Faithful Church.* Scottdale, Penn.: Herald, 1978.

Boston, Rob. "Different Doctrine." *Church and State* 42, no. 8 (September 1989): 175–76.

Boswell, John. *Christianity, Social Tolerance and Homosexuality.* Chicago: University of Chicago Press, 1980.

Bromiley, Geoffrey W. *God and Marriage.* Grand Rapids: Eerdmans, 1980.

Brown, Peter. *The Body and Society: Men, Women and Sexual Renunciation in Early Christianity.* New York: Columbia University Press, 1988.

Brunner, Emil. *The Divine Imperative.* Philadelphia: Westminster, 1947.

Cahill, Lisa Sowle. *Between the Sexes.* Philadelphia: Fortress Press, 1985.

Clement of Alexandria. *The Stromata, or Miscellanies.* Edited by Alexander Roberts and James Donaldson. In *The Ante-Nicene Fathers: Translation of the Writings of the Fathers Down to A.D. 325.* Grand Rapids: Eerdmans, 1962.

Coleman, Peter. *Christian Attitudes to Homosexuality.* London: SPCK, 1980.

Congregation for the Doctrine of the Faith. "Instruction on Respect for Human Life in its Origin and on the Dignity of Procreation: Replies to Certain Questions of the Day." Vatican City: Congregation for the Doctrine of the Faith, Feb. 22, 1987.

Cooper, Robert M. "Intimacy." *St. Luke's Journal of Theology* 30 (March 1987): 113–24.

Davidson, Richard M. "Theology of Sexuality in the Song of Songs." *Andrews University Seminary Studies* 27, no. 1 (Spring 1989): 1–19.

DeJong, Peter, and Donald R. Wilson. *Husband and Wife.* Grand Rapids: Zondervan, 1979.

DeLamater, John, and Patricia MacCorquodale. *Premarital Sexuality: Attitudes, Relationships, Behavior.* Madison: University of Wisconsin Press, 1979.

Demant, V. A. *Christian Sex Ethics.* New York: Harper and Row, 1963.

De Young, James B. "The Meaning of 'Nature' in Romans 1 and Its Implications for Biblical Proscriptions of Homosexual Behavior." *Journal of the Evangelical Theological Society* 31, no. 4 (1988): 429–41.

Diamond, Milton, and Arno Karlen. *Sexual Decisions.* Boston: Little, Brown and Co., 1980.

Duin, Julia. *Purity Makes the Heart Grow Stronger.* Ann Arbor, Mich.: Vine Books, 1988.

Dwyer, John C. *Human Sexuality: A Christian View*. Kansas City, Mo.: Sheed and Ward, 1987.

Erdman, Charles. *The First Epistle of Paul to the Corinthians*. Philadelphia: Westminster, 1928.

Everett, Craig A. "Introduction." *Journal of Divorce* 12, no. 2–3 (1989): 1.

Fee, Gordon. *The First Epistle to the Corinthians*. Grand Rapids: Eerdmans, 1987.

Fielding, Ellen Wilson. "Love and Marriage." *Human Life Review* 14, no. 4 (Fall 1988): 70–76.

Findlay, Steven. "What Do Infertility Clinics Really Deliver?" *U.S. News and World Report* (April 3, 1989): 74–75.

Fletcher, Joseph. *Situation Ethics: The New Morality*. Philadelphia: Westminster, 1966.

Ford, Norman M. *When Did I Begin? Conception of the Human Individual in History, Philosophy and Science*. Cambridge: Cambridge University Press, 1988.

Foucault, Michael. *The Use of Pleasure*. Vol. 2 of *The History of Sexuality*. New York: Pantheon Books, 1985.

Friedman, Robert. "The Psychoanalytic Model of Male Homosexuality: A Historical and Theoretical Critique." *The Psychoanalytic Review* 73, no. 4 (Winter 1986): 483–519.

Friedrich, Otto. "A Legal, Moral, Social Nightmare." *Time* 124, no. 11 (Sept. 10, 1984): 54–56.

Frymer-Kensky, Tikva. "Law and Philosophy: The Case of Sex in the Bible." *Semeia* 45 (1989): 89–101.

Fuchs, Eric. *Sexual Desire and Love*. New York: Seabury Press, 1983.

Gardella, Peter. *Innocent Ecstasy*. New York: Oxford, 1985.

Garland, Diana S. Richmond, and David E. Garland. *Beyond Companionship—Christians in Marriage*. Philadelphia: The Westminster Press, 1986.

Gerber, Aaron H. *Biblical Attitudes on Human Sexuality*. Great Neck, N.Y.: Todd and Honeywell, 1982.

Gerstenberger, Erhard, and Wolfgang Schrage. *Woman and Man. Biblical Encounters Series*. Nashville: Abingdon, 1980.

Getz, Gene A. *The Measure of a Family*. Glendale, Calif.: Gospel Light, Regal Books, 1976.

Gibbs, Nancy. "The Baby Chase." *Time* 134, no. 15 (Oct. 9, 1989): 86–89.

Gilligan, Carol. *In a Different Voice*. Cambridge, Mass.: Harvard University Press, 1982.

Goergen, Donald. *The Sexual Celibate*. New York: Seabury, 1974.

Greenberg, David. *The Construction of Homosexuality*. Chicago: University of Chicago Press, 1988.

Grenz, Stanley J. "What Is Sex For?" *Christianity Today* (June 12, 1987): 22–23.

Grobstein, Clifford, et al. "Special Report: Freezing Embryos: Policy Issues." *The New England Journal of Medicine* 312, no. 24 (1985): 1584–88.

Hall, Elizabeth. "When Does Life Begin? A Conversation with Clifford Grobstein." *Psychology Today* 23, no. 9 (September 1989): 43–46.

Hamilton, William D. "Sex and Disease." In *The Evolution of Sex*. Edited by George Stevens and Robert Bellig. San Francisco: Harper and Row, 1988.

Hanigan, James P. *Homosexuality: The Test Case for Christian Sexual Ethics*. Mahwah, N.J.: Paulist, 1988.

Hanna, Jack "Sexual Abandon." *Maclean's* 102, no. 39 (Sept. 25, 1989): 48.

Harvey, John. "The Traditional View of Homosexuality as Related to the Pastoral Situation of Homosexual Persons." Quoted by Eileen Flynn. *AIDS: A Catholic Call for Compassion*. Kansas City, Mo.: Sheed and Ward, 1985.

Hatterer, Lawrence J. "What Makes a Homosexual?" Condensed from *McCall's* (July 1971) in *The Reader's Digest* (September 1971): 60–63.

Hays, Richard. "Relations Natural and Unnatural: A Response to John Boswell's Exegesis of Romans 1." *Journal of Religious Ethics* 14, no. 1 (Spring 1986): 184–215.

Heth, William A. "Unmarried 'For the Sake of the Kingdom' (Matthew 19:12) in the Early Church." *Grace Theological Journal* 8, no. 1 (1987): 55–88.

Hettlinger, Richard. *Growing Up with Sex*. New York: Seabury, 1971.

———. *Living with Sex*. New York: Seabury, 1966.

———. *Sex Isn't That Simple*. New York: Seabury, 1974.

Hoffman, Mark S., ed. *The World Almanac and Book of Facts 1990*. New York: Pharos Books, 1989.

Hoffman, Wendell W., and Stanley J. Grenz. *AIDS: Ministry in the Midst of an Epidemic*. Grand Rapids: Baker, 1990.

Holmes, Urban T. "The Sexuality of God." In *Male and Female: Christian Approaches to Sexuality*. Edited by Ruth Tiffany Barnhouse and Urban T. Holmes III. New York: Seabury, 1976.

Horner, Tom. *Sex in the Bible*. Rutland, Vt.: Charles E. Tuttle, 1974.

Isaacs, Florence "High-Tech Pregnancies" *Good Housekeeping* 202 (February 1986): 79–82.

Jenson, Joseph. "Human Sexuality in the Scriptures." In *Human Sexuality and Personhood*. Chicago: Franciscan Herald Press, 1981.

Jersild, Paul T., and Dale A. Johnson, eds. *Moral Issues and Christian Response*. 3rd ed. (1983), 4th ed. (1988). New York: Holt, Rinehart and Winston, 1988.

Jewett, Paul K. *Man as Male and Female*. Grand Rapids: Eerdmans, 1975.

Johnson, Ron, and Deb Brock. "Gender-Specific Therapy." *Journal of Psychology and Christianity* 7, no. 4 (Winter 1988): 50–60.

Johnson, Otto, ed. *The 1989 Information Please Almanac*. Boston: Houghton Mifflin Company, 1989.

Jones, Stanton L., and Don E. Workman. "Homosexuality: The Behavioral Sciences and the Church." *Journal of Psychology and Theology* 17, no. 3 (1989): 213–25.

Joy, Donald M. *Rebonding: Preventing and Restoring Damaged Relationships.* Waco, Tex.: Word, 1986.

Kalland, Lloyd A. "View and Position of the Christian Church—An Historical Review." In *Birth Control and the Christian.* Edited by Walter O. Spitzer and Carlyle L. Saylor. Wheaton, Ill.: Tyndale House, 1969.

Kass, Leon. "New Beginnings in Life." In *The New Genetics and the Future of Man.* Edited by M. Hamilton. Grand Rapids: Eerdmans, 1972.

Katchadourian, Herant A., and Donald T. Lunde. *Fundamentals of Human Sexuality.* 2nd ed. New York: Holt, Rinehart and Winston, 1975.

Kirkendall, Lester Allen. *Premarital Intercourse and Interpersonal Relations.* New York: Julian Press, 1961.

———. "Understanding the Male Sex Drive." In *Sex in the Adolescent Years.* Edited by Isadore Rubin and Lester A. Kirkendall. New York: Association Press, 1968.

Kosnik, Anthony, chairperson. *Human Sexuality—New Directions in American Catholic Thought.* New York: Paulist, 1977.

Kotva, Joseph J., Jr. "Scripture, Ethics, and the Local Church: Homosexuality as a Case Study." *Conrad Grebel Review* 7, no. 1 (Winter 1989): 41–61.

Lacayo, Richard. "Nobody's Children." *Time* 134, no. 15 (Oct. 9, 1989): 91–95.

Lance, Darrell. "The Bible and Homosexuality." *American Baptist Quarterly* 8, no. 2 (1989): 142–43.

Lawton, Kim A. "Confrontation's Stage Is Set." *Christianity Today* 33, no. 11 (Aug. 18, 1989): 36–38.

Lebacqz, Karen. "Appropriate Vulnerability: A Sexual Ethic for Singles." *Christian Century* 104, no. 15 (May 1987): 435–38.

Leo, John. "The Revolution Is Over." *Time* 123, no. 15 (April 9, 1984):74–83.

Lewis, C. S. *The Four Loves.* London: Collins, 1960.

Livingood, John M., M.D., ed. *National Institute of Mental Health Task Force on Homosexuality: Final Report and Background Papers.* Rockville, Md.: National Institute of Mental Health, 1972.

Luck, William F. *Divorce and Remarriage.* San Francisco: Harper and Row, 1987.

Luther, Martin. *Lectures on Genesis.* Vols. 2, 3, 4 of *Luther's Works.* Edited by Jaroslav Pelikan. St. Louis: Concordia, 1958, 1960, and 1964.

McDowell, Janet Dickey. "Ethical Implications of In Vitro Fertilization." *Christian Century* (Oct. 19, 1983): 936–38.

McMurrin, Sterling M. *The Theological Foundations of the Mormon Religion.* Salt Lake City: University of Utah Press, 1965.

McNeill, John J. *The Church and the Homosexual* (Kansas City, Mo.: Sheed, Andrews, and McMeel, 1976.

Maccoby, Eleanor E. "Women's Intellect." In *The Potential of Woman.* Edited by Seymour M. Farber and Robert H. L. Wilson. New York: McGraw-Hill, 1963.

Mackin, Theodore. *Divorce and Remarriage*. New York: Paulist, 1984.

———. *Marriage in the Catholic Church*. New York: Paulist, 1982.

———. *The Marital Sacrament*. New York: Paulist, 1989.

———. *What Is Marriage?* New York: Paulist, 1982.

Maslow, Abraham. "Self-Esteem (Dominance-Feeling) and Sexuality in Women." In *Sexual Behavior and Personality Characteristics*. Edited by M. F. DeMartino. New York: Grove, 1966.

Masters, William H., and Virginia E. Johnson. *Homosexuality in Perspective*. New York: Bantam Books, 1982.

Mead, Margaret. *Male and Female*. New York: William Morrow and Co., 1967.

Medved, Diane. *The Case Against Divorce*. New York: Donald I. Fine, 1989.

Meier, Paul D. "Counseling Homosexuals." *Fundamentalist Journal* 4, no. 3 (March, 1985): 20–21.

Meredith, Nikki. "The Gay Dilemma." *Psychology Today* 18, no. 1 (January 1984): 56–62.

Micks, Marianne H. *Our Search for Identity*. Philadelphia: Fortress Press, 1982.

Miller, Barbara. "Baby Harvest: Year Two-thousand Twenty." *Contemporary Philosophy* 12, no. 7 (January 1989): 29–30.

Miller, Keith, and Andrea Wells Miller. *The Single Experience*. Waco, Tex.: Word, 1981.

Moberly, Elizabeth. *Homosexuality: A New Christian Ethic*. Greenwood, S.C.: Attic Press, 1983.

Moore, James F. *Sexuality and Marriage*. Minneapolis: Augsburg, 1987.

Morrison, Eleanor S., and Vera Borosage. *Human Sexuality: Contemporary Perspectives*. Palo Alto, Calif.: Mayfield Publishing Company, 1977.

Muller, H. J. "Means and Aims in Human Genetic Betterment." In *The Control of Human Heredity and Evolution*. Edited by T. M. Sonneborn, New York: Macmillan, 1965.

Muto, Susan Annette. *Celebrating the Single Life*. Image Books, Garden City, N.Y.: Doubleday, 1985.

Neaves, William B., and Priscilla W. Neaves. "Moral Dimensions of *In Vitro* Fertilization." *Perkins Journal* 39, no. 1 (January 1986): 10–23.

Nelson, James B. *Embodiment*. Minneapolis: Augsburg, 1978.

———. *The Intimate Connection*. Philadelphia: Westminster, 1988.

Nixon, Rosemary. "The Priority of Perfection." *The Modern Churchman*, 27, no. 1 (1984): 30–37.

O'Neill, Nena, and George O'Neill. *Open Marriage: A New Life Style for Couples*. New York: Avon, 1972.

Origen. *On First Principles*. Book IV of *Origen, The Classics of Western Spirituality*. Translated by Rowan A. Greer. New York: Paulist Press, 1979.

Ozar, David T. "The Case Against Thawing Unused Frozen Embryos." *Hastings Center Report* 15, no. 4 (August 1985): 7–12.

Packard, Vance. *The Sexual Wilderness*. New York: David McKay Co., 1968.

Parrinder, Geoffrey. *Sex in the World's Religions*. New York: Oxford, 1980.

Parsons, Talcott. "The Normal American Family." Reprinted in *Sourcebook in Marriage and the Family*. Edited by Marvin B. Sussman. 3rd ed. Boston: Houghton Mifflin, 1968.

Patton, Michael S. "Twentieth-Century Attitudes Toward Masturbation." *Journal of Religion and Health* 25, no. 4 (Winter 1986): 291–302.

Payette-Bucci, Diane. "Voluntary Childlessness." *Direction* 17, no. 2 (Fall 1988): 26–41.

Phipps, William E. *Recovering Biblical Sensuousness*. Philadelphia: Westminster, 1978.

Plato. *Republic* 5:457D–460D. Translated by Paul Shorey. In *The Collected Dialogues of Plato*. Edited by Edith Hamilton and Huntington Cairns. Princeton: Princeton University Press, 1961.

Pope Pius XI. "Casti Connubii." *Eighteen Encyclicals of Social Reconstruction*. Vol. 2 of *Social Wellsprings*. Edited by Joseph Husslein. Milwaukee: The Bruce Publishing Company, 1942.

Ramm, Bernard L. *The Right, the Good and the Happy*. Waco, Tex.: Word, 1971.

Rhymes, Douglas. *No New Morality*. Indianapolis: The Bobbs-Merrill Company, Inc., 1964.

Richards, Larry. *How Far Can I Go?* Chicago: Moody, 1969.

Ryken, Leland. "Were the Puritans Right about Sex?" *Christianity Today* (April 7, 1978): 13–18.

Sachs, Andrea. "Swinging-and-Ducking-Singles." *Time* 132, no. 10 (Sept. 5, 1988): 54.

Sanday, Peggy Reeves. *Female Power and Male Dominance*. New York: Cambridge University Press, 1981.

Sanford, John A. *The Invisible Partners*. New York: Paulist, 1980.

Scanzoni, Letha Dawson. *Sexuality*. Philadelphia: Westminster, 1984.

———. *Sex Is a Parent Affair*. Glendale, Calif.: Regal Books, 1973.

Scanzoni, Letha Dawson, and Virginia Mollenkott. *Is the Homosexual My Neighbor?* San Francisco: Harper and Row, 1978.

Sheppard, Sharon. "Sexual Attitudes and Practices of BGC Teens." *The Standard* 79, no. 10 (November 1989): 38–39.

Sidey, Ken. "Kids Get the Message: It's Okay to Say No." *Christianity Today* 33, no. 14 (Oct. 6, 1989): 40.

Small, Dwight Hervey. *Christian: Celebrate Your Sexuality*. Old Tappan, N.J.: Fleming H. Revell, 1974.

————. *Design for Christian Marriage.* Westwood, N.J.: Fleming H. Revell, 1959.

Smedes, Lewis B. *Caring and Commitment.* San Francisco: Harper and Row, 1988.

————. *Sex for Christians.* Grand Rapids, Eerdmans, 1976.

Smith, Joseph. *History of the Church of Jesus Christ of Latter-day Saints, Period I.* Edited by B. H. Roberts. 2nd ed. Salt Lake City: Deseret News Press, 1950.

Smith, Mark S. "God Male and Female in the Old Testament: Yahweh and His 'Asherah.'" *Theological Studies* 48 (June 1987): 333–40.

Solnick, Robert L., ed. *Sexuality and Aging.* Rev. ed. Los Angeles: University of Southern California Press, 1987.

Spence, Janet T., and Robert L. Helmreich. *Masculinity and Femininity.* Austin: University of Texas Press, 1978.

Spong, John Shelby. *Living in Sin?* San Francisco: Harper and Row, 1988.

Stafford, Tim. "Coming Out." *Christianity Today* 33, no. 11 (Aug. 18, 1989): 16–21.

————. "Intimacy: Our Latest Sexual Fantasy." *Christianity Today* 31, no. 1 (Jan. 16, 1987): 12–27.

————. "The Abortion Wars." *Christianity Today* 33, no. 14 (Oct. 6, 1989): 16–20.

————. *The Sexual Christian.* Wheaton, Ill.: Victor Books, 1989.

Stone, Lawrence. "Sex in the West." *The New Republic* (July 8, 1985): 25–37.

Sturtevant, A. H. *A History of Genetics.* New York: Harper and Row, 1965.

Sulloway, Alvah W. *Birth Control and Catholic Doctrine.* Boston: Beacon Press, 1959.

Symons, Donald. *The Evolution of Human Sexuality.* New York: Oxford University Press, 1979.

Tavard, George H. "Theology and Sexuality." *Women in the World's Religions, Past and Present.* Edited by Ursula King. New York: Paragon, 1987.

————. *Woman in Christian Tradition.* South Bend: University of Notre Dame Press, 1973.

Taylor, Elizabeth. "Are You My Mother?" *Time* 134, no. 15, (Oct. 9, 1989): 90.

Taylor, Rhena. *Single and Whole.* Downers Grove, Ill.: InterVarsity, 1984.

Terrien, Samuel L. *Till the Heart Sings.* Philadelphia, Fortress Press, 1985.

Thielicke, Helmut. *Sex.* Vol. 3 of *Theological Ethics.* Edited by William A. Loranth. Grand Rapids: Eerdmans, 1964.

Thomas, David M. *Christian Marriage—A Journey Together.* Vol. 5 of *Message of the Sacraments.* Edited by Monika Hellwig. Wilmington, Del.: Michael Glazier, Inc., 1983.

Trebilcot, Joyce. "Two Forms of Androgynism." In *"Femininity," "Masculinity," and "Androgyny."* Edited by Mary Vetterling-Braggin. Totowa, N.J.: Rowman and Allanheld, 1982.

Trible, Phyllis. *God and the Rhetoric of Sexuality.* Philadelphia: Fortress Press, 1978.

Udry, J. Richard. *The Social Context of Marriage*. Philadelphia: J. B. Lippincott, 1966.

Ukleja, P. Michael. "Homosexuality and the Old Testament." *Bibliotheca Sacra* 140, no. 559 (1983): 259–66.

Van Regenmorter, John, and Sylvia Van Regenmorter, and Joe S. McIlhaney, Jr., M.D. *Dear God, Why Can't We Have a Baby?* Grand Rapids: Baker, 1986.

Wallerstein, Judith S., and Sandra Blakeslee. *Second Changes: Men, Women, and Children a Decade After Divorce*. New York: Ticknor and Fields, 1989.

Walters, William, and Pete Singer, eds. *Test Tube Babies: A Guide to Moral Questions, Present Techniques and Future Possibilities*. Melbourne: Oxford University Press, 1982.

Warnack, Mary, ed. *A Question of Life: The Warnack Report on Human Fertilization and Embryology*. New York: Basil Blackwell Ltd., 1984.

Warren, Mary Anne. "The Abortion Struggle in America." *Bioethics* 3, no. 4 (1989): 320–32.

Wiebe, Phillips H. "Jesus' Divorce Exception." *Journal of the Evangelical Theological Society*. 32, no. 3 (September 1989): 327–33.

Wright, David F. "Homosexuals or Prostitutes?" *Vigiliae Christianae* 38, no. 2 (1984): 125–53.

Yarbrough, O. Larry. *Not Like the Gentiles*. SBL Dissertation Series 80. Atlanta: Scholars Press, 1985.

Yoder, Bruce, and Imo Jeanne Yoder. *Single Voices*. Scottdale, Penn.: Herald, 1982.

Index of Biblical References

Index of Names

Index of Subjects